China's New Global Strategy

Rising as a global power and regarding the existing world order unjust and unreasonable enough to meet the interests of both itself and other emerging powers, China has demanded reform to global governance, and taken new initiatives using its new quotient of wealth and influence to draw countries into its orbit. This comprehensive volume focuses on the two most important of these initiatives: the Belt and Road Initiative (BRI), launched in 2013 to strengthen China's connectivity with a large part of the world through infrastructure and economic development; and the Asian Infrastructure Investment Bank (AIIB), created in 2015, which represented China's effort in the reconstruction of the international development rules. This book explores how these two initiatives are central to China's emerging global strategy.

The authors examine China's geopolitical and geo-economic motivations and domestic political dynamics in launching these two initiatives. They also investigate the responses from the major foreign partners involved in both initiatives. This book will be of great interest to students, academics and researchers of China's emerging global strategy. It comprises articles originally published in the *Journal of Contemporary China*.

Suisheng Zhao is Professor and Director of the Center for China-US Cooperation in the Josef Korbel School of International Studies at the University of Denver, USA, and founding editor of the *Journal of Contemporary China*.

China's New Global Strategy

The Belt and Road Initiative (BRI) and Asian
Infrastructure Investment Bank (AIIB), Volume I

Edited by
Suisheng Zhao

LONDON AND NEW YORK

First published 2020
by Routledge
2 Park Square, Milton Park, Abingdon, Oxon, OX14 4RN

and by Routledge
52 Vanderbilt Avenue, New York, NY 10017

Routledge is an imprint of the Taylor & Francis Group, an informa business

First issued in paperback 2021

British Library Cataloguing in Publication Data
A catalogue record for this book is available from the British Library

ISBN13: 978-0-367-32149-9 (hbk)
ISBN13: 978-1-03-209174-7 (pbk)

Typeset in Myriad Pro
by Newgen Publishing UK

Publisher's Note
The publisher accepts responsibility for any inconsistencies that may have arisen during the conversion of this book from journal articles to book chapters, namely the inclusion of journal terminology.

Disclaimer
Every effort has been made to contact copyright holders for their permission to reprint material in this book. The publishers would be grateful to hear from any copyright holder who is not here acknowledged and will undertake to rectify any errors or omissions in future editions of this book.

Contents

Citation Information   vii
Notes on Contributors   ix

Introduction – The BRI and AIIB as China's New Global
Strategy: Motivations, Domestic Politics and International Responses   1
Suisheng Zhao

PART I
Geopolitics and Geo-economic Motivations behind the BRI/AIIB

1 Motivation behind China's 'One Belt, One Road' Initiatives and
   Establishment of the Asian Infrastructure Investment Bank   3
   Hong Yu

2 The One Belt One Road and the Asian Infrastructure Investment
   Bank: Beijing's New Strategy of Geoeconomics and Geopolitics   19
   Kevin G. Cai

3 Beyond Balancing: China's approach towards the Belt and Road Initiative   36
   Weifeng Zhou and Mario Esteban

4 Could 'Belt and Road' be the Last Step in China's Asian Economic Integration?   51
   Cheng King and Jane Du

5 Strategic Reassurance in Institutional Contests: Explaining China's
   Creation of the Asian Infrastructure Investment Bank   71
   Zheng Chen and Yanchuan Liu

6 China's Silk Road Economic Belt Initiative: Network and Influence
   Formation in Central Asia   87
   Jeffrey Reeves

PART II
China's Domestic Politics and the BRI

7   The Domestic Politics of the Belt and Road Initiative and its Implications   104
    Baogang He

8   Overseas Port Investment Policy for China's Central and Local Governments
    in the Belt and Road Initiative   120
    Jihong Chen, Yijie Fei, Paul Tae-Woo Lee and Xuezong Tao

PART III
Responses from Foreign Partners

9   Regional Responses to China's Maritime Silk Road Initiative in Southeast Asia   140
    Shaofeng Chen

10 The Political Economy of a Rising China in Southeast Asia: Malaysia's
    Response to the Belt and Road Initiative   158
    Hong Liu and Guanie Lim

11 Myanmar's Role in China's Maritime Silk Road Initiative   174
    J. Mohan Malik

12 Deconstructing the China-Pakistan Economic Corridor: Pipe Dreams Versus
    Geopolitical Realities   191
    Jeremy Garlick

    Index   206

Citation Information

The following chapters were originally published in the *Journal of Contemporary China*. When citing this material, please use the original page numbering for each article, as follows:

Chapter 1

Motivation behind China's 'One Belt, One Road' Initiatives and Establishment of the Asian Infrastructure Investment Bank
Hong Yu
Journal of Contemporary China, volume 26, issue 105 (May 2017) pp. 353–368

Chapter 2

The One Belt One Road and the Asian Infrastructure Investment Bank: Beijing's New Strategy of Geoeconomics and Geopolitics
Kevin G. Cai
Journal of Contemporary China, volume 27, issue 114 (November 2018) pp. 831–847

Chapter 3

Beyond Balancing: China's approach towards the Belt and Road Initiative
Weifeng Zhou and Mario Esteban
Journal of Contemporary China, volume 27, issue 112 (July 2018) pp. 487–501

Chapter 4

Could 'Belt and Road' be the Last Step in China's Asian Economic Integration?
Cheng King and Jane Du
Journal of Contemporary China, volume 27, issue 114 (November 2018) pp. 811–830

Chapter 5

Strategic Reassurance in Institutional Contests: Explaining China's Creation of the Asian Infrastructure Investment Bank
Zheng Chen and Yanchuan Liu
Journal of Contemporary China, volume 27, issue 114 (November 2018) pp. 795–810

Chapter 6

China's Silk Road Economic Belt Initiative: Network and Influence Formation in Central Asia
Jeffrey Reeves
Journal of Contemporary China, volume 27, issue 112 (July 2018) pp. 502–518

Chapter 7

The Domestic Politics of the Belt and Road Initiative and its Implications
Baogang He
Journal of Contemporary China, volume 28, issue 116 (March 2019) pp. 180–195

Chapter 8

Overseas Port Investment Policy for China's Central and Local Governments in the Belt and Road Initiative
Jihong Chen, Yijie Fei, Paul Tae-Woo Lee and Xuezong Tao
Journal of Contemporary China, volume 28, issue 116 (March 2019) pp. 196–215

Chapter 9

Regional Responses to China's Maritime Silk Road Initiative in Southeast Asia
Shaofeng Chen
Journal of Contemporary China, volume 27, issue 111 (May 2018) pp. 344–361

Chapter 10

The Political Economy of a Rising China in Southeast Asia: Malaysia's Response to the Belt and Road Initiative
Hong Liu and Guanie Lim
Journal of Contemporary China, volume 28, issue 116 (March 2019) pp. 216–231

Chapter 11

Myanmar's Role in China's Maritime Silk Road Initiative
J. Mohan Malik
Journal of Contemporary China, volume 27, issue 111 (May 2018) pp. 362–378

Chapter 12

Deconstructing the China-Pakistan Economic Corridor: Pipe Dreams Versus Geopolitical Realities
Jeremy Garlick
Journal of Contemporary China, volume 27, issue 112 (July 2018) pp. 519–533

For any permission-related enquiries please visit:
    www.tandfonline.com/page/help/permissions

Notes on Contributors

Kevin G. Cai is an Associate Professor of East Asian Studies at Renison University College at the University of Waterloo, Canada.

Jihong Chen is a Professor and Department Chair of Waterway Transportation in the College of Transport and Communications at Shanghai Maritime University, China. He is also Maritime Expert Member at the Science and Technology Committee of Shanghai Municipal Transport Commission, and Director of the Chinese Association of Productivity Science.

Shaofeng Chen is Associate Professor with the School of International Studies at Peking University (PKU), China, and is also responsible for the PKU-Sciences Po Dual Master's Degree in International Relations.

Zheng Chen is an Associate Professor at the School of International and Public Affairs at Shanghai Jiao Tong University, China.

Jane Du has been affiliated with the East Asian Institute of the National University of Singapore.

Mario Esteban is Professor of East Asian Studies at the Autonomous University of Madrid, Spain, and Senior Analyst at the Elcano Royal Institute in Madrid, Spain.

Yijie Fei is a Postgraduate of the College of Transport and Communications at Shanghai Maritime University, China.

Jeremy Garlick is an Assistant Professor, specialising in China's international relations and diplomacy, at the University of Economics Prague, Czech Republic.

Baogang He is Alfred Deakin Professor and Personal Chair in International Relations in the School of Humanities and Social Sciences in the Faculty of Arts and Education at Deakin University, Australia, and Honourable Professor at Huazhong Normal University, China.

Cheng King has been affiliated with Sun Yat-Sen University, China, and the East Asian Institute at the National University of Singapore.

Paul Tae-Woo Lee is a Professor of Maritime Transport and Logistics at Ocean College at Zhejiang University, China. He is editor-in-chief of the *Journal of International Logistics and Trade* and associate editor of *TR-E*.

Guanie Lim is a Research Fellow at Nanyang Centre for Public Administration at Nanyang Technological University, Singapore.

Hong Liu is the Tan Kah Kee Endowed Professor of Public Policy and Global Affairs, the Chair of the School of Social Sciences, and Director of Nanyang Centre for Public Administration at Nanyang Technological University, Singapore.

Yanchuan Liu is a Research Fellow at Evidence for Policy Design at the John F. Kennedy School of Government at Harvard University, USA.

J. Mohan Malik is Professor of Asian Security at the Daniel K. Inouye Asia–Pacific Center for Security Studies in Honolulu, Hawaii, USA.

Jeffrey Reeves is Vice-President of Research for the Asia Pacific Foundation of Canada.

Xuezong Tao is an Assistant Professor in the College of Transport and Communications at Shanghai Maritime University, China.

Hong Yu is a Senior Research Fellow at the East Asian Institute at the National University of Singapore.

Suisheng Zhao is Professor and Director of the Center for China-US Cooperation in the Josef Korbel School of International Studies at the University of Denver, USA, and founding editor of the *Journal of Contemporary China*.

Weifeng Zhou is a PhD Candidate in Political Science and International Relations at the Autonomous University of Madrid, Spain.

Introduction – The BRI and AIIB as China's New Global Strategy

Motivations, Domestic Politics and International Responses

Suisheng Zhao

Rising as a global power, China has regarded the existing world order unreasonable enough to meet the interests of China and other emerging powers. Using its new quotient of wealth and influence, China has taken new initiative to reform the global governance to enhance its great power aspiration. This book focuses on the two most important initiatives that China started after President Xi came to office in 2012. One is the Belt and Road Initiative (BRI) launched in 2013 as President Xi's signature foreign policy to strengthen China's connectivity with a large part of the world through infrastructure construction and economic development. The other is the Asian Infrastructure Investment Bank (AIIB), created in 2015 under Beijing's leadership to fill the gap of infrastructure investments in developing countries and reconstruct the rules of international development.

This book is composed of three parts. The first part examines China's geopolitical and geo-economic motivations behind the two initiatives. In spite of the official rhetoric of providing public goods, these two initiatives are designed to serve China's geopolitical and geo-economic interests. As a huge stimulus package to help overcome the nation's domestic economic problems, the BRI and AIIB also aim to promote Chinese influence in the region and beyond, weaken the U.S. dominance in the regional and global economy, and reform global governance. These two initiatives are interrelated. While the BRI centers on the development of inter-connectivity of infrastructure to reflect China's ascendance in the global arena, the AIIB is to serve as the spearhead of the BRI to facilitate and accelerate infrastructure improvement in the region and beyond by providing capital loans and technical services. Seeking to form a China-centered bargaining coalition, the BRI and AIIB may help Beijing reshape global governance and transform the existing international system in a way that reflects China's values, interests, and status. Putting China at the center of geo-economics and geopolitics on the world stage, these two initiatives are central to China's emerging global strategy.

The second part of the book explores China's domestic political dynamics in the launching of the BRI. To achieve the grand objectives of the two initiatives, China has to overcome not only international challenges but also domestic barriers. The authors in Part II focuses on the domestic politics of the BRI and find that the BRI is permeated by underlying and interrelated tensions that derive from China's domestic political dynamics. One such dilemma is that the size of the BRI and the limited ability of governance through control and mobilization have inevitably put a huge burden on the Chinese economy and bureaucracy. Under the double-level governance of the central and local governments, discrepancies, disjointed actions, and gaps inevitably arise between the policies launched by the central and local governments. Local governments often think more about parochial interests and favor huge investments without considering their positions in a national strategy. In the meantime, Chinese political institutions currently lack mechanisms to correct potential mistakes committed by top leaders. The BRI may pose a nightmare for China if it opens a great strategic hole which sucks away China's resources or falls into a sort of Chinese geopolitical overstretching, as other empires did in the past.

The third part of the book looks at the responses from the regional and global partners involved in the BRI. Beijing may assume that economic development coupled with good will will be enough to make the BRI a success. But the effective implementation of the BRI largely depends on the response of China's partners, large and small, and requires much more than simply rhetoric and good will. While the political elites in many countries, particularly relatively weak and small state, are adept in engaging with China's initiatives to advance their key projects and furthering their own agenda, the responses of a huge number of countries have inevitably been varied. While China's partners may welcome China's investments and expertise, cross-border infrastructure projects are difficult to implement as they require complex and often protracted negotiations over proposed routes, development rights, financing and investment returns. China cannot assume that the growth through gigantic infrastructure investments, which drove China's economic success in the past, is a panacea and embraced automatically by other countries because many countries have doubts about issues in sovereignty, autonomy, local employment, and the economic returns from Chinese investments. To an extent, these concerns stem from the BRI's inherently bilateral nature by which China draws these countries into its orbit. With shared and conflicting interests, BRI countries' reactions to the BRI are inevitably mixed, both longing for and dreading Chinese investment. The challenge for China is how to respond and address the concerns of the BRI countries.

1 Motivation behind China's 'One Belt, One Road' Initiatives and Establishment of the Asian Infrastructure Investment Bank

Hong Yu

ABSTRACT

The 'One Belt, One Road' (OBOR) initiatives form the centerpiece of the Chinese leadership's new foreign policy. The OBOR initiatives are a reflection of China's ascendance in the global arena, economically, politically, and strategically. Developing inter-connectivity of infrastructure development forms a central part of China's OBOR initiatives. The Asian Infrastructure Investment Bank (AIIB) aims to facilitate and accelerate infrastructure improvement in the region by providing capital loans and technical services. The AIIB will serve as the spearhead of China's OBOR initiatives. The AIIB and OBOR initiatives have put China at the center of geoeconomics and geopolitics in the region and beyond, a position from which it hopes to strengthen its economic ties with other Asian countries. The new Silk Road initiatives also provide a channel for Chinese companies and capital to invest in other countries by leveraging China's strengths in infrastructure development, financial power and manufacturing capacity. The OBOR initiatives and the AIIB could change the economic and political landscape of Asia, the most dynamic and economically vibrant region of the twenty-first century. However, China faces serious challenges, both internally and externally, in implementing these initiatives.

China Unveils its 'One Belt, One Road' Initiatives

During Chinese President, Xi Jinping's visit to Kazakhstan and Indonesia in October 2013, he outlined China's ambitious plans for the so-called 'Silk Road Economic Belt' and 'Maritime Silk Road of the Twenty-First Century' respectively, contemporary versions of the centuries-old Silk Road trade routes. On land, the 'Silk Road Economic Belt' would mainly target Central Asia and Europe, while the Maritime Silk Road would mainly target Southeast, South and North Asia. These two initiatives were eventually combined into the 'One Belt, One Road' initiative (OBOR), with China as its hub.

This is to be a far-reaching strategy with regional and global implications for decades to come; as such it has attracted increasing interest among government officials, academia and the business community.

Since the announcement of the OBOR strategy the Chinese government has been conducting a charm offensive towards Asian and other countries along the historical Silk Road route, fully mobilizing its political, economic and diplomatic resources in order to forge a positive image of the New Silk Road strategy among the international community.

China's OBOR initiatives are rooted in history and inspired by the historic Silk Road (丝绸之路), an extensive network of maritime and land routes for trade, communication and cultural exchanges that once linked China with the countries of Asia, Middle East, and Africa to Europe. It fell into disuse around the 1600s after a few glorious centuries. The Chinese authority describes Southeast Asia as an important commercial hub along the maritime Silk Road route, playing an indispensable role in expanding China's external trade with the outside world. In the early fifteenth century, under the command of Admiral Zheng He, the Ming emperor dispatched a series of naval expeditions and treasure ships to foreign countries, reaching as far as the South China Sea, Indian Ocean and the African continent.[1] Hence, the trade links between China and its neighboring littoral states in the region were established in ancient times. China is now keen for this historical Silk Road to be revived.

However, Zheng He's main mission was not to promote trade and build friendly relations with countries and regions along the route, but instead to demonstrate China's sea power and the formidable imperial rule of Emperor Yongle.[2] In fact, most of the maritime trade across the Silk Road routes was not initiated by the Chinese, and imperial China's trade with the Southeast Asian littoral states was limited, as was its maritime prowess. The historian Wang Gungwu's studies show that expansion of the Chinese empire had been consistently landwards and Chinese rulers were consistently passive about forging maritime contact with the outside world, despite sporadic maritime trade links with Southeast Asian ports during Emperor Yongle's era. After his death, his successors showed little interest in maritime trade with the outside world. The Dutch and Portuguese played an important role in maritime trade with Southeast Asia along the Silk Road, whilst by the eighteenth century the British had started to play a dominant role in the maritime routes in the region.[3]

The Chinese government is eager to strengthen China's political influence and promote closer economic integration with its neighboring Asian nations via improvement of physical inter-regional connectivity under the framework of the OBOR strategy. To support implementation of the OBOR strategy, China led the establishment of the Asian Infrastructure Investment Bank (AIIB). The AIIB and the new Silk Road initiatives demonstrate that China is now starting to take on a leadership role to reflect its position as a rising global power. The AIIB and OBOR initiatives have made China the center of geoeconomics and geopolitics in the region and beyond. China is a central actor both in the region and on the world's economic and political stage. China's rising geo-economic power means that it is now the largest trading and economic partner for most of the Asian countries.

Whilst geopolitics and geoeconomics are different concepts with different meanings, the two are closely interrelated. The concept of geopolitics is defined as 'an old expression shaped by both academic and popular usages going back to imperial concerns with the links between geography, state territoriality, and world power politics.' In contrast, geo-economics is a relatively new concept, 'geoeconomic visionaries tend as a result to anticipate capitalist inclusion rather than the expulsion or containment of evil others. Their focus is on networks not blocs, connections not walls, and transborder ties instead of national territories.'[4] In essence, geopolitics studies the influence of such aspects as military, political, human resources and other hard power elements on the policy of a state, particularly its foreign policy. Meanwhile geo-economics focuses more on economic space, covering transportation connectivity, networks, commerce, trade, investment, and financial and economic strengths. Geo-economics concerns a nation's pursuit of strong economic performance and sustainable economic competitiveness. However, geopolitics and are two sides of the same coin, the political dimension of geoeconomics being strongly intertwined with the competitive economic dimension of geopolitics.

---

[1]Daniel C Waugh, 'The silk roads in history', *Expedition* 52(3), (2011), pp. 9-22; Jeremy Page, "Chinese territorial strife hits archaeology," *The Wall Street Journal*, 2 December 2013, accessed 19 February 2014, http://online.wsj.com/news/articles/SB10001424052702 3044705045791648732581594 10.
[2]Gungwu Wang, 'China and South-East Asia 1402–1424', in *Studies in the Social History of China and South-East Asia*, eds. Jerome Ch'en and Nicholas Tarling (Cambridge: Cambridge University Press, 1970), pp. 375-405.
[3]Gungwu Wang, 'The China Seas: becoming an enlarged Mediterranean', in *The East Asian 'Mediterranean: Maritime Crossroads of Culture, Commerce and Human Migration*, ed. Angela Schottenhammer, (Wiesbaden: Harrassowitz Verlag, 2008), pp. 7–22. Gungwu Wang, 'Southeast Asia: imperial themes', *New Zealand Journal of Asian Studies* 11(1), (2009), pp. 36–48.
[4]Matthew Sparke, 'Geopolitical fears, geoeconomic hopes, and the responsibilities of geography', *Annals of the Association of American Geographers* 97(2), (2007), pp. 339–340.

China has leveraged its formidable economic power to pursue its long-term strategic geopolitical goals. China aims to further deploy its growing national capacity and utilize its economic and financial power to expand its geopolitical influence in the region and overseas. The countries along the Silk Road routes will thus be brought into China's economic orbit. Graham Allison comments:[5]The preeminent geostrategic challenge of this era is not violent Islamic extremists or a resurgent Russia. It is the impact that China's ascendance will have on the U.S.-led international order, which has provided unprecedented great-power peace and prosperity for the past 70 years.

The rise of China as a formidable global economic power is enabling it to expand its geopolitical influence. The implementation of OBOR initiatives will give China greater access to energy and other natural resources, from countries such as Turkmenistan, Kazakhstan and Russia, and enormous markets along the Silk Road route to power sustained economic growth at home and advance its national economic interests abroad. The infrastructure development, trade and economic initiatives of the Silk Road strategy will reinforce China's geopolitical position in the region and throughout the world.

Although the OBOR strategy and the establishment of the AIIB have received much international media attention, these topics have rarely been exposed to academic scrutiny. What is the motivation and rationale behind China's new Silk Road strategy and the establishment of the AIIB? What will be the role of the AIIB in the OBOR initiatives? What major challenges face China in implementing this grand strategy? This article intends to address these serious issues.

For the completion of this article, the author made two fieldwork trips to Guangxi and Yunnan provinces, China, in May and June 2014. Many of the analyses and views in this article are based on the author's interviews with local officials and scholars, and personal experiences.

This article is divided into six sections. The current part presents an Introduction to China's OBOR initiatives. The second section analyzes the motivation and rationale behind China's new Silk Road initiative. The third section discusses the motivation behind China's plan to establish the AIIB. The fourth section provides analysis on the race for founding membership of the AIIB and the United States' reaction to the bank. The fifth section presents the main challenges China faces in implementing this grand initiative. The final section presents concluding thoughts.

Motivation and Rationale behind China's OBOR Initiatives

Since introducing the OBOR initiative, the Chinese government has been criticized on the grounds that the initiative is too vague a concept and might just be an example of hollow government rhetoric.[6] Against this backdrop, on 28 March 2015, China's National Development and Reform Commission (NDRC), Ministry of Commerce and Ministry of Foreign Affairs jointly released the lengthy 'Vision and Actions on Jointly Building the Silk Road Economic Belt and 21st Century Maritime Silk Road[7] (the Blueprint) outlining relevant frameworks, principles and action plans. Although still short on some detail, this Blueprint provides the clearest overall picture yet of the Silk Road strategy and demonstrates China's serious attempt to materialize its grand vision.

The new Silk Road initiatives represent Xi's most ambitious foreign policies, demonstrating a new policy direction for China and its aspirations for global ascendancy. The OBOR initiatives are a reflection of China's ascendance as well as her growing power in the global arena. China's new initiatives are pragmatic, being driven by economic, historical and strategic motivations. As China is a one-party ruled country, the process of foreign policy formulation lacks transparency and is hidden from the outside world, although the other political Parties, academia and the business community may play a consultative role.

---

[5]Graham Allison, 'The Thucydides Trap: are the US and China headed for war?' the Atlantic, 24 September 2015, accessed 14 December 2015, http://www.theatlantic.com/international/archive/2015/09/united-states-china-war-thucydides-trap/406756/.

[6]Lucio Blanco Pitlo III, "China's 'One Belt. One Road' to where?" The Diplomat, 17 February 2015, accessed 28 March 2015, http://thediplomat.com/2015/02/chinas-one-belt-one-road-to-where/.

[7]Ministry of Foreign Affairs of the People's Republic of China, 'Vision and Actions on Jointly Building Silk Road Economic Belt and 21st Century Maritime Silk Road,' 28 March 2015, accessed 2 April 2015, http://www.fmprc.gov.cn/mfa_eng/zxxx_662805/t1249618.shtml.

Compared with the previous era, China's foreign policy direction has changed substantially over the past several years, in particular after 2008, and it is now more proactive, assertive and globally-driven. Against the backdrop of domestic economic slowdown, boosting Chinese economic growth has been one of the main drivers of foreign policy decision-making in Xi's China. The domestic economic situation is a major consideration in the making and implementation of China's OBOR initiatives. Given the rising regional interdependency of the globalization era, the OBOR initiatives are an important tool for Beijing to flex its financial muscle to advance China's economic interests abroad.

More importantly, China's proactive foreign policy has been influenced by the increasing sense of national pride that has accompanied the emergence of China as a global power and the world's second largest economy. The Chinese people by and large have become more confident about their nation.[8] Meanwhile, the Chinese leaders have been increasingly responsive to this popular nationalism. Zhao Suisheng argues that the Chinese government has become more accountable to popular nationalist calls since 2008 in terms of its muscular foreign policy, which he referred to as a 'strident turn' for China.[9]

The transformation of China's foreign policy began late in the era of Hu Jintao, the former Chinese President. As its economic and financial power accumulated, China began to engage in multilateral regional cooperation platforms. Hence, China's proactive foreign policy under the current leader Xi is a reflection of continuity rather than radical change. Nevertheless, like their predecessors, the new Chinese leaders need to show innovation in foreign policy by announcing new policies that will distinguish their leadership strategy and advance China's national interests abroad in a fast changing international environment. The OBOR initiatives form a centerpiece of China's new foreign strategy under Xi Jinping, in particular with regard to its neighboring countries in Asia.

By pushing for the OBOR initiatives, the Chinese government has rebranded and integrated the various existing regional cooperation mechanisms to facilitate regional economic integration and advance its national interests through improvement of inter-regional connectivity. These cooperation mechanisms include the Shanghai Cooperation Organization (SCO), ASEAN Plus China (10+1), China-ASEAN (Association of Southeast Asian Nations) Expo, Asia-Pacific Economic Cooperation (APEC), and Greater Mekong Sub-region Economic Cooperation (GMS). Through its active role in relation to these cooperation mechanisms, China seeks to gain support from the respective countries in promoting the OBOR initiatives.

The scale and pace of change in China's foreign policy under Xi have been unprecedented and have surprised many China watchers. Fravel once predicted that 'Xi and the new Politburo Standing Committee may not launch new initiatives of their own for perhaps one or two years.... Chinese foreign policy under Xi Jinping is likely to remain inherently reactive and not proactive.'[10] The ascendancy of China in the global arena and Xi's initiation of a new foreign policy agenda in such a short period of time have astonished both the region and onlookers in the West. The new Silk Road and AIIB proposals demonstrate China's capability to develop its own initiatives for financial and economic governance in the region.

China has now turned a corner in its foreign policy decision-making, and is determined to reshape the world order rather than be shaped by the changing world. Compared with his predecessors, Xi has abandoned China's long-held policy of 'keeping a low profile in international affairs' adhered to since the 1980s by the previous leader Deng Xiaoping. China's foreign policy is now more centralized, proactive and even aggressive. Xi has centralized foreign policy-making power under his own direction since he came to power in 2012, chairing the Central Leading Group for Foreign Affairs, the highest authority for foreign policy decision-making in China, which demonstrates his strong man image and his ambitious vision.

[8]Shaun Breslin, 'China and the global order: signaling threat or friendship?', *International Affairs* 89(3), (2013), pp. 615–634.
[9]Suisheng Zhao, 'Foreign policy implications of Chinese nationalism revisited: the strident turn', *Journal of Contemporary China* 22(82), (2013), pp. 535–553.
[10]Taylor Fravel, 'Foreign policy under Xi Jinping,' *The Diplomat*, 23 November 2012, accessed 10 December 2015, http://thediplomat. com/2012/11/foreign-policy-under-xi-jinping/.

One of the major objectives of China's foreign policy towards Asia is to maintain friendly neighborhood relations by promoting regional economic integration and improving regional connectivity, in order to achieve primacy in the region and beyond. In 2014, during a Chinese central government conference on foreign affairs, Xi Jinping remarked that China needs to develop a 'distinctive diplomatic approach befitting its role as a major country'.[11] The Chinese government accords Asia high priority in its foreign policy. As shown in the empirical findings by Ramasamy *et al.*, over the last decade Asia has accounted for more than 50% of total stock of China's outward foreign investment.[12]

It is understandable that China felt obliged to take a low-profile, passive approach to foreign policy when it was a poor developing nation with many thorny domestic issues and limited financial resources. However, over the past two decades China has become far more powerful than in Deng's era, and it is now able to project its power in Asia and beyond. With its rise as a global power after three decades of economic reform and opening up, China has started to take a more proactive foreign policy stance to safeguard its domestic development, and to advance its national strategic and economic interests abroad. Xi views the change to China's foreign policy as necessary to match its ascendancy as the rising global power. Xi intends that China will one day become a rule-shaper in the global arena and regain a position of pre-eminence in the world.

From the economic perspective, this strategy serves three main purposes for China. First, through promoting its OBOR strategy, China is keen to help Asian countries to modernize their infrastructure and improve cross-border transport and other crucial infrastructure facilities. This in turn will help China to forge strong bilateral trade and economic integration with its Asian neighbors.

Connectivity is the shortcut to economic prosperity. Economic geography theorists have long argued the importance of infrastructure development in overcoming backward geographical conditions and reducing the high costs of production in landlocked countries.[13] Infrastructure provides the foundation for industrial and economic prosperity. For example, the comparative cross-regional study by Calderón and Servén describes the significant contribution made by infrastructure development to economic growth in Sub-Saharan Africa.[14]

China is convinced that its new Silk Road strategy will boost regional trade and economic development in Asia through inter-regional infrastructure improvement and industrial transfer. In particular, high-speed railway connectivity and maritime trade via deep-water ports and harbors are viewed as key pre-conditions for economic take-off and prosperity. China's ports lead the world in global shipping and cargo transportation. In 2014, Shanghai ranked as the largest exporter of containerized goods worldwide, whilst ten of China's ports were included among the world's top 20 container ports.[15] China's superiority in this field of commerce provides the foundation for building close maritime ties with other countries along the Silk Road routes, and achieving further transport cooperation with Asian countries in the future.

China's economic growth is powered by its massive export-oriented manufacturing industries, while it has to import large amounts of intermediate components and raw resources to power these industries. As the transport of these raw materials and semi-finished goods to China largely depends on maritime shipping, a secure and reliable maritime trade shipping line is crucial to China.

---

[11]Ministry of Foreign Affairs of People's Republic of China, *The Central Conference on Work Relating to Foreign Affairs was held in Beijing*, 29 November 2014, accessed 4 June 2015, http://www.fmprc.gov.cn/mfa_eng/zxxx_662805/t1215680.shtml.

[12]Bala Ramasamy, Matthew Yeung and Sylvie Laforet, 'China's outward foreign direct investment: location choice and firm ownership', *Journal of World Business* 47, (2012), pp. 17–25.

[13]Gerald Kraft, John R. Meyer and Jean-Paul Valette, *The Role of Transportation in Regional Economic Development* (London: D.C. Health and Company, 1971). Spiros Bougheas, Panicos O. Demetriades and Edgar L.W. Morgenroth, 'Infrastructure, transport costs and trade', *Journal of International Economics* 47, (1999), pp. 169–189. J. Vernon Henderson, Zmarak Shalizi and Anthony J. Venables, 'Geography and development', *Journal of Economic Geography* 1, (2001), pp. 81–105.

[14]César Calderón and Luis Servén, 'Infrastructure and economic development in Sub-Saharan Africa', *Journal of African Economies* 19(AERC Supplement 1), (2010), pp. i13–i87.

[15]American Association of Port Authorities, 'World Port Rankings 2014', 2014, accessed 11 September 2016, http://www.aapa-ports.org/unifying/content.aspx?ItemNumber=21048.

From the Chinese perspective, relocating some excessive production capacity to neighboring Southeast Asian Silk Road countries where there is a demand will also be beneficial to their economies and accelerate local industrialization, through engaging in bilateral infrastructure, trade and investment cooperation and tapping into China's huge domestic markets. China also needs to engage with other fast emerging Asian markets, to power sustainable domestic economic development.

Second, in seeking to gain more profits and expand their global business operations, Chinese companies have strong incentives under the OBOR initiatives to invest their capital in other nations and implement a 'going-out' strategy. China is eager to participate in the construction of port and other related facilities in this region as such outward infrastructure investment will boost its manufacturing investment and hence its economic growth.

The Silk Road countries will provide new markets for China's enormous excess of manufactured products and construction capacity. Although China is pursuing more balanced economic growth in which domestic consumption will play a major role, this is a very difficult task and it will take time. The export sector is thus still essential to boost the Chinese economy and domestic industrial development. The export of 'Made in China' goods to the Asian countries will help to absorb many of China's manufactured goods, such as iron and steel, aluminum, shipbuilding products, cement and flat-panel glass, which will help to address domestic production overcapacity and stimulate domestic economic growth through upgrading of its industries.

Thirdly, the OBOR initiatives could enable China's vast inland western regions such as Xinjiang and Yunnan to improve internal economic integration and participate in global trade. Implementing these initiatives will improve inter-regional connectivity of the land-locked western regions and allow them direct access to port facilities in neighboring countries. As an example, Yunnan Province needs cross-border economic links in order to achieve rejuvenation and economic prosperity. Its land connectivity with the ASEAN will be strengthened through cooperation on expressway and railways, and development of its ports and harbor-related and airport infrastructure.

Yunnan borders three ASEAN countries, Myanmar, Laos and Vietnam, and is a short distance from India and Bangladesh in South Asia, Thailand and Cambodia in Southeast Asia. This geographical advantage enables Yunnan to serve as the international gateway or connector for China, Southeast Asia and South Asia. Yunnan could become a key littoral or gateway for China's OBOR strategy.

Fourth, from the historical perspective, the rationale behind China's OBOR initiative is to revive its historical Silk Road. The Silk Road initiatives echo the so-called 'China Dreams' of the great revival of the Chinese nation, which was first announced by President Xi Jinping in November 2012,[16] and has been reiterated by the Chinese leaders in their speeches thereafter. The Chinese leadership sees the OBOR proposal as an important step on the road to reclaiming China's historical global position.

Many China observers and analysts argue that the OBOR strategy is China's version of the Marshall Plan, whereby United States (US) loans and investment helped to rebuild Europe after World War II. In fact, China's ambition far exceeds that of the Marshall Plan. Whilst the Marshall Plan was restricted in scope to the region of Europe, China's new Silk Road strategy is globally-oriented: from the geographical perspective it stretches across 60 countries along envisioned routes extending through Asia, Middle East, Europe and even Africa, and could potentially generate an even greater international impact.

Establishment of the China-led AIIB

Inter-connectivity infrastructure development forms a central part of China's OBOR strategy. The AIIB, which has its headquarters in Beijing, will spearhead the strategy by facilitating and accelerating infrastructure improvement in the region by providing capital loans and technical services. The AIIB was formally launched during a signing ceremony attended by the 21 Asian founding member countries.

---

[16] 'China's Future: Xi Jinping and the Chinese dream,' *The Economist*, 1 May 2013, accessed 20 February 2014, http://www.economist.
com/news/leaders/21577070-vision-chinas-new-president-should-serve-his-people-not-nationalist-state-xi-jinping.

Xi Jinping personally met the heads of delegations from these 21 states, and hailed the establishment of the AIIB as an important development for Asia.

According to the articles of agreement (AOA)[17] of the bank, China will hold a total voting share of over 26% due to its contribution of US$29.78 billion. China is the largest investor in the AIIB and its largest shareholder. As written in the AOA, at least 75% of total votes are required in order to amend the AOA, adjust the capital shares of regional members, increase the capital base of the bank and make other major changes. Thus, China has the de facto veto power in the bank.

With over US$3.5 trillion in foreign exchange reserves, China has plentiful financial resources for aiding infrastructure development in underdeveloped nations in the region. The establishment of the AIIB is a reflection of China's push for outward investment globally. China is winning over many developing countries in Asia, Africa and Latin America with preferential loans and grants for infrastructure development. Since the announcement of the AIIB proposal, many Asian countries have been eager to gain financial assistance from China for large-scale public infrastructure projects that they are incapable of self-funding. The AIIB is hence an important financial tool for China in increasing its geoeconomic influence in the region and increasing the international momentum of the OBOR strategy.

China's motivation for establishment of the AIIB is based both on external and internal considerations. From the external perspective, one of the main drivers is the urgent need among Asian countries for investment for infrastructure development. Many developing Asian countries are faced with the task of upgrading their totally inadequate and inefficient road, air transport, port and railroad infrastructure, which is a key barrier to achieving local economic take-off and regional integration. As shown in the global competitiveness index published by the World Economic Forum in 2013,[18] the majority of Southeast Asian and South Asian countries come out very poorly in international comparisons of quality of transportation and other critical infrastructure.

For such countries, infrastructure underdevelopment is a major obstacle to economic advancement. Frequently-occurring electricity and water shortages, inadequate and outdated infrastructure facilities have not only held back ordinary people's living standards, but also impeded local industrialization and foreign investment. According to the report published by the Japan External Trade Organization (JETRO) in 2014, inadequate infrastructure remains the biggest challenge for the investment environment in the region.[19] These countries are therefore unable to meet the infrastructure demand created by their increasing middle-class populations and the rapid urbanization within the region. For example, by 2020, Thailand, Malaysia, Philippines and Indonesia will between them have 40 million new urban residents[20] and will need massive investment in infrastructure as well as much technical and professional assistance in order to unlock their full development potential.

As a case in point, aged and inadequate port infrastructure has made intra and inter-regional maritime transportation extremely costly in many Asian countries and impeded their formation of maritime cooperation with China. Moreover, they lack the financial resources to upgrade their existing facilities. For instance, the Director General of the Cambodia Chamber of Commerce states that Cambodia badly needs more foreign investment to construct deep-water ports and other infrastructure facilities to accommodate large-scale cargo ships.[21]

However, the World Bank and the Asian Development Bank (ADB) combined do not have adequate capacity to meet this huge investment demand, whilst the high-risks and long construction cycles of infrastructure development projects have deterred private investors. Against this backdrop, the aim of the AIIB is to fill this investment gap regarding infrastructure construction in Asian countries. This

---

[17]AIIB, 'Asian Infrastructure Investment Bank Articles of Agreement', pp. 1–34, accessed 8 December 2015, http://www.aiib.org/uploadfile/2015/0814/20150814022158430.pdf .

[18]World Economic Forum, *The Global Competitiveness Report 2013-2014* (Geneva, Switzerland, 2013), pp. 1–551.

[19]JETRO, '2014 JETRO global trade and investment report: on making Japan a base for international business circulation,' 7 August 2014, accessed 14 December 2015, https://www.jetro.go.jp/en/news/releases/2014/20140807856-news.html.

[20]Goldman Sachs, 'ASEAN's half a trillion dollar infrastructure opportunity,' *Asia Economics Analyst Issue* 13/18, (May 2013).

[21]'Interview: China's "Maritime Silk Road" initiative vital to further enhance ties with ASEAN: Cambodian exports,' *Xinhua News*, 18 January 2014, accessed 20 February 2014, http://news.xinhuanet.com/english/indepth/2014-01/18/c_133055311_2.htm.

bank will provide a new financial tool for China, and funding Asian connectivity-related infrastructure projects will be its priority.

Moreover, the AIIB represents China's response to its frustration with the slow pace of reform of the international financial system. As the world's second largest economy, China is now a net capital surplus exporter and seeks a bigger stake in the West-dominated international financial system through the implementation of these bold reforms. In 2015, despite the total value of China's Gross Domestic Product (GDP) (US$10.98 trillion) being more than double that of Japan (US$4.12 trillion), the World's third largest economy, and more than 60% of the US (US$17.94 trillion), the world's largest economy,[22] as of December 2015, China's total holding in the ADB was, for instance, only 6.45%, whilst Japan and the US held 15.62% and 15.51% respectively.[23] Furthermore, the US has power of veto in the World Bank and the IMF, whilst Japan has power of veto in the ADB.

Hence, China's shareholding and voting power in these multilateral organizations has failed to match the global power shift towards the east and its status as the rising global power. China's limited voting power implies it has little influence in the decision-making process of the World Bank, the IMF (International Monetary Fund) and the ADB. China is therefore prepared to demand more say in these organizations in return for supplying Chinese capital to fund existing multilateral institutions such as the IMF for assisting countries with liquidity crises.

Against this backdrop, China has adopted a two-pronged strategy for reform of the existing global financial system. On the one hand, China is allying with other emerging economies, primarily the BRICS countries (Brazil, Russia, India, China and South Africa) which have a shared perception of being underrepresented in the current West-dominated economic system and a shared objective to work together for international financial reforms. On the other hand, China has taken the step of creating its own international financial organizations such as the AIIB. China is putting more pressure on the West to accelerate the process of international financial reforms by challenging the dominant role of the World Bank and the ADB in funding transportation and other infrastructure projects in Asia.

From the internal perspective, the AIIB provides a channel for investment of Chinese capital in other countries. The OBOR strategy will expand the scope and depth of Chinese companies' investment and business activities in the region. China has demonstrated its economic clout through pouring billions of dollars in investment into developing Asian countries, in fields ranging from infrastructure construction, agricultural production, mining and manufacturing to service and retail business.

With Beijing's full backing, Chinese companies, most of which are state-owned, have been proactive in implanting the OBOR initiatives, and they already have made huge investments in transportation and other infrastructure projects located in the Silk Road countries. Investment in ports is a case in point. Chinese firms have constructed many container ports and been granted exclusive management rights. These ports are located in strategic positions along China's Silk Road, which enables China to control transportation of goods and people (Table 1).

The construction of large-scale port projects in the region, some already completed, others under construction, or yet to be constructed will help China to diversify its energy and raw materials supply overseas and safeguard its national energy and economic security. The Chinese government has pushed forward the long-term new Silk Road strategy to increase China's global influence and its global leadership role.

Moreover, the implementation of a new Silk Road strategy will help to revive China's slowing domestic economy by boosting foreign trade and China's outward investment. This strategy will also allow China more time and room for pursuing industrial restructuring and upgrading. The slowdown in the Chinese economy has resulted in a serious problem of domestic production overcapacity in China's heavy industries. Participating in the infrastructure projects financed by the AIIB will help to absorb

---

[22]'Country gross domestic product 2015,' *World Development Indicators Database*, World Bank (July 2016).
[23]Asian Development Bank, 'ADB annual report 2015,' April 2016, accessed 10 August 2016, http://www.adb.org/documents/adb-annual-report-2015.

Table 1. List of investment by Chinese companies in container ports along the Silk Road route.

Country	Container port	Chinese company	Shareholding ratio of Chinese company
Malaysia	Kuantan Port	Guangxi Beibu Gulf Port Group	40%
Singapore	Singapore Container Port	COSCO Pacific	49%
Myanmar	Kyaukphyu Port	China National Petroleum Corporation (CNPC)	50.9%
Sri Lanka	Colombo International Container Terminal	China Merchants Holdings (International)	85%
	Hambantota Container Port	China Harbor Engineering Corporation	65%
Pakistan	Gwadar Port	China Overseas Port Holding Company	40-year lease agreement for operating and managing port
Egypt	Safaga Port	COSCO Pacific	20%
Djibouti	Djibouti Container Port	China Merchants Holdings (International)	23.5%
Israel	Haifa New Port	Shanghai International Port Group	25-year lease agreement for operating and managing port
Greece	Piraeus Container Port	COSCO Pacific	35-year lease agreement for operating and managing port
Italy	Naples Container Port	COSCO Pacific	50%
Belgium	Port of Antwerp	COSCO Pacific	25%

Source: Author.

China's massive production overcapacity at home in manufacturing, infrastructure construction and related industries.

Race for Founding Membership of the AIIB and the US Reaction to the AIIB

In early March 2015, the United Kingdom (UK) government announced its decision to join the AIIB and lend money to the bank, a decision that was based on its national economic interests. Britain wants a share of the potentially huge infrastructure construction market in Asia, and seeks to strengthen London's role as a key international financial center by tapping into the rapid economic growth of China and the other emerging Asian economies.[24]

The UK was the first major developed western country to join the China-led AIIB, and this was a symbolic move in terms of attracting other developed Asian and non-Asian countries to join the bank. Germany, France, Italy, among many other European countries, and Australia, South Korea and Israel, which are close allies of the US, soon followed in the UK's footsteps and announced their decision to seek founding membership of the AIIB.

The US has not signed up for the AIIB, reiterating its concerns over whether the AIIB will achieve sufficiently high standards of corporate governance, and questioning the structure of the organization, lending procedure, and environmental and social safeguards. The US perceives the AIIB as serving as a vehicle for China to project its economic influence across Asia. The US government believes that the China-led AIIB will not work in harmony with the World Bank, the IMF and the ADB and will challenge the West-dominated international financial order. The US government has therefore exerted diplomatic pressure on its close allies not to join the AIIB.[25] In a rare criticism of UK policy, the US government expressed its unhappiness and disappointment over the UK's move to join the AIIB, with a US government official reportedly telling the *Financial Times* that 'we are wary about a trend toward constant accommodation of China, which is not the best way to engage a rising power'.[26]

---

[24]'UK support for China-backed Asia Bank prompts US concern,' *BBC News*, 13 March 2015, accessed 28 March 2015, http://www.bbc.com/news/world-australia-31864877.

[25]*The Economist*, 'China on the world stage: a bridge not far enough,' 21 March 2015, accessed 7 April 2015, http://www.economist.com/node/21646746/print.

[26]Geoff Dyer and George Parker, 'US attacks UK's "constant accommodation" with China,' *Financial Times*, 12 March 2015, accessed 7 April 2015, http://www.ft.com/cms/s/0/31c4880a-c8d2-11e4-bc64-00144feab7de.html#axzz3WaYUeVoe.

Whilst Washington has concerns over the perceived threat to its superpower status in the region and around the world, some analysts believe that China is the only rising power that can challenge the hegemonic power of the US. As stated by the following remark from China experts:

> The most important factor is the decline of US power. While the United States remains the most powerful state today, its decline has been much faster than many have expected. The United States has been strong in all aspects since World War II, but now it remains strong only in the military force.[27]

The US fears that China's real intention in founding the AIIB might be to replace the Western-dominated financial architecture with a China-centric regional and international financial system. During his State of the Union Address to Congress in January 2015, US President Obama made the following remark attacking China:[28]

> But as we speak, China wants to write the rules for the world's fastest-growing region. That would put our workers and our businesses at a disadvantage. Why would we let that happen? We should write those rules.

However, the Chinese government has repeatedly said that the AIIB is complementary to the existing regional and international financial systems, and it will cooperate closely with the existing multilateral development organizations in the region. China argues that rather than seeking to replace the functions and role of existing international banking organizations, the AIIB will learn from the best practice of these organizations.

The major multilateral development institutions have all said that they will work with the AIIB in providing loans and sharing their professional expertise in order to construct much needed infrastructure in the region. Although the AIIB will find it hard to avoid competition with the existing international organizations in financing infrastructure projects, the infrastructure construction market is large enough for the AIIB, World Bank and the ADB to compete amicably.

The US's traditional allies, despite the risk of offending Uncle Sam, are suddenly rushing eastwards towards China. *The Economist* comments: 'China has won, gaining the support of American allies not just in Asia but in Europe, and leaving America looking churlish and ineffectual'.[29] In addition, Lawrence Summers, a former US Treasury Secretary and former President of Harvard University, and hence an influential public figure, strongly argued that US government policy on the China-led AIIB had been misguided, and asked the US government to review its global economic policies. In an article published by *The Washington Post* on 6 April 2015,[30] he stated:

> This past month may be remembered as the moment the United States lost its role as the underwriter of the global economic system. … But I can think of no event since Bretton Woods comparable to the combination of China's effort to establish a major new institution and the failure of the United States to persuade dozens of its traditional allies, starting with Britain, to stay out.

There are 57 countries in total serving as the Prospective Founding Members (PFMs) for the AIIB. The fact that so many Asian and non-Asian countries are seeking to become PFMs of the AIIB is a remarkable achievement for China. China itself underestimated the popularity of the bank, as the President of the AIIB, Jin Liqun made what now appears a very modest estimate that China hoped that up to 37 countries would either be PFMs or applicants by 31 March 2015. The race for AIIB founding membership among non-Asian developed countries has suddenly transformed the AIIB from potentially a regional financial organization, into a banking organization of global reach and perspective. China's proactive foreign policy and its formidable geoeconomic power and influence are transforming the region and beyond.

[27]Yongnian Zheng and Wen Xin Lim, 'The Challenging Geopolitical Landscape and China's World Order', *EAI Background Brief 1051*, August 19, 2015, National University of Singapore, p. 5.

[28]'*Remarks by the President in State of the Union Address*', White House, 20 January 2015, accessed 4 June 2015, https://www.whitehouse.gov/the-press-office/2015/01/20/remarks-president-state-union-address-january-20-2015.

[29]*The Economist*, 'The Asian Infrastructure Investment Bank: the infrastructure gap', 21 March 2015, accessed 7 April 2015, http://www.economist.com/node/21646740/print.

[30]Lawrence Summers, 'The US may have lost its role as the world's economic leader', *The Washington Post*, 6 April 2015, accessed 4 June 2015, http://www.businessinsider.com/larry-summers-the-us-has-lost-its-role-as-the-worlds-economic-leader-2015-4.

Challenges to China's New Silk Road Initiatives and the AIIB

China faces both internal and external challenges to implementation of its OBOR initiatives. From the internal perspective, China has yet to establish an effective central leadership structure to coordinate Silk Road-related activities and the various government departments have failed to come up with unified strategy for implementing the OBOR proposals abroad. For example, the Ministry of Commerce is primarily interested in bilateral trade and investment, whilst the NDRC is primarily concerned with inter-regional infrastructure construction projects with the region. Intensifying local competition represents an additional concern for China, as two southwestern Chinese provinces, Yunnan and Guangxi, both claim to be China's gateway towards Southeast Asia and are engaged in intense competition over preferential policies from the Chinese central government.[31]

A lack of inter-organizational and central-local coordination could not only delay implementation of the state's Silk Road plans, which are already dogged by red tape and bureaucracy, but could also cause confusion in Asian countries as to who is in charge of the Silk Road proposal and with whom they should negotiate. As Wang Jisi rightly points out,[32] 'Almost all institutions in the central leadership and local governments are involved in foreign relations to varying degrees, and it is virtually impossible for them to see China's national interest the same way or to speak with one voice. These differences confuse outsiders as well as the Chinese people.' Such problems over unity and communication could undermine China's efforts to promote its grand strategy.

From the external perspective, the biggest challenge to China's Silk Road initiatives derives from external issues and is political rather than economic. China hopes to use these OBOR initiatives to forge close economic cooperation with the Silk Road countries and boost their economic growth by improving infrastructure connectivity and increasing trade and investment. However, due to their suspicion over China's real intention, the Asian countries' reactions to the OBOR initiatives have been mixed. The reactions from the ASEAN countries, the US, Japan and India are particularly crucial to the implementation of the OBOR initiatives and its overall effectiveness. Meanwhile, China has failed to cultivate the necessary strategic and political trust among these respective parties over the new Silk Road strategy.

First, although China's bilateral trade and economic ties with the ASEAN countries are increasing, relations between China and many member countries have been damaged by ongoing maritime disputes in the South China Sea (SCS). The OBOR initiatives could be seen as a reflection of China's growing maritime power and its aim to project its sea power and naval capabilities globally. Some scholars believe that the main purpose of the maritime Silk Road proposal is to safeguard China's maritime trade route along the SCS, which is vital to its importation of energy and resources.[33]

In May 2014, the Philippines condemned China's action on land reclamation to build new facilities on a SCS reef that is the subject of a dispute between the two countries.[34] On 11 May 2014, several large-scale rallies and protests took place in Vietnam's major cities, where people vented their anger over a deepwater oil drilling operation conducted by a state-owned Chinese company in disputed waters of the SCS.[35] These protests were reportedly the largest anti-China protests in Vietnam in recent years.

China has massively stepped up its efforts in land reclamation and infrastructure construction activities in the SCS in the past few years, and its increasing assertiveness in the SCS is a signal to the ASEAN that China will not hesitate to safeguard its territorial sovereignty and protect its maritime interests, taking unilateral action if necessary. The ASEAN countries have consequently become very wary of any move made by China in the region. China's perceived aggressive behavior has not helped its attempts

---

[31]Mingjiang Li, 'Local Liberalism: China's provincial approaches to relations with Southeast Asia', *Journal of Contemporary China* 23(86), (2014), pp. 275–293.

[32]Jisi Wang, 'China's search for a grand strategy: a rising great power finds its way', *Foreign Affairs* 90(2), (2011), pp. 68–79.

[33]Michael Crisp, 'The great Chinese sea power debate: a review essay', *Journal of Contemporary China* 19(63), (2010), pp. 201–212.

[34]Manuel Mogato, 'Philippines says China appears to be building an airstrip on disputed reef', *Reuters*, 13 May 2014, accessed 15 May 2014, http://www.reuters.com/article/2014/05/14/us-philippines-china-reef-idUSBREA4D00K20140514.

[35]Andrew Browne, 'Beijing pays a price for assertiveness in South China Sea', *Wall Street Journal*, 13 May 2014, accessed 15 May 2014, http://online.wsj.com/news/articles/SB10001424052702303627504579558913140862896.

to establish cooperative relations with its neighbors in the region. From the ASEAN perspective, China's growing military power is widely perceived as a threat to free movement of cargo and a form of deterrence to endorse its sovereignty claim over the SCS. As one scholar points out, China's vast size, her huge market potential and growing military capabilities have presented both opportunities and threats to the ASEAN.[36]

With the rise of China as a global power, these Asian countries are concerned that China will become more aggressive and eventually use or threaten to use force to solve its territorial disputes with neighboring countries. The ASEAN therefore welcomes the United States''pivot to Asia' strategy as a hedge or counterbalance against the rise of China, whilst China views the actions and maritime claims by the Philippines and Vietnam in the SCS as a challenge to its territorial integrity and 'core interest'.

These territorial disputes surrounding the SCS show no signs of being resolved in the near future and are seen as the major obstacle to the deepening of bilateral relationships.[37] Despite pledges by the leaders of both China and the ASEAN member states to strengthen bilateral cooperation, China-ASEAN relations remain fragile and fraught with contention and competition.

Indeed, the ASEAN has warned that China's involvement in the construction of large-scale critical infrastructure could threaten regional security. Some neighboring Asian countries are suspicious of whether China will use its increasing formidable economic and political power for the good of Asia and the world, or to become a regional or global hegemon. Such skepticism among Asian nations about China's real motivation and intentions could deter these countries from cooperating fully with OBOR initiatives on infrastructure development, which could jeopardize the operations of the AIIB and the implementation of China's grand plans. China has to convince the Asian countries that implementation of the OBOR initiatives is a win-win situation for both parties.

China needs to work with the small Asian countries in a more equal and collaborative manner, as these countries would certainly resent being seen as passive recipients of China's proposals. China has on occasions focused unilaterally on its own interests and failed to consult or communicate properly with the ASEAN side. Guangxi officials, meanwhile, have expressed surprise that their 'Nanning – Singapore Economic Corridors' initiative proposed in 2006 has failed to attract support from the ASEAN countries, even though China is willing to provide a large portion of the funding for inter-regional transportation construction. They regard Vietnam as being over-concerned about its national security and territorial sovereignty in relation to this proposal.[38] However, from the perspectives of the ASEAN countries, they are keen to avoid economic over dependence on China at a time of increasing territorial disputes between China and some ASEAN member states, in light of China's growing assertiveness in foreign policy.

Second, the US and its allies may present a fundamental obstacle to China in implementation of the OBOR initiatives. The US and China appear to have increasingly divergent views on their respective strategic roles in the region and worldwide, with each country suspicious of the other's strategic and political intentions. The US fears that the rise of China will challenge US interests and reshape the West-dominated world order, whilst China is concerned that the US will restrain the rise of China.[39] Since Xi came to power in 2012, he has repeatedly called for an equal relationship with the US, under the framework of a 'new type of major power relationship'. Nevertheless, the US has largely ignored such calls, as it is intent on retaining its status as the world's sole superpower.

---

[36]Khai Leong Ho, 'Rituals, risks and rivalries: China and ASEAN in the coming decades', *Journal of Contemporary China* 10(29), (2001), pp. 683–694.

[37]Kok-Kheng Emile Yeoh, 'Forward China: foreign relations and maritime conflict', *International Journal of China Studies* 2(3), (2011), pp. 551–553.

[38]The following remarks were made by a senior local official in Guangxi with responsibility for Guangxi's trade and economic cooperation with the ASEAN countries, during an interview with the author.

[39]Cheng Li, 'A new type of major power relationship?', *Georgetown Journal of International Affairs*, Brookings Institution, 26 September 2014, accessed 9 December 2015, http://www.brookings.edu/research/interviews/2014/09/26-new-type-power-relationship-li. Biwu Zhang, 'Chinese perceptions of US return to Southeast Asia and the prospect of China's peaceful rise', *Journal of Contemporary China* 24(91), (2015), pp. 176–195.

Despite its rising international status, China is not yet ready to challenge the US-led Western primacy, and needs to acknowledge the limitations of its power. Neither should it exaggerate the decline in strength of the US or underestimate its resilience. The US economy is still much larger than that of China, the former's per capita GDP being more than seven times higher than the corresponding figure for China. Furthermore, America still leads the world in terms of technological capability, innovation, science and military might, due in no small part to its ability to attract a plentiful supply of skilled talent to its shores.

The US and its allies are however concerned that China is aiming to establish a Sino-centric regional order by means of the OBOR initiatives. Intense competition in Asia and beyond, between the US as the established superpower and China as the rising global power is emerging. To counterbalance the rise of China and its increasing prominence in the region, the US is implementing its high-profile 'Pivot to Asia' strategy to strengthen its military alliances, and reinforce its economic ties with the region.

From the economic dimension, the US is pushing hard for the TPP (Trans-Pacific Partnership) in the region, from which China is excluded. On the military and security side, US moves to increase military cooperation with the Philippines and Vietnam, its naval deployment to Singapore, and new troop rotation to Australia have caused concern for China. In the eyes of many Chinese scholars and policymakers, the US 'pivot to Asia' strategy is essentially a tool for the US to reinforce regional security alliances and its dominance in the Asia-Pacific region, primarily to counteract the rise of China.

Thirdly, the Japan factor presents a challenge for China, as Sino–Japan relations are becoming increasingly geopolitically competitive and confrontational. Bilateral relations between Japan and China had already been soured by various issues deriving from unresolved historical war legacies due to Japan's invasion of China, the Yasukuni Shrine, military rivalry, territorial disputes in the Diaoyu/Senkaku Islands, and infrastructure competition in the region. Tension between the two countries has been at its highest since the end of World War II in 1945, causing alarm bells to ring in Beijing.

Believing that membership of the AIIB would create a new competitor for the ADB and dilute its dominance of infrastructure development in the region, Japan has not signed up for the AIIB or endorsed China's OBOR initiatives. To compete with China on steering infrastructure projects in the region, the Japanese government proposed the "Partnership for quality infrastructure investment for Asia's future", pledging funding of US$110 billion in May 2015. Both Japan and China perceive infrastructure building in Asia as big business and a platform to demonstrate regional prominence.

Given that Japan's population is ageing rapidly and its domestic market is shrinking, accessing foreign markets is crucial to sustain corporate growth for Japanese companies. The typically intense competition between Tokyo and Beijing over infrastructure construction is demonstrated by the bidding battle for the construction of the Jakarta-Bandung high-speed railway in Indonesia, which was eventually won by China. China is intent on exporting its high-speed railway technology and other high-tech infrastructure equipment throughout the region and beyond.[40]

The ASEAN countries are the prime field for the contest between China and Japan. Although the overall volume of bilateral trade between China and ASEAN countries has, since 2009, been higher than the corresponding figure for Japan–ASEAN, Japan is still the more important trading partner for ASEAN countries such as Indonesia and the Philippines. In addition, for ASEAN countries, Japan is the most important source of foreign investment, and China's outward investment to the ASEAN is far lower in value than that of Japan.

Private business in Japan has invested far more heavily than China in the region, aided by institutional and policy support from the Japanese government and relevant trade-promotion agencies such as the JETRO. The lure of low-cost manufacturing sites has made Southeast Asia one of the top destinations

---

[40]Hong Yu, 'China's eagerness to export its high-speed rail expertise to ASEAN members', *The Copenhagen Journal of Asian Studies* 32(2), (2014), pp. 13–36.

for Japanese investors.[41] China accounted for 7.2% of global outward FDI (foreign direct investment), while the US and Japan accounted for 24% and 9.6% of the global outward FDI.[42]

Fourth, China has to address the challenge that the rise of India in the region presents to its implementation of the OBOR initiatives. India is perceived as a 'Swing State' and has yet to buy in to China's OBOR initiative. Despite Xi's personal visit to India in 2014, India merely made the diplomatic gesture of saying it would consider China's proposal.

China–India relations are perceived as among the most important yet complicated bilateral regions in Asia.[43] Some scholars even suggest that power rivalry between India and China is inevitable in the future.[44] The two countries were briefly engaged in a boarder war in 1962, and India has still not forgotten the humiliation of its defeat by China in that war. Furthermore, territorial disputes in the Himalaya region have yet to be resolved. India fears that China's OBOR initiatives are in essence an updated version of 'the string of pearls' to contain the development of India and project China's naval power in the Indian Ocean.

Certain ongoing large infrastructure construction projects in the Indian Ocean under the Silk Road initiatives have only served to reinforce India's suspicions. These projects include the Gwadar Port in Pakistan, Colombo Port City in Sri Lanka, and Kyaukpyu Port in Myanmar. India is especially concerned about the increasing Chinese presence in South Asia and the Indian Ocean, which Indian regards as its sphere of influence. India will assume that the real rationale behind the Chinese government's initiative is to expand China's maritime and political interests in the Indian Ocean and project the Chinese navy's power overseas. Conceivably, concerns over threats to its national security will make it hard for India to permit Chinese companies to construct large-scale critical infrastructure on its soil.

Hence, despite China becoming India's top trading partner, Indian politicians and strategists fear that China's plans for cross-border infrastructure construction under the OBOR strategy will enable India's giant neighbor to gain regional dominance over India in the Indian Ocean and South Asian continent, as a part of China's 'strategic encirclement' strategy. Raja Mohan comments that it is an open secret that Indian security and army circles strongly oppose any such China-initiated infrastructure project on national security grounds.[45] India is concerned that China might use these infrastructure facilities for military purposes, to build a blue water naval fleet. In 2014, India was shocked by the docking of a nuclear-powered Chinese submarine in Colombo International Container Terminal, Sri Lanka.

Due to India's strategic location and its emergence as a regional power, it is vital for China to bring India on board in order to implement the OBOR initiatives successfully, particularly in relation to the Bangladesh-China-India-Myanmar Economic Corridor. The existing territorial disputes and other security issues between China and India need to be resolved. China also has to convince India that its cross-border infrastructure facilities are purely commercially-driven and that bilateral cooperation is a win-win situation.

Fifth, although China founded the AIIB and is its largest shareholder, it is not a Chinese bank and neither does it belong to China. The Chinese leaders may want newly established multilateral financial institutions such as the AIIB under Chinese control. Nevertheless, the bank has 56 other PFMs and more new members will join in the future, which will put pressure on China to increase the operational transparency of the bank and stick to strict lending principles by ensuring environmental and social safeguards are adhered to in financing infrastructure projects.

[41]Sarah Teo and Bhubhindar Singh, eds, *Impact of The Sino-Japanese Competitive Relationship on ASEAN as a Region and Institution*, Policy Report, (Singapore: S. Rajaratnam School of International Studies, Nanyang Technological University, 2014), pp. 1–28.

[42]JETRO, '*2014 JETRO Global Trade and Investment Report*'.

[43]David Scott, 'India's role in the South China Sea: geopolitics and geoeconomics in play', *India Review* 12(2), (2013), pp. 51–69.

[44]Jagannath P Panda, 'Competing realities in China-India multilateral discourse: Asia's enduring power rivalry', *Journal of Contemporary China* 22(82), (2013), pp. 669–690.

[45]C. Raja Mohan, 'Chinese takeaway: One Belt, One Road', *The Indian Express*, 13 August 2014, accessed 12 September 2014, http://indianexpress.com/article/opinion/columns/chinese-takeaway-one-belt-one-road/99/.

The success of the AIIB largely depends on the participation and cooperation of other member states. This will constrain any attempts by China to advance its national interests or unilaterally change the existing international financial system. As Xi Jinping himself admitted, 'The AIIB is an international financial institution whose rules of operation are decided by its members through consultation, not by China alone'.[46] The participation of other major countries will stifle China's ability to establish a Sino-centric financial and economic order that would give China free rein in regional development.

Last but not least, investing in large-scale inter-regional infrastructure projects will be a highly risky business for the AIIB, from both a political and economic perspective, especially as it is still in its nascent stage. Given that many countries in the region are underdeveloped and economically backward, it is important to ascertain their capability to repay any loans from the bank.

Many of the potential inter-connectivity infrastructure projects in the region are driven by government rather than industry-oriented; hence the very long time it could take for any potential economic return to be realized raises serious questions over the financial sustainability of these projects. In the case of the China–Pakistan Economic Corridor, the crucial Gwadar Port project, for example, will involve territory in Balochistan, one of the most insecure and volatile region in Pakistan. China should, therefore, not underestimate the potential security challenges it faces in Pakistan and other terrorism-ridden countries in the implementation of the OBOR strategy.

From the political perspective, domestic political instability, change of government policy, regime change or government transition after elections in other countries could make previously signed and binding infrastructure contracts difficult to implement, causing them to be suspended or even scrapped entirely. The Myitsone hydropower project in Myanmar is a case in point. In September 2011, the Burmese government suddenly ordered the suspension of this huge China-funded hydroelectric power project.

Concluding Remarks

In recent years, China has been extremely keen to project its rising power and expand its global influence through implementing new foreign policies and forging close trade and economic cooperation with other countries. This marks a major departure from the long-held international affairs policy of 'hiding one's capabilities, biding one's time and focusing on domestic development'. The Chinese government's OBOR strategy forms a cornerstone of its new foreign policy. By leveraging its financial power and strong manufacturing and infrastructure development capacity, China's new Silk Road strategy is likely to have far-reaching political and socio-economic implications at home and abroad in years to come.

The OBOR initiative goes far beyond investment cooperation and economic interests as it has clear political and strategic underpinnings. The promotion of the new Silk Road strategy and the establishment of the AIIB are reflections of the rise of China as a global power and will draw other Asian countries deeper into China's orbit of development. The OBOR initiative will therefore advance China's strategic, political and economic interests in Asia as well as countries along this Silk Road route.

OBOR will help China to deal with the domestic problem of industrial overcapacity and speed up industrial restructuring and technological upgrading at home. To provide financial backing for the Silk Road strategy, China has proposed the establishment of the AIIB to spearhead China's OBOR initiatives.

Nevertheless, the Chinese government will encounter serious internal and external challenges to the implementation of this grand strategy. These challenges have proven so great that there has been little real progress despite the initiative attracting huge international attention and China's efforts to increase its momentum. It is consequently still too early to assess the success of the Silk Road strategy.

The effective implementation of the OBOR initiatives largely depends on the response of China's neighbors, large and small, and will require much more than simply rhetoric and good will. The Chinese government has to focus on consultation in order to explain the Silk Road initiatives in detail to its

---

[46]'Exclusive Q&A with Chinese President Xi Jinping,' *Reuters*, 17 October 2015, accessed 14 December 2015, http://www.reuters.com/article/us-china-britain-xi-q-a-idUSKCN0SC03920151018.

prospective partners, and that this strategy will not be for the benefit of China alone. To avoid percep-tions of unilateralism on the part of the other member countries, China must allow the other players full participation and a sense of ownership of the OBOR initiatives.

Acknowledgment

The author would like to thank two anonymous reviewers for their constructive comments and suggestions on this article.

Disclosure statement

No potential conflict of interest was reported by the author.

2 The One Belt One Road and the Asian Infrastructure Investment Bank

Beijing's New Strategy of Geoeconomics and Geopolitics

Kevin G. Cai

ABSTRACT

While generally seen as China's foreign economic initiatives designed to promote regional and global economic cooperation, the One Belt One Road (OBOR) and the Asian Infrastructure Investment Bank (AIIB) have been launched by Beijing as a grand economic and diplomatic strategy, which is designed and pursued not only to overcome the nation's domestic economic problems but also to help promote Chinese influence in the region and beyond, weaken the US dominance in the regional and global economy, and minimize the effects of Washington's policy of containing China. The OBOR and AIIB initiatives will inevitably bring significant impact on the economic architecture in multiple important areas, which would in turn have strategic implications in the region and beyond.

Since Xi Jinping came into office as General Secretary of the Chinese Communist Party (CCP) and the State President in late 2012 and early 2013, Beijing has been making significant adjustment to its foreign policy in a number of important policy areas, reflecting the changed conditions in both the domestic and external settings in the context of the rising Chinese power.[1] It is against this background that Beijing has launched two significant diplomatic initiatives, the One Belt One Road (OBOR) and the Asian Infrastructure Investment Bank (AIIB). While the OBOR and the AIIB are generally seen as Beijing's foreign economic initiatives designed to promote regional and global economic cooperation, the driving forces and the impact of these two initiatives are not limited to economic spheres. As a matter of fact, Beijing's twin initiatives of the OBOR and the AIIB could be better understood as an important part of Beijing's overall foreign policy adjustment under Xi Jinping, which have represented some most significant moves in China's diplomatic history.

This paper attempts to examine Beijing's dual initiatives of the OBOR and the AIIB, explore the major driving forces behind them, and assess the impact of these two initiatives on regional and global economics, politics and security.

The paper is organized as follows. Section 1 provides an overview of Beijing's OBOR and the AIIB initiatives and their progress by the time this paper is completed. Section 2 analyzes the driving forces behind Beijing's launching of the two initiatives. Section 3 discusses how these two initiatives have been received in the region and beyond. The concluding section assesses the implications of the OBOR and the AIIB on regional and global economics, politics and security.

---

[1]Kevin G. Cai, 'China's foreign policy adjustment under Xi Jinping', *China's World* 1(2), (2015), pp. 31–41.

Beijing's OBOR and AIIB initiatives on the move

Never before in its diplomatic history has the People's Republic of China ever actively launched any initiative comparable to the OBOR and the AIIB. Obviously, Beijing under the new leader Xi Jinping has moved to pursue these two initiatives in direct response to both the economic and diplomatic imperatives as a result of the changed domestic and external conditions. In the meantime, it also reflects Beijing's rising confidence in exercising its rapidly increased power in dealing with those issues that are of vital importance for the country's economic well-beings and national security.

The OBOR initiative, which is fully known as the Silk Road Economic Belt and the Twenty-first century Maritime Silk Road, was first proposed by Chinese leader Xi Jinping when he visited Kazakhstan and Indonesia, respectively, in September and October 2013. While the One Belt includes the countries that are located on the historical Silk Road through Central Asia, West Asia, the Middle East and Europe, the One Road makes the initiative extend to cover South Asia, Southeast Asia, Oceania and Africa (see OBOR Map). While over 60 countries are said to be located along the route of the OBOR initiative (see Table 1), many other countries outside the OBOR route are also involved or are considering getting involved in OBOR projects.

OBOR Map

Table 1. The countries along the route of the OBOR.

Regions	Countries
Northeast Asia (2)	China, Mongolia
Southeast Asia (10)	Brunei, Cambodia, Indonesia, Laos, Malaysia, Myanmar, the Philippines, Singapore, Thailand, Vietnam
South Asia (7)	Bangladesh, India, Nepal, Pakistan, Bhutan, Maldives, Sri Lanka
Central Asia (9)	Afghanistan, Armenia, Azerbaijan, Georgia, Kazakhstan, Kyrgyzstan, Tajikistan, Turkmenistan, Uzbekistan
Middle East (15)	Bahrain, Egypt, Iran, Iraq, Israel, Jordan, Kuwait, Lebanon, Oman, Palestine, Qatar, Saudi Arabia, Syria, United Arab Emirates, Yemen
Central and Eastern Europe (23)	Albania, Belarus, Bosnia and Herzegovina, Bulgarian, Croatia, Cyprus, Czech, Estonia, Greece, Hungary, Latvia, Lithuania, Macedonia, Moldova, Montenegro, Poland, Romania, Russia, Serbia, Slovakia, Slovenia, Turkey, Ukraine

Note: While there is no official list of OBOR countries yet, this list of countries is widely circulated in the Chinese media as covered by the OBOR initiative.

The OBOR initiative as a whole was originally proposed as a plan for the construction of a network of infrastructure projects for the vast areas of the OBOR through Chinese investments, including roads, railways, oil and natural gas pipelines, telecommunications, electricity projects, ports and other coastal infrastructure projects. In support of this initiative, Xi Jinping further announced in November 2014 a plan to create a $40 billion fund, called the Silk Road Fund, which was later established on 29 December 2014. In May 2015, the China Development Bank, one of the country's policy banks, further announced that as part of its efforts to boost the OBOR initiative, it would invest more than $890 billion dollars in over 900 projects involving 60 countries to connect Asia and Europe by creating six corridors, namely, the China–Mongolia and Russia corridor, the New Eurasian Land Bridge corridor, the China and Central and West Asia corridor, China and the Indo–China Peninsula corridor, the China and Pakistan corridor, and the Bangladesh, China, India and Myanmar corridor.[2] As such, the ambitious OBOR initiative is dubbed 'China's Marshall Plan'.[3] According to one estimate, if the whole plan were fully implemented, it would cost as high as $8 trillion.[4]

Furthermore, on 28 March 2015, the Chinese government released an official document, 'Vision and Actions on Jointly Building Silk Road Economic Belt and Twenty-first century Maritime Silk Road,' providing a more detailed plan for the initiative and clearly moving the initiative well beyond infrastructure construction to comprehensive economic cooperation between China and the rest of Eurasia, Oceania and Africa. According to the document, in addition to infrastructure development, the initiative would also promote policy coordination, financial integration, the use of Renminbi (RMB) by other countries, liberalization of trade and investment, creation of information and communication networks, and people to people connectivity in the vast areas of East and Southeast Asia, Oceania, South Asia, Central Asia, Europe and Africa.

On 14–15 May 2017, China hosted the first OBOR summit, the OBOR Forum in Beijing, during which Xi Jinping further pledged to provide an additional ￥100 billion ($14.5 billion) for the Silk Road Fund, while the China Development Bank and Export-Import Bank would, respectively, set up new lending schemes of ￥250 billion ($36.2 billion) and ￥130 billion ($18.8 billion) in support of OBOR projects. In addition, China would also provide ￥60 billion ($8.7 billion) for humanitarian aid focusing on food, housing, health care and poverty alleviation.[5] A second OBOR Forum has been scheduled for 2019.

Largely in support of the OBOR initiative, Beijing also launched another significant initiative, the AIIB around the same time. The AIIB was first proposed by the Chinese leader Xi Jinping in October 2013 as a development bank dedicated to lending for infrastructure projects in Asia. Thereafter, there were bilateral and multilateral discussions and consultations on core principles and key elements of the proposed bank, which led to the official launching of the bank on 4 October 2014 with a Memorandum of Understanding (MOU) being signed by 22 of 57 original founding members, called Prospective Founding Members (PFMs). The Chief Negotiators Meeting (CNM) was then established by the PFMs as the forum to negotiate on the AIIB's Articles of Agreement and other related issues. Through five CNMs of negotiations and discussions, the text of the AIIB's Articles of Agreement (Articles), the legal framework, was finalized and adopted on 22 May 2015. By 29 June 2015, the Articles was signed by 50 of the 57 PFMs in Beijing, and by 31 December 2015, all 57 PFMs signed the Articles. Following the ratification of the AIIB's Articles of Agreement by 17 member states, representing 50.1% of the bank's capital stock, the AIIB entered into force on

---

[2]He Yini, 'China to invest $900 billion in Belt and Road Initiative', *China Daily*, 28 May 2015, available at http://usa.chinadaily.com.cn/business/2015-05/28/content_20845687.htm (accessed 6 April 2017); Hazrat Hassan, 'China 6 magical economic corridor', Foreign Policy News, 14 August 2016. available at http://foreignpolicynews.org/2016/08/14/china-6-magical-economic-corridor/ (accessed 20 April 2017).

[3]'China's "Marshall Plan:" Xi Jinping bids to take leadership away from the U.S', *The Wall Street Journal*, 11 November 2014, available at http://online.wsj.com/articles/chinas-marshall-plan-1415750828 (accessed 10 May 2017).

[4]Willy Lam Wo-lap, 'Getting lost in "One belt, one road"', ejisight, 12 April 2016, available at http://www.ejinsight.com/20160412-getting-lost-one-belt-one-road/(accessed 10 November 2017).

[5]Shannon Tiezzi, 'What did china accomplish at the belt and road forum?' *The Diplomat*, 16 May 2017, available at http://thediplomat.com/2017/05/what-did-china-accomplish-at-the-belt-and-road-forum/ (accessed 17 May 2017).

25 December 2015. By 4 August 2016, the Articles had been ratified by all the 57 PFMs with their instruments deposited.[6] By April 2018, the AIIB's total membership had reached 84, including 20 prospective members.[7]

The AIIB has a registered capital of $100 billion, over 31% of which comes from China. As the largest stakeholder, China therefore holds 26.6% of voting power, which marks a milestone in China's bid to play a more active role in global governance and development.[8] Dubbed as China's 'World Bank' for the Asia-Pacific region, the AIIB is widely seen as Beijing's efforts to provide an alternative to the postwar US-dominated financial institutions like the International Monetary Fund (IMF) and the World Bank. It is also viewed as a challenge to the Asian Development Bank (ADB), dominated by the USA and Japan.[9]

Beijing's twin initiatives of the OBOR and the AIIB are highly complementary. In less than 3 years since these two initiatives were launched, both the OBOR and the AIIB had become fully operational. The total amount of direct investment by Chinese companies in the countries along the OBOR route had reached more than $66 billion in a period of 2013 – mid 2017.[10] Most prominent among these OBOR infrastructure investment projects that are currently underway are the $45 billion China–Pakistan Economic Corridor (CPEC) project and the $7.2 billion harbor project – Melaka Gateway Port in Malaysia, to name but two. In the meantime, by August 2017, the China Development Bank and the Export Import Bank of China had provided over $110 billion of loans in support of OBOR projects and the Silk Road Fund had invested over $6 billion in OBOR projects, while the China Export and Credit Insurance Corporation had covered over $320 billion of exports and investment for OBOR projects. Moreover, China had signed currency swap agreement with 22 countries and areas under the OBOR with a total amount reaching ￥1 trillion ($157.5 billion).[11]

Similar vigorous investment projects financed by the AIIB have also been underway. In its first two years of operation, the AIIB approved $1.13 billion loans in 2016 and $3.3 billion in 2017.[12] In terms of projects, by 2 April 2018, the AIIB had already approved 35 infrastructure projects for financing that involve 12 countries and a fund (see Table 2) In the meantime, by 2 April 2018, 13 other proposed projects had been under consideration by the AIIB for funding (see Table 3). It is important to note that the majority of these infrastructure investment projects have been approved or under consideration for financing by the AIIB in conjunction with the World Bank, the ADB and other international financial institutions to reduce the risk. On the other hand, joint financing by the AIIB also allows the World Bank, the ADB and other financial institutions to be able to finance more development projects for developing countries. It is expected that in the first five to six years, the AIIB will lend $10–$15 billion a year. This said, it is important to point out that the AIIB is still incomparable to the ADB in terms of the amount of loans lent. For example, the ADB approved $17.5 billion of loans in 2016 and $19.1 billion in 2017, more than 8 times the approved loans provided by the AIIB during the same period. In the meantime, it is also interesting to note that China has borrowed more from the ADB than it has lent through the AIIB.[13]

---

[6]AIIB, http://euweb.aiib.org/html/aboutus/introduction/Membership/?show=0.

[7]Ibid., available at https://www.aiib.org/en/about-aiib/governance/members-of-bank/index.html (accessed 2 April 2018).

[8]Ibid.

[9]Despite that, however, the registered capital of the AIIB is only about 50% of the World Bank and 2/3 of the ADB.

[10]The State Council Information office of the PRC, '中国企业对沿线国家直接投资逾600亿美元'('The direct investment of Chinese companies along the OBOR route has reached over $60 billion'), 12 May 2017, available at http://www.scio.gov.cn/xwfbh/xwbfbh/wqfbh/35861/36661/zy36665/Document/1551718/1551718.htm and http://www.scio.gov.cn/m/31773/35507/35519/Document/1561190/1561190.htm (accessed 18 June 2017).

[11]Ibid.

[12]Salvatore Babones, 'China's AIIB expected to lend $10-15B a year, but has only managed $4.4B In 2 Years', Forbes, 16 January 2018, https://www.forbes.com/sites/salvatorebabones/2018/01/16/chinas-aiib-expected-to-lend-10-15b-a-year-but-has-only-managed-4-4b-in-2-years/#6cc11c6007f1 (accessed 18, 2018).

[13]Ibid.

Table 2. AIIB-approved projects for financing by 9 February 2018 (US$ million).

	Country/region	Project	Cost of project	Fund provided by AIIB	Other sources	Approval date
1	Bangladesh	Bangladesh Bhola IPP	$271	$60	Not specified	9 February 2018
2	China	Beijing Air Quality Improvement and Coal Replacement Project	$761.10	$250	Beijing Municipality ($228.33), China CDM Fund[a] ($$30), Beijing Gas ($252.77)	8 December 2017
3	Oman	Broadband Infrastructure Project	$467	Not specified	Not specified	8 December 2017
4	India	Bangalore Metro Rail Project – Line R6	$1,785	$335	Borrower ($867), EIB[b] ($583)	8 December 2017
5	Philippines	Metro Manila Flood Management Project	$500	$207.60	Borrower ($84.79), WB[c] ($207.60)	27 September 2017
6	Emerging Asia	IFC Emerging Asia Fund	$640	$150	IFC[d] ($150), Other Investors ($340)	27 September 2017
7	India	Transmission System Strengthening Project	$303.47	$100	ADB[e] ($50), POWERGRID[f] ($153.47)	27 September 2017
8	Egypt	Egypt Round II Solar PV Feed-in Tariffs Program: Al Subh Solar Power	$70–75	$17.5–19	IFC and others ($41), Balance covered by equity	4 September 2017
9	Egypt	Egypt Round II Solar PV Feed-in Tariffs Program: Enara SunEdison	$70–75	$17.5–19	IFC and others ($41), Balance covered by equity	4 September 2017
10	Egypt	Egypt Round II Solar PV Feed-in Tariffs Program: TBEA Enara	$70–75	$17.5–19	IFC and others ($41), Balance covered by equity	4 September 2017
11	Egypt	Egypt Round II Solar PV Feed-in Tariffs Program: Alcazar Energy Egypt Solar 1	$70–75	$17.5–19	IFC and others ($41), Balance covered by equity	4 September 2017
12	Egypt	Egypt Round II Solar PV Feed-in Tariffs Program: Delta for Renewable Energy	$70–75	$17.5–19	IFC and others ($41), Balance covered by equity	4 September 2017
13	Egypt	Egypt Round II Solar PV Feed-in Tariffs Program: ARC for Renewable Energy	$70–75	$17.5–19	IFC and others ($41), Balance covered by equity	4 September 2017
14	Egypt	Egypt Round II Solar PV Feed-in Tariffs Program: Arinna Solar Power	$35–40	$12–14	IFC and others ($18), Balance covered by equity	4 September 2017
15	Egypt	Egypt Round II Solar PV Feed-in Tariffs Program: Winnergy for Renewable Energy Projects	$35–40	$12–14	IFC and others ($18), Balance covered by equity	4 September 2017
16	Egypt	Egypt Round II Solar PV Feed-in Tariffs Program: Phoenix Power 1	$70–75	$17.5–19	IFC and others ($41), Balance covered by equity	4 September 2017
17	Egypt	Egypt Round II Solar PV Feed-in Tariffs Program: SP Energy	$70–75	$17.5–19	IFC and others ($41), Balance covered by equity	4 September 2017
18	Egypt	Egypt Round II Solar PV Feed-in Tariffs Program TAQA Arabia for Solar Energy	$70–75	$17.5–19	IFC and others ($41), Balance covered by equity	4 September 2017
19	India	Gujarat Rural Roads (MMGSY) Project	$658	$329	Gov't of Gujarat ($329)	4 July 2017
20	Tajikistan	Nurek Hydropower Rehabilitation Project, Phase I	$350	$60	WB ($225.7), UDB[g] ($40), Financial Gap ($24.3)	15 June 2017
21	India	India Infrastructure Fund	$750	$150	Other Investors ($600)	15 June 2017
22	Georgia	Batumi Bypass Road Project	$315.2	$114	Borrower ($87.2), ADB ($114)	15 June 2017
23	India	Andhra Pradesh 24x7 – Power For All	$571	$160	Gov't of Andhra Pradesh ($171), WB ($240)	2 May 2017

(Continued)

Table 2. (Continued).

	Country/region	Project	Cost of project	Fund provided by AIIB	Other sources	Approval date
24	Bangladesh	Natural Gas Infrastructure and Efficiency Improvement Project	$453	$60	ADB (167) Government ($226)	22 March 2017
25	Indonesia	Dam Operational Improvement and Safety Project II	$300	$125	WB ($125) Government ($50)	22 March 2017
26	Indonesia	Regional Infrastructure Development Fund Project	$406	$100	Government ($203) WB ($103, including $3 million in grant from SECO[h] channeled via WB)	22 March 2017
27	Azerbaijan	Trans Anatolian Natural Gas Pipeline Project	$8,600	$600	WB ($800) EBRD[i] & EIB ($2,100) Borrower ($2,100) Commercial Borrowings ($3000)	21 December 2016
28	Oman	Duqm Port Commercial Terminal and Operational Zone Development Project	$353.33	$265	SEZAD[j] ($88.33)	8 December 2016
29	Oman	Railway System Preparation Project	$60	$36	OGLG[k] ($24)	8 December 2016
30	Myanmar	Myingyan 225 MW Combined Cycle Gas Turbine (CCGT) Power Plant Project	Data unavailable	$20	IFC ($ unavailable) ADB ($ unavailable) Others ($ unavailable)	27 September 2016
31	Pakistan	Tarbela 5 Hydropower Extension Project	$823.5	$300	WB ($390) Government ($133.5)	27 September 2016
32	Indonesia	National Slum Upgrading Project	$1,743	$216.5	WB ($216.5) Borrower ($1,310)	24 June 2016
33	Pakistan	National Motorway M-4 (Shorkot-Khanewal Section) Project	$273	$100	ADB ($100) DFID[l] ($34) Government ($39)	24 June 2016
34	Bangladesh	Distribution System Upgrade and Expansion Project	$262.29	$165	Government ($79.4) EA[l] ($17.89)	24 June 2016
35	Tajikistan	Dusbanbe–Uzbekistan Border Road Improvement Project	$105.9	$27.5	EBRD ($62.5) Government ($15.9)	24 June 2016

Source: Compiled from AIIB, accessed 2 April 2018, https://www.aiib.org/en/projects/approved/index.html.

[a]China Clean Development Mechanism Fund.
[b]European Investment Bank.
[c]World Bank.
[d]International Finance Corporation.
[e]Asian Development Bank.
[f]Power Grid Corporation of India Limited.
[g]Eurasian Development Bank
[h]Swiss Secretariat for Economic Affairs
[i]European Bank for Reconstruction and Development.
[j]Special Economic Zone Authority of Duqm.
[k]Oman Global Logistics Group.
[l]Department for International Development (UK).
Executing Agency.

Table 3. Proposed projects under consideration by AIIB for financing by 9 February 2018 (US$ million).

	Country	Project	Estimated cost of project	Fund requested of AIIB	Other sources	Estimated date of board consideration
1	Uzbekistan	Railway Electrification Project (Bukhara-Urgench-Khiva)	$339.1	$168.2	UTY[a] ($170.9)	September 2018
2	Uzbekistan	Power Transmission Project in Tashkent	$30	$25	JSC[b] Uzbekenergo ($5)	November 2018
3	Laos	National Road 13 Improvement and Maintenance Project	$128	$40	WB[c] ($40) Nordic Development Fund ($9.5) Gov't of Laos ($38.5)	September 2018
4	Turkey	Tuz Golu Gas Storage Expansion Project	$2,500	$600	WB ($600) BOTAS[d] ($1,300)	June 2018
5	Sri Lanka	Solid Waste Management Project	$274	$115	Borrower ($44) WB ($115)	April 2018
6	Indonesia	Strategic Irrigation Modernization and Urgent Rehabilitation Project	$578	$250	Borrower ($78) WB ($250)	April 2018
7	India	West Bengal Major Irrigation and Flood Management Project	$413	$145	WB ($145) Gov't of West Bengal ($123)	September 2018
8	Sri Lanka	Climate Resilience Improvement Project – Phase II	$155+ local cost (TBD)	$77.5	WB ($77.5) Government (local cost/TBD)	March 2018
9	India	National Investment and Infrastructure Fund	$2,100	$200	Government ($1,000) Other investors (900)	1st Quarter of 2018
10	India	Madhya Pradesh Rural Connectivity Project	$502	$141	Borrower ($150) WB ($211)	March 2018
11	India	Amaravati Sustainable Capital City Development Project	$715	$200	WB ($300) Gov't of Andhra Pradesh ($215)	March 2018
12	India	Mumbai Metro Line 4 Project	$2,224	$500	Borrower ($1,524) Co-financiers to be arranged by AIIB ($200)	March 2018
13	Georgia	280 MW Nenskra Hydropower Plant	$1,083	$100	ADB[e], EBRD[f], EIB[g], KDB[h] ($758) Balance covered by Equity	April 2018

Source: Compiled from AIIB, accessed 2 April 2018, https://www.aiib.org/en/projects/proposed/index.html.
[a]Uzbekiston Temir Yollari.
[b]Joint-Stock Company.
[c]World Bank.
[d]Boru Hatları ile Petrol Taşıma A.Ş.
[e]Asian Development Bank.
[f]European Bank for Reconstruction and Development.
[g]European Investment Bank.
[h]Korea Development Bank.

The driving forces of Beijing's OBOR initiative and AIIB initiative

While Beijing continues to emphasize its traditional diplomatic principles of sovereignty and non-interference in launching both the initiatives, the OBOR and the AIIB are seemingly intended by Beijing to pursue not only its economic objectives but also its diplomatic and security objectives. There are clearly both important economic and geopolitical driving forces behind Beijing's twin initiatives. By launching these two initiatives, Beijing hopes to achieve its multiple economic, diplomatic and strategic objectives.

First of all, the OBOR and the AIIB initiatives are designed to help Beijing address its rising domestic economic challenges in multiple areas, most important of which are the slowed economic growth, huge industrial overcapacity and the underdevelopment of the nation's southern and western provinces. By initiating the OBOR and the AIIB, Beijing hopes to find a new stimulus of economic growth through expanding the external markets for Chinese goods, overcoming the worsening problem of the nation's industrial overcapacity,[14] and promoting the economic development of the nation's underdeveloped southern and western areas through increasing infrastructure construction. This would therefore help cushion the effects of deepening economic slowdown of the country and promoting more balanced development between the country's prosperous coastal areas and poorer inland/peripheral areas. Besides, the projects under the OBOR may also help provide many less viable large state enterprises and banks, which are experiencing difficulty implementing market-oriented reforms, with a new opportunity to survive. Moreover, a large number of investment projects under the OBOR could also help expand financing channels in China, moving away from primarily relying on bank loans for investment financing to more diversified forms of financing, bond issuing in particular. This would in turn provide a further stimulus for China's financial reforms and an opening of the country's capital market, thus making financing more diversified and optimizing capital allocation in the Chinese economy.

Secondly, the two initiatives also reflect Beijing's efforts to promote the reform of the existing international economic system dominated by the USA so as to allow China to play a more important role. As an integral part of the post-Mao Chinese leadership's economic reform policy that was initiated in the late 1970s, Beijing started to adopt an opening policy to integrate the country into the capitalist world economy. As an important step of this opening policy, China resumed its membership in the IMF and the World Bank in 1980 and joined the ADB in 1986, but primarily on terms that had been set by developed countries, the USA in particular. Given its weak economic position at the time, China unavoidably had a very limited voice and influence in these institutions. Over time, however, as China gradually gained economic power as a result of rapid economic growth, Beijing was increasingly disappointed with US and Western dominance in these institutions. Thus, around 2005 China started to push for the reform of the existing international institutions, the IMF and the World Bank in particular. In a statement to the IMF in 2005, the Governor of the Bank for China stated that: 'the two institutions (the IMF and the World Bank) should reform their own governance structure, increasing participation of developing countries in decision making. In doing so, the increasing strength of developing countries as a whole should be reflected, and the views of all member countries expressed in a balanced way, to ensure that the policies of the two institutions will be in the interest of the vast developing countries as well as the world at large. At the same time, the two institutions should also stick to their development mission and professionalism, and resist any attempt or practice to politicize their businesses.'[15] In Beijing's view, the existing international economic system can no longer reflect the new reality of the changed balance of economic power in the world economy, hence needs a reform.[16]

Beijing's call for the reform of the existing international economic system, however, can hardly be echoed and supported by the status-quo-powers, the USA in particular. It is under such circumstances that China has tried to advance the establishment of new institutions outside the existing system to bypass the USA-dominated existing system and to increase Beijing's influence in the regional and global economic arena. Both the OBOR and the AIIB initiatives have precisely been launched within this geoeconomic background. It is in this sense that the OBOR and the AIIB initiatives would inevitably help enable China to play a more active role in global governance and development and weaken the US dominance in the existing international system. In a similar fashion, the two initiatives would also help weaken the Japan-dominated ADB over time.

---

[14]China's most important industrial sectors of overcapacity include steel, coal, plate glass, cement, electrolytic aluminum, shipbuilding, photovoltaics, wind power and petrochemicals.

[15]IMF, 'Press Release No. 13', September 24–25, 2005, available at http://www.imf.org/external/am/2005/speeches/pr13e.pdf (accessed 7 May 2017).

[16]For an account of China's relationship with and evolving role in the IMF, see Bessma Momani, 'China at the international monetary fund. Continued engagement in its drive for membership and added voice at the IMF executive board', *Journal of Chinese Economics* 1(1), (2013), pp.125–150.

However, it is important to point out that although China has been moving to establish new international institutions and schemes like the OBOR and the AIIB as a way to increase its influence in the regional and global economy,[17] Beijing has neither intention nor ability to completely replace the existing system with a new one and that the existing system, generally speaking, still works quite well for China, although China is not satisfied with some of the practices and rules of the system. By initiating these new moves, Beijing primarily seems to hope to exert pressure on the USA so that the existing system could be reformed in a way that would let China have a voice more commensurate with its economic power. In his speech to commemorate the 95th anniversary of the Chinese Communist Party on 1 July 2016, Xi Jinping made it quite clear that the world order should be decided not by one country or a few but by the people of all countries through consultations and that China will actively participate in the building of a global governance system and contribute to the improvement of global governance.[18]

Thirdly, the two initiatives could also help promote the use of the RMB by other countries, thus expanding the role of the RMB as an international currency. Particularly, the OBOR would help promote the use of the RMB by the countries that receive OBOR investment. It is expected that the OBOR would bring as high as $10 trillion of investment in infrastructure construction and the RMB will inevitably function as a major currency of investment in this regard. The OBOR will also help boost China's foreign trade, thus further promoting the global use of the RMB.[19] Similarly, given China's position as the largest contributor to the capital pool of the AIIB, the AIIB will similarly help promote the use of the RMB in its funded projects.

Fourthly, the OBOR and the AIIB were launched by Beijing as a diplomatic and strategic move as well in the face of new geopolitical and security challenges in the context of the changing geopolitical setting in the Asia-Pacific region in the first two decades of the 2000s. The geopolitical and security environment in the region was generally favorable for China to concentrate on economic development with minimal explicit geopolitical and security challenges from outside in the 1980s through the early 2000s, largely because a rising China was not quite seen as a real or imminent threat yet by others in the region. By the early 2010s, however, the rise of Chinese power, its military power in particular, had become all the more evident and real, which inevitably made the status-quo powers and neighboring states increasingly concerned. It is within this context that the Obama administration started to adopt a new Asia policy, dubbed 'Asia pivot' and 'rebalancing,' which, in Beijing's eyes, is clearly intended to contain a rising China. In the meantime, there were, in Beijing's view, growing 'deliberate' moves by some East Asian neighbors on highly sensitive issues of territorial disputes in the East and South China Seas, the most significant move of which was Japan's nationalization of the Diaoyu Islands/Senkaku Islands in September 2012. Under such circumstances, Beijing has started to adjust its foreign policy by adopting a more comprehensive diplomatic strategy that involves both 'sticks' and 'carrots.' On the one hand, Beijing has dropped its previous *tao guang yang hui* (low-profile) foreign policy, which was initially introduced by Deng Xiaoping in the 1980s, and moved to take a more active and even assertive policy to directly respond to the rising external challenges. On the other hand, however, Beijing, by using its increased economic power and wealth as a diplomatic weapon, has provided huge economic incentives for Asian states to develop closer cooperation with China. The OBOR and AIIB initiatives have been launched precisely against this backdrop as an important part of Beijing's overall foreign policy adjustment under the leadership of Xi Jinping. A regional 'infrastructure gap' estimated

---

[17]A good example of China's efforts in this respect at the global level is the BRICS-initiated New Development Bank. As a crucial member of the BRICS, China has played a very important role in the establishment of the New Development Bank (formerly called BRICS Development Bank), which will be headquartered in Shanghai.

[18]'Xi: China to contribute wisdom to global governance', *China Daily*, 1 July 2016, available at http://www.chinadaily.com.cn/china/2016-07/01/content_25933506.htm (accessed 23 November 2017).

[19]'人民币国际化遇挑战 一带一路如何助力'('How the OBOR helps RMB meet the challenge of its internationalization') dwnews, 19 June 2016, available at http://economics.dwnews.com/news/2016-06-19/59747274.html (accessed 2 April 2017).

at least in the amount of $8 trillion[20] makes Beijing's two initiatives all the more attractive to many countries in the region. Obviously, huge carrots like the OBOR and the AIIB would help compromise Washington's 'containment' policy in the name of Asia pivot and rebalancing and help soften and mitigate the 'shock' brought about by Beijing's more determined and assertive policy in the East and South China Seas. Although the new US President Trump's China policy is still in the process of being finalized, it can well be expected that containing the rising influence of China in the region would still be a major theme of Trump's policy towards Beijing. This is clearly reflected in the Trump administration's newly endorsed 'Indo-Pacific' concept following an official four-party meeting that involved the USA, Japan, Australia and India in Manila on 12 November 2017 during Trump's 12-day, five-country trip to East Asia.[21] The 'Indo-Pacific' concept is believed to have been adopted by the Trump administration to replace the previous administration's Asia pivot and rebalancing policy as Trump's new strategy of quadrilateral alliance of the USA, Japan, Australia and India to counter a rising China.[22] It is in this sense that the OBOR and AIIB initiatives are not just economic projects, but more importantly, they are also Beijing's diplomatic and strategic maneuver, clearly and deliberately intended to mitigate the effects of US policy of containing China.

To pursue the analysis further, it is China's philosophical belief that the conflicting national interests would become all the more prominent and unmanageable if nation-states shared no common interests. It is in this sense that the OBOR and the AIIB are deliberately designed to help develop and expand common interests between China and other countries, particularly those that are currently involved in territorial disputes with China in the South China Sea and those that are fearful of a rising Chinese power. As such, it is Beijing's hope that the two initiatives will help reduce the tensions derived from the territorial disputes in the South China Sea and create a more amiable atmosphere and an opportunity for effectively managing these disputes and preventing them from becoming out of control, potentially even solving these disputes with the countries involved. In a broader sense, the initiatives could help further strengthen Beijing's third world diplomacy.

Finally, it is important to note that some of the OBOR projects can also help China obtain more economic security in the face of increasing external challenges, particularly in the context of the rising tensions in the South China Sea and, in the eyes of Beijing, a geopolitically increasingly less trustworthy Singapore, which is strategically located in the Strait of Malacca, a vital shipping route for China with its huge volumes of foreign trade (including 80% of its imported oil) having to pass through it.[23] As such, investment in energy and mineral resources, particularly in Central Asia, could help reduce China's reliance on commodities imported from overseas through the Strait of Malacca. Similarly, investment in infrastructure in Pakistan (the $450 billion CPEC that links Pakistan's Gwadar Port to China's Kashi (Kashgar) in particular) and in Malaysia (notably, the Melaka Gateway Port, a $7.2 billion harbour project in Malacca that aims to overtake Singapore as the largest port in the region and that would even directly connect to the South China Sea if new railways were going to be constructed on Malay Peninsula) would also help China reduce its

[20]ADB, 'Public-private partnership operational plan 2012–2020', available at https://www.adb.org/documents/public-private-partnership-operational-plan-2012-2020 (accessed 20 February 2018).

[21]Ankit Panda, 'US, Japan, India, and Australia hold working-level quadrilateral meeting on regional cooperation', *The Diplomat*, 13 November 2017, available at https://thediplomat.com/2017/11/us-japan-india-and-australia-hold-working-level-quadrilateral-meeting-on-regional-cooperation/ (accessed 14 November 2017).

[22]Bhavan Jaipragas, 'Why is the U.S. calling asia-Pacific the Indo-Pacific? Donald Trump to "Clarify"', South China Morning Post, 7 November 2017, available at http://www.scmp.com/week-asia/politics/article/2118806/why-us-calling-asia-pacific-indo-pacific-trump-clarify (accessed 19 February 2018).

[23]For Beijing's growing distrust of Singapore, see Nahui Chen and Xue Li, 'Lee Kuan Yew's Legacy for China-Singapore relations', *The Diplomat*, 5 December 2016, available at http://thediplomat.com/2016/12/lee-kuan-yews-legacy-for-china-singapore-relations/ (accessed 10 December 2016); Maria Siow, 'There may be trouble ahead for China and Singapore', *South China Morning Post*, 26 August 2016, available at http://www.scmp.com/week-asia/politics/article/2006266/there-may-be-trouble-ahead-china-and-singapore (accessed 20 June 2017).

heavy dependence on the Strait of Malacca, which China's economic well-being now so significantly hinges on.[24]

In the context of the changing domestic and external conditions, China has launched the OBOR and AIIB initiatives as a grand economic and diplomatic strategy, using the nation's growing economic power and expanding wealth as a leverage. This strategy is designed and pursued not only to overcome the nation's domestic problems by exporting the overcapacity of industrial production to developing countries in Central Asia, South Asia, Southeast Asia and East Africa, but also to help promote Chinese influence in the region and beyond, weaken the US dominance in the regional and global economy, and minimize the effects of Washington's policy of containing China. Particularly, from a geopolitical perspective, Beijing, through these innovative and vigorous initiatives, is offering a large number of Asian and Asia-Pacific countries with huge amounts of highly attractive economic benefits and opportunities. These initiatives are deliberately planned to neutralize the policies of many of the countries in the region towards the US–Chinese rivalry, hence, minimizing the effects of Washington's Asia-Pacific policy, which in Beijing's eyes is intended to contain China and Chinese influence in the Asia-Pacific region. In the meantime, the initiatives will also help China increase and consolidate its position and influence in vast areas of the Asia-Pacific, Central Asia and well beyond.

In brief, Beijing under the leadership of Xi Jinping has made the OBOR and the AIIB part of the centerpiece of the nation's foreign policy and economic strategy.

Regional and global responses

Beijing's twin initiatives of the OBOR and the AIIB have received mixed responses from the region and beyond. Generally speaking, Beijing's initiatives are welcomed by most developing countries in the region, which are in need of infrastructure investment, as well as by major international organizations. By April 2018, over 80 countries and international organizations had signed agreements with China on cooperation under the OBOR initiative. Even many countries in Africa, Latin America and South Pacific are enthusiastic about Beijing's initiative, seeking the possibility of being covered by the OBOR projects.[25] Particularly significant is that on 19 September 2016, the UN Development Program signed an OBOR memorandum with China, the first such memorandum that China had signed with an international organization. By this, the UN officially got involved in promotion of OBOR projects.[26] Furthermore, the first OBOR Forum hosted by Beijing on 14–15 May 2017 was attended by leaders from 29 countries and representatives from over 130 countries, as well as the heads of the UN, the IMF and the World Bank. While developing countries are mostly enthusiastic about the OBOR, major developed countries are, however, mostly suspicious of the intention of China's initiative, seeing the OBOR as Beijing's scheme of expanding its influence in the region and beyond with its rising power.[27] This contrast in views on China's OBOR initiative

[24]For the CPEC, see Daniel S. Markey and James West, 'Behind China's Gambit in Pakistan', Council on Foreign Relations, 12 May 2016, available at http://www.cfr.org/pakistan/behind-chinas-gambit-pakistan/p37855 (accessed 24 December 2016); also see the official website of the CPEC, http://cpec.gov.pk/ (accessed 20 June 2017); for the Malacca harbour project, see 'Chinese companies to help Malaysia build new deep sea port in Malacca', Xinhua, 19 October 2016, available at http://news.xinhuanet.com/english/2016-10/20/c_135768342.htm (accessed 24 June 2017) and 'Malacca harbour plan raises questions about China's strategic aims', The Straits Times, 14 November 2016, available at http://www.straitstimes.com/asia/se-asia/malacca-harbour-plan-raises-questions-about-chinas-strategic-aims (accessed 24 June 2017).

[25]'Transcript: President Xi addresses the 2018 Boao Forum for Asia in Hainan,' U.S.-China Perception Monitor, 11 April 2018, available at https://www.uscnpm.org/blog/2018/04/11/transcript-president-xi-addresses-2018-boao-forum-asia-hainan/ (accessed 12 April 2018); The State council information office of the PRC, available at http://www.scio.gov.cn/m/31773/35507/35519/Document/1561190/1561190.htm (accessed 19 February 2018).

[26]National Development and Reform Commission (NDRC) of the People's Republic of China, available at http://wss.ndrc.gov.cn/gzdt/201609/t20160920_818935.html (accessed 28 May 2017).

[27]BBC (Chinese), '美亚欧大国纷纷反制"一带一路"四面楚歌' ['Major Powers in America, Asia and Europe counter the OBOR one after another and the initiative is under fire from all quarters'], 19 February 2018, available at http://www.bbc.com/zhongwen/simp/world-43120078 (accessed 20 February 2018).

between most developing countries and major developed counties seems inevitable, as developing countries mostly see the initiative primarily from the perspective of economic development, while major developed countries tend to interpret it from the perspective of geopolitics and geoeconomics.

In contrast to the OBOR that receives mixed responses, the AIIB has generally obtained positive responses from both developing countries and most developed countries. Developing countries are positive about the AIIB initiative because they believe that the AIIB will provide them with an additional source of financing in support of their economic development. On the other hand, most developed countries are also positive about Beijing's AIIB initiative, in contrast to their suspicion of the OBOR. This is largely because the AIIB as a multilateral institution would be governed in a multilateral fashion, although China has the largest voting power given the proportion of its capital subscriptions. This is very different from the OBOR, which, as a national scheme that is unilaterally operated by Beijing, could easily be used to pursue its own national agenda and to promote its own national interests. As such, not only all the major emerging new economies, including India, South Africa, Brazil, Egypt and Argentina, timely joined the AIIB, but most developed countries in Western Europe and the Asia-Pacific joined the China-led AIIB one after another, despite Washington's opposition. By early April 2018, the AIIB had a total membership of 84 (including prospective members), well surpassing the ADB with 67 members.

In observing global and regional responses to Beijing's two initiatives, it is interesting to note that there have been gradual adjustments in attitudes of both the USA and Japan (China's major global and regional rivals) towards the OBOR and AIIB initiatives over time. Generally speaking, both Washington and Tokyo had initially maintained strong reservation on both the OBOR and the AIIB, suspicious of Beijing's intentions behind these two initiatives. Since early 2017, however, both powers have been subtly modifying their attitude and/or policy on Beijing's two initiatives, a process that is still going on and subject to further observation.

In the first place, Washington's reaction to Beijing's One Belt One Road initiative had been quite ambivalent under the Obama administration. Initially, Washington had concerns about Beijing's One Belt plan, seeing it as Beijing's political and economic expansion into Central Asia and beyond. But later Washington became 'cautiously positive' of the One Belt, at least as related to Central Asia, seeing the possible positive effects of China's large-scale investments for the development of infrastructure in Central Asia. This point was clearly reflected in a talk by US Deputy Secretary of State Antony J. Blinken on 31 March 2015, who explicitly stated that Beijing's One Belt plan could be complementary to Washington's Central Asia policy and that the two countries could coordinate their policies towards Central Asia.[28] While the true reason why Washington switched from its previous negative view of China's One Belt to a more positive one is unknown, it is very likely that Washington had to accept the reality of rising Chinese influence in Central Asia and try to find a model of cooperation with Beijing (like a G-2 model) in a region where Chinese influence could no longer be stopped while US influence could hardly be exerted effectively.[29] Besides, it was also likely that Beijing's rising influence in Central Asia was seen as a less significant challenge to Washington's overall global strategic and security interests, particularly as compared to the Asia-Pacific region. It was even possible that Washington hoped that Beijing's increased attention to Central Asia and beyond through the One Belt would help divert and/or weaken its attention to the Asia-Pacific, a core region that was seen as fundamentally geopolitically and strategically important for the USA.

In contrast to its 'positive' view of Beijing's One Belt, the Obama administration, on the other hand, was very negative of the One Road, which was primarily directed at the Asia-Pacific region.

---

[28]U.S. Department of State, 'State's blinken on a vision for central Asia', IIP Digital, 31 March 2015, available at http://translations.state.gov/st/english/texttrans/2015/04/20150401314506.html#axzz4H7Sl7RzL (accessed 12 October 2017).
[29]Shanghai center for SCO Studies of Shanghai Social Sciences Academy, Brief of Shanghai Cooperation Organization (SCO) Studies, 2, 10 April 2016.

As the Asia-Pacific was a key region that was of political and strategic importance for the USA, Washington's primary policy objective in the Asia-Pacific was to contain the expansion of Chinese power and the rising Chinese influence through (1) the adjustment of its Asia policy by adopting Asia rebalancing and Asia pivot strategy and (2) explicit and implicit alliance with those countries in the region that were fearful of a rising China. It is against this backdrop that Washington's suspicion of and opposition to Beijing's One Road can be better understood.

Similarly, the Obama administration also maintained 'reservation' on Beijing's AIIB initiative on the ground that the AIIB might not reach the high standards and international norms of such international institutions, obviously fearing that the AIIB would challenge and weaken the US influence and dominance in international monetary affairs.

Since Trump came into office as the US president on 20 January 2017, however, Washington has been subtly modifying its attitude and policy towards Beijing's OBOR and AIIB initiatives. Immediately after Trump's election as the US president, James Woolsey, a senior adviser to Trump on national security and intelligence, wrote an opinion piece published in Hong Kong's *South China Morning Post* on 10 November 2016, noting that Donald Trump could be expected to give a 'much warmer' response to China's 'One Belt, One Road' trade initiative than President Obama, and that the Obama administration's rejection of the China-led AIIB was a 'strategic mistake.'[30]

Woolsey's anticipation was later confirmed in some way when the Trump administration decided to send its senior officials to attend Beijing's OBOR Forum on 14–15 May 2017.[31] While Washington's modified attitude and policy on Beijing's OBOR initiative should reflect the Trump administration's different understanding of this issue as compared with the Obama administration, however, it was also clearly the direct result of the Trump-Xi's first submit on 6–7 April 2017, during which the two leaders reached an agreement, the so-called 100-Day Action Plan, in an attempt to achieve a more balanced trade between the two countries. It is within this context that Washington's modified attitude towards Beijing's OBOR can be seen as part of the efforts of both powers to improve their overall bilateral relations, economic relations in particular. Despite this modified attitude towards the OBOR, however, it could still be well expected that Washington would hardly be truly supportive of an initiative that would help its major rival, China increase its regional and global influence. This is most recently reflected in an emerging idea of establishing a rival joint regional infrastructure investment scheme that would involve the USA, Australia, Japan and India in an attempt to counter China's spreading influence as a result of the OBOR.[32] Obviously, this joint regional infrastructure investment idea exactly matches the Trump administration's newly endorsed Indo-Pacific concept for regional security through a quadrilateral alliance as discussed in the previous section.

On the other hand, the Trump administration also seems to have moved away from the Obama administration's critical view on Beijing's AIIB initiative, particularly given the fact that the AIIB has now been well-established and fully operational, involving all the major economic powers with the exception of the USA and Japan. Although the Trump administration's policy towards the AIIB is still subject to being more explicitly and fully unfolded, it should not be unexpected if Washington eventually decides to pursue some kind of cooperation with the AIIB.

In a similar fashion, Tokyo has also recently started a subtle process of adjustment of its policy towards Beijing's OBOR and AIIB. Japan has suffered from strained relations with China in recent years as a result of a territorial conflict over the disputed islands in the East China Sea, controversies

---

[30]Cited from Fortune, 'A top Trump adviser is rebuking Obama for giving Asia's "World Bank" the cold shoulder', 10 November 2016, available at http://fortune.com/2016/11/10/donald-trump-aiib-china-trade-one-belt-road/ (accessed 12 October 2017).

[31]William Ide and Saibal Dasgupta, 'US to attend China's belt and road forum', VOA, 12 May 2017, available at https://www.voanews.com/a/us-to-attend-china-belt-and-road-forum/3849761.html (accessed 18 June 2017).

[32]Phillip Coorey, 'Australia mulls rival to China's "belt and road" with US, Japan, India', *Financial Review*, 18 February 2018, available at http://www.afr.com/news/australia-mulls-rival-to-chinas-belt-and road with us japan india-20100210-li0w7k3 (accessed 19 February 2018).

over how the recent history of Japan's imperialist war in Asia should be interpreted, and profound mutual distrust between these two regional powers. Consequently, Tokyo had been consistently skeptical about and opposed to Beijing's OBOR and AIIB initiatives for fear that China's rising influence would eclipse Japan's influence in the region and beyond.[33] However, starting in May 2017, Japan seemed to adjust its policy on both of Beijing's initiatives. This policy modification was reflected in Tokyo's decision to send Toshihiro Nikai, the secretary-general of Japan's ruling Liberal Democratic Party (LDP) and a figure who was second only to Japanese prime minister Abe, to attend the OBOR forum of 14–15 May 2017. On 5 June 2017, Japanese prime minister Abe further expressed for the first time his intention for Japan to cooperate with China on the OBOR initiative if certain conditions are met.[34] Around the same time, Abe also dramatically reversed his previous attitude of suspicion of the AIIB by stating on 15 May 2017 that Japan would consider joining the AIIB if questions surrounding its projects' environmental impacts and other issues were resolved.[35]

Obviously, Tokyo's change of policy towards Beijing's twin initiatives is primarily due to the changed external circumstances. In the first place, the fact that both the OBOR and the AIIB have been attracting a growing number of countries is exerting a growing pressure on Japan. Even more importantly, it is Washington's modification of policy towards Beijing's initiatives under the Trump administration that has finally forced Tokyo to change its course of policy. After coming into office, Trump not only dropped the Trans-Pacific Partnership (TPP), but also decided on 11 May 2017 to send his representatives to attend Beijing's OBOR Forum of 14–15 May. This brought Japan an imperative that if Japan did not follow to get involved in the OBOR, it would inevitably be isolated. Similarly, the AIIB expanded rapidly after its founding, likely becoming the most important source of infrastructure investment in the region replacing the ADB. As such, if Japan fails to join, it would likely be isolated. Under such circumstances, there was a rising consensus among the Japanese elite that Japan should join the AIIB ahead of the USA. In a further analysis, in the context of the aborted TPP, joining the OBOR could obviously help Japan export its overcapacities of production. Moreover, a more positive policy towards Beijing-led OBOR and AIIB would also help Japan mend strained relations with China. Despite this, however, geopolitical concerns should continue to bother Tokyo. It is in this sense that the idea of creating a joint regional infrastructure investment scheme with the USA, Australia and India should be quite attractive to Japan to rival China's OBOR initiative.

Finally, it is interesting to note that as a major developing country and China's largest neighbor in Asia, India has an ambivalent attitude towards Beijing's twin initiatives of the OBOR and AIIB. On the one hand, New Delhi is very positive about Beijing's AIIB initiative and has timely joined the AIIB, obviously seeing the AIIB as a useful additional source for India's much needed funds in support of its infrastructure investment. This policy of New Delhi on the AIIB is clearly reflected in the statistical data on the investment projects that have been submitted to the AIIB for consideration for funding as well as the investment projects that have already been approved by the AIIB for financing. For example, out of 35 projects that had been approved for funding by the AIIB by April 2018, 5 projects were from India with a combined amount of finance from the AIIB reaching $1.074 billion; in the meantime, 5 more Indian projects are currently under consideration by the AIIB for financing (see Tables 2 and 3). On the other hand, India's attitude towards Beijing's OBOR initiative is quite suspicious and even critical, largely for geopolitical and security concerns. Particularly, New Delhi fears that rising infrastructure investment in South Asia from China through the OBOR would not only help weaken its

[33]Hidehito Fujiwara, 'One belt, one road: A Japanese perspective', *The Newsletter* 74, (Summer 2016), International Institute for Asian Studies, available at http://iias.asia/the-newsletter/article/one-belt-one-road-japanese-perspective (accessed 20 March 2017); Tridivesh Singh Maini, 'Japan's effort to counter China's silk road', The Globalist, 6 April 2016, available at http://www.theglobalist.com/japan-effort-to-counter-china-silk-road-india/ (accessed 20 June 2017); Saori N. Katada, 'At the crossroads: The TPP, AIIB, and Japan's Foreign economy strategy', Asia Pacific Issues, Analysis from the East-West Center, 125, May 2016.
[34]'Abe: Japan may cooperate in "One Belt, One Road"', The Japan News by *The Yomiuri Shimbun*, 6 June 2017, available at http://the-japan-news.com/news/article/0003743639 (accessed 18 June 2017).
[35]Kyodo, 'Japan would consider joining China-led AIIB if doubts are dispelled, Abe says', 16 May 2017, available at http://www.japantimes.co.jp/news/2017/05/16/business/japan-consider-joining-china-led-aiib-doubts-dispelled-abe-says/#.WUcvY2iyyIU (accessed 18 June 2017).

own dominance in what India sees as its backyard, but also undermine the country's national security. In this respect, the $45 billion CPEC project, which runs through the part of Kashmir that is under control by Pakistan, is even seen as a direct challenge to India's sovereignty claim over the disputed region. The over 2-month border stand-off between the two countries in a plateau that lies between China, India's northeastern state of Sikkim and Bhutan (June 18 through 28 August 2017) could at least partly be seen as reflecting New Delhi's concerns. Consequently, it could be well expected that the idea of forming a joint infrastructure investment mechanism with the USA, Japan and Australia to counter China's OBOR would likely be welcomed by India.

Conclusion

China's OBOR and AIIB initiatives have now been fully operational and increasingly influential. The launching of the two initiatives can be viewed as a new round of China's opening policy since the post-Mao economic reform was initiated in the late 1970s. When the post-Mao opening policy was first introduced by Deng Xiaoping in the late 1970s, it was primarily designed to help the nation enter the capitalist world economy by joining the existing international economic system and by bringing in foreign capital, technology and know-how in support of Beijing's efforts to achieve the objective of the nation's modernization. This new round of opening policy in the form of the OBOR and the AIIB reflects Beijing's intention and efforts to play a more important role in the regional and global economy and to reconfigure new governance structure of the existing international economic order dominated by developed countries, the USA in particular. The twin initiatives of the OBOR and the AIIB are a clear reflection of China's growing capacity and economic clout that Beijing under Xi Jinping's leadership possesses and intends to use to pursue China's geopolitical and geoeconomic objectives. This represents recent evidence of the rise of Chinese power.

China's efforts to implement the OBOR and AIIB initiatives will inevitably have a significant impact on the economic architecture in multiple important areas, including patterns of regional trade, investment and infrastructure development, which would in turn have strategic impact on the region and beyond.[36] Generally speaking, the OBOR and the AIIB will likely have the following implications on economics, politics and security in the region and the world at large.

In terms of economics, if successfully implemented, the projects under the OBOR and the AIIB could help promote regional economic growth, development and integration. As the gap between supply and demand for infrastructure spending in Asia is as high as $8 trillion by 2020,[37] the OBOR and the AIIB will inevitably play a significant role in regional infrastructure development and economic growth. Economic growth in turn could help strengthen the political institutions and political and social stability in the region.

Over the medium to long term, successful implementation of the initiatives could help promote regional economic integration, boost trade and financial flows within the vast region that is covered by the OBOR and the AIIB, and expand a China-centered pattern of trade, investment, and infrastructure. This development would inevitably place China in a central and leading position in regional economic relations, which would in turn enhance Beijing's diplomatic leverage in this vast region. Furthermore, the OBOR and the AIIB would also help to more closely link the markets of Asia and Africa with not only products made in China moving more freely into these markets but also products made by Chinese-invested companies in Asia and Africa moving into the Western markets at even lower costs.

In finance, China has bypassed the World Bank by lending unilaterally under the OBOR and multilaterally through the AIIB to developing countries in support of regional infrastructure

---

[36]Scott Kennedy and David A. Parker, 'Building China's "One belt, one road"', Center for Strategic & International Studies, 3 April 2015, available at https://www.csis.org/analysis/building-china%E2%80%99s-%E2%80%9Cone-belt-one-road%E2%80%9D (accessed 23 July 2017).

[37]See Footnote 20.

projects. This, together with the New Development Bank (formerly known as the BRICS Development Bank) that is designed to finance development in emerging economies, would inevitably weaken the prominence of the World Bank and the ADB.

Furthermore, the OBOR and the AIIB will likely develop into a new model of economic cooperation, involving the Association of Southeast Asian Nations (ASEAN), the Shanghai Cooperation Organization (SCO), the South Asian Association for Regional Cooperation (SAARC), the Eurasian Economic Union (EAEU), and potentially a China–Japan–South Korean economic grouping, and promote the integration of Asia in which China will play a very important role.

In terms of geopolitics, there is no doubt that the OBOR and the AIIB will inevitably help enhance Beijing's influence over the vast areas of Eurasia. Moreover, China's involvement in constructing regional information technology infrastructure could bring China additional channels for exerting its influence in the region. Although China has tried to downplay the political implications of the initiatives, emphasizing the economic win-win nature of the OBOR and the AIIB, the initiatives will unavoidably bring important foreign policy implications for a number of powers in the region, including the USA, Japan, Russia, India and ASEAN countries. The USA and Japan as the status-quo powers in the region are particularly concerned about China's rising influence in the Asia-Pacific; Russia is concerned about China's influence in Central Asia, which Moscow views as its sphere of influence; India is concerned with China's influence in Sri Lanka, Bangladesh, Nepal, Bhutan and Maldives, which New Delhi sees as its backyards, as well as in Pakistan, which is India's rival in the South Asian subcontinent; and finally, the ASEAN as a regional grouping is concerned about China's influence in some of its member states, which would weaken its one voice with which the grouping would speak on many important regional issues, and even weaken the unity of the organization. Hence, China's OBOR and AIIB initiatives will inevitably increase geopolitical rivalry in the region, thus making the already complicated political, security and economic issues in the region even more complex.

From the Chinese perspective, however, the OBOR and the AIIB initiatives have so far brought some initial positive results in regional geopolitics and geoeconomics as Beijing had hoped for. Particularly, in one very important aspect, Beijing's 'carrot' diplomacy in the form of the OBOR and AIIB initiatives has already, to a great extent, helped ease China's tensions with the Philippines, a country that had been until very recently most uncompromising over its territorial dispute in the South China Sea with China. As a result, despite Manila's sweeping victory over an arbitration case against China over the territorial dispute in the South China Sea following the tribunal's ruling that was released on 12 July 2016, the new president, Rodrigo Duterte, who took office on 30 June 2016, has dramatically reversed his predecessor's China policy regarding the territorial dispute and agreed to reopen talks with Beijing without even referring to the tribunal's ruling following his state visit to China on 18–21 October 2016. What is even more dramatic is that President Duterte has even claimed to separate from the USA and adopt an independent foreign policy. In return for Duterte's reconciliatory policy, Beijing has immediately promised to provide huge economic benefits, which the Philippines is desperately in need of.[38] Although there are various speculations among analysts on the true motives of Duterte in reversing his predecessor's China policy, it is clear that Beijing's 'carrot' diplomacy seems to work, at least for the short and medium term.

Finally, the successful implementation of the OBOR and AIIB initiatives also implies the recognition and acceptance of China's model of development by the developing world, which further helps lay a solid foundation for China to become a true global superpower in the near future. It is in this sense that the OBOR and the AIIB indeed represent an important part of Beijing's overall global geoeconomic and geopolitical strategy.

---

[38]CNN, 'In China, Duterte announces split with US: "America has lost"', 20 October 2016, available at http://www.cnn.com/2016/10/20/asia/china-philippines-duterte-visit/ (accessed 26 June 2017); PhilNews, 'Pres. Duterte Brings Home $24 Billion Worth of Funding & Investment Pledges from China', 22 October 2016, available at http://www.philnews.xyz/2016/10/pres-duterte-brings-home-24-billion-funds-chinese.html (accessed 26 June 2017).

Disclosure statement

No potential conflict of interest was reported by the author

3   Beyond Balancing

China's approach towards the Belt and Road Initiative

Weifeng Zhou and Mario Esteban

ABSTRACT
This article explores the motivations and calculations behind China's Belt and Road Initiative. It argues that China's efforts to enhance regional multilateral cooperation across the Eurasian space through the BRI are strongly motivated by a multifaceted grand strategy. First, China makes use of the BRI as a vehicle of soft balancing to frustrate the US containment and encirclement of China, and undermine its dominance in Eurasia and beyond. Second, China intends to promote alternative ideas and norms and build its role as a normative power through the BRI for fostering the legitimacy of its rising power. Third, China seeks to form a bargaining coalition through the BRI and AIIB to reshape global governance and transform the existing international system in a way that reflects its values, interests and status. Overall, the BRI serves as a decisive strategic maneuver for China to ensure security and promote power status in the international order, moving from a rule-taker to rule-maker.

Introduction

Over the past three decades, China has considerably enhanced its comprehensive national strength and emerged as a regional and global power. China's mounting prominence in the international arena triggered a debate about China's rise and its implications for the existing international system.[1] Meanwhile, Chinese foreign policy experienced a dramatic shift from bilateralism and multilateralism to regional multilateralism.[2] Since the late 1990s, China has become a major actor in initiating, developing and institutionalizing multilateral cooperation mechanisms such as ASEAN Plus Three, ASEAN Plus One, Shanghai Cooperation Organization (SCO), East Asia Summit and Trilateral Cooperation.[3] In 2013, China launched the Belt and Road Initiative (BRI), namely the Silk Road Economic Belt and the Twenty-first Century Maritime Silk Road, to promote regional multilateral cooperation in the Eurasian space. The

---

[1] G. John Ikenberry, 'The rise of China and the future of the West: can the liberal system survive?', *Foreign Affairs* 87(1), (2008), pp. 23–37; Thomas J. Christensen, 'Fostering stability or creating a monster? The rise of China and U.S. policy toward East Asia', *International Security* 31(1), (2006), pp. 81–126; Aaron L. Friedberg, 'The future of U.S.–China relations: is conflict inevitable?', *International Security* 30(2), (2005), pp. 7–45.

[2] On regional multilateralism in Chinese foreign policy, see Emilian Kavalski, *China and the Global Politics of Regionalization* (London: Routledge, 2016); Guoguang Wu and Helen Lansdowne, *China Turns to Multilateralism: Foreign Policy and Regional Security* (London: Routledge, 2007).

[3] See Suisheng Zhao, 'China's approaches toward regional cooperation in East Asia: motivations and calculations', *Journal of Contemporary China* 20(68), (2011), pp. 53–67; Cheng-Chwee Kuik, 'Multilateralism in China's ASEAN policy: its evolution, characteristics, and aspiration', *Contemporary Southeast Asia* 27(1), (2005), pp. 102–122; Jingdong Yuan, 'China's role in establishing and building the Shanghai Cooperation Organization (SCO)', *Journal of Contemporary China* 19(67), (2010), pp. 855–869.

BRI is considered Beijing's most ambitious foreign policy initiative and is creating a new global geopolitical map, since the Initiative not only promises a mega geoeconomic agenda to deepen regional economic cooperation along the Silk Road, but also sets up a great power strategy to advance China's geopolitical and geostrategic interests in Eurasia and beyond. In particular, this diplomatic maneuver signals a significant shift in Chinese foreign policy from 'Keeping a Low Profile' (*taoguang yanghui*) to 'Striving for Achievement' (*yousuo zuowei*).[4] The ideas of China renaissance (*mingzu fuxing*) and Chinese dream (*zhongguo meng*) introduced by Chinese President Xi Jinping embodied the key element of China's global ambition. This article addresses the two main questions: why does China as a rising power become increasingly enthusiastic for regional multilateralism and what are the strategic calculations behind China's BRI?

The rise of China is one of the most prominent events of the twenty-first century. Some scholars argue that China's growing enthusiasm for regional multilateralism is closely associated with its changing role in the international system.[5] Indeed, there is a consensus among the scholars and policymakers in both Washington and Beijing that China's rising economic and military capabilities enable it to play a greater role in global affairs and promote its great power status. At the same time, China's growing power makes it the most credible challenger to the US's global dominance and has triggered a Sino–US strategic rivalry. The intensifying Sino–US competition presents Beijing with a stark dilemma of how to manage its relations with Washington for ensuring security and achieving its peaceful rise.

This article argues that China's embrace of regional multilateralism in Eurasia is not only driven by neorealist thought, but also shaped by constructivist and neoliberal logics that are respectively linked to power balancing, normative influence and institutional transformation. In particular, regional multilateral cooperation that enhances the nexus of economic, political and security relations serves as a vital instrument for China to tackle security challenges in pursuit of its peaceful rise.[6] Accordingly, China's approach towards the BRI is strongly motivated by a multifaceted grand strategy: adopting a soft balancing strategy to frustrate the US containment of China and undermine its power and influence, promoting China's soft power and building its role as a normative power through the promotion of alternative ideas and norms, and reshaping global governance in a way that reflects China's values, interests and status.

To further explore the motivations and calculations behind China's BRI, this article is divided into seven sections. Section I gives a brief overview of China's activism in regional multilateral cooperation and the BRI. Section II looks into the concept of regional multilateralism based on the three international relations theories: neorealism, neoliberalism and constructivism. Section III illustrates China's geoeconomic, geopolitical and geostrategic interests in promoting regional multilateral cooperation within the BRI. Section IV explores the logic of China's use of the BRI as a vehicle of soft balancing to counter the US containment strategy and undermine its dominance. Section V provides insight into China's endeavor to build its role as a normative power and foster the legitimacy of its rising power through the promotion of alternative ideas and norms within the BRI. Section VI deals with China's attempts to forge a bargaining coalition and reshape global governance through the BRI and the Asian Infrastructure Investment Bank (AIIB). Section VII presents some conclusions by highlighting the potential risks and challenges of BRI.

---

[4]See Xuetong Yan, 'From keeping a low profile to striving for achievement', *The Chinese Journal of International Politics* 7(2), (2014), pp. 153–184.
[5]See Shaun Breslin, 'China's emerging global role: dissatisfied responsible great power', *Politics* 30(1), (2010), pp. 52–62; David Shambaugh, 'China engages Asia: reshaping the regional order', *International Security* 29(3), (2004), pp. 64–99; Avery Goldstein, 'The diplomatic face of China's grand strategy: a rising power's emerging choice', *The China Quarterly* 168(12), (2001), pp. 835–864; Yunling Zhang, *China and Asian Regionalism* (Singapore: World Scientific Publishing, 2010).
[6]Avery Goldstein and Edward Mansfield, *The Nexus of Economics, Security, and International Relations in East Asia* (California: Stanford University Press, 2012).

Regional Multilateralism and International Relations Theories

Regional multilateralism was defined by Robert Keohane as the practice of coordination, cooperation and collaboration in certain policy areas among three or more states through ad hoc agreements, conventions and arrangements under the provisions of international institutions, organizations and regimes.[7] Regional multilateralism as a subset of multilateralism emphasizes the common, universal and reciprocal norms and rules to coordinate specific policy areas within regional multilateral settings. At present, regional multilateral cooperation has gone far beyond trade and become a multidimensional mechanism encompassing economic, political, security and cultural aspects. Building on the existing literature, the changing balance of global power is identified as one of the main factors explaining the emergence of regional multilateralism.[8]

From a neorealist perspective, international institutions are often viewed as means of statecraft of powerful states and play a vital role in shaping a hierarchical power structure in the international system.[9] For example, the Bretton Woods institutions have great significance in consolidating US hegemonic status and global influence. However, regional multilateral institutions have different implications for a rising power and for an existing hegemon, since they can either be used to increase the power of the former at the expense of the latter or be used to socialize the former into the latter's preferred regime and mechanism. Three neorealist assumptions provide explanations to the rationale of China's growing engagement in regional multilateral institutions: bargaining power,[10] institutional balancing[11] and counter-containment.[12] The first argument suggests that regional multilateral settings enable China to take advantage of asymmetric power and raise its bargaining power over other regional and international actors, advancing its interests. The second argument asserts that China has incentives to form a balancing coalition through regional multilateral institutions to counter the perceived threats. The third argument finds that promoting regional multilateral cooperation can be a strategic maneuver to frustrate the US containment of China and enhance Beijing's position in the power competition.

Neoliberalism argues that states pursue absolute gains rather than relative gains to other states and the international institutions facilitating cooperation and compromise between states can produce absolute gains for all their members. Neoliberal institutionalism assumes that states advance their overall interests with a commitment to strengthen cooperation within international institutions or regimes, since those institutions or regimes can not only reduce costs, form preferences and monitor processes, but also overcome collective action problem, facilitate problem-solution and achieve goals.[13] Accordingly, while regional multilateral cooperation helps enhance strategic interdependence among the states and reshape the balance of power at regional and global levels, regional multilateral initiatives can be used strategically and tactically as a vehicle of soft balancing against a potential or existing hegemon.

While neorealists and neoliberalists underline 'war and power' and 'interest and cooperation' respectively, constructivists take into consideration two key elements shaping the international order: identity and norm.[14] Constructivist scholars have argued that creating political identity and promoting certain 'normative values' seem to be of primary importance for the states to establish regional multilateral

---

[7]Robert O. Keohane, 'Multilateralism: an agenda for research', *International Journal* 45(4), (1990), p. 731.
[8]See Stephan Keukeleire and Bas Hooijmaaijers, 'The BRICS and other emerging power alliances and multilateral organizations in the Asia–Pacific and the global South: challenges for the European Union and its view on multilateralism', *Journal of Common Market Studies* 52(3), (2014), pp. 582–599.
[9]Kenneth Waltz, 'Structural realism after the Cold War', *International Security* 25(1), (2000), pp. 5–41.
[10]See Ann Kent, *Beyond Compliance: China, International Organizations and Global Security* (Stanford, CA: Stanford University Press, 2007).
[11]For example, see Kai He, 'Institutional balancing and international relations theory: economic interdependence and balance of power strategies in Southeast Asia', *European Journal of International Relations* 14(3), (2008), pp. 489–518.
[12]See Marc Lanteigne, *China and International Institutions: Alternate Paths to Global Power* (London and New York: Routledge, 2005).
[13]Robert O. Keohane, *After Hegemony: Cooperation and Discord in the World Political Economy* (Princeton, NJ: Princeton University Press, 1984).
[14]Audie Klotz and Cecelia M. Lynch, *Strategies for Research in Constructivist International Relations* (New York: M.E. Sharpe, 2007).

regimes and institutions.[15] The interaction between actors, states or institutions helps create, promote and justify political identities which legitimize the power of those actors, states and institutions in the existing international system. International cooperation amongst and between actors and states also promotes international norms as international institutions or regimes possess a set of rules, processes and principles to facilitate the convergence of interest, objective and action.[16] Accordingly, we contend that the interaction between Beijing and other Eurasian actors within the BRI helps to promote alternative ideas and norms, build Beijing's soft and normative power and enhance the legitimacy of its rising power in the international society.

China's Strategy Towards Eurasia and the BRI

During his state visits to Kazakhstan and Indonesia in 2013, Chinese President Xi Jinping proposed establishing the BRI, including the land-based and the sea-based Silk Roads, to promote regional connectivity and multilateral cooperation. The land routes start in China's Central and Western regions, pass through Central Asia, West Asia, Central and Eastern Europe and end in Western Europe. The maritime routes connect China's coastal regions and Europe through the South China Sea, the Indian Ocean, the Persian Gulf and the Mediterranean Sea. The BRI involves 65 countries across Asia, Europe and Africa,[17] and represents 70% of the world's population and more than 40% of the world's GDP. The Initiative offers not only a multilateral mechanism to enhance economic, political and cultural ties between China and other Eurasian countries, but also a venue to strengthen cooperation with the existing regional multilateral groups such as the SCO, ASEAN, European Union, Asia–Europe Meeting, Eurasian Economic Union, South Asian Association for Regional Cooperation and the Gulf Cooperation Council.

The BRI sets up an ambitious agenda to deepen multilateral cooperation across the Eurasian continent and promote prosperity and development of all countries along the BRI. According to a statement released by the National Development and Reform Commission, the BRI will enhance regional multilateral cooperation on five pillars: '(i) strengthen policy dialogue; (iii) strengthen trade facilitation; (iv) strengthen financial cooperation; (v) strengthen people-to-people exchanges'.[18] Along with the BRI, China created the AIIB and the Silk Road Fund to provide financial support to the BRI projects. In May 2017, Beijing formalized the BRI by hosting the first Belt and Road Forum for International Cooperation in Beijing that resulted in a large number of cooperation agreements signed by more than 50 countries.[19] China's efforts to promote multilateral cooperation through the BRI are motivated by a desire to advance its geoeconomic, geopolitical and geostrategic interests in Eurasia and beyond.

China's Geoeconomic Interests

The BRI is strongly driven by geoeconomic factors. First, the Western Development Strategy, which was enacted in 1999 to accelerate economic development in China's western regions, is given a priority by Chinese leaders. Poor infrastructure, inadequate investment and development imbalance have not only impeded economic development but also posed a threat to political stability in China's western regions. Second, China's economic growth has suffered a slowdown since 2012 and unprecedentedly declined to 6.7% in 2016, recording a historic low level in the past 25 years. In this respect, the problem of how

---

[15]Björn Hettne, 'Globalization and the new regionalism: the second great transformation', *Globalism and the New Regionalism* 1, (1999), pp. 1–24.
[16]Stephen D. Krasner, *International Regimes* (Ithaca, NY: Cornell University Press, 1983).
[17]The BRI is an open and inclusive initiative including but not limited to the 65 countries; please see Hong Kong Trade Development Council, 'Country profile: the Belt and Road', *Hong Kong Trade Development Council*, available at: http://beltandroad.hktdc.com/en/country-profiles/country-profiles.aspx (accessed 12 August 2017).
[18]National Development and Reform Commission, *Vision and Actions on Jointly Building Silk Road Economic Belt and 21st-Century Maritime Silk Road*, The State Council of China, (28 March 2015), available at: http://en.ndrc.gov.cn/newsrelease/201503/t20150330_669367.html (accessed 10 August 2017).
[19]'List of deliverables of belt and road forum', *Xinhua News Agency*, (15 May 2017), available at: http://news.xinhuanet.com/english/2017-05/15/c_136286376.htm (accessed 12 August 2017).

to sustain stable economic growth is placed at the top of Chinese policymakers' agenda. In November 2013, the Central Committee of the Communist Party of China decided to build a more open economic system by deepening market integration and developing a new trade strategy, and promote multilateral cooperation by constructing the Silk Road Economic Belt and the Maritime Silk Road.[20]

Through the BRI, China seeks to establish closer economic ties between its western regions and Central Asia, Southeast Asia and South Asia by developing infrastructure, promoting trade and enhancing interconnectivity. China has proposed to set up seven economic corridors along the BRI: China–Mongolia–Russia Economic Corridor; New Eurasian Land Bridge; China-Central and West Asia Economic Corridor; China–Indo–China Peninsula Economic Corridor; China–Pakistan Economic Corridor; Bangladesh–China–India–Myanmar Economic Corridor; and China–India–Nepal Economic Corridor. This not only creates huge investment opportunities for Chinese firms and tackles China's industrial overcapacity, but also stimulates development of China's western regions and revives its sluggish economy.[21] Until May 2017, a total of 1,676 infrastructure projects involving highway, high-speed rail, electricity grid, port facilities, and gas and oil pipelines have been contracted to consolidate regional connectivity, which is clearly a geoeconomic imperative.[22]

With the BRI, China also intends to forge a stronger Eurasian linkage between Asia and Europe, two of the world's most dynamic markets.[23] As of May 2017, the Eurasian rail network has connected 28 Chinese cities directly with 29 cities in 11 European countries. Meanwhile, China also proposed establishing a land–sea express route linking the port of Piraeus, one of the largest container ports in Europe and a gateway between the Middle East, the Balkans, European markets and Xinjiang. That enables Beijing not only to increase access to regional markets, promote Renminbi internationalization, diminish excessive foreign reserves and diversify energy suppliers and routes, but also to translate its growing economic power into political power.

China's Geopolitical Interests

In 1904, the British geographer Halford Mackinder wrote a paper on 'The Geographical Pivot of History', arguing that the country ruling the heartland of Eurasia would dominate the world.[24] Along the same lines, the American geostrategist Zbigniew Brzezinski wrote:

> … How America 'manages' Eurasia is critical. A power that dominates 'Eurasia' would control two of the world's three most advanced and economically productive regions. A mere glance at the map also suggests that control over 'Eurasia' would almost automatically entail Africa's subordination, rendering the Western Hemisphere and Oceania geopolitically peripheral to the world's central continent. About 75 percent of the world's people live in 'Eurasia', and most of the world's physical wealth is there as well, both in its enterprises and underneath its soil. 'Eurasia' accounts for about three-fourths of the world's known energy resources.[25]

China, one of the two Eurasian great powers (namely China and Russia), not only has a stake in Eurasia but also possesses great advantage to win friends, build power and expand influence across the continent. As an integral part of China's peripheral strategy, the regional multilateral mechanism serves as a vital diplomatic tool for Beijing not merely to ensure access to resources and markets but also to advance its key geopolitical objectives. By enhancing regional multilateral cooperation within the ASEAN Plus Three and SCO, Beijing has established its prominent role in East Asia and Central Asia. The BRI allows Beijing to further expand its influence in other parts of Eurasia such as South Asia, West Asia, the Middle East and Europe. Given China's historic role in Eurasia, the fundamental purpose of rebuilding

[20]'Decision of the Central Committee of the Communist Party of China on some major issues concerning comprehensively deepening the reform', *The People's Net*, (29 January 2014), available at: http://en.people.cn/90785/8525422.html (accessed 10 August 2017).
[21]Yiping Huang, 'Understanding China's Belt & Road Initiative: motivation, framework and assessment', *China Economic Review* 40, (2016), pp. 314–321.
[22]See 'List of deliverables of belt and road forum', *Xinhua News Agency*.
[23]See Nicola Casarini, 'When all roads lead to Beijing: assessing China's new Silk Road and its implications for Europe', *The International Spectator* 51(4), (2016), pp. 95–108.
[24]Halford Mackinder, 'The geographical pivot of history', *The Geographical Journal* 23(4), (1904), pp. 421–437.
[25]Zbigniew Brzezinski, *The Grand Chessboard: American Primacy and its Geostrategic Imperatives* (New York: Basic Books, 1998), p. 31.

the ancient Silk Road through the BRI is to reaffirm its geopolitical interests in the Eurasian space, revive the 'Moment of Glory' of Chinese civilization and regain its great power status.[26]

The BRI is vital to advance China's geopolitical interests in three aspects: energy security; geopolitical influence; and maritime interests. First, since China is heavily dependent on energy imports from the Persian Gulf,[27] the New Eurasian Land Bridge and China-Central and West Asia Economic Corridor allow it to forge stronger energy ties with Russia and Central Asian states and reduce its reliance on energy imports from the Persian Gulf. The China–Pakistan Economic Corridor and Bangladesh–China–India–Myanmar Economic Corridor will facilitate China's energy imports from the Persian Gulf and Africa via gas and oil pipelines and reduce its dependence on the Malacca Strait where the US can exert great influence. Second, the Land Silk Road helps expand Beijing's geopolitical influence across the continent. Regional connectivity and multilateral cooperation that help enhance asymmetric interdependence enable Beijing not only to leverage its power and influence over other Eurasian partners to its strategic interests, but also to broaden its strategic hinterland and geopolitical space. Third, the Maritime Silk Road helps Beijing to build its maritime power and expand influence in the Indian Ocean for improving maritime security and advancing its maritime interests. For example, China's heavy investment in Hambantota Port (Sri Lanka), Gwadar Port (Pakistan) and Kyaukpyu port (Myanmar) allows Beijing to reinforce its naval presence in the Indian Ocean, ensure the security of its trade and energy routes, and foster its role as a maritime power.[28]

China's Geostrategic Interests

The BRI is also shaped by rising geostrategic competition in the Asia–Pacific. Traditionally, China regarded East Asia as its primary geopolitical focus and sought to build its power and influence in the region. When Beijing's growing economic and military power was perceived as a challenge to American preponderance, Washington announced a 'Pivot to Asia' strategy to reaffirm its strategic interests in Asia and contain China's rising influence.[29] Washington sought to build a 'C-shaped ring of encirclement' around China by linking the East China Sea, Taiwan Strait, South China Sea, Malacca Strait and Indian Ocean for limiting China's influence in the first island chain and constraining China's expansion into the Indian and Pacific Oceans. Washington also set an aggressive economic agenda to counter China's rising economic power through the conclusion of the Trans-Pacific Partnership (TPP),[30] which has however been abandoned by US President Trump.[31] In this context, the BRI can be seen as a 'Pivot to Europe' strategy to counterbalance the US's 'Pivot to Asia',[32] breaking US containment of China and undermining its dominance. Wang Jisi, a prominent International Relations scholar at Peking University, argued that the BRI is not merely a 'Marching West' strategy to advance China's geostrategic interests in Eurasia, but also a geostrategic rebalance to the US's 'Pivot to Asia'.[33]

The BRI illustrates a profound shift in Chinese foreign policy from 'Keeping a low profile' to 'Striving for achievement'. Throughout the 1980s, 1990s and 2000s, Deng Xiaoping's 'Keeping a low profile' was a basic principle guiding Chinese foreign policy and played a crucial role in fostering a favorable

[26]Valerie Hansen, *The Silk Road: A New History* (New York: Oxford University Press, 2012).

[27]Charles E. Ziegler, 'The energy factor in China's foreign policy', *Journal of Chinese Political Science* 11(1), (2006), pp. 1–23.

[28]Christopher Len, 'China's 21st Century Maritime Silk Road Initiative, energy security and SLOC access', *Maritime Affairs: Journal of the National Maritime Foundation of India* 11(1), (2015), pp. 1–18.

[29]Evan Braden Montgomery, 'Contested primacy in the Western Pacific: China's rise and the future of U.S. power projection', *International Security* 38(4), (2014), pp. 115–149.

[30]Evelyn S. Devadason, 'The Trans-Pacific Partnership (TPP): the Chinese perspective', *Journal of Contemporary China* 23(87), (2012), pp. 462–479.

[31]Office of Press Secretary of the White House, *Presidential Memorandum Regarding Withdrawal of the United States from the Trans-Pacific Partnership Negotiations and Agreement*, The White House, (23 January 2017), available at: https://www.white-house.gov/the-press-office/2017/01/23/presidential-memorandum-regarding-withdrawal-united-states-trans-pacific (accessed 10 August 2017).

[32]Theresa Fallon, 'China's pivot to Europe', *American Foreign Policy Interests* 36(3), (2014), pp. 175–182.

[33]Jisi Wang, 'Xijin: Zhongguo Diyuan Zhanlue de Zai Pingheng' ['Marching West: China's geopolitical rebalancing strategy'], *Huanqiu Shibao* [*Global Times*], (17 October 2012), available at: http://opinion.huanqiu.com/opinion_world/2012-10/3193760.html (accessed 10 August 2017).

international environment for China's modernization process. Some Chinese scholars argue that such a strategy has become outdated when Washington's containment policy has not only endangered China's security environment but also limited China's ability to project power in its periphery.[34] In particular, the decline of American power provided an opportunity for China to play a greater role in global affairs. After Xi Jinping took power, Beijing adopted a more assertive foreign policy to advance its regional and global interests.[35] Thus, the BRI is strongly driven by three factors: first, China makes use of the BRI as a vehicle of soft balancing to undermine American power by establishing asymmetric interdependence, enhancing strategic reassurance over its Eurasian partners, and deterring the formation of any anti-China coalition and 'anyone but China' club. Second, China seeks to promote soft power and build its role as a normative power, increasing the legitimacy of its rising power. Third, China intends to reshape global governance and transform the existing international system in a way that reflects its values, interests and status.

Soft Balancing Against the US

Soft balancing theorists point out that secondary power may adopt a soft balancing strategy to counter the perceived threats from the hegemon through economic, political, diplomatic and institutional means, since the traditional hard balancing is too costly and risky.[36] As regional multilateral regimes help overcome collective action problems and facilitate cooperation towards common interests and objectives, secondary powers have a strong incentive to initiate, utilize or dominate regional multilateral institutions and cooperation to counter coercion and threat from a superior power. This especially applies to Sino–US competition. With limited military capabilities, it would be quite unwise for Beijing to undertake traditional hard balancing against the American hegemony. Accordingly, China is strongly motivated to pursue a soft balancing strategy against the US through institutional methods.

While China's rise is seen as a challenge to American dominance in the Asia–Pacific,[37] Washington's 'Pivot to Asia' strategy is a direct response to China's growing role.[38] The TPP and Transatlantic Trade and Investment Partnership (TTIP) that don't include Beijing can be seen as an updated version of US strategic containment of China, since Washington attempts to build an 'anyone but China' club by forging Transatlantic and Transpacific links to interconnect East Asia, North America and the European Union. As China's economy is heavily dependent on Asian, European and American markets, the US's intention to reshape the global trading regime through the TPP and the TTIP is to limit China's access to those markets, 'choke' its economic growth, undermine Beijing's ability to expand its influence regionally and globally, and constrain its continued rise.[39] According to Richard Baldwin, a country or region that has been excluded from a preferential agreement is strongly motivated to join a similar bloc or build a

---

[34]For example, see Kai He and Huiyun Feng, 'Xi Jinping's operational code beliefs and China's foreign policy', *The Chinese Journal of International Politics* 6(3), (2013), pp. 209–231; Yan, 'From keeping a low profile to striving for achievement', pp. 153–184; Feng Zhu and Peng Lu, 'Be strong and be good? Continuity and change in China's international strategy under Xi Jinping', *China Quarterly of International Strategic Studies* 1(1), (2015), pp. 19–34.

[35]Theresa Fallon, 'The New Silk Road: Xi Jinping's grand strategy for Eurasia', *American Foreign Policy Interests* 37(3), (2015), pp. 140–147.

[36]On the soft balancing theory, see Robert Pape, 'Soft balancing against the United States', *International Security* 30(1), (2005), pp. 7–45; Thazha V. Paul, 'Soft balancing in the age of US primacy', *International Security* 30(1), (2005), pp. 46–71; Stephen G. Brooks and William C. Wohlforth, 'Hard times for soft balancing', *International Security* 30(1), (2005), pp. 72–108; He, 'Institutional balancing and international relations theory'.

[37]See Christopher Layne, 'The unipolar illusion: why new great powers will rise', *International Security* 17(4), (2009), pp. 5–51; Jeffrey W. Legro, 'What China will want: the future intentions of a rising power', *Perspective on Politics* 5(5), (2007), pp. 515–534; Robert G. Sutter, 'Assessing China's rise and US leadership in Asia: growing maturity and balance', *Journal of Contemporary China* 19(65), (2010), pp. 591–604.

[38]Hilary Clinton, 'America's Pacific century', *Foreign Policy* 189, (2011), pp. 56–63; David Beitelman, 'America's Pacific pivot', *International Journal* 67(4), (2012), pp. 1073–1094.

[39]Ashley J. Tellis, 'The geopolitics of the TTIP and the TPP', *Adelphi Series* 54(450), (2014), pp. 93–120; Devadason, 'The Trans-Pacific Partnership (TPP)', pp. 462–479; Michael J. Green and Matthew P. Goodman, 'After TPP: the geopolitics of Asia and the Pacific', *The Washington Quarterly* 38(4), (2015), pp. 19–34; Roberto Bendini, *EU and US Trade Policy and its Global Implications: TPP, TTIP und China*, Directorate-General for External Policies, (7 July 2014), available at: http://www.europarl.europa.eu/RegData/etudes/briefing_note/join/2014/522349/EXPO-INTA_SP%282014%29522349_EN.pdf (accessed 12 August 2017).

new bloc to counterbalance the negative effect of being excluded.[40] Therefore, the BRI is considered a response to Washington's attempt to create new trading blocs that exclude China.[41]

The BRI that goes far beyond a pure trade agenda can be seen as a bold geoeconomic initiative to advance Beijing's geopolitical and geostrategic goals. Thus, this initiative keeps its relevance even if Trump decided to withdraw from the TPP. As regional multilateral cooperation provides a new approach to establish an interests-based coalition between China and other Eurasian partners, the BRI can serve as a vehicle of soft balancing for Beijing to counterbalance American preponderance without provoking it directly. The logic of undertaking a strategy of soft balancing against the US through the BRI lies in establishing strategic interdependence, reassuring Eurasian partners of the peaceful intention of China's rising power, deterring the formation of any form of anti-China coalition or 'anyone but China' club.

China's increasing economic power is the key to understand how the BRI is used by Beijing as a means of soft balancing against the US. Given the size and dynamism of the Chinese economy, promoting regional economic cooperation and integration within the BRI will enhance asymmetric economic interdependence between Beijing and other Eurasian countries, making those countries much more dependent on Beijing economically than vice versa. Such asymmetric economic interdependence enables Beijing to translate its economic power into political power, leverage its influence over those Eurasian countries to its strategic interests,[42] and undermine the US dominance in Eurasia and beyond.

Figure 1 shows how China's trade volume with 65 BRI countries has risen much more dramatically than the US's trade volume with them. The share of China's trade with the BRI countries in its total trade jumped sharply from 19% to 26% between 2005 and 2014, whereas the share of the US's trade with those countries in its total trade only experienced a small increase from 13% to 15%. In the meanwhile, China has replaced the US as the world's largest trading nation in 2012 and almost become the largest trading partner of all the BRI countries. The picture is quite similar when looking at Foreign Direct Investment (FDI). According to the World Investment Report 2016 by the United Nations Conference on Trade and Development (UNCTAD), China became the world's second largest investor in 2015.[43] Figure 2 indicates that China's outward FDI into the BRI countries has constantly risen from only 9.08 billion in 2006 to 109.77 billion in 2015, constituting 75% of its total outward FDI for that year. After the launching of the BRI, China's outward FDI into the BRI countries has increased from 75.94 billion in 2013 to 109.77 billion in 2015 while its outward FDI into the rest of the world almost remained unchanged during the same period.

Despite its repeated commitment to peaceful rise, China's growing power and influence has generated a great deal of mistrust, anxiety and fear in the region. Those who perceive China's rise as a threat are more likely to shape a balancing coalition or 'anyone but China' club to contain China's expanding influence through isolation, marginalization and boycotting.[44] In this context, Beijing's efforts to enhance regional multilateral cooperation within the BRI can not only reassure Eurasian countries of the peaceful nature of its rising power but also deter those countries to form an anti-China coalition or join the US-led alliance against China. Therefore, the BRI provides a pragmatic way for China to reassure its partners, deter its rivals, and undermine the US power and influence without stirring up a war.

The South China Sea issue offers a good example of how the BRI serves as a means of soft balancing for China to undermine US power and influence. In July 2016, the Permanent Court of Arbitration (PCA)

[40]Richard Baldwin, *A Domino Theory of Regionalism*, NBER Working Papers No. 4465, National Bureau of Economic Research, (September 1993), available at: http://www.nber.org/papers/w4465.pdf (accessed 10 August 2017).

[41]William H. Overholt, 'One belt, one road, one pivot', *Global Asia* 10(3), (2015), pp. 1–8.

[42]See He, 'Institutional balancing and international relations theory', pp. 489–518; Miles Kahler and Scott L. Kastner, 'Strategic uses of economic interdependence: engagement policies on the Korean Peninsula and across the Taiwan Strait', *Journal of Peace Research* 43(5), (2006), pp. 523–541; Paul A. Papayoanou, *Power Ties: Economic Interdependence, Balancing, and War* (Ann Arbor, MI: Michigan University Press, 1999).

[43]United Nations Conference on Trade and Development (UNCTAD), *World Investment Report 2016* (Geneva: United Nations, 2016), available at: http://unctad.org/en/PublicationsLibrary/wir2016_en.pdf (accessed 10 August 2017).

[44]On the dynamic relations between Beijing, Washington and other Asian states, see Evelyn Goh, 'Great powers and hierarchical order in Southeast Asia: analyzing regional security strategies', *International Security* 32(3), (2008), pp. 113–157; Suisheng Zhao and Xiong Qi, 'Hedging and geostrategic balance of East Asian countries toward China', *Journal of Contemporary China* 25(100), (2016), pp. 485–499.

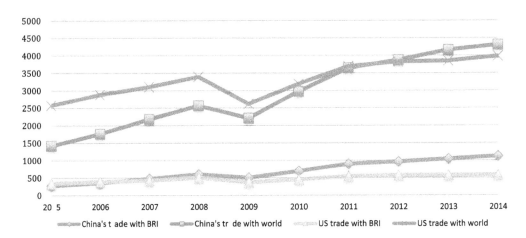

Figure 1. China and US trade with BRI countries and world during 2005–2014 (in billion US$). Sources: National Bureau of Statistics of China, http://data.stats.gov.cn; The International Trade Administration, US Department of Commerce, http://www.trade.gov.

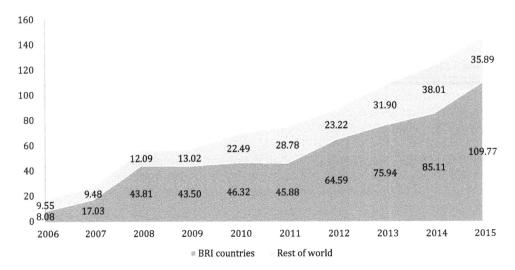

Figure 2. China's outward FDI into BRI countries and the world during 2006–2015 (in billion US$). Source: 2015 Statistical Bulletin of China's Outward Foreign Direct Investment.

issued a ruling in favor of a US-backed Philippine challenge to China's territorial claims in the South China Sea despite strong opposition from Beijing. Meanwhile, Washington's Asian and European allies who have close economic ties with Beijing are unwilling to endorse the PCA ruling. For example, the EU failed to issue a timely statement on the ruling as Athens and Budapest blocked such a EU statement criticizing Beijing.[45] These two countries' growing dependence on Chinese investment and their eagerness to play a pivotal role in the BRI caused them reluctantly to annoy Beijing. Although the EU finally reached a common position after three days of difficult negotiation, Brussels only issued a vague and neutral statement acknowledging the PCA ruling without direct reference to Beijing.[46] Similarly, ASEAN

---

[45]Georgi Gotev, 'EU unable to adopt statement upholding China Sea ruling', *Euroactive*, (14 July 2016), available at: http://www.euractiv.com/section/global-europe/news/eu-unable-to-adopt-statement-upholding-south-china-sea-ruling/ (accessed 10 August 2017).

[46]Theresa Fallon, *The EU, the South China Sea, and China's Successful Wedge Strategy*, CSIS, (13 October 2016), available at: https://amti.csis.org/eu-south-china-sea-chinas-successful-wedge-strategy/ (accessed 10 August 2017).

failed to issue a joint statement upholding the PCA ruling[47] as the stances of ten ASEAN countries were deeply divided: (1) Laos and Cambodia opposed the ruling; (2) Thailand, Myanmar, Malaysia (as one of claimants), Brunei (as one of claimants), Indonesia (as one of claimants) and Singapore (as the US's ally) maintained a neutral position; (3) the Philippines and Vietnam supported the ruling. After Rodrigo Duterte took power, the Philippines' stance on the South China Sea disputes experienced a stunning reversal. While Manila desires to gain Chinese investment and aid and join the Maritime Silk Road for improving infrastructures and boosting growth, Duterte not only decided to suspend the PCA ruling but also agreed to resolve disputes through a bilateral dialogue,[48] accommodating Beijing's strategic interests at the expense of Washington.

Building Soft and Normative Power

As China's rapid economic growth has facilitated a dramatic increase in its military might and international security presence, its growing hard power has fueled the perceptions of the 'China Threat' that make it difficult to expand its influence regionally and globally. Chinese policymakers realized that China's rise to great power status relies not only on formidable hard power but also on soft power.[49] Thus, Beijing is keen to promote its soft power through various means, including not only culture and public diplomacy but also economic and diplomatic levers such as aid, investment and participation in or creation of regional multilateral organizations and institutions.[50] Enhancing soft power through regional multilateral cooperation does not merely assist Beijing in increasing its global image and international prestige as a peaceful, benign and responsible power,[51] but also helps persuade others to accept and recognize its rising power status in the international community, facilitating its peaceful rise.[52]

Jay Jackson defined normative power as the potential influence over others' activity and behavior through the power of norms and stressed the '*domain* and *range*' of legitimate behavior.[53] While power shifts often prompt normative transformation in the international system, China, as a rising power, has a strong motive to promote political identity and legitimacy of its rising power and build its role as a normative power through the promotion of alternative ideas, rules and norms in international fora.[54] More importantly, Beijing's efforts to construct its identity as a normative power will increase its normative authority and legitimacy at the expense of Washington and consolidate its role as a great power in the international system.[55]

Regional multilateral initiatives such as the BRI are essential to produce common rules, promote alternative norms and socialize ideas of interactive cooperation for bolstering Beijing's soft power and

---

[47]Louise Watt, 'Recent developments surrounding the South China Sea', *Associated Press*, (7 August 2017), available at: https://www.washingtonpost.com/world/asia_pacific/recent-developments-surrounding-the-south-china-sea/2017/08/07/f3d2d97a-7b30-11e7-b2b1-aeba62854dfa_story.html (accessed 10 August 2017).

[48]Dongyang Zhu, 'Duterte's visit presents overdue opportunity for China–Philippines rapprochement', *Xinhua News Agency*, (18 October 2016), available at: http://news.xinhuanet.com/english/2016-10/18/c_135762185.htm (accessed 12 August 2017).

[49]On soft power, see Joseph S. Nye Jr, 'The changing nature of world power', *Political Science Quarterly* 105(2), (1990), pp. 177–192.

[50]Chin-Hao Huang, *China's Soft Power in East Asia: A Quest for Status and Influence?*, NBR Special Report 42 (Washington: The National Bureau of Asian Research, 2013); Gregory G. Holyk, 'Paper tiger? Chinese soft power in East Asia', *Political Science Quarterly* 126(2), (2011), pp. 223–254; Joshua Kurlantzick, *Charm Offensive: How China's Soft Power is Transforming the World* (New Haven, CT: Yale University Press, 2007).

[51]Georgiana Boboc, 'The Belt and Road Initiative: China's soft power strategy', *China Daily*, (5 July 2017), available at: http://www.chinadaily.com.cn/opinion/2017beltandroad/2017-06/05/content_29618551.htm (accessed 12 August 2017).

[52]Xin Li and Verner Worm, 'Building China's soft power for a peaceful rise', *Journal of Chinese Political Science* 16(1), (2011), pp. 69–89; Ian Hall and Frank Smith, 'The struggle for soft power in Asia: public diplomacy and regional competition', *Asian Security* 9(1), (2013), pp. 1–18.

[53]Jay Jackson, 'Normative power and conflict potential', *Sociological Methods & Research* 4(2), (1975), pp. 237–239; Ian Manners, 'Normative power Europe: a contradiction in terms?', *Journal of Common Market Studies* 40(2), (2002), pp. 235–258.

[54]See Emilian Kavalski, 'The struggle for recognition of normative powers: normative power Europe and normative power China in context', *Cooperation & Conflict* 48(2), (2013), pp. 247–267; Emilian Kavalski, 'The shadows of normative power in Asia: framing the international agency of China, India, and Japan', *Pacific Focus* 29(3), (2014), pp. 303–328.

[55]Xuetong Yan, 'The rise of China and its power status', *Chinese Journal of International Politics* 1(1), (2006), pp. 5–33; Deborah Welch Larson and Alexei Shevchenko, 'Status seekers. Chinese and Russian responses to U.S. primacy', *International Security* 34(4), (2001), pp. 63–95.

building its role as a normative power. In November 2014, at the Central Conference on Work Relating to Foreign Affairs, Xi Jinping emphasized the importance of building the BRI in the following terms:

> We should seek other countries' understanding of and support for the Chinese dream, which is about peace, development, cooperation and win–win outcomes. What we pursue is the wellbeing of both the Chinese people and the people of all other countries … We should make more friends while abiding by the principle of non-alignment and build a global network of partnership. We should increase China's soft power, give a good Chinese narrative, and better communicate China's message to the world.[56]

Since the end of World War II, the principle of Westphalian sovereignty has become the cornerstone of contemporary international relations and the liberal international order. However, the norms of Westphalian sovereignty were eroded by the global competition between the US and the Soviet Union during the Cold War. These norms have also been undermined in the post-Cold War era when Washington sought to create an American-led liberal hegemonic order, and have undergone a normative shift in international relations from a Westphalian to a post-Westphalian model. The Five Principles of Peaceful Coexistence that China initiated together with India and Myanmar in 1954 are not only a basic norm governing China's foreign policy and international relations,[57] but also a major source of China's normative power. At the 60th anniversary of the Five Principles of Peaceful Coexistence, Chinese President Xi Jinping stressed that:

> These five principles, as an integrated, interconnected, and indivisible concept, capture the essence of today's international relations, and can apply to relations among all countries regardless of their social system, stage of development or size. Principles have effectively upheld the rights and interests of the developing world and have played a positive role in building a more equitable and rational international political and economic order.[58]

Promoting the Five Principles of Peaceful coexistence is not only an effort to oppose any imposition of norms and values on others and interference in other countries' domestic affairs, but also an attempt to enhance China's role as a normative power that champions an international order based on the concept of Westphalian sovereignty and peaceful coexistence. Establishing and enhancing regional multilateral cooperation within the BRI is part of Beijing's efforts to diffuse those norms and ideas across the continent. The vision and action plan for the BRI upholds the Five Principles of Peaceful Coexistence and adds:

> The Initiative is harmonious and inclusive. It advocates tolerance among civilizations, respects the paths and modes of development chosen by different countries, and supports dialogues among different civilizations on the principles of seeking common ground while shelving differences and drawing on each other's strengths, so that all countries can coexist in peace for common prosperity.[59]

More recently, in his speech at the opening ceremony of the Belt and Road Forum for International Cooperation in Beijing, Xi Jinping underlined the importance of upholding the Five Principles of Peaceful Coexistence in implementing the BRI:

> China will enhance friendship and cooperation with all countries involved in the Belt and Road Initiative on the basis of the Five Principles of Peaceful Co-existence. We are ready to share practices of development with other countries, but we have no intention to interfere in other countries' internal affairs, export our own social system and model of development, or impose our own will on others. In pursuing the Belt and Road Initiative, we will not resort to outdated geopolitical maneuvering. What we hope to achieve is a new model of win–win cooperation. We have no intention to form a small group detrimental to stability, what we hope to create is a big family of harmonious co-existence.[60]

The BRI provides Beijing with great opportunities to promote those norms among countries and regions along the Silk Road. In a joint statement issued by Chinese and Serbian leaders in June 2016,

[56]'Xi eyes more enabling international environment for China's peaceful development', Xinhua News Agency, (24 November 2014), available at: http://news.xinhuanet.com/english/china/2014-11/30/c_133822694_4.htm (accessed 12 August 2017).

[57]Xinbo Wu, 'Four contradictions constraining China's foreign policy behavior', Journal of Contemporary China 10(27), (2001), pp. 293–301; Qimao Chen, 'New approaches in China's foreign policy: the post-Cold War era', Asian Survey 33(3), (1993), pp. 237–251.

[58]Fu Peng, 'Five principles of peaceful coexistence not outdated: Chinese President', Xinhua News Agency, (28 June 2014), available at: http://news.xinhuanet.com/english/china/2014-06/28/c_133445548.htm (accessed 12 August 2017).

[59]See National Development and Reform Commission, Vision and Actions on Jointly Building Silk Road Economic Belt and 21st-Century Maritime Silk Road.

[60]'President Xi's speech on work together to build the Silk Road Economic Belt and the 21st Century Maritime Silk Road', Xinhua News Agency, (14 May 2017), available at: http://news.xinhuanet.com/english/2017-05/14/c_136282982.htm (accessed 12 August 2017).

the two countries not only agreed to promote regional connectivity between China and Central and Eastern European countries (CEEs) within the BRI, but also 'pledged to respect and support each other in choosing development paths and policies according to their national conditions, and in issues of core interests and common concern, based on the principles of mutual respect, equality and non-interference in internal affairs'.[61] One week later, at a trilateral meeting of leaders of China, Russia and Mongolia in Tashkent, Xi Jinping, Vladimir Putin and Tsakhiagiin Elbegdorj agreed to boost trilateral cooperation within the BRI and construct the China–Russia–Mongolia Economic Corridor. And Putin said: 'Russia, China and Mongolia are friendly neighbors based on equality, respect and mutual benefit'[62] that certainly conforms to the spirit of the Five Principles. Also during Aung San Suu Kyi's visit to Beijing in August 2016, the two leaders issued a joint statement[63] saying that the two sides agreed to push forward China–Myanmar 'Paukphaw' friendship, China–Myanmar comprehensive strategic cooperative partnership and the Bangladesh–China–India–Myanmar Economic Corridor within the BRI on the basis of the Five Principles of Peaceful Coexistence.

In line with the Five Principles, China also proposed new ideas and concepts such as Peaceful Rise, Peaceful Development, Harmonious World and Community of Common Destiny to enhance its soft power. The concepts of peaceful rise and peaceful development were first proposed by Chinese scholar Zheng Bijian[64] and then reiterated by Chinese President Hu Jintao to rebut against the 'China Threat' theory. Hu Jintao also proposed the idea of building a harmonious world to enhance Beijing's normative narrative and its role as a peaceful power.[65] Along with the BRI, Xi Jinping proposed the concept of a community of common destiny, underlining that 'the world has increasingly grown into a community where one's destiny is interwoven with that of another' and China is working to promote common development and prosperity of all countries towards building a community of shared interests, destiny and responsibility.[66] It helps Beijing to build its soft and normative power and strengthen its role as a responsible global power.

Reshaping Global Governance

Robert Gilpin argues that 'as its relative power increases, a rising state attempts to change the rules governing the system'.[67] Indeed, while China grows more powerful, the country becomes increasingly dissatisfied with the status quo. As a result, Beijing seeks to reshape global governance and transform the existing international system in a way that reflects its values, interests and status. Many realist scholars believe that the Sino–US power competition will inevitably lead to a war and thus China cannot rise peacefully.[68] This article will challenge this viewpoint by illustrating how China attempts to transform the US-dominated global system and promote its international status in a peaceful way, which is embedded in regional multilateralism. Randall Schweller and Xiaoyu Pu contend that a peer competitor that does not possess the military capabilities to directly challenge the US hegemony through hard balancing seeks to create a new international order by shaping a revisionist counter-hegemonic

---

[61]'China, Serbia publish blueprint for upgrading partnership', *Xinhua News Agency*, (18 June 2016), available at: http://news.xinhuanet.com/english/2016-06/18/c_135447513.htm (accessed 12 August 2017).

[62]'China, Russia, Mongolia endorse development plan on economic corridor', *Xinhua News Agency*, (24 June 2016), available at: http://news.xinhuanet.com/english/2016-06/24/c_135461510.htm (accessed 12 August 2017).

[63]Ministry of Foreign Affairs, *Joint Press Release between the People's Republic of China and the Republic of the Union of Myanmar*, Ministry of Foreign Affairs of China, (20 August 2016), available at: http://www.fmprc.gov.cn/mfa_eng/zxxx_662805/t1390889.shtml (accessed 12 August 2017).

[64]Bijian Zheng, 'China's "peaceful rise" to great-power status', *Foreign Affairs* 84(5), (2005), pp. 18–24.

[65]See 'Chinese President calls for building harmonious world', *Xinhua News Agency*, (24 September 2009), available at: http://news.xinhuanet.com/english/2009-09/24/content_12104060.htm (accessed 10 January 2017).

[66]'Xi's World vision: a community of common destiny, a shared home for humanity', *Xinhua News Agency*, (15 January 2017), available at: http://news.xinhuanet.com/english/2017-01/15/c_135983586.htm (accessed 10 August 2017).

[67]Robert Gilpin, *War and Change in World Politics* (Princeton, NJ: Princeton University Press, 1981), p. 187.

[68]See Graham Allison, *Destined for War: Can America and China Escape Thucydides's Trap?* (Boston, MA: Houghton Mifflin Harcourt, 2017); Zbigniew Brzezinski, 'Can China avoid the Thucydides trap?', *New Perspectives Quarterly* 31(2), (2014), pp. 31–33; John I Mearsheimer, 'Can China rise peacefully?', *The National Interest*, (25 October 2014), available at: http://nationalinterest.org/commentary/can-china-rise-peacefully-10204 (accessed 10 August 2017).

coalition and delegitimizing the hegemon's global authority.[69] Therefore, China has a strong motive to forge an interest-based coalition to reshape the global governance system by either joining existing multilateral institutions or initiating new multilateral institutions.[70]

Since the end of World War II, the Western-dominated global multilateral institutions, such as the International Monetary Fund (IMF), the World Bank and the World Trade Organization, have played a central role in global governance. However, the Bretton Woods system has become increasingly problematic when the balance of global economic power is shifting from established powers to emerging powers. The creation of the G-20 after the 2008 global financial crisis not only symbolized a relative decline of US global economic power, but also reflected a growing consensus on reshaping the existing global governance system. China and other emerging powers have a strong desire to promote the fundamental transformation of the US-dominated global system towards a more inclusive and equitable international order.[71] At a work conference on foreign affairs in November 2014, Chinese President Xi Jinping said:

> We should strengthen unity and cooperation with other developing countries and closely integrate our own development with the common development of other developing countries. We should advance multilateral diplomacy, work to reform the international system and global governance, and increase the representation and say of China and other developing countries.[72]

Given that China is still too weak to challenge the US's global leadership alone, the BRI spanning 65 countries across Asia, Europe and Africa allows Beijing to form a bargaining coalition and shape a 'community of shared interests' towards reshaping the global governance system. As an integral part of the BRI, the AIIB has offered a good example of how China seeks to reshape global financial governance through the creation of new multilateral institutions. In 2013, China announced plans to launch the AIIB in order to meet enormous investment demand in BRI infrastructure projects, making it the first developing country seeking to create a multilateral financial institution. While Washington heavily lobbied its allies not to join the bank, George Osborne, British Chancellor of the Exchequer, surprisingly announced in March 2015 that the UK would join the AIIB. That astonished the whole world including Washington and triggered a domino effect. When the AIIB started operations in January 2016, the bank had 57 founding members, including Washington's closest allies such as the UK, Germany, France, Australia, Israel and South Korea. After only six months, Canada, as the US's closest ally, also announced its decision to join the AIIB. Currently, the AIIB has expanded its membership to 80 and become the world's third largest multilateral financial institution after the IMF and the World Bank.

For a very long time, Western countries have dominated the agenda-setting, veto authority and discourse in global financial institutions. Beijing persistently pushed for quota reforms of the IMF and the World Bank giving China and other emerging economies more voting power to better reflect the changes in global economic power, but failed. Soon after the launching of the AIIB, everything began to change. In December 2015, the IMF conceded to include the Renminbi as the fifth currency in its Special Drawing Rights basket. Two weeks later, the US congress finally approved the IMF quota reform after five years of blocking. As a result, China's voting power in the IMF increased from 2.98% in 2006 to 6.11% in 2016 and ranked in third place after the US (16.53%) and Japan (6.16%).[73] Meanwhile, China's voting power in the World Bank also increased from 2.77% to 4.64% in 2016 and ranked in third place

[69]See Randall L. Schweller and Xiaoyu Pu, 'After unipolarity: China's visions of international order in an era of U.S. decline', *International Security* 36(1), (2011), pp. 41–72.

[70]On the legitimacy of global governance, see Jan Aart Scholte, 'Towards greater legitimacy in global governance', *Review of International Political Economy* 18(1), (2011), pp. 110–120; James Brassett and Eleni Tsingou, 'The politics of legitimate global governance', *Review of International Political Economy* 18(1), (2011), pp. 1–16.

[71]See Joseph Y. S. Cheng, 'China's approach to BRICS', *Journal of Contemporary China* 24(92), (2015), pp. 357–375.

[72]'Xi eyes more enabling international environment for China's peaceful development', *Xinhua News Agency*.

[73]See more details at: IMF Members' Quotas and Voting Power, and IMF Board of Governors, *International Monetary Organization*, (5 July 2016), available at: https://www.imf.org/external/np/sec/memdir/members.aspx (accessed 10 August 2017).

after the US (16.63%) and Japan (7.19%).[74] The AIIB is not merely a response to the poor governance of global financial institutions, but also a catalyst for shaping a new global financial order, enabling Beijing to play a greater role in the global financial system.

The AIIB is the first multilateral financial institution created and ruled by emerging and developing countries. Although the environmental and social framework of the AIIB is inspired by the best practices of multilateral institutions such as the World Bank and the IMF, there exists a difference in norms and rules between them. At the 2015 China Development Forum in Beijing, China's Finance Minister Lou Jiwei commented on the governance and operational rules of AIIB, saying that 'the AIIB is a multilateral institution led by developing countries. We need to consider their needs and sometimes the West puts forwards some rules that we don't think are optimal'.[75] Indeed, the Western-dominated multilateral financial institutions have long been criticized for imposing additional conditions such as privatization and liberalization on loans to developing countries.[76] The China-led AIIB not only provides an alternative to the existing Western-dominated multilateral institutions, but also serves as a promising instrument to shape a bargaining coalition to transform the existing global governance system and boost Beijing's global role from rule-taker to rule-maker.[77]

While Obama stressed the importance of the TPP by stating: 'we can't let countries like China write the rules of the global economy',[78] China is playing a key role in shaping a new international economic order. As a rule-taker, China has benefited enormously from the existing international order and its rules and norms. When China's interests become global, China desires to play a greater role in global governance. As the US-dominated global system has no space left for any emerging power which might challenge its hegemonic status, it presents Beijing with a real dilemma on how to advance its global interests, transform the existing international system and establish its role as a global rule-maker. Establishing the BRI and AIIB is part of Beijing's efforts not only to reshape global governance and strengthen its global leadership role, but also to delegitimize the US-dominated system and create a fairer and more inclusive international order. Thus, China is neither a pure status quo power nor a revisionist power, since Beijing, as the largest beneficiary of the existing international order, has no intentions or capabilities to replace the US hegemonic position and overthrow the existing order. Instead, China struggles for a revision of the US-established international order through the transformation of the global governance system, achieving its peaceful rise to great power status.

Conclusion: Big Ideas, Great Opportunities and Potential Challenges

China's approach towards the BRI is strongly motivated by a multifaceted grand strategy in search of security, influence and status. As regional multilateral cooperation provides a peaceful way to transform the existing international system and avoid a classic 'Thucydides Trap', the BRI serves as a strategic maneuver for Beijing to advance its foreign policy goals. First, the BRI is strategically and tactically used by Beijing as a vehicle of soft balancing against the US, as regional multilateral cooperation allows Beijing to establish asymmetric interdependence over other Eurasian partners, to reassure those partners of the peaceful nature of its rising power and to deter the formation of any anti-China coalition or 'anyone but China' club. Second, China

---

[74]See International Bank for Reconstruction and Development Subscriptions and Voting Power of Member Countries, *World Bank*, (1 July 2016), available at: http://siteresources.worldbank.org/BODINT/Resources/2780271215524804501/IBRDCountryVotingTable. pdf (accessed 10 August 2017).

[75]'Caizheng Buzhang Lou Jiwei jiu Yatouhang Fanbo Yakaihang Hangzhang: Xifang Guize Bingfei Zuijia' ['Chinese Finance Minister Lou Jiwei responds to the President of Asian Development Bank: Western rules may be not best for AIIB'], *Guancha* [*The Observer*], (22 March 2015), available at: http://www.guancha.cn/economy/2015_03_22_313149.shtml (accessed 10 August 2017).

[76]James Raymond Vreeland, *The International Monetary Fund: Politics of Conditional Lending* (London and New York: Routledge, 2007); Susanne Lütz and Matthias Kranke, 'The European rescue of the Washington Consensus? EU and IMF lending to Central and Eastern European Countries', *Review of International Political Economy* 21(2), (2014), pp. 310–338.

[77]See Xiao Ren, 'China as an institution-builder: the case of the AIIB', *Pacific Review* 29(3), (2016), pp. 435–442; Chao Xi, 'From rule-taker to rule-maker: China and international banking regulation', in Friedl Weiss and Kammel Armin, eds, *The Changing Landscape of Global Financial Governance and the Role of Soft Law* (Leiden: Brill, 2015), pp. 312–336; Philip Stephens, 'Now China starts to make the rules', *Financial Times*, (28 May 2015), available at: https://www.ft.com/content/9dafcb30-0395-11e5-a70f-00144feabdc0 (accessed 10 August 2017).

[78]*Statement by the President on the Trans-Pacific Partnership*, Office of the Press Secretary of the White House, (5 October 2015), available at: https://www.whitehouse.gov/the-press-office/2015/10/05/statement-president-trans-pacific-partnership (accessed 12 August 2017).

seeks to promote alternative ideas and norms and build its role as a normative power through the BRI for enhancing the legitimacy of its rising power at the expense of US normative authority and legitimacy. Third, China attempts to form a bargaining coalition through the BRI and AIIB for reshaping the global governance system and enhancing its global leadership role in the existing international order.

Although the BRI will significantly strengthen China's role on the world stage, this ambitious initiative faces potential challenges including geopolitical rivalry, security threats, territorial disputes and political risks. First, the geopolitical rivalry arising from China's expanding global role may pose a potential challenge to the BRI. New Delhi's negative position towards the China–Pakistan Economic Corridor and its boycott of the Belt and Road Forum for International Cooperation illustrates this point.[79] Second, potential security threats might impair regional connectivity and cooperation in the Eurasian space as the BRI covers unstable regions such as the Middle East and Central Asia. Third, territorial disputes, especially in the South China Sea, could undermine Beijing's efforts to promote regional multilateral cooperation among the countries along the BRI.[80] As the South China Sea is at the core of the Maritime Silk Road, overlapping sovereignty claims over the disputed islands and waters might pose a great obstacle to multilateral cooperation between China and other Asian countries. Fourth, political turbulence in the conflicted and failed states along the BRI brings political risks and uncertainty to the implementation of the BRI projects.

While the world order is undergoing a dramatic change, the recent Belt and Road Forum for International Cooperation, attended by more than 1,500 representatives from over 130 countries and 70 international organizations, demonstrates Beijing's ambition for a more prominent global leadership role. As the Trump Administration's anti-globalization sentiment and 'America first' doctrine have raised doubts about the US's leadership role in the liberal economic order, the BRI provides the impetus for a new wave of globalization that enables China to play a greater global role in the new international economic order. The BRI that aims to promote the common development and prosperity of all the countries not only manifests China's commitment to a peaceful rise, but also presents a Chinese vision for a new world order based on harmonious and peaceful coexistence.

Acknowledgments

We are grateful to the editor Suisheng Zhao and two anonymous referees for their helpful comments and suggestions. This research article is a chapter of Weifeng Zhou's doctoral dissertation titled *Beyond the Balance of Power: The Logic of China's Engagement in Regional Multilateralism'.*

Disclosure statement

No potential conflict of interest was reported by the authors.

Funding

This research was supported by the Spanish Ministry of Economy, Industry and Competitiveness [grant number I+D project CSO2017-82921-P].

---

[79]*Official Spokesperson's Response to a Query on Participation of India in OBOR/BRI Forum*, Ministry of External Affairs of the Government of India, (13 May 2017), available at: http://www.mea.gov.in/media-briefings.htm?dtl/28463/Official_Spokespersons_response_to_a_query_on_participation_of_India_in_OBORBRI_Forum (accessed 10 August 2017).

[80]William A. Callahan, 'China's "Asia Dream": the Belt Road Initiative and the new regional order', *Asian Journal of Comparative Politics* 1(3), (2016), pp. 226–243.

4 Could 'Belt and Road' be the Last Step in China's Asian Economic Integration?

Cheng King and Jane Du

ABSTRACT

This article assesses the role of China's 'Belt and Road' initiative (BRI) in the country's intended global economic integration. Particular attention is paid to China's capital penetration of Asian markets, with an empirical assessment of the structure of Asian markets from the perspective of foreign trade, foreign direct investment (FDI) and intergovernmental aid. The success of China's new opening-up initiative will be largely contingent on Asian markets' recognition of Chinese products and capital: its trade with potential cooperative countries and its FDI and intergovernmental aid to them fall behind those of the developed countries that are China's major cooperative partners in/outside Asia. China's ongoing Asian economic strategy thus faces competition and will need to integrate the BRI into the current framework of international economic cooperation.

Introduction

This article assesses China's 'Belt and Road' Initiative (BRI) and its feasibility in Asia, paying particular attention to Asian markets' recognition of Chinese capital. The terms 'belt' and 'road' refer to the historical inland and maritime Silk Roads (operating from the Han dynasty in the second century BC to the early Tang dynasty in the eighth century AD, and since the eighth century respectively) with which China was mainly involved as a product exporter. By the late Qing period in the late nineteenth and early twentieth century, China's major silk road merchandise, tea and silk, had gradually lost its competitiveness to products from British India, British Ceylon and Japan, downgrading China's trading position and reducing its involvement in the Asian economy. After suffering long domestic instability and economic backwardness under the Manchu, Republican and Mao governments, in the early 1980s Deng Xiaoping proactively reopened China's economy and reintegrated it with Asian industrialisation.

With more than three decades of fast economic growth since the 1980s, the 'belt and road' concept was reintroduced in 2013. In the present context, this goes far beyond its original form as a mere trading of products. It is a new opening-up strategy for China's much greater participation in the global economy, particularly in Asia.[1]

In the preliminary stage, China is committed to expanding existing and exploring the potential for new economic cooperation so that its industries can offset the negative impact of declining external demand due to the current weak and uncertain global economy. The success of the BRI depends on how successfully Chinese capital penetrates, in the first instance, the Asian market.

---

[1] Increased foreign trade and international economic integration lead to higher domestic income and enhance a country's overall economic growth. See Bhagwati Jagdish, In Defence of Globalization (Oxford University Press, 2004), pp.64–65.

A realistic view of the BRI emphasizes some of the Chinese government's urgent demands, generated by its current economic situation. They are the result of China's long-term motivation to grow its economy and its involvement in Asia's post-war industrialisation, which have crafted the country's rapid development over the past three decades. Some economies in Asia lack sufficient capital investment for development, and ideally Chinese capital investment in these economies can be increased to fulfil Asian market demand for capital investment. It may be too optimistic to suppose that Asia's capital-absorptive capacity can absorb as much capital investment as China can provide through BRI: in fact China itself is the largest Asian FDI recipient economy, and without China, Asia's capital absorptive capacity is largely reduced and concentrated in several emerging economies which may already have long-term cooperative investment partners other than China. This presents a challenge for China's large outpouring of capital to the rest of Asia.[2]

Sufficient capacity to absorb capital inflows aside, there is a huge difference between meeting domestic market demand and meeting overseas market demand. The overseas market may not provide the necessary stability to allow the trading of products across borders easily[3] or to guarantee returns on capital investment. There are trade and investment criteria to consider when China chooses recipient countries for its BRI.

Although China is the second-largest economy in the world, its per capita gross domestic product (GDP) is only that of medium-ranking developing Asian countries. The upper capacity of BRI investment is therefore limited by China's own economic ability. Once this reaches its upper limit for foreign investment, a further increase in capital requirement will generate pressure on the country's domestic use of capital. The marginal capital requirement at this point therefore will determine the success of the BRI, and China will need to make efficient use of its limited resources in order to maximize its capital return.

As discussed in the following text, when selecting partner countries for cooperation, certain economic criteria need careful consideration: the proposed partner-country's level of development compared to China; its existing economic links with China; and the size of its population, as rapid population growth can easily offset per capita investment and foreign capital may play a less important role in the proposed partner-country's economic development – as it does in China itself – and this kind of dilution effect is not ideal for China or for the BRI. With such development and population constraints, China's infrastructure-focused initial investment may go to less-populous Asian countries whose economic development is inferior to its own.

After analysing these criteria, feasibility studies are necessary. Put simply, the partner-country's capacity to consume the product and to absorb China's capital investment will eventually determine how far China integrates with the Asian economy and how much further it can go. Current Asian trade structures and China's participation in them, FDI, and aid networks could be reinvented to help China to adopt its new BRI role. The challenge that it faces in penetrating Asian markets is largely unknown: Asia may not be able to ensure China's share in its trade and investment markets when faced with plenty of investment options offered by other investors (i.e. developed economies). China's new opening-up initiative will need to conform to Asian growth trajectories to ensure that the recipient countries make efficient use of Chinese goods and capital, thereby minimising local uncertainties for China.

This work is inspired by studies that link China's new opening-up goals to its economic behaviour. The BRI is a newly emerged topic and still lacks specifics, and little research has addressed it. Several studies in the field of economics assess the initiative mainly by estimating its potential benefits, an approach that commonly refers to China's expanding trade with other Asian countries,[4] higher capacity for investment and better external environment.[5] A cost-benefit

---

[2]Besides China, Vietnam and Thailand rank amongst the top countries absorbing capital inflows for infrastructure construction.

[3]James E. Anderson and Eric van Wincoop, 'Trade costs', Journal of Economic Literature 42(3), (2004), pp. 691–751.

[4]Justin Lin, 'One belt and one road and free trade zones: China's new opening-up initiatives', Frontiers of Economics in China 10(4), (2015), pp. 585–590.

[5]The Economist Intelligence Unit, 'Prospects and challenges on China's "one belt, one road": a risk assessment report', (2015), available at http://www.eiu.com/public/topical_report.aspx?campaignid=OneBeltOneRoad (accessed 8 April 2018).

analysis is routinely conducted as a proxy for any inquiry into returns on investment. The question that remains is whether and to what extent Asian countries can help China to achieve its economic goals. This article is intended to help to fill this gap in the scholarship.

Certain methodological concerns that emerged from this analysis may be beyond control. Details of China's BRI investment plans regarding its cooperation with potential destination countries are lacking, with only some elements from different routes on the 'belt' and 'road' traceable in the *Vision and Actions on Jointly Building Silk Road Economic Belt and 21st-Century Maritime Silk Road*,[6] (hereinafter 'the Action Plan'). This study prefers using cross-country data to an individual country case study: although the latter could supply comprehensive information about a certain economy, cross-country studies using the same source and calibre of statistics can more accurately reflect the overall feasibility of China's BRI investment plan. However, macro data on some countries involved in the Action Plan (i.e. Iraq and Myanmar) is lacking due to war and political instability.

The data used in this work came mainly from official sources such as China's National Bureau of Statistics, the World Bank's World Development Indicators, and the International Monetary Fund (IMF) database. This research starts its observation from 2004, when the Chinese government encouraged large state-owned enterprises (SOEs) to invest abroad and the country's overseas investment started to boom. This research built a dataset based on China and other Asian economies' GDP, population, trade, FDI and intergovernmental aid from 2004 to 2015, and used macro data (e.g. on GDP and population) to detect Asia's current growth trajectories and which Asian countries meet the BRI's initial criteria of partnership such as the development and population conditions. This article analyses the composition of trade, investment and aid in Asian destination countries to identify China's contribution to their local economic development and hence China's current competitiveness in Asia.

The results show that China's economic competitiveness in Asia is still weak. China's total trade volume with potential BRI partner-countries falls behind that of developed economies. The scale of Chinese capital available is unlikely to compete with Organisation for Economic Co-operation and Development (OECD) and United Nations (UN)-led FDI and aid systems. In the near future China will face competitions and will have to integrate BRI with the framework of the current international economic system. Additionally, to pursue its own economic growth China will need to identify a good balance between its Asian economic strategy and its global economic cooperation.

Section 2 of this article analyses the growth trajectories of Asian economies from the 1960s to the 2010s; section 3 analyses the criteria and constraints that China considers when choosing BRI partner countries; section 4 looks at China's share in influencing Asia's current growth from the perspective of trade, FDI and intergovernmental aid; and section 5 presents the conclusions drawn.

Asia and China's growth momentum

Geographic division and trajectories of asian growth

Geopolitically, Asia can be divided into five sub-regions: East Asia,[7] Central Asia,[8] West Asia (also known as the Middle East),[9] Southeast Asia[10] and South Asia.[11] Compared to Europe, Asia's sub-

---

[6]The National Development and Reform Commission, Ministry of Foreign Affairs, and Ministry of Commerce and the State Council, 'Vision and actions on jointly building silk road economic belt and 21st-Century maritime silk road', 28 March 2015, available http://en.ndrc.gov.cn/newsrelease/201503/t20150330_669367.html (accessed 8 April 2018)

[7]Japan, South and North Korea, Taiwan, Mongolia and China.

[8]Turkmenistan, Kyrgyzstan, Uzbekistan, Tajikistan, Kazakhstan and Afghanistan. Sometimes Afghanistan is also classified as a South Asian country.

[9]West Asia covers a large number of countries, mainly in the Middle East. Geographically, it includes Armenia, Azerbaijan, Bahrain, Cyprus, Egypt (the Sinai Peninsula), Georgia, Iran, Iraq, Israel, Jordan, Kuwait, Lebanon, Oman, Palestine, Qatar, Saudi Arabia, Syria, Turkey, the United Arab Emirates and Yemen.

[10]Southeast Asia mainly consists of Indochina and the Malay Archipelago, covering Vietnam, Laos, Cambodia, Thailand, Myanmar, Malaysia, Indonesia, Brunei, the Philippines, East Timor and Singapore.

[11]The Indian subcontinent countries occupy the main South Asian land mass which includes India, Pakistan, Bangladesh, Nepal, Bhutan, Sri Lanka and the Maldives.

regions are relatively independent.[12] Within each, geographic, cultural and ethnic factors predominantly form the close intraregional relationships. After World War II, Asia's interregional integration emerged from three structural changes: Japan's post-war industrialisation and subsequent marginal industrial transfer[13]; the rapid economic boom in the Middle East after the 1970s oil price shock; and the Cold War ideological conflict and tension experienced by some Asian countries.[14]

The first change, Japan's post-war industrialisation and subsequent diffusion of technology, caused waves of economic growth: from the 1960s to the 1970s it triggered the rise of the Four Asian Tigers,[15] and further, propelled a remarkable economic transition in China from the 1980s onwards. Most economies that first benefited from Asia's industrialisation were those in East Asia, with industrialisation diffusing outwards to their neighbours.

The second change, the boom of resource-rich countries in Asia as a consequence of the 1970s energy price spikes due to the oil crisis, raised the incomes of many Asian oil-producing countries to those of moderately and highly developed economies.[16] After the 2000s the rich resources of these Asian economies not only acted as a buffer, protecting them from fiscal troubles, but also supported their fast economic growth, even in the post-2008 global recession.

The third factor that shaped Asia's growth pattern was the tension caused by the Cold War. Besides its direct occupation of and military intervention in Central Asia,[17] the Soviet Union spread its ideological roots into the East (i.e. China and North Korea) and to a set of Warsaw Pact observer countries in Southeast Asia.[18] In South Asia, Socialist ideology dominated India's economic policy-making until the 1990s.

However, there are important distinctions between Japanese-led industrialisation and ideological and resource-led income increases and decreases. The latter two were passively accepted by Asian economies. For example, not even the elites in countries such as China and India realized the consequences of accepting the socialist ideology of central planning economy, which blocked the possibility of growth based on market-oriented industrialisation. Small countries such as Saudi Arabia and Cambodia had very limited room to develop their own growth paths, which were either constrained by their natural endowments or decided by the superpowers.

Under the impact of these three structural changes, Asia had two main strands to its economic momentum (Figure 1). The first was recovery and growth in countries that had gained ideological independence from the Soviet Union. Most economies that have experienced huge Soviet influence and intervention or have recently drifted away from Cold War ideology have long been economically stagnant,[19] whereas those that have broken away (i.e. China and Vietnam) show great potential. The other strand is the geographic extension of an increase in per capita GDP that spread from Japan and the Middle East to their surrounding areas. This is particularly true of Japan's industrialisation, whose first wave led to the 'East Asian Miracle', and the further diffusion of this phenomenon from these economies to their neighbours, which is known as the second wave of

---

[12]BRI's final destination.

[13]Kojima Kiyoshi, Direct Foreign Investment: A Japanese Model of Multination Business Operations (London: Groom Helm, 1978).

[14]This refers mainly to the political and military tension between the United States and the former Soviet Union.

[15]The Four Asian Tigers are Hong Kong, Singapore, South Korea and Taiwan. These economies registered exceptionally high performances in rapid industrialisation and economic growth from the early 1960s to the 1990s.

[16]In the 1970s the world economy encountered two serious energy crises: the 1973 oil crisis and the 1979 energy crisis. Both were directly caused by interruptions to the export of crude oil from Middle Eastern countries. In 12 years from 1970 to 1981, the Brent crude oil price increased sharply from US$2 to $39 per barrel. After more than two decades of fluctuation since the 1980s, on 15 July 2008 the oil price reached a historical high at US$147 per barrel. The dramatic rise in the price of crude oil quickly raised Asia's oil-producing economies to high-income status, contributing the most to the post-war boom in the resource-rich economies (i.e. the Middle East).

[17]Geographically, Central Asia was part of the Russian Empire and later the Soviet Union until its independence in the 1990s. The Soviet-Afghan War in Central Asia lasted from 1979 to 1989. Before the collapse of the former Soviet Union in 1991, Central Asia was under restrictive Soviet control and was also known as Soviet Central Asia.

[18]In Southeast Asia, Vietnam, Laos and Cambodia (as well as Mongolia in East Asia) were also influenced by Soviet ideology, becoming observer countries of the Warsaw Pact.

[19]i.e. Afghanistan and North Korea.

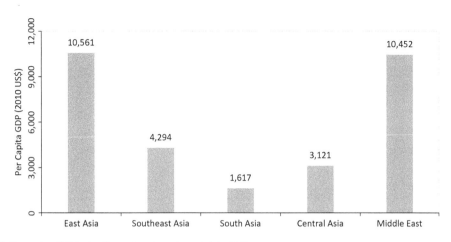

Figure 1. Per capita GDP in the five main sub regions of Asia, 2015.

Source: World Bank, World Development Indicators, available at: http://databank.worldbank.org/data/home.aspx.

Asian industrialisation. This industrialisation facilitated the interregional integration of economies in Asia, with Southeast Asia currently riding the crest of the third wave.

China's remarkable economic growth corroborates both strands.

Waves of Asian industrialisation

Compared with the rise of resource-based economies in West and Central Asia, growth in most East and Southeast Asian economies has benefited from the same Japanese industrialisation. This growth based on the extent of the industrialisation of an economy is firm and solid, and has been at the root of Asia's continued economic expansion.

The first wave of Asian growth in Japan and the Four Asian Tigers (see the 1960s and 1970s panels in Figure 2) slowed in the late 1980s, when these economies began to transfer their low-end industries to Asia's industrializing economies, triggering labour-intensive industrialisation in economically inferior countries in Asia throughout 1990s and 2000s. China's economic development largely occurred during the second wave of Asia's industrial technology diffusion (see the 1980s, 1990s and 2000s panels in Figure 2). Its growing integration with the Asian economy has led to significant changes in the composition of trade and regional investment in Asia. However, since the 2008 financial crisis the world's economy has slowed significantly. Second-wave industrialising countries started to transfer their own low-end industries to economically inferior countries. The high energy prices did not fall immediately after 2008 but remained relatively high for at least three years, buffering some resource-rich Asian economies (see Turkmenistan and Mongolia in the 2010s panels in Figure 2). Resource-based growth and Southeast Asian industrialisation kick-started a third wave of Asian growth (see e.g. Laos and Cambodia in the 2000s and 2010s panels in Figure 3). First- and second-wave economies would have to capitalise on these rising sources of growth to sustain their economy; China's BRI was launched for much the same reasons.

Japanese-style industrialization is the most solid way for Asia to escape the low- and middle-income trap, and may be the best way for countries not endowed with rich resources to achieve a high level of income. Such marginal industrial transfer, however, has particular features. The first is that industrialisation diffuses from economies with high labour costs to those with low labour costs. Throughout these waves, leading economies always transfer their low-end industries to economically inferior economies. Industrial frontiers can make domestic low-value-added industries high-value-added again when investing overseas. Here a key to the generation of Asia's industrial waves is labour costs, which create an international flow of capital. During this process dormant labour in recipient

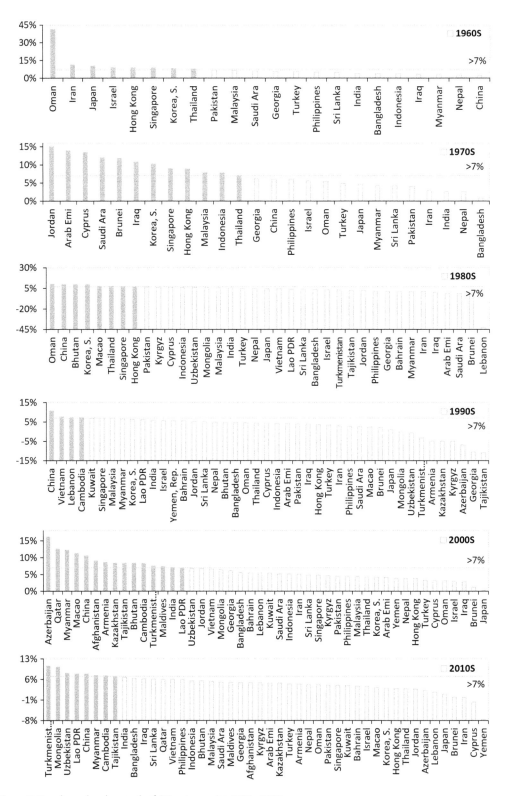

Figure 2. Decade-on-decade growth of Asian economies, 1960s–2010s.

Source: World Bank, World Development Indicators, available at: http://databank.worldbank.org/data/home.aspx

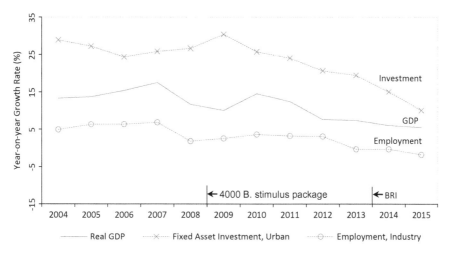

Figure 3. Investment, employment and GDP growth rates in China, 2004–2015.
Source: National Bureau of Statistics of China.

economies is aroused by cross-country capital flows, and in the long term their own labour price appreciates.

Usually this move of industries across countries is accompanied by large-scale trade and capital flows between the originating and the recipient economy. Most of Asia's industrial shifts involve a restructuring of the production chain, which sees economies that industrialized earlier redistributing part of their production capacity to neighbouring Asian economies.[20] When such a redistribution takes place, booms in intermediate product flows can be observed, as happened between Japan and the Four Asian Tigers in the first wave, and between the Tigers and China in the second.

The slowing of the Chinese economy

Three decades of rapid growth have transformed China from a low- to an upper-middle-income economy. From 1980 to 2010, the country's real national income increased 17-fold, with real per capita GDP increasing 12-fold.[21] Nevertheless, after a real average growth rate of 10.4% throughout the 2000s, the Chinese State Council's Report on the Work of the Chinese Government in early 2012 showed that the country was keenly aware of its slowing economic growth,[22] with its real GDP growth rate falling quickly to 7.9% over 2 years and further to 6.9% in 2015. The 2008–2010 investment boom led to chronic oversupply in many Chinese industries. The growth of GDP and urban fixed asset investment continued to slow down in 2015, while industrial employment progressively declined by 0.3% and 1.8% in 2014 and 2015 respectively (Figure 3). Such economic data indicates that China's industrial capacity is more than sufficient to meet its domestic needs, allowing for significant amounts of industrial capacity to be allocated overseas.[23]

Unlike the cases of Japan and the Four Asian Tigers, the slowing down of China's economy came earlier than expected and before the country had completed its overall industrialisation. The growth rate is crucial to the Chinese government and its 1.4 billion people, who largely expect

[20]This could be seen as a measure to counter the 'border effects' or 'border costs' (e.g. James E. Anderson and Eric van Wincoop, 'Gravity with gravitas: A solution to the border puzzle', American Economic Review 93(1), (2003), pp.170-192).
[21]As the yearly official GDP deflator is unknown, a fixed-base cumulative consumer price index (1978 = 100) was used here as a deflator to calculate the year-on-year real GDP growth rate.
[22]The State Council's Report of the Work of the Chinese Government, delivered at the Fifth Session of the Eleventh National People's Congress, 5 March 2012, available at http://en.people.cn/90785/7759779.html (accessed 8 April 2018)
[23]This oversupply also forces enterprise to cut prices to maintain their market share, further exacerbating the average profit performance of the local industry.

the country's economic growth to improve their living standard. In the current economic situation the Chinese government faces two major challenges: finding markets for its industrial overcapacity, and finding new sources of economic growth.

Constraints to BRI

A common feature of the Asian development model is that industrialisation-based growth patterns require proper capital (and technology diffusion with capital flows) and goods flows to facilitate industry upgrades at each stage. China's *de facto* labour costs have increased more than 30-fold in the past three decades, and China can now be expected to move its marginal industries overseas in search of lower labour inputs that will give rise to large-scale capital and goods outflows.

Although the financing of the BRI is backed by the Asian Infrastructure Investment Bank (AIIB), China, as the biggest beneficiary country of the 57 founder members,[24] is expected to bear the bulk of the cost as a major power. Like all overseas investment, even though China has strongly advanced its economic status in Asia its total capital investment is largely constrained by its own economic capabilities. Low- and middle-income Asian industrialising countries are therefore better potential partners for China's BRI, as their labour costs are lower and their economies better integrated with Asia's regional economic network, making their growth even more stable than that of those that have not yet started their industrialisation.

Developmental and population constraints

The entire BRI investment plan currently lacks specifics. What is certain is that China views '[infrastructural] facilities connectivity' as 'a priority area' for the implementation of BRI, as indicated by the officially released Action Plan. Infrastructure matters, as it triggers economic growth; however, a country's infrastructure is largely determined by its level of industry.

When China became the largest economy in Asia its per capita GDP was still a fraction of that of the large economies. According to World Bank data, China remains a medium-ranking developing economy amongst all Asian economies (see Figure 4). With such developmental constraints, China's first efforts at investing in infrastructure are thus most likely to be made in Asian economies that are economically inferior to itself (shaded in grey in Figure 4), ruling out 21 economies in Asia.

There are risks to such investment, as fast population growth can easily offset per capita investment, as mentioned. Thus populous countries require large-scale investment from China to fill the gap in their per-capita infrastructural requirements. As the BRI necessitates China setting aside a certain sum for loans to developing economies, it is unlikely that China will concentrate its investment on a small number of particularly populous countries. Even if it has the capacity to provide sufficient capital for infrastructural investment in the four most populous countries in South and Southeast Asia – Bangladesh, Pakistan, Indonesia and India (see Figure 5) – as it has in Pakistan,[25] the outcome of BRI investment in these countries can be expected to be limited.

BRI partnership

Growth and population constraints vary widely amongst Asian economies, with the less-populous developing countries generally enjoying sound per-capita growth, followed by populous countries (see Figures 4 and 5). These less-populous developing economies have largely committed to BRI's initial objective of helping to construct China's neighbouring countries' infrastructure.

The BRI covers most countries in Central, South, Southeast and West Asia. Taking into account the economic factors – development level and size of population – around 22 countries, mainly

---

[24]A total of 37 nations have been approved as founder members of AIIB, including China
[25]Since the 1965 Indo-Pakistani War, Pakistan has received a huge amount of investment from China.

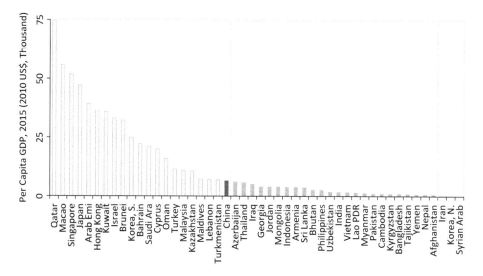

Figure 4. Per capita GDP among Asian countries/economies, 2015.

Source: World Bank, World Development Indicators, available at: http://databank.worldbank.org/data/home.aspx.

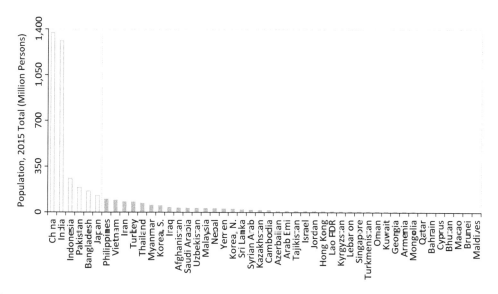

Figure 5. Populations of Asian countries/economies, 2015.

Source: World Bank, World Development Indicators, available at: http://databank.worldbank.org/data/home.aspx.

low- and middle-income developing economies in Asia,[26] are the likely partners at the initial stage.[27] However if the crisis in Iran, Iraq and the Syrian Arab Republic continues, the instability may spread to Jordan, leaving 18 BRI countries, as indicated on the map (Figure 6).

---

[26]As indicated in Figure 6.

[27]Taking into account population growth, the initial stage excludes Bangladesh, Pakistan, Indonesia and India. However, as Pakistan is long-term cooperative country with China based on political reasons, its inclusion will hardly be influenced by BRI. Thus with the exception of Pakistan, the current population growth rate in Bangladesh, Indonesia and India may pose a great challenge to the Chinese government's fiscal situation if China intends to change these countries' current infrastructure conditions through BRI. Populous countries are thus excluded from the calculation for a more accurate estimation of BRI's prospects.

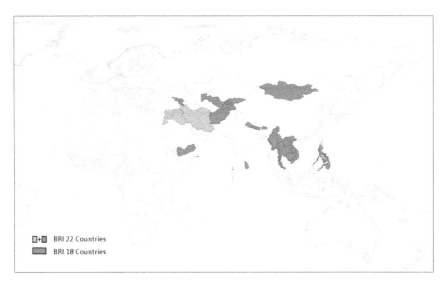

Figure 6. Distribution of BRI 18 and BRI 22 countries in Asia.
Source: Illustrated by the authors using the results of Figures 4 and 5.

Recognition of Chinese capital in asia

China's pursuit of BRI investment faces severe limitations, due not only to its own outward investment capability but also to the Asian destination economies' capacity for capital absorption. In particular, Chinese investment in the 22 target countries will inevitably encounter fierce competition from other countries with a long history of investment in Asia. The share of Asia's capital-absorptive capacity that China must acquire to accommodate BRI investment is unknown and difficult to predict at the initial stage. China may be forced to crowd out existing investors if its targeted developing Asian economies cannot increase their capital absorption capacity quickly in the near future.

Alternatively China will have to resort to channelling its fast-expanding industrial overcapacity, which is almost certain to outstrip domestic need in the coming years, into existing trade and investment channels to resolve its overcapacity problem. Either way, being a significant individual investor or a major player in existing international channels would facilitate China's integration of Asia's low- and middle-income developing countries with the China-led Asian economic circle.

China's BRI investment in targeted countries in Asia will have to be in the form of trade, FDI and intergovernmental aid, the three channels traditionally adopted by developing Asian countries. The success of the initiative is thus highly dependent on China's market share of products and capital in Asia, and particularly in Asia's developing economies.

International trade

The total trade volume of China's imports and exports has increased rapidly since the Hu-Wen era which encouraged Chinese firms to expand trade and economic cooperation overseas from the mid-2000s to the early 2010s. The four-trillion stimulus package has further boosted China's industrial production and foreign trade. According to its National Bureau of Statistics, China's total trade volume tripled from US$1154.6 billion in 2004 to $3953.0 billion in 2015, of which trade in Asia represented 53.0%. However, China's foreign trade in Asia is largely concentrated in Hong Kong, Japan, South Korea and Taiwan, which accounted for 27.5% of the country's total volume of global trade.

The BRI 22 countries' share of China's total foreign trade has risen steadily in the past two decades (see Table 1). The group was China's fifth-largest trading partner before 2006. In 2014 and

Table 1. Trade partners' ranking in China's total trade volume, 1998–2015

Rank	1998	2003	2007	2008	2012	2013	2014	2015
1	Japan	Japan	US	US	US	US	US	US
2	US	US	Japan	Japan	BRI 22	Hong Kong	BRI 22	BRI 22
3	Hong Kong	Hong Kong	Hong Kong	BRI 22	Hong Kong	BRI 22	Hong Kong	Hong Kong
4	S. Korea	S. Korea	BRI 22	Hong Kong	Japan	Japan	Japan	Japan
5	Taiwan	BRI 22	S. Korea	S. Korea	S. Korea	S. Korea	S. Korea	S. Korea
6	BRI 22	Taiwan	Taiwan	Taiwan	Taiwan	Taiwan	Taiwan	Taiwan
7	Germany	Germany	Germany	Germany	Germany	Germany	Germany	Germany

Source: National Bureau of Statistics, *Zhongguo Maoyi Waijing Tongji Nianjian* [*China Trade and External Economic Statistical Yearbook*] (Beijing: China Statistics Press. 1990–2016 editions).

2015 it rose steadily to second, with about 3.5% less trade than the United States, in China's total trade volume.

Optimistically, if all 22 countries continue to grow based on the average of their own top three records in the past ten years, their combined GDP is expected to reach about as much as US$4500 billion by 2025. In the event that the crisis in Iraq, Iran and Syria continues and spreads to neighbouring Jordan, the left 18 countries could still have a chance of achieving a combined GDP of about US$3000 billion by 2025. Furthermore, in terms of a bilateral foreign trade multiplier,-[28] the total volume of trade between China and low- and middle-income Asian economies will be higher than that of estimated Sino-Korean trade in 2025.[29] As a group, Asia's developing countries have out-performed other developing economies by a wide margin in terms of trade.

The ranking of the BRI 22 group in China's total trade volume has risen quickly (see Table 1), meaning that these countries have the potential to absorb China's ongoing industrial overcapacity. However, China's shares in each individual country's trade vary significantly. Its trade with Kyrgyzstan, Myanmar, Mongolia and Tajikistan has been significant, accounting for about 50% of their trade volume in 2015 (see Figure 7). These countries are contiguous with China and hence convenient for trade; China's trade with them is mostly associated with energy and mineral resources, particularly in the cases of Kyrgyzstan and Mongolia.

The largest proportion of Asia's developing-economy trade is carried out with developed economies. In the past ten years the trade between developing Asia and advanced economies has remained at about 60% of Asia's total trade volume. Of the total trade volume between developing Asia and other developing economies, a quarter is energy-based. Non-fuel trade accounted for 30% of developing Asia's total trade in 2014 (see Figure 8). This 30% includes some non-resource-originating developing economies with trade potential comparable to China's, such as India. On the assumption that trade dependence very much hinges on the importing country's population and is relatively stable in the short term, China's non-fuel trade with Asia's low- and middle-income developing economies is very limited. The development of Asia's foreign trade remains focused on advanced economies and resource-originating countries.

Between 2004–2014, while Asian developing countries' imports of non-fuel products increased 3.5-fold, the growth rate of fuel product imports increased by 5.7 times. This shows that developing Asia has less potential for non-fuel imports from other developing economies compared with fuel trade. As the BRI is to help China explore new overseas markets to offset the negative impact of declining external demand, developing Asia's capacity to absorb China's ongoing industrial over-supply, mostly of non-fuel industrial products, may not be very satisfactory.

---

[28]To estimate the bilateral trade volume between China and each of the BRI 22 target countries by 2025, the average value of the foreign trade multiplier between China and each country since the 2008 financial crisis was used. Unlike other economic indicators, foreign trade volume in the short term (say, ten years) is relatively stable.

[29]The same method was applied to estimate Sino-Korean trade using estimated GDP (the average over ten years) with the average foreign trade multiplier calculated from the 2008–2015 data. This article included only the BRI 18 countries to exclude resource trade between China and the four gulf countries.

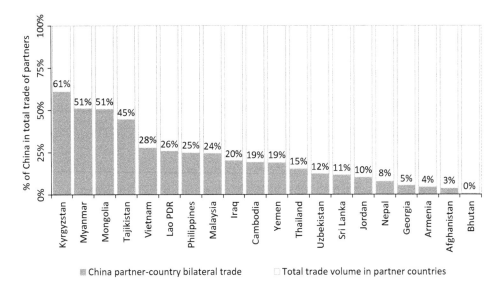

Figure 7. China's share in partner countries' total trade volume, 2015.

Source: World Bank, World Development Indicators, available at: http://databank.worldbank.org/data/home.aspx.

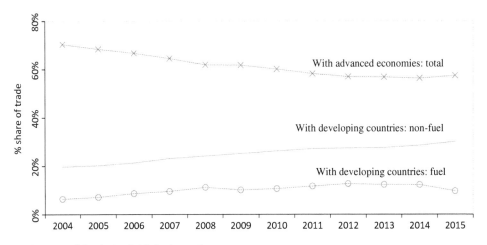

Figure 8. Structure of developing Asia's foreign trade.

Source: CEIC, World Trend Plus Database. available at: https://www.ceicdata.com/en/products/worldtrendplus-database.

Outward foreign direct investment

Strong growth in outward foreign direct investment (OFDI) in recent years suggests that China has the capacity to provide sufficient funds to lead initial BRI investment in Asia. After the mid-2000s, when the government encouraged large SOEs to invest abroad, China's OFDI grew more than eight-fold from US $5.5 billion in 2004 to US$145.7 billion in 2015 (see Figure 9). Since 2012 it has ranked as the world's third-largest source country for OFDI.

The importance of the BRI 22 countries in China's total OFDI cannot be overrated. In 2014, all 22 countries together accounted for only 4.6% of China's total OFDI, then dropping to 1.8% in 2015 (see Figure 9).[30] Even including the developing economies in the Association of Southeast

---

[30]According to the 2014 Statistical Bulletin of China's Outward Foreign Direct Investment, China's OFDI to the 22 BRI target countries totalled US$5.5 billion, 4.6% of its entire OFDI in 2014.

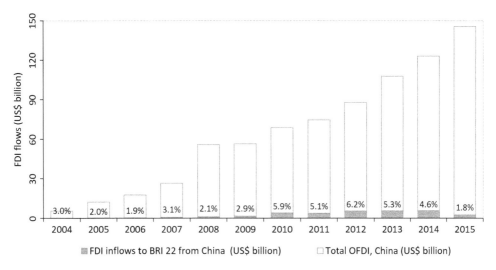

Figure 9. The BRI 22 countries' share in China's total OFDI, 2004–2015.

Source: Ministry of Commerce, *Zhongguo Duiwai Zhijie Touzi Tongji Gongbao* [Statistical bulletin of China's outward foreign direct investment], (Beijing: China Statistical Press, 2011–2016 editions).

Asian Nations (ASEAN), a bloc with which China has perhaps the very close economic cooperation in Asia, China's OFDI flow decreased by 20.6% from 2013 to 2015 after the BRI strategy was announced. This contrasts with the 39.7% increase in China's combined OFDI to the United States, Australia and Europe in the same period.

In 2015 Asia continued to be the world's top FDI-recipient region, accounting for nearly 39.8% of global FDI inflows, according to the UN Conference on Trade and Development.[31] Total net inflows to Asian developing economies amounted to US$541 billion in 2015, 15.6% higher than in 2014 and 25.5% higher than in 2013. The global slump in FDI inflow around 2012 did not seem to affect the lure of investing in the Asian market.[32]

China's OFDI has expanded rapidly since the early 2000s, and the plummeting global asset prices during the 2008 financial crisis boosted it further (see Figure 10). According to Statistical Bulletin of China's Outward Foreign Direct Investment,[33] the country's non-financial outflows to Asia approximated US$108.4 billion in 2015, 15.4% of total FDI inflows received in Asia in that year.

However, China's OFDI in Asia is largely concentrated on Hong Kong, which receives US $89.8 billion of Asia's US$108.4 billion (2015). Part of China's OFDI to Hong Kong includes the Chinese government benefit of corporate tax reduction for 'overseas investors' when their Hong Kong subsidiaries invest back in mainland China, while the other significant part is for tax avoidance purpose or to channel money out of China to third destinations through Hong Kong. Excluding Hong Kong, the rest of Asia's share in China's total OFDI outflow dropped sharply from 74.4% (Figure 11(a)) to 12.8% (Figure 11(b)): higher than Europe's 4.9%, but slightly lower than the combined size of North and Latin America's FDI inflows from China at 16.1%.

Of the total Chinese FDI inflows to Asia excluding Hong Kong, more than 30% went to a few developed economies including Singapore (56.1%), South Korea (7.1%) and Japan (1.3%). China's OFDI to Asia's developing countries only accounted for 5.8% of its total nominal OFDI in 2015. This

[31]United Nations Conference on Trade and Development, 'World Investment Report 2016: Investor Nationality: Policy Challenges', 22 June 2016, available at http://unctad.org/en/PublicationsLibrary/wir2016_en.pdf (accessed 8 April 2018).
[32]Global FDI inflows had declined from US$1,500 billion in 2011 to US$1,350 billion in 2012, an 18% drop.
[33]Ministry of Commerce, Zhongguo Duiwai Zhijie Touzi Tongji Gongbao [Statistical Bulletin of China's Outward Foreign Direct Investment] (Beijing: China Statistical Press, 2016).

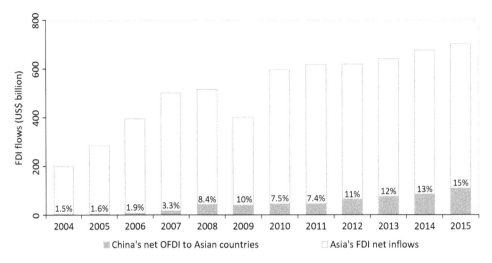

Figure 10. Share of China in Asia's total FDI inflows, 2004–2015.

Source: Ministry of Commerce, *Zhongguo Duiwai Zhijie Touzi Tongji Gongbao* [Statistical bulletin of China's outward foreign direct investment], (Beijing: China Statistical Press, 2011–2016 editions); National Development Council, *Taiwan statistical data book* (Taipei: National Development Council, 2004–2016 editions); World Bank, World Development Indicators, available at: http://databank.worldbank.org/data/home.aspx.

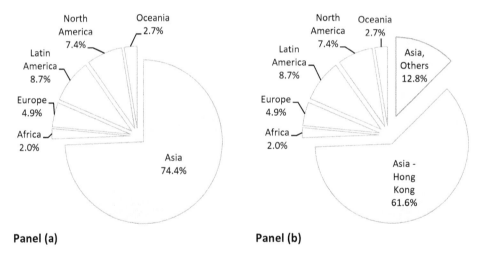

Panel (a)   Panel (b)

Figure 11. OFDI, China 2015.

Source: Ministry of Commerce, *Zhongguo Duiwai Zhijie Touzi Tongji Gongbao* [Statistical bulletin of China's outward foreign direct investment], (Beijing: China Statistical Press, 2011–2016 editions).

figure includes some upper-middle-income developing economies with a per-capita GDP comparable to that of China such as Iran, Kazakhstan and Thailand. Discounting these from the calculation, China's overseas investment in Asia's low- and middle-income developing economies amounted to only US$9.0 billion,[34] 8.3% of its total OFDI in 2015 and 1.3% of the total inflow of FDI that Asia received in the same year (see Table 2).

From 2010 to 2015, while total FDI inflows to Asia increased by 17.8%, China's share of investment in the 22 BRI countries remained at below 1% (of Asia's total FDI inflows), showing that China's competitiveness in all the initial BRI target countries together is stable but low.

---

[34] According to the 2015 Statistical Bulletin of China's Outward Foreign Direct Investment, the amount of Chinese FDI inflows to the 22 BRI Asian developing economies totalled US$2.7 billion.

Table 2. Percentage of FDI inflows from China to selected Asian economies, by host economy, 2004–2015 (US$ millions)

	2004		2005		2006		2007		2008	
(a) China's OFDI to Asia	3,019		4,484		7,767		16,600		43,557	
(b) Asia's FDI inflows	200,039		285,210		394,392		500,495		515,676	
	FDI inflows	% in (a)	FDI inflows	% in (a)	FDI inflows	% in (a)	FDI inflows	% in (a)	FDI inflows	% in (a)
Developed economies										
Hong Kong	2628	87%	3420	76%	6931	89%	13,732	83%	38,640	89%
Singapore	48.0	1.6%	20.3	0.5%	132.2	1.7%	397.7	2.4%	1,551	3.6%
Japan	15.3	0.5%	17.2	0.4%	39.5	0.5%	39.0	0.2%	58.6	0.1%
S. Korea	14.1	0.5%	6.5	0.1%	27.3	0.4%	56.7	0.3%	96.9	0.2%
Taiwan	—	—	—	—	-0.0	0.0%	-0.1	0.0%	-0.1	0.0%
Upper-middle-income economies										
Kazakhstan	2.3	0.1%	94.9	2.1%	46.0	0.6%	279.9	1.7%	496.4	1.1%
Thailand	23.4	0.8%	4.8	0.1%	15.84	0.2%	76.4	0.5%	45.5	0.1%
Iran	17.6	0.6%	11.6	0.3%	65.8	0.8%	11.4	0.1%	-34.5	-0.1%
	FDI inflows	% in (b)	FDI inflows	% in (b)	FDI inflows	% in (b)	FDI inflows	% in (b)	FDI inflows	% in (b)
Low- and middle-income economies										
BRI 22	164.3	0.1%	240.3	0.1%	343.2	0.1%	814.8	0.2%	1,182	0.2%
BRI 18	147.4	0.1%	227.5	0.1%	283.1	0.1%	813.7	0.2%	1,221	0.2%

	2009		2010		2011		2012		2013		2014		2015	
(a) China's OFDI to Asia	40,417		44,931		45,513		64,854		75,709		85,229		108,416	
(b) Asia's FDI inflows	401,511		595,782		617,168		618,372		641,582		675,995		701,801	
	FDI inflows	% in (a)	FDI inflows	% in (b)	FDI inflows	% in (a)	FDI inflows	% in (a)	FDI inflows	% in (a)	FDI inflows	% in (b)	FDI inflows	% in (a)
Developed economies														
Hong Kong	35,601	88%	38,505	86%	35,655	78%	51,238	79%	62,824	83%	70,867	83%	89,790	83%
Singapore	1,414	3.5%	1,119	2.5%	3,269	7.2%	1,519	2.3%	2,033	2.7%	2,814	3.3%	10,452	9.6%
Japan	84.1	0.2%	338	0.8%	149.4	0.3%	210.7	0.3%	434.1	0.6%	394.5	0.5%	240.4	0.2%
S. Korea	265.1	0.7%	-721.7	-1.6%	341.7	0.8%	942.4	1.5%	268.8	0.4%	548.9	0.6%	1325	1.2%
Taiwan	0.0	0.0%	17.4	0.0%	11.1	0.0%	112.9	0.2%	176.7	0.2%	183.7	0.2%	267.1	0.2%
Upper-middle-income economies														
Kazakhstan	66.8	0.2%	36.1	0.1%	581.6	1.3%	2,996	4.6%	811.5	1.1%	-40.1	0.0%	-2510	-2.3%
Thailand	49.8	0.1%	699.9	1.6%	230.1	0.5%	478.6	0.7%	755.2	1.0%	839.5	1.0%	407.2	0.4%
Iran	124.8	0.3%	511.0	1.1%	615.6	1.4%	702.1	1.1%	745.3	1.0%	592.9	0.7%	-550	-0.5%
	FDI inflows	% in (c)	FDI inflows	% in (b)	FDI inflows	% in (b)	FDI inflows	% in (b)	FDI inflows	% in (b)	FDI inflows	% in (b)	FDI inflows	% in (b)
Low- and middle-income economies														
BRI 22	1,643	0.4%	4,026	0.7%	3,844	0.6%	5,471	0.9%	5,678	0.9%	5,706	0.8%	2,668	0.4%
BRI 18	1,513	0.4%	3,458	0.6%	3,107	0.5%	4,617	0.7%	4,920	0.8%	5,014	0.7%	3,208	0.5%

Sources: National Bureau of Statistics of China, *Zhongguo Jiage Tongji Nianjian* [China price statistical yearbook] (Beijing: China Statistics Press, 1981–2016 editions); World Bank, World Development Indicators, available at: http://databank.worldbank.org/data/home.aspx; CEIC, China Premium Database, available at: https://www.ceicdata.com/en/products/china-economic-database; Ministry of Commerce, *Zhongguo Duiwai Zhijie Touzi Tongji Gongbao* [Statistical bulletin of China's outward foreign direct investment] (Beijing: China Statistical Press, 2011–2016 editions); National Development Council, *Taiwan Statistical Data Book* (Taipei: National Development Council, 2004–2016 editions).

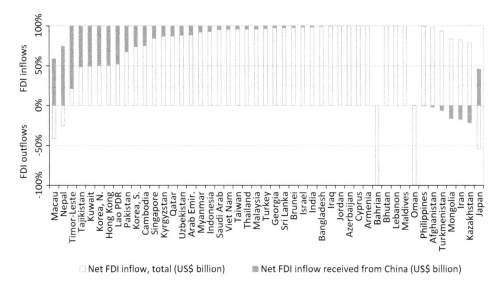

Figure 12. Share of China in FDI inflows in Asia by host economy, 2015.

Source: Ministry of Commerce, *Zhongguo Duiwai Zhijie Touzi Tongji Gongbao* [Statistical bulletin of China's outward foreign direct investment] (Beijing: China Statistical Press, 2011–2016 editions); World Bank, World Development Indicators, available at: http://databank.worldbank.org/data/home.aspx.

However, as Asia's developing economies vary significantly in size, China's OFDI in some specific low- and middle-income countries is still of particular importance. Figure 12 shows that the amount of China's FDI in Nepal, Timor and Tajikistan exceeded half of these countries' net FDI inflows in 2015, and those in North Korea, Lao, Pakistan and Cambodia by a quarter.

Chinese investment in Lao and Cambodia has always been generous, as the two countries link China to Southeast Asia and ports along the maritime route connecting China with West Asia. Its investment in Tajikistan is generally resource-based (oil, natural gas and mineral stones) and market-seeking (industrial products). Despite an encouraging record, China's 2.7% effective investment share of Asia's total FDI inflows (excluding Hong Kong) shows that it faces great competitive pressure and has a long way to go before it can fully compete with other countries investing in the region.

Official developmental assistance

Although government-led investment will take the lead in infrastructure construction to increase the absorption capacity of the host economies and spur non-government FDI, foreign aid is another important source of capital inflow, especially in low- and middle-income Asian economies.

China's share of bilateral aid to each country remains unknown because its available aid data does not reflect recipient countries individually. According to the World Bank's World Development Indicators, aid flowing to Asia in 2005–2014 totalled US$883.5 billion. Since 2005 Asia's aid inflow has come from three major sources: direct bilateral intergovernmental aid from Development Assistance Committee (DAC) members[35] ; Official Developmental Assistance (ODA), donated mainly by advanced economies; and development assistance from major UN donor agencies (see Figure 13).

From 2005 to 2014, direct bilateral aid from DAC members outstripped all other sources, contributing 60.3% of aid flows to Asia.[36] In the same period, ODA for developing Asia totalled

---

[35]DAC is an international committee acting under the auspices of the OECD.
[36]From 2005 to 2014, net bilateral aid flows from DAC donors to Asia's developing economies totalled US$532 billion.

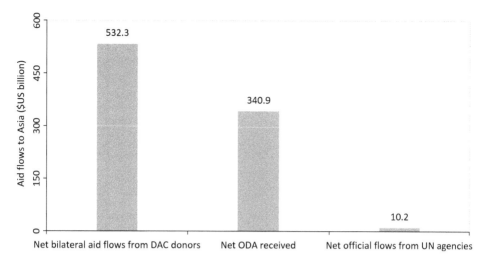

Figure 13. Total net inflows of foreign assistance to Asia, 2005–2014.

Source: World Bank, World Development Indicators, available at: http://databank.worldbank.org/data/home.aspx.

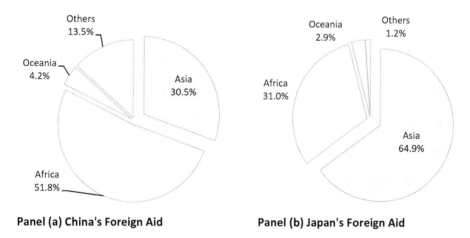

Panel (a) China's Foreign Aid   **Panel (b) Japan's Foreign Aid**

Figure 14. China and Japan's distribution of foreign aid, 2010–2012.

Source: Information Office of the State Council of China, 'China's foreign aid 2014', *Chinese Government White Paper*, (10 July 2014), available at: http://english.gov.cn/archive/white_paper/2014/08/23/content_281474982986592.htm; Ministry of Foreign Affairs of Japan, 'Japan's official development assistance 2012', *Japanese Government White Paper*, (30 July 2013), available at: http://www.mofa.go.jp/policy/oda/white/2012/html/index.html; Ministry of Foreign Affairs of Japan, 'Japan's official development assistance 2013', *Japanese Government White Paper*, (2 May 2014), available at: http://www.mofa.go.jp/policy/oda/white/2013/html/index.html.

US$340.9 billion, $191.4 billion less than direct bilateral aid. Aid from UN agencies, the third-largest source, was worth US$10.2 billion, or 1.2% of total aid to Asia in this period (see Figure 13). Among the 29 current DAC members[37] only two Asian countries, Japan and South Korea, participate as foreign aid donors. As China is not a DAC member its intergovernmental aid is not categorised with DAC aid (the first source in Figure 13); in addition, it is not easy to for China's aid capital to flow through the ODA system, the second largest source of foreign assistance to Asia, as it has mainly been dominated by developed economies.

---

[37]DAC currently has 29 members: Australia, Greece, Poland, Austria, Iceland, Portugal, Belgium, Ireland, Slovak Republic, Canada, Italy, Slovenia, Czech Republic, Japan, Spain, Denmark, South Korea, Sweden, the European Union, Luxembourg, Switzerland, Finland, the Netherlands, the United Kingdom, France, New Zealand, the United States, Germany and Norway.

Table 3. Ranking on net foreign aid, China versus DAC members, 2005–2013

Rank	2005	2007	2009	2011	2013
1	US	US	US	US	US
2	Japan	Germany	France	Germany	UK
3	UK	France	Germany	UK	Germany
4	Germany	UK	UK	France	Japan
5	France	Japan	Japan	Japan	France
6	Netherlands	Netherlands	Spain	Netherlands	China
7	Italy	Spain	Netherlands	Sweden	Sweden
8	Canada	Sweden	Sweden	Canada	Norway
9	Sweden	Canada	Norway	Australia	Netherlands
10	Spain	Italy	Canada	Norway	Canada
11	Norway	Norway	Italy	China	Australia
12	Denmark	Australia	China	Italy	Italy
13	Belgium	Denmark	Denmark	Spain	Switzerland
14	Switzerland	China	Australia	Switzerland	Denmark
15	Australia	Belgium	Belgium	Denmark	Belgium
16	Austria	Austria	Switzerland	Belgium	Spain
17	China	Switzerland	Finland	Finland	S. Korea

Source: Naohiro Kitano and Yukinori Harada, 'Estimating China's Foreign Aid 2001–2013', *Journal of International Development* 28(7), (2016), pp. 1050–1074.

Table 4. China's net and gross foreign aid during 2003–2013 (US$ million)

Year	Bilateral net foreign aid	Multi-government expenditure from international organisations	Total net foreign aid	Total gross foreign aid
2003	650	91	741	743
2004	161	120	948	972
2005	202	133	1,161	1,194
2006	362	149	1,433	1,481
2007	755	171	2,204	2,270
2008	635	205	2,408	2,498
2009	1,174	212	3,109	3,223
2010	1,627	257	3,629	3,773
2011	1,891	280	4,507	4,705
2012	2,552	394	5,710	6,003
2013	3,484	699	7,092	7,462

Sources: Ministry of Finance, *Zhongguo Caizheng Nianjian* [Finance yearbook of China] (Beijing: China's Finance Magazine Press, 1991–2016 editions); Naohiro Kitano and Yukinori Harada, 'Estimating China's Foreign Aid 2001–2013', *Journal of International Development* 28(7), (2016), pp. 1050–1074; Information Office of the State Council of China, 'China's foreign aid 2014', *Chinese Government White Paper*, (10 July 2014), available at: http://english.gov.cn/archive/white_paper/2014/08/23/content_281474982986592.htm.

China's intergovernmental aid status has risen rapidly in recent years. It hovered below 17th place until 2005. In 2012 and 2013 it rose quickly to sixth place,[38] although not a DAC member (Table 3).

Statistics show that in 2010–2012 the Chinese government contributed US$14 billion to the development of developing economies,[39] an average of US$4.8 billion each year. In 2013 there was a sharp increase to US$7.5 billion, and in the near future China is expected to further increase its sum to catch up with the only Asian country among the top five DAC donors: Japan (Tables 3 and 4). Chinese foreign aid does not go solely to Asia. The latest white paper *China's Foreign Aid* (2014) reported that Africa received 52% (US$7.5 billion) of China's foreign aid. During 2010–2012 China's aid to Asia (US$4.4 billion) made up just 31% of its total aid (see Figure 14(a)).

---

[38]Naohiro Kitano and Yukinori Harada, 'Estimating China's foreign aid 2001–2013', Journal of International Development 28(7), (2016), pp. 1050–1074.

[39]Information Office of the State Council of the People's Republic of China, 'China's foreign aid 2014', Chinese Government White Paper, 10 July 2014, available at http://english.gov.cn/archive/white_paper/2014/08/23/content_281474982986592.htm (accessed 8 April 2018).

As China's largest aid competitor in Asia, in 2010–2012 Japan granted a total amount of US$16.3 billion to Asian developing economies, approximately two-thirds of its total global ODA (Figure 14 (b)). China's contribution pattern was the opposite; although its aid capacity and ranking has seen dramatic growth, its competitiveness in the Asian aid market has fallen far behind that of Japan. Even if the new opening-up initiative can successfully establish a new official aid system between China and the rest of Asia, China's total development aid is difficult to catch up with that of the EU and the United States in the near future (e.g. the OECD's DAC); even in Asia, it will be difficult to crowd out Japan's importance in Asia's official intergovernmental aid system.

Conclusion

In 2011, after three decades of fast economic growth, the size of China's economy exceeded that of Japan. As the largest economy in Asia, China has steadily progressed in its effort to broaden economic cooperation in developing Asia. Excess industrial investment capacity and a slowing economy have pushed the country to take a proactive stance in order to establish a China-led economic circle in this region in the form of the BRI. If implemented successfully, the initiative will help China to expand its overseas markets and find new sources to support its future economic growth. Fundamentally, however, the success of China's BRI is largely contingent on Asian markets' recognition of Chinese products and capital.

The two largest trading groups with developing Asia are advanced economies and resource-originating countries. Developing Asia's capacity to absorb China's ongoing industrial oversupply may not be as satisfactory as expected. Further, China's investment is concentrated on several neighbouring economies (e.g. Laos and Cambodia). China's OFDI or intergovernmental aid to low- and middle-income Asia remains low. To change this, China needs a fasting expanding business/ fiscal capacity to increase its share of FDI and aid to developing economies in Asia, and this is unlikely to happen within a short period. In BRI countries where long-term cooperative relations with other investor countries and donor organisations (e.g. OECD and UN agencies) have long existed, China may have to compete in terms of the amount of aid that it provides to crowd out competitors.

It may also need to conduct a study of the profitability of such efforts, given that the volume of trade between China and the 22 BRI countries is usually less than its trade with the EU or the United States. China's investment capacity is difficult to compete with FDI and aid from the OECD- and UN-led systems. Even in Asia, China faces immense difficulty crowding out Japan's existing importance.

China's BRI is thus fraught with obstacles. It faces cooperation-based competition and will need to integrate the BRI into the current framework of international economic cooperation. Intensifying its competition for investment in Asia may affect its partnerships with competitors in other markets.

While China's new opening-up BRI has been launched with a loud fanfare, the path ahead is largely unknown and unpredictable. Asia, as the first stop along the belt and the road, is vital to China's success. China will need to maintain a realistic balance between its ambitious Asian economic strategy and its global economic cooperation.

Acknowledgements

This paper is dedicated to the memory of Professor John Wong, who passed away last month. It is gratifying that we have been able to honor him with work which he made many insightful comments on.

Disclosure statement

No potential conflict of interest was reported by the authors.

5 Strategic Reassurance in Institutional Contests

Explaining China's Creation of the Asian Infrastructure Investment Bank

Zheng Chen and Yanchuan Liu

ABSTRACT

The Asian Infrastructure Investment Bank (AIIB) has been widely conceived as a Chinese effort to promote reforms of global financial governance. While the existing literature of contested multilateralism tends to focus on the problem of threat credibility, this article highlights the necessity of strategic reassurance in institutional contests. To facilitate incremental reforms of the existing order, rising powers like China need not only to pose credible challenge towards established institutions, but also to demonstrate their benign intentions and commitment to future cooperation. Besides revealing strength and resolve, the creation of a new multilateral regime helps rising powers to signal their self-restraints and reassure other powers. Consequently, the institutional configuration of new multilateral organizations involves a trade-off between the dual needs for threats and reassurance. Chinese behaviours in creating the AIIB can be explained through this framework.

Introduction

Ever since the global financial crisis in 2008, Beijing has been actively constructing new multilateral financial regimes that are at least partially competing with pre-existing institutions.[1] Nonetheless, while pioneering the creation of parallel institutions, Beijing remains an active member in the Bretton Woods regimes. Those China-led new institutions also cooperate closely with and adopt practices frequently from their established counterparts. A paramount case of Beijing's activism is the creation of the Asian Infrastructure Investment Bank (AIIB), which has generated various speculations on Chinese motivations behind. With a focus on economic rationales, some analyses underscore Asia's huge demand for infrastructure investment and China's need to export its industrial overcapacity to tackle the domestic slowdown.[2] Many others emphasize geopolitical motivations, arguing that the bank is a part of China's

---

[1]Injoo Sohn, 'Between confrontation and assimilation: China and the fragmentation of global financial governance', *Journal of Contemporary China* 22(82), (2013), pp. 630–48; Sebastian Heilmann et al., 'China's shadow foreign policy: Parallel structures challenge the established international order', *MERICS China Monitor*, No.18, (2014), available at: http://blog.merics.org/fileadmin/templates/download/china-monitor/China_Monitor_No_18_en.pdf (accessed 16 January 2017); James F. Paradise, 'The role of "parallel institutions" in China's growing participation in global economic governance', *Journal of Chinese Political Science* 21(2), (2016), pp. 149–75.

[2]Hongying Wang. 'The Asian Infrastructure Investment Bank: A new Bretton Woods moment? A Total Chinese Triumph?' *CIGI Policy Brief*, No. 59, (2015), available at: https://www.cigionline.org/sites/default/files/policy_brief_no_59.pdf (accessed 28 February 2017).

[3]Amitai Etzioni, 'The Asian Infrastructure Investment Bank: A case study of multifaceted containment', *Asian Perspective* 40(2), (2016), pp. 173–196; Xiao Ren, 'China as an institution-builder: The case of the AIIB', *The Pacific Review* 29(3), (2016), pp. 435–42; Hong Yu, 'Motivation behind China's "One Belt, One Road" initiatives and establishment of the Asian Infrastructure Investment Bank', *Journal of Contemporary China* 26(105), (2017), pp. 353–368; Martin A. Weiss, *Asian Infrastructure Investment Bank (AIIB)* (Washington, DC: Congressional Research Service, 2017); Lai-Ha Chan and Pak K. Lee, 'Power, ideas and institutions: China's Emergent footprints in global governance of development aid', *CSGR Working Paper* No. 281/17, Centre for the Study of Globalisation and Regionalisation, University of Warwick, 2017, available at: http://www2.warwick.ac.uk/fac/soc/pais/research/researchcentres/csgr/papers/281-17.pdf. (accessed 1 August 2017).

balancing efforts against the U.S. 'Pivot to Asia' strategy.[3] A growing number of scholars suggest that Beijing's primary interest lies in soft power and institutional influence.[4] The AIIB is conceived as a bargaining instrument for Beijing to promote reforms in global financial governance, as it signals Beijing's discontent with the existing regimes and a warning that China has both the capacity and resolve to bypass the system if necessary.[5]

All of these factors have played a role in Beijing's creation of the AIIB. However, China's practices in creating AIIB are more complicated, and several puzzles remained. First, if China has enough resolve and strength to pose credible challenges already, why did Beijing fail to achieve the desired reforms in the first place? Second, if the AIIB was primarily a result of Chinese economic and geopolitical ambitions, Beijing could have pursued those projects on a purely bilateral, state-to-state basis, which would guarantee it more policy autonomy. When a variety of tools exist, why did China choose to bear the cost of creating a new multilateral bank? What is the added value of a new multilateral regime? Finally, while the AIIB is widely regarded as a Chinese 'external innovation' to challenge the existing U.S.-led institutions, why does the AIIB also mirror and cooperate with the World Bank and the Asian Development Bank (ADB) so closely?[6]

This article addresses the aforementioned puzzles through the lens of bargaining theory in International Relations (IR). It argues that even when rising powers can pose credible threats, serious commitment problems associated with rapid power shifts may obstruct reforms within existing institutions by exacerbating distrusts between rising and established powers. Meanwhile, new multilateral institutions can act as commitment devices for rising powers to ease the problem. Besides magnifying strength and demonstrating resolve, delegating power to multilateral organizations helps rising states signal self-restraints to reassure other states. In turn, rising powers' dual needs for credible threats and reassurance shape the institutional configuration of those new multilateral organizations they created. As observers have generally agreed, the AIIB was partially meant to strengthen the credibility of potential Chinese options to withdraw its support for the existing Bretton Woods institutions. However, China also needs and has sought to reassure other states by adopting an inclusive approach in developing the AIIB. This reassurance function is a distinctive value of a new multilateral development bank (MDB) while the AIIB's institutional configurations clearly reflected this consideration.

This article contributes to the emerging literature of contested multilateralism and China's strategies towards international institutions in two important ways. First, while existing explanations of institutional adaption tend to emphasize the problem of threat credibility, this article elaborates on the necessity of strategic reassurance for emerging powers. It thus highlights the value of new multilateral institutions in helping rising powers credibly signal their self-restraints. Second, analysing the AIIB within a broader context of Beijing's pursuit of a peaceful rise, this article elaborates on China's dual considerations about threats and reassurance in its creation of the AIIB. More specifically, it is in China's strategic interest to reassure other states by tying its own hands in the new multilateral organization.

The rest of the article proceeds as follows. The next section maps out the interplay between new regime creation and reforms of the existing order through the lens of bargaining theory. It explains the stagnation of reforms within existing institutions with an emphasis on commitment problems associated with power shifts rather than threat credibility. It then highlights the dual functions of new multilateral regimes in posing challenges and granting reassurance, followed by an illustration

---

[4]Rebecca LaForgia, 'Listening to China's multilateral voice for the first time: Analysing the Asian Infrastructure Investment Bank for soft power opportunities and risks in the narrative of "Lean, Clean and Green"', *Journal of Contemporary China* 26(107), (2017), pp. 633–649; Kai He, 'Contested regional orders and institutional balancing in the Asia pacific', *International Politics* 52 (2), (2015), pp. 208–222.

[5]Helmut Reisen, 'Will the AIIB and the NDB help reform multilateral development banking?' *Global Policy*, 6(3), (2015), pp. 297–304; Xiaoyu Pu and Clayton Cleveland, 'Exit, voice, and AIIB: Shifting powers and reaction mechanisms of institutional change'(Paper presented in ISA annual convention 2017 in Baltimore, Maryland, February 22–25, 2017).

[6]G. John Ikenberry and Darren Lim, *China's Emerging Institutional Statecraft* (Washington, D.C.: Brookings Institution), 13 April 2017, available at: https://www.brookings.edu/research/chinas-emerging-institutional-statecraft/ (accessed 6 January 2018).

of how the tension between these two considerations shapes the configuration of new institutions. After that, the empirical section examines how China encountered the commitment problem and managed to balance the dual needs of threats and reassurance in constructing the AIIB. The article concludes with some further thoughts.

Power transition and strategic reassurance in institutional contest

This section develops a theoretical framework about the commitment problems in institutional contests between rising powers and established powers to highlight the importance of strategic reassurance on the development of a new institution. In the anarchic international system, a dissatisfied rising powers must bargain with established powers to increase its institutional benefits and privileges.[7] It could choose whether to promote reforms of existing institutions or to withdraw from them. In turn, the established powers can either accommodate or contain the rising power's 'revisionist' efforts. Following Albert Hirschman's classic work *Exit, Voice, and Loyalty*, recent studies conceptualize the creation of new multilateral institutions as an 'exit' move (or an outside option), whose realization can be prevented by changes within the established institutions.[8] Meanwhile, 'voice' (promoting reforms of the established institutions) is similarly costly, but it provides a share of the surplus from avoiding 'exit' for each side.[9] A state will have more leverage when it has better outside options than its counterparts.[10] The rising power can negotiate better terms if it can make a credible threat of 'exit' to undermine the existing institutions' effectiveness.[11] The credibility of such a threat forms the main condition of institutional adaptions.[12] This is the mechanism that many analyses of the AIIB have relied on.

Commitment problems in institutional reform bargaining

In light of Hirschman's model, however, a rising power needs not to actually implement its outside (or 'exit') options to promote reform. Since at least one side will suffer utility loss if the bargaining fails, theoretically, a bargaining range emerges for a compromise.[13] Nonetheless, in reality as in the AIIB case, states sometimes create new institutions even when a compromise is in both sides' interests. James Fearon, Rebert Powell and others have developed two explanations of why states engage in costly conflicts when a bargaining range exists: information asymmetries and commitment problems.[14] Existing works on contested multilateralism emphasize the credibility of threats.[15] If a state that is not intent on replacing existing institutions nonetheless believes that other states have underestimated its strength and resolve, it may initiate an actual 'exit' to demonstrate its capabilities and determination.

[7]Christina J. Schneider, 'Weak States and Institutionalized Bargaining Power in International Organizations', *International Studies Quarterly* 55(2), (2011), pp. 331–55.

[8]Albert O. Hirschman, *Exit, Voice, and Loyalty: Responses to Decline in Firms, Organizations, and States* (Harvard: Harvard University Press, 1970); Joseph Henri Jupille, Walter Mattli, and Duncan Snidal, *Institutional Choice and Global Commerce* (Cambridge: Cambridge University Press, 2013).

[9]Scott Gehlbach, 'A formal model of exit and voice', *Rationality and Society* 18(4), (2006), pp. 395–418.

[10]Schneider, 'Weak states and institutionalized bargaining power in international organizations'; Randall W. Stone, *Controlling Institutions: International Organizations and the Global Economy* (Cambridge: Cambridge University Press, 2011); Allison Carnegie, 'States held hostage: Political hold-up problems and the effects of international institutions', *American Political Science Review* 108(1), (2014), pp. 54–70; Philip Lipscy, 'Explaining institutional change: Policy areas, outside options, and the Bretton Woods institutions', *American Journal of Political Science*, 59(2), (2015), pp.341–56.

[11]Johannes Urpelainen and Thijs Van de Graaf, 'Your place or mine? Institutional capture and the creation of overlapping international institutions', *British Journal of Political Science* 45(4), (2015), pp. 799–827.

[12]Bernhard Zangl, Frederick Heußner, Andreas Kruck, and Xenia Lanzendörfer, 'Imperfect adaptation: How the WTO and the IMF adjust to shifting power distributions among their members', *The Review of International Organizations* 11(2), (2016), pp. 171–96.

[13]Gehlbach, 'A formal model of exit and voice'.

[14]James D. Fearon, 'Rationalist explanations for war', *International Organization* 49(3), (1995), pp. 379–414; Robert Powell, 'Bargaining theory and international conflict', *Annual Review of Political Science* 5(1), (2002), pp.1–30.

[15]Julia C. Morse and Robert O. Keohane, 'Contested multilateralism', *The Review of International Organizations* 9(4), (2014), pp. 385–412.

However, the problem of threat credibility is insufficient to explain the failure of institutional reform bargaining when states have both incentives and means to communicate effectively. According to the information problem logic, competing states might withhold important private information about their own relative power, making it difficult to reach a settlement. Nonetheless, unlike what happens in military conflicts, this might not be so serious an obstacle in issue areas such as development finance, whereby states have limited incentives and capabilities in deceiving and bluffing each other. Economic information is more openly shared. To achieve greater say in a regime, an actor has to make concrete contributions. Rising states also have other channels to disrupt the function of existing institutions to pose credible threats. As in the IMF reform case, China's growing financial power and economic influence is widely acknowledged. Its capability to disrupt the liberal international economic order might even be exaggerated by western powers. In this case, the problem lies less in private information but mutual distrust due to rapid power shifts.[16]

This observation highlights the other source of bargaining failure: commitment problems. Commitment problems refer to situations whereby at least one side expects the others to violate the terms of a settlement. To reach an agreement, actors must commit to certain courses of action. An obstacle arises when these promises are not credible, since some of the players have incentives and means to renege on what they previously agreed to. In the anarchic system of international politics, rapid and uncertain power shifts make it even more difficult for relevant parties to forge binding long-term contracts.[17] As previous studies have revealed, while the strengthening of an 'exit' option would enhance the power of 'voice,' it would also make the 'voice' option relatively less attractive.[18] Established powers would suspect that the rising power would demand further revisions in the future or abuse its strength even after receiving significant concessions. Moreover, privileges in international institutions are strategic assets. Redistributions imply different strengths and asymmetrical benefits for the negotiating parties in future. The established power thus refrains from making concessions. Even when those challenger's 'exit' options are credible, a dominant state may prefer to live with the current arrangement.[19]

Institutional reforms thus tend to happen only when the current regime are suffering serious difficulties. To induce cooperation, the established powers, in temporarily weak positions, might accommodate rising powers to a certain degree. However, this requires a series of institutional concessions across several periods during which established powers might expect the power distribution to shift back in their favour. As other states would suspect, once recovering from their temporary difficulties, the established powers would renege on previous concessions.

Consequently, in the shadow of the rapid and uncertain shifts of power, institutional reform bargaining between rising and established powers faces serious commitment problems. States might agree on how to divide today's pie, but they cannot credibly commit to future divisions. In fact, if the power distribution shifts fast enough, few settlements would be time-consistent.[20] As each side has an incentive to renege, it is difficult to achieve mutual trust. Thus, even when the threats from rising powers are credible, reform negotiations might be trapped in stagnation. When this happens, rising powers may prefer founding alternative regimes.

The dual task of the new institution

The previous section suggests reform bargaining might fail even when neither the rising nor the established powers want to abandon existing regimes and no serious information asymmetry

---

[16]Branislav L. Slantchev, 'The power to hurt: Costly conflict with completely informed states', *American Political Science Review* 97(1), (2003), pp. 123–133.

[17]Robert Powell, 'Commitment problems and shifting power as a cause of conflict', in Michelle R. Garfinkel and Stergios Skaperdas, eds., *The Oxford Handbook of the Economics of Peace and Conflict* (Oxford: Oxford University Press, 2012), pp.43–58.

[18]Gehlbach, 'A formal model of exit and voice'.

[19]Robert Powell, 'Bargaining and learning while fighting', *American Journal of Political Science*, 48(2), (2004), pp 344–361

[20]Powell, 'Commitment problems and shifting power as a cause of conflict'.

exists. New questions arise then: As rising powers have various tactics to exercise 'exit' and fulfil their goals, why do they create new multilateral institutions? What is this option's distinctive value?

The answer lies in a new institution's dual potential as inside and outside options, and particularly its utilities in reassuring other states and easing commitment problems. Building new institutions do not necessarily end the rising power's efforts to reform existing regimes. Although 'voice' and 'exit' are substitutes initially, they become complements once the 'exit' option becomes available and attractive.[21] Even when they are unattractive as an outside option in full sense, new institutions could also be used as an inside option to improve one's bargaining position.

In the bargaining literature, a player's inside option is the payoff that it obtains during the bargaining process when the relevant parties are temporarily in disagreement.[22] The development of new institutions offers rising powers additional leverage in a tortuous negotiation process, as they now enjoy alternative multilateral tools of coordination, monitoring and enforcement to achieve policy objectives. In this scenario, rising powers develop seemingly redundant alternative regimes to escape from the deadlocks in institutional reforms and fetch additional leverage vis-à-vis established powers or status-quo institutions.[23]

Investing in the new regime, however, raises another risk of negotiation breakdown in the power shift process. The development of alternative regimes whereby rising powers dominate might send unintended signals that lead others to exaggerate the rising powers' aggressiveness. While new institution can steadily increase the emerging power's influence so that someday it can fulfil its long-term goal of overthrowing the established order, this prospect attracts suspicions and containment from other powers.[24]

Rising powers thus face a dual task of compellence and reassurance in institutional contests. This coincides with the key components of any successful coercive diplomacy: states must use clear threats and credible assurance in combination to force target countries to do something or dissuade them from undesirable behaviour.[25] On the one hand, rising powers should pose credible threats to hold up contributions to and even disrupt the operation of established institutions. Meanwhile, the other, at least equally important, task is to reassure that once other states (the current hegemon in particular) make the demanded concessions, they would act as stakeholders and provide more public goods.

It is rational for rising powers to balance threats with reassurance. Otherwise, they would run the risk of incurring unnecessary obstructions and conflicts. Established powers might suspect that rising powers would overtake their leadership and revise the existing rules. Small states and middle powers would be anxious about the prospect of being dominated by new players. For the smooth and sustainable development of the new institution, rising powers should assure other states that their intentions are limited and predictable while the exercise of their influence is, at least to some acceptable degree, circumscribed.

Dealing with this dual task of posing threat and granting reassurance is difficult, but creating new multilateral organizations offers distinctive benefits. First, the availability of alternative organizations increases the credibility of the rising powers' threats to disrupt pre-existing arrangements. These multilateral institutions would also help rising powers to magnify their influence and transform momentary power advantages into a durable flow of benefits. Moreover, the creation and operation of new institutions involves heavy burdens of coalition building.[26] This is a costly process that tests and signals a state's resolve and strength.

---

[21]Hirschman,*Exit, Voice, and Loyalty*; Gehlbach, 'A formal model of exit and voice', p. 402.

[22]Abhinay Muthoo, *Bargaining Theory with Applications* (Cambridge: Cambridge University Press, 1999).

[23]Scott L. Kastner, Margaret M. Pearson, and Chad Rector, 'Invest, hold up, or accept? China in multilateral governance', *Security Studies* 25(1), (2016), pp. 142–79.

[24]Pu and Cleveland, 'Exit, voice, and AIIB'.

[25]Schelling, *The Strategy of Conflict*; James W. Davis, *Threats and Promises: The Pursuit of International Influence* (Baltimore: Johns Hopkins University Press, 2000).

[26]Jupille, Mattli, and Snidal, *Institutional Choice and Global Commerce*.

Nonetheless, the most distinctive value of creating new multilateral institutions, in comparison with other modes of 'exit,' lies in reassuring other states by signalling the challengers' benign intentions and commitment to cooperation. Existing studies of foreign policy signalling suggest that a commitment would be more credible if it creates the possibility that states will become locked into some positions and will refrain from reneging because of significant sunk costs and audiences costs.[27] Combining this logic with insights from neoliberal institutionalism theories in IR, this article suggests that the deliberate development of new multilateral institutions provides a reliable mechanism through which rising powers like China could credibly signal their benign intentions and self-restraints.

Here, the ability to generate costs of reneging is critical. Multilateral regimes provide cost-effective frameworks of exchanges that generate reliable information for the assessment of states' reputation. They offer an extra mechanism through which a government could credibly commit to public goods provision and alleviate worries about cheating or bad faith.[28] Delegating power to international organizations also sets disciplines and helps a rising power to mitigate other states' fear of power abuse, while inducing them to accommodate its increasing influence.[29] In the absence of functioning electoral systems and free press, which serve as commitment devices at the domestic level, non-democracies would rely more on international mechanisms to set self-constraints and signal commitments to reassure other players.

To achieve this goal, as G. John Ikenberry suggested, power states can adopt several measures in the configuration of new institutions. Ikenberry's various discussions focused on the hegemon but rising powers can also resort to 'opening itself up' and 'tying itself down' to make their exercises of power more predictable and accessible to other states.[30] Here, 'opening itself up' means making the new institution's operations more transparent to other players and providing access for them to have an influence, thereby reducing their suspicions.[31] With regard to 'tying itself down,' besides delegating a certain degree of decision-making power to a multilateral organization, the rising state could establish institutional links between the new organization and established regimes. In effect, binding institution arrangements create constraints on the way power can be exercised, rendering asymmetric power relations less exploitative.[32] Through these methods, a rising state reassures others that there will be limits on its exercises of growing influences.

Nonetheless, incentives to grant reassurance are not unconditional. Rising states face difficult trade-offs on whether and how to develop a new multilateral institution. In agreeing to abide by the rules of a multilateral organization, a state accepts some constraints on its freedom of action for long-term interests. However, temptations to excise power unilaterally and maintain autonomy always exist. Reassurance measures might also erode the effectiveness of threats. No clear-cut choice exists. The option of creating new multilateral organizations will appeal to a state only when it sees the benefits from self-restraints and reassurance exceed the costs of losing autonomy and threat effectiveness. The higher the risks of containment by established powers, the more willing the rising powers become to grant reassurance. A closer examination of the evolving political

[27] James D. Fearon, 'Signaling foreign policy interests: Tying hands versus sinking costs', *Journal of Conflict Resolution* 41(1), (1997), pp. 68–90.

[28] Barbara Koremenos, 'Contracting around international uncertainty', *The American Political Science Review* 99(4), (2005), pp. 549–65; B. Peter Rosendorff and Helen V. Milner, 'The optimal design of international trade institutions: Uncertainty and escape', *International Organization* 55(4), (2001), pp. 829–57.

[29] Kenneth. W. Abbott and Duncan. Snidal, 'Why states act through formal international organizations', *Journal of Conflict Resolution* 42(1), (1998), pp. 3–32.

[30] G. John Ikenberry, *After Victory: Institutions, Strategic Restraint, and the Rebuilding of Order after Major Wars* (Princeton: Princeton University Press, 2001).

[31] Jon Elster, *Institutional Design in Post-Communist Societies: Rebuilding the Ship at Sea* (Cambridge: Cambridge University Press, 1998), p. 15.

[32] Joseph M. Grieco, 'State interests and institutional rule trajectories: A neorealist interpretation of the Maastricht Treaty and European Economic and Monetary Union', *Security Studies* 5(3), (1996), p. 200, Abbott and Snidal, 'Why states act through formal international organizations'.

context would help explain variations and evolutions in a state's design of new multilateral regimes.

In sum, the obstacle to the adaptions of existing institutional arrangements arises not only from threat credibility problems but also commitment problems inherent in the power shifts process. To promote redistributive reforms of any existing order, rising powers face a dual task of signalling threat and reassurance. The development of new institutions provides them with a proper tool for this dual purpose, while the tension between threat and reassurance shapes how rising powers design and configure these new institutions. As political contexts vary, the development of alternative institutions has complex strategic origins, multiple functions and different institutional configurations.

This bargaining framework suggests following theoretical propositions, which are distinctive from existing studies, to answer the puzzles in the introductory section.

(1) Even when the challenge from rising powers is credible, established powers would still obstruct rising powers' reform efforts out of their anxiety about the settlement's implications for future power distribution.
(2) While there are other options of 'exit' to pose credible threats, a reform-oriented rising power might prefer creating new multilateral institution since this option could act both as an inside option and a commitment device to facilitate adjustments of the existing order.
(3) The institutional configuration of new multilateral regimes involves a trade-off between the needs to pose a threat and grant reassurance. A reform-oriented rising power would adopt an inclusive and self-restrained approach in configuring new multilateral organizations to reassure other states.

The empirical examination of the AIIB case below testifies to the aforementioned arguments by answering three puzzles raised at the beginning of the article.

China's creation of the AIIB and the bank's developments

Empirically, this article examines China's creation of the AIIB. For years, Beijing had largely kept a low profile in international financial institutions.[33] As China's economic influence grows, Beijing's discontent about these institutions became apparent in the early 2000s. The global financial crisis in the fall of 2008 further stimulated an uptick in criticisms from Chinese officials on two issues: China's underrepresentation in the IMF and the dominance of the U.S. dollar as a reserve currency.[34] In the subsequent years, Beijing actively pressed the issue of IMF vote shares reform through the G20 process.[35] It also openly linked the under-representation of emerging markets and developing countries to the World Bank's legitimacy.[36]

While it continues to call for reforms of the IMF and the World Bank, Beijing proposed the AIIB in October 2013. The bank officially commenced operation in January 2016 and it has now grown to 84 approved members from around the world. Introduced as an alternative source of infrastructure financing for developing countries, the AIIB has great potential to bring new priorities, principles

---

[33]Gregory Chin, 'The emerging countries and China in the G20: Reshaping global economic governance', *Studia Diplomatica* 63 (2), (2010), p. 109.

[34]Ming Zhang, 'China's new international financial strategy amid the global financial crisis', *China & World Economy* 17(5), (2009), pp. 22–35.

[35]'China Urges Actions to Reform Global Financial System', *Xinhua News*, (7 July 2009), available at: http://news.xinhuanet.com/english/2009-07/09/content_11681665.htm (accessed 6 August 2017).

[36]"Statement by Shi Yaobin, Vice Minister of Finance, the People's Republic of China, Joint Ministerial Committee of the Boards of Governors of the Bank and the Fund on the Transfer of Real Resources to Developing Countries, 96th Meeting,' *World Bank*, (14 October 2017), available at: http://siteresources.worldbank.org/DEVCOMMINT/Documentation/23715170/DC2017-0003.pdf (accessed 15 January 2018).

and procedures into multilateral development assistance and compete with U.S.-led world financial institutions including the IMF and the World Bank, as well as the Japan-led ADB.

Commitment problems, the reform deadlock and the AIIB's creation

The AIIB was created against the backdrop of China's frustration with the slow pace of reform of the pre-existing international financial system. Although it has become a stakeholder in Breton Woods institutions, Beijing remains dissatisfied with their workings. The increasing weight of China and other emerging economies remains inadequately reflected in those focal institutions. For instance, right before the 2010 reform plan, China had a disproportionately low share of only 3.81% of voting right in the IMF quota system. European countries, in contrast, were allocated 27.5%.[37] As the world's second largest economy, China had a voting share of 4.42% in the World Bank, compared to 16.4% for the U.S. and 7.9% for Japan.[38] Similarly, Japan and the U.S. play a dominant role within the ADB.[39] As of December 2016, China's total holding in the ADB was only 6.4%, whereas Japan and the U.S. each held 15.6% respectively.[40]

Despite China's strong advocacy, its attempts to reshape the global financial order have largely been frustrated by the developed economies. G20 leaders had agreed in 2009 to reform the governance of the IMF and the World Bank, and the executive boards of both organizations decided to modify voting power distribution in 2010.[41] In the following 5 years, however, the reform plan failed to be carried out. As the western powers are recovering from the financial crisis, the prospect for more balanced representation in the near future appears bleak.

It is now widely believed that a significant reason why emerging powers, China in particular, initiated the New Development Bank and AIIB was their shared frustration with the deadlock in reforming Bretton Woods institutions.[42] Ironically, the main obstruction facing the IMF reform plan came from Washington, even though it was the European countries not the U.S. that would lose voting share. The Republican-dominated U.S. House of Representatives blocked the reform plan for years.[43] Implementing the reform would not increase total U.S. financial commitments to the IMF. The share of U.S. voting power at the IMF falls only slightly, and Washington would still maintain its unique veto power over most policy decisions. Nonetheless, many American legislators were sceptical about the emerging economies' commitment to the established norms of international financial institutions, and suspected that these countries may prefer strategies less aligned with those of the U.S.[44]

---

[37]'Acceptances of the proposed amendment of the articles of agreement on reform of the executive board and consents to 2010 quota increase', *International Monetary Fund*, (29 December 2016), available at: http://www.imf.org/external/np/sec/misc/consents.htm#a2%5D (accessed 6 August 2017).

[38]Amitai Etzioni, 'The Asian Infrastructure Investment Bank: A case study of multifaceted containment', *Asian Perspective* 40(2), (2016), pp. 173–96.

[39]Daniel Yew Mao Lim and James Raymond Vreeland, 'Regional organizations and international politics: Japanese influence over the Asian Development Bank and the UN Security Council', *World Politics* 65(1), (2013), p. 48.

[40]'Shareholders,' *Asian Development Bank*, (31 December 2016), available at: https://www.adb.org/site/investors/credit-funda mentals/shareholders (accessed 6 August 2017).

[41]'IMF Quota and Governance Reform Elements of an Agreement', *International Monetary Fund*, (31 October 2010), available at: https://www.imf.org/external/np/pp/eng/2010/103110.pdf (accessed 6 August 2017).

[42]See Shawn Donnan, 'US congress moves closer to approving long-stalled IMF reforms', *Financial Times*, (16 December 2015), available at: https://www.ft.com/content/bee64f68-a412-11e5-873f-68411a84f346 (accessed 30 September 2016); Jonathan Dove, 'The AIIB and the NDB: The end of multilateralism or a new beginning?' *The Diplomat*, (26 April 2016), available at: http://thediplomat.com/2016/04/the-aiib-and-the-ndb-the-end-of-multilateralism-or-a-new-beginning/ (accessed 6 August 2017).

[43]Dries Lesage, Peter Debaere, Sacha Dierckx, and Mattias Vermeiren, 'IMF reform after the crisis', *International Politics* 50(4), (2013), pp. 553–78; Jacob Vestergaard and Robert H. Wade, 'Protecting power: How Western States retain the dominant voice in the World Bank's governance', *World Development* 46, (2013), pp. 153–64.

[44]Jeffrey Frankel, 'IMF reform and isolationism in the US Congress', *East Asia Forum*, (29 January 2014), available at: http://www.eastasiaforum.org/2014/01/29/imf-reform-and-isolationism-in-the-us-congress (accessed 6 August 2017); Rebecca M. Nelson and Martin A. Weiss, 'IMF reform: Issues for congress', *Congressional Research Service Report*, (9 April 2015), available at: http://digital.library.unt.edu/ark:/67531/metadc505420/m1/1/high_res_d/R42844_2015Apr09.pdf (accessed 6 August 2017).

Washington has long been urging Beijing to behave as a 'responsible stakeholder' by contributing more to global governance.[45] Nonetheless, the U.S. seems reluctant to sacrifice its own authority and privileges to accommodate China.[46] Because of its deep-rooted distrust of China's political system and rapidly rising power, it suspected that Beijing would disrupt established practices after gaining more institutional authority.[47] In fact, ever since the financial crisis, there has been increasing sensitivity among U.S. elites to China's alleged attempts to take advantage of U.S. difficulties.[48] They demonstrate growing anxiety about the erosion of U.S. superiority, with China widely regarded as the most prominent challenger.[49] The obstruction of the IMF reform reveals Washington's suspicion towards China's bid for more institutional influence.

China's move to create the AIIB is a part of the 'price' paid for this reluctance of accommodation.[50] After the U.S. Congress's repeated refusals to approve the IMF reform plan, the deadlock led China to suspect that advanced economies had reneged on their earlier promise of reform.[51] The establishment of the AIIB and other new financial institutions reflect both Beijing's dissatisfaction about its inadequate representation and its frustration with the slow pace and grim prospect of reform.[52]

It was, however, not the problem of threat credibility that prevented the desired reforms of the IMF. China has clearly accumulated enough economic clout to exploit opportunities in development finance. A striking feature of the AIIB is its concentration on funding infrastructure projects, an area where existing institutions have proved inadequate.[53] The 'thirst for infrastructure funding' in the world in general and Asia in particular has been widely acknowledged.[54] The existing multilateral lending institutions such as the World Bank and the ADB lack the capacity to satisfy this huge demand.[55] The inadequacy of pre-existing regimes provides Beijing with a great opportunity to bypass them.

Beijing also has remarkable lending capability to compete with existing institutions. By the end of 2013, China had a huge foreign-exchange reserve of US$ 3.82 trillion, with about 1.4 trillion invested in U.S. treasury bonds.[56] In the face of domestic criticisms on the low cost-effectiveness of purchasing U.S. Treasury bonds, Beijing had great incentive to use its capital in more constructive ways.[57] Meanwhile, as the world's second-largest economy, China has already become a global

[45]Thomas J. Christensen, *The China Challenge: Shaping the Choices of a Rising Power* (New York: WW Norton & Company, 2015).
[46]Robert B. Zoellick, 'Whither China: From membership to responsibility?', *US Department of States*, (21 September 2005), available at: https://2001-2009.state.gov/s/d/former/zoellick/rem/53682.htm (accessed 6 January 2018).
[47]Jonathan Weisman, 'At global economic gathering, U.S. primacy is Seen As Ebbing', *The New York Times*, (17 April 2015), available at: http://www.nytimes.com/2015/04/18/business/international/at-global-economic-gathering-concerns-that-us-is-ceding-its-leadership-role.html (accessed 6 August 2017).
[48]Kenneth G. Lieberthal and Jisi Wang, 'Addressing U.S.-China strategic distrust', *Brookings Institute*, (30 March 2012), available at: https://www.brookings.edu/research/addressing-u-s-china-strategic-distrust/ (accessed 6 August 2017).
[49]Graham Allison, 'The thucydides trap: Are the U.S. and China headed for war?', *The Atlantic*, (24 September 2015), available at: http://www.theatlantic.com/international/archive/2015/09/united-states-china-war-thucydides-trap/406756/ (accessed 6 August 2017).
[50]Nelson and Weiss, 'IMF reforms: Issues for congress'; 'U.S. Allies, Lured by China's Bank', *The New York Times*, (20 March 2015), available at: http://www.nytimes.com/2015/03/20/opinion/us-allies-lured-by-chinas-bank.html (accessed 6 August 2017).
[51]'China urges IMF reform implementation', *Xinhuaa News Net*, (14 March 2013), available at: http://news.xinhuanet.com/english/china/2013-03/14/c_124460626.htm (accessed 6 August 2017); 'China urges implementation of IMF Quota reform business', *China Daily*, (18 April 2015), available at: http://www.chinadailyasia.com/business/2015-04/18/content_15252633.html (accessed 6 August 2017).
[52]'A bridge not far enough', *The Economist*, (21 March 2015), available at: http://www.economist.com/news/leaders/21646746-america-wrong-obstruct-chinas-asian-infrastructure-bank-bridge-not-far-enough (accessed 6 August 2017).
[53]Reisen, 'Will the AIIB and the NDB help reform multilateral development banking?'.
[54]Asian Development Bank, *Infrastructure for a Seamless Asia*, (2009), available at: http://www.adb.org/publications/infrastructure-seamless-asia (accessed 6 August 2017); Raffaele Della Croce, P. Schieb, and B. Stevens, 'Pension funds investment in infrastructure: A survey', *International Futures Programme, OECD*, (2011), available at: http://www.oecd.org/futures/infrastructureto2030/48634596.pdf (accessed 6 August 2017); Biswa N. Bhattacharyay, Masahiro Kawai, and Rajat Nag, *Infrastructure for Asian Connectivity* (Cheltenham: Edward Elgar Publishing, 2012).
[55]'Why China is creating a new "World Bank" for Asia', *The Economist*; Steinbock, 'American exceptionalism and the AIIB debacle'.
[56]Yong Wang, 'China's economic challenges: Grappling with a "New Normal"', *Global Asia* 3(4), (2014), pp. 12–17.
[57]Daniel Drezner, 'Bad debts: Assessing China's financial influence in great power politics', *International Security* 34(2), (2009), pp. 7–45.

lender.[58] In fact, its two giant policy banks, the China Development Bank and the Export-Import Bank of China (C-EXIM), already hold more assets than the combined sum of the assets of the West-backed MDBs.[59] For borrowers seeking to avoid the strictures of the Bretton Woods framework, China provides an attractive alternative source of funding. Development finance thus is an area where China could pose credible threats with existing policy tools.[60]

In sum, China's decision to found a new multilateral bank reflects its frustration with the glacial pace of global financial governance reform, which is largely due to the commitment problem associated with the power transition process. China obviously can pose credible threat to contest in the area of development finance where existing structures are insufficient. Because of the U.S. Congress's suspicion of China's future behaviours, the reform process came to a halt. This in turn stimulated China's decision to create the AIIB.[61]

The AIIB as an inside option

While creating the AIIB, Beijing has never ceased its advocacy for reforms of the Bretton Woods institutions. China is still the third largest funder of the ADB, the AIIB's closest competitor, and plays an increasingly active role in the World Bank and the IMF. Chinese officials have continued to request these institutions to fulfil their promise of more realistic representation of developing countries.[62] Beijing is using its new regimes not to replace those existing institutions, but to hedge risks and exert competitive pressure to stimulate reforms. While the adaption of pre-existing financial institutions remains stagnant, the AIIB helps China to pursue its economic goals in a more effective way and to offset the loss from the lack of representation in the Bretton Woods system. This in turn strengthens China's position in promoting reforms of the existing governance structure. The AIIB improves China's inside option in the continued bargaining.

MDBs such as the AIIB have two significant advantages. MDBs can provide economic and regional expertise as well as improved monitoring of project spending, thereby promoting more efficient use of creditors' money. Meanwhile, they also enjoy a degree of autonomy from participating governments.[63] In comparison with other modes of investment, the AIIB's multilateral nature helps ease external suspicions that China is using its growing economic clout to pursue unilateral geopolitical ambitions. It disciplines China's behaviour by tying Beijing's hands to a multilaterally agreed code of conduct, which would help to increase credibility and reduce moral hazard of lending. China is now a net capital surplus exporter. Previous attempts to diversify China's foreign investment portfolio, however, have resulted in sizeable losses.[64] Beijing expects to utilize the lending experience and specialized expertise of its peers

---

[58]Ngaire Woods, 'Whose Aid? Whose influence? China, emerging donors and the silent revolution in development assistance', *International Affairs* 84(6), (2008), pp. 1205–1221.

[59]Rohini Kamal and Kevin Gallagher, 'China goes global with development banks', *Bretton Woods Project*, (5 April 2016), available at: http://www.brettonwoodsproject.org/2016/04/20508/ (accessed 6 August 2017).

[60]Gui Qing Koh, 'Exclusive: China's AIIB to offer loans with fewer strings attached—sources', *Reuters*, (1 September 2015), available at: http://www.reuters.com/article/us-aiib-china-loans-idUSKCN0R14UB20150901 (accessed 6 August 2017).

[61]As an anonymous reviewer points out, it is possible that the frustration of the reform just offered an excuse for China to legitimatize its creation of the AIIB and made the bank attractive and consequently successful. This is an interesting argument. However, although the genuine intention of the Chinese government is difficult to ascertain, it does not challenge the article's argument that the deadlock in reforming the exiting regimes is the key background of the AIIB's creation.

[62]Xiaochuan Zhou, 'IMFC statement by the Honorable Zhou Xiaochuan, Governor, People's Bank of China' *International Monetary Fund*, (11 October 2014), available at: https://www.imf.org/External/AM/2014/imfc/statement/eng/chn.pdf (accessed 6 August 2017); Xiaochuan Zhou, 'IMFC statement by ZHOU Xiaochuan, Governor, People's Bank of China', *International Monetary Fund*, (9 October 2015), available at: https://www.imf.org/External/spring/2015/imfc/statement/eng/chn.pdf (accessed 6 August 2017).

[63]Dani Rodrik, 'Why is there multilateral lending?', *National Bureau of Economic Research Working Paper*, (1995), doi:10.3386/w5160.

[64]'Rich but Rash', *The Economist*, (31 January 2015), available at: http://www.economist.com/news/finance-and-economics/21641259-challenge-world-bank-and-imf-china-will-have-imitate-them-rich (accessed 6 August 2017); James Kyneg and Gabriel Wildau, 'China. With friends like these', *Financial Times*, (17 March 2015), available at: https://www.ft.com/content/2bb4028a-cbf0-11e4-aeb5-00144feab7de (accessed 6 August 2017).

through the AIIB to share risks, reduce moral hazards and increase China's foreign investment efficiency.[65]

The AIIB also helps to promote China's geopolitical interests in a smarter way. The bank was established against the backdrop of a shift in China's strategic orientation, as policymakers sought to improve both the popularity and effectiveness of Chinese overseas investment. In particular, the launch of the AIIB coincided with China's ambitious Belt and Road Initiative (BRI).[66] The BRI serves multiple economic purposes, such as exporting China's economic overcapacity and making efficient use of its abundant foreign exchange reserve.[67] The key political consideration of the BRI is to shift China's geopolitical priority to Eurasia in response to the American 'pivot' to the Asia-Pacific, which Beijing perceives as targeting China.[68] The BRI is also designed to cultivate closer neighbourhood relations and promote Chinese influence through the 'improvement of physical inter-regional connectivity'.[69] While the bank is not created solely for the BRI, an important function of AIIB is to spearhead BRI-related projects.[70]

Reassurance consideration and the AIIB's institutional development

However, other states and the existing international institutional order also influence Beijing's practices. Chinese policymakers have been propelled to adjust their original plans to ease obstructions and attract other states' cooperation. The reassurance consideration in turn shaped the AIIB's institutional configurations.

After the AIIB was proposed in late 2013, Beijing fully mobilized its diplomatic resources to promote the programme. It also developed several institutional features to the bank to attract partners. For instance, Beijing introduced a founding member privilege into the bank's voting system, assigning more power to early birds than to latecomers. In addition, similar to the ADB, the AIIB distinguishes regional members from non-regional members. Finally, all countries, members and non-members alike, are able to bid for projects. The bank also hires staff from non-member countries. These features are designed to increase the bank's attractiveness and inclusiveness.

Nonetheless, the bank still encountered serious suspicions and obstructions. China had attempted to invite Japan and offered the vice president position, but Tokyo showed no interest.[71] Meanwhile, Washington not only openly opposed the AIIB, but also exerted diplomatic pressure on its allies such as Japan, South Korea and Australia to not join the bank.[72] It reiterated several arguments to justify its opposition.[73] One query is whether the AIIB would achieve sufficiently high standards of corporate governance, lending procedure, and environmental and social safeguards.

---

[65]Mikko Huotari and Sandra Heep, 'Learning geoeconomics: China's experimental financial and monetary initiatives', *Asia Europe Journal* 14(2), (2016), pp. 153–71; 'AIIB outbound investment agenda is key to China's economic rebalancing', *South China Morning Post*, (19 May 2015), available at: http://www.scmp.com/comment/insight-opinion/article/1802993/aiib-outbound-investment-agenda-key-chinas-economic (accessed 6 August 2017).

[66]'Vision and actions on jointly building silk road economic belt and 21st-Century maritime silk road', National Development and Reform Commission, (28 March 2015), available at: http://en.ndrc.gov.cn/newsrelease/201503/t20150330_669367.html (accessed 6 August 2017).

[67]Xiao Ren, 'China as an Institution-Builder'; Yong Wang, 'Offensive for defensive: The belt and road initiative and China's new grand strategy', *Pacific Review* 29(3), (2016), pp. 455–63; Hong Yu, 'Motivation behind China's "One Belt, One Road"'.

[68]Robert S. Ross, 'Problem with the Pivot: Obama's New Asia policy is unnecessary and counterproductive', *Foreign Affairs* 91(6), (2012), pp. 70–82; Yong Wang, 'The politics of the TPP are Plain: Target China', *Global Asia* 8(1), (2013), pp. 54–56; Jisi Wang, 'China in the middle', *The American Interest*, (2015), available at: http://www.the-american-interest.com/2015/02/02/china-in-the-middle (accessed 8 January 2017); Ren, 'China as an institution-builder', p. 436.

[69]Bala Ramasamy, Matthew Yeung, and Sylvie Laforet, 'China's outward foreign direct investment: Location choice and firm ownership', *Journal of World Business* 47(1), (2012), pp. 17–25; Yu, 'Motivation behind China's "One Belt, One Road" initiatives and establishment of the Asian Infrastructure Investment Bank.'

[70]Mike Callaghan and Paul Hubbard, 'The Asian Infrastructure Investment Bank: Multilateralism on the silk road', *China Economic Journal* 9(2), (2016), pp. 116–39.

[71]Shintaro Hamanaka, 'Insights to great powers' Desire to establish institutions: Comparison of ADB, AMF, AMRO and AIIB', *Global Policy* 7(2), (2016), pp. 288–92.

[73]The Economist, 'A bridge not far enough'.

[73]Etzioni, 'The Asian Infrastructure Investment Bank'.

Another concern concentrated on the possibility that the AIIB would weaken the enforcement mechanism of existing lending regimes.[74]

The more serious, unstated tension stems from the suspicion that China will use the new bank as a vehicle to project its economic influence in development finance and to pursue geopolitical ambitions.[75] In the eyes of critics, the AIIB also serves as China's strategic ploy to disrupt U.S. global leadership.[76] In particular, critics worried that China would develop its own rules and standards in project lending, thereby undermining the liberal norms underlying the Bretton Woods system.[77] President Obama clearly expressed this anxiety: 'China wants to write the rules for the world's fastest-growing region. That would put our workers and our businesses at a disadvantage. Why would we let that happen? We should write those rules'.[78] As a result, the U.S. government openly obstruct the establishment of the AIIB.

Despite obstruction by the U.S., the AIIB appealed to many other states including traditional U.S. allies. The U.S. containment of the AIIB started to collapse in early March 2015 after the U.K. announced its intention to join the AIIB as a founding member.[79] Germany, France, Italy, Australia, South Korea and Israel soon followed the U.K.'s footsteps to seek founding membership. At the end, 57 countries obtained founding member status at the AIIB. This 'victorious campaign against American-led scepticism' was a pleasant surprise for Beijing.[80] The AIIB also attracted countries from Latin America (e.g. Brazil) and Africa (e.g. Egypt). The bank's diverse membership transformed it from a regional organization into a development bank of global reach and perspective. The more China proves capable of steering the AIIB, the more credible is its threat to tilt the balance of authority away from the existing regimes.

Nonetheless, it is also in Beijing's interest to not have the AIIB collide with the existing order and upset other countries. The rise of China has inspired considerable suspicion but China still benefits from and relies on working within the current international order. Integration into the global economy is indispensable for China's economic growth, which is vital for its domestic stability. Moreover, establishing its credential as a responsible power is important for Beijing to reassure its neighbours and beyond to avoid strategic containment.[81] In general, China avoids actions that directly challenge U.S. hegemony.[82] Noticeably, while arguing that an institutional contest between China and the U.S. is emerging, Chinese officials and scholars also emphasize that such a contest is not a zero-sum game and that Beijing should provide pursue an inclusive and cooperative approach to win political legitimacy.[83]

---

[74]Jane Perlez, 'China creates a World Bank of its own, and the U.S. Balks', *The New York Times*, (4 December 2015), available at: http://www.nytimes.com/2015/12/05/business/international/china-creates-an-asian-bank-as-the-us-stands-aloof.html (accessed 6 August 2017); Etzioni, 'The Asian Infrastructure Investment Bank'.

[75]Steinbock, 'American exceptionalism and the AIIB debacle'.

[76]Fareed Zakaria, 'China's growing clout', *The Washington Post*, (13 November 2014), available at: https://www.washingtonpost.com/opinions/fareed-zakaria-chinas-growing-clout/2014/11/13/fe0481f6-6b74-11e4-a31c-77759fc1eacc_story.html?utm_term=.6d9a8a292c63 (accessed 6 August 2017); Rebecca Liao, 'Out of the Bretton Woods', *Foreign Affairs*, (27 July 2015), available at: https://www.foreignaffairs.com/articles/asia/2015-07-27/out-bretton-woods (accessed 6 August 2017); Robert Kahn and Eleanor Albert, 'A bank too far?', *Council on Foreign Relations*, (17 March 2015), available at: http://www.cfr.org/global-governance/bank-too-far/p36290 (accessed 6 August 2017).

[77]Rebecca M. Nelson, *Multilateral Development Banks: Overview and Issues for Congress*, Congressional Research Service Report R41170 (Washington, DC: Congressional Research Service 2015), pp. 17–18.

[78]Barack Obama, 'Remarks by the President in state of the union address', *Whitehouse.Gov*, 20 January 2015, available at: https://www.whitehouse.gov/the-press-office/2015/01/20/remarks-president-state-union-address-january-20-2015 (accessed 6 August 2017).

[79]'UK support for China-backed Asia bank prompts US concern', *BBC News*, (13 March 2015), available at: http://www.bbc.co.uk/news/world-australia-31864877 (accessed 6 August 2017); Geoff Dyer and George Parker, 'US attacks UK's "Constant Accommodation" with China', *Financial Times*, (12 March 2015), available at: https://www.ft.com/content/31c4880a-c8d2-11e4-bc64-00144feab7de (accessed 6 August 2017).

[80]'The Infrastructure Gap', *The Economist*, (21 March 2015), available at: http://www.economist.com/news/asia/21646740-development-finance-helps-china-win-friends-and-influence-american-allies-infrastructure-gap (accessed 6 August 2017).

[81]Susan L. Shirk, *China: Fragile Superpower* (Oxford: Oxford University Press, 2007).

[82]Robert S. Ross and Feng Zhu, *China's Ascent: Power, Security, and the Future of International Politics* (Ithaca: Cornell University Press, 2008).

[83]Li Wei, *Zhidu zhizhan: Zhanlve jinzhen shidai de zhongmei guanxi* [Struggle for Institutions: Sino-U.S. Relations in An Era of Strategic Competition] (Beijing: Shehui kexue wenxian chubanshe, 2016).

Throughout the construction of the AIIB, Beijing worked hard to ease suspicions and reassure other powers on the new bank's goals and intentions. The multilateral nature of the bank affords China more effective tools to convince other powers than other option could. Over the course of the AIIB's evolution, Beijing made various further adjustments in the bank's institutional configuration. Ever since the AIIB was proposed, people raised questions about the bank's governance, staffing, lending standards, while the Bank was questioned as 'a bank of China, by China and for China'.[84] Beijing has been striving to ease these anxieties, making strenuous efforts to clarify the bank's goal and operational rules.[85] In the face of concerns about China's veto power within the AIIB, both the spokesperson of China's Ministry of Foreign Affairs and the Finance Ministry's chief negotiator for the AIIB declared that 'the issue of China seeking or forgoing the one-vote veto power did not exist'.[86]

Realist sceptics may question these statements as pure rhetoric and suspect that the bank is merely a multilateral cover for Beijing. However, as things turned out, AIIB's member states enjoy significant influence on the bank's developments. At its early start in spring 2015, the AIIB was expected to raise US$100 billion as initial total capital, with China contributing half of the amount. Such a design would give China 50% of the total voting power. However, the bank now has many more member states than Beijing had expected. The U.K.'s decision to become a founding member of the AIIB encouraged other advanced European economies to follow suit. Eventually, the size of the AIIB's founding membership increased from 21 to 57. The unexpected expansion of the AIIB's membership unavoidably diluted China's share and influence. At the end, China's capital share decreased to 30.34% when the bank was set up. Nonetheless, Beijing welcomed this expansion as a diplomatic success which strengthened the bank's legitimacy and credibility.[87]

China temporarily enjoys decisive influence over the AIIB, holding a total voting share around 26%.[88] Since major decisions at the AIIB require a super majority of 75%, Beijing was slightly above the de facto veto level.[89] However, China's dominant influence would decline or even disappear with the AIIB's further expansion. In 2017, the Bank announced the approval of another 27 prospective members, bringing the total approved membership from 57 to 84.[90] As AIIB expects more new and full members in the future, Chinese voting power would be weakened further. Nonetheless, Beijing seems willing to relinquish its de facto veto in support of the bank's matura-tion. In fact, in the negotiation stage, Beijing reportedly offered to forgo its veto power in exchange for Japan's and America's participation.[91] Besides, Beijing has clearly stated that the future pre-sident of the AIIB needs not to be a Chinese citizen. The bank has also been inclined to fill its pay roll with former World Bank and ADB officials.[92] These arrangements help to ease concerns about Chinese dominance in the newly established institution.

During the early stage of the establishment of the AIIB, Chinese officials often linked the AIIB and the BRI together, indicating that the bank would support the implementation of the BRI initiative.[93] Over

---

[84]Takatoshi Ito, 'The future of the Asian infrastructure Investment Bank: Concerns for transparency and governance', *Centre on Japanese Economy and Business, Columbia Business School Occasional Pa*per series 72, (2015), available at: https://doi.org/10.7916/D8WS8SFD (accessed 25 July 2017), p. 3.

[85]'Reversion to the Mean', *The Economist*, (26 September 2015), http://www.economist.com/news/asia/21667964-chinas-new-infrastructure-bank-has-gained-wide-support-lending-will-be-tougher-reversion (accessed 25 July 2017).

[86]Ren, 'China as an Institution-Builder', p. 438.

[87]Lingling Wei and Bob Davis, 'China forgoes veto power at New Bank to Win Key European nations' Support', *Wall Street Journal*, (23 March 2015), available at: http://www.wsj.com/articles/china-forgoes-veto-power-at-new-bank-to-win-key-european-nations-support-1427131055 (accessed 25 July 2017).

[88]Callaghan and Hubbard, 'The Asian Infrastructure Investment Bank', p. 129.

[89]Wei and Davis, 'China forgoes veto power at New Bank to win key European Nations' support.'

[90]'AIIB approves membership of Cook Islands, Vanuatu, Belarus and Ecuador', The Asian Infrastructure Investment Bank, available at: https://www.aiib.org/en/news-events/news/2017/20171219_001.html (accessed 6 January 2018).

[91]Ming Wan, *The Asian Infrastructure Investment Bank: The Construction of Power and the Struggle for the East Asian International Order* (New York: Palgrave Macmillan, 2016), p. 19.

[92]Gregory T. Chin, 'Asian Infrastructure Investment Bank: Governance innovation and prospects', *Global Governance* 22(1), (2016), p. 15; Wan, *The Asian Infrastructure Investment Bank*, pp. 54–55.

[93]Yun Sun, 'China and the evolving Asian Infrastructure Investment Bank', in Daniel Bob, ed., *Asian Infrastructure Investment Bank: China as Responsible Stakeholder* (Washington: Sasakawa Peace Foundation USA, 2015), pp. 27–42.

time, this expression has been toned down as international concerns over Chinese domination grow. To reassure other states, Chinese officials has intentionally created a distance between the AIIB and the BRI since mid-2015. President Jin Liqun has sought on various occasions to clarify China's position that while the Bank would support BRI projects, the AIIB is 'an MDB that must serve the interests of all of its members', and it 'would finance infrastructure projects in all emerging market economies even though they don't belong to the Belt and Road initiative'.[94]

While delinking the AIIB from BRI in the official parlance, Beijing seeks to establish institutional links between the new bank and those established regimes. China repeatedly asserted that the AIIB is complementary to and will cooperate closely with existing multilateral financial institutions. Officials of the ADB and the World Bank have also extended a welcome to the new bank, saying that they will work with the AIIB in providing loans and share their professional expertise.[95] In May 2016, for instance, the AIIB and ADB signed a memorandum of understanding to strengthen cooperation through co-financing, knowledge sharing and joint policy dialogues and consultations.[96] As of December 2017, the AIIB has approved 24 projects, including 16 co-financed with other MDBs—nine with the World Bank Group (including the International Finance Corporation) and five with the ADB.[97] These linkages with existing regimes helped ease suspicions about the AIIB.

Moreover, in response to concerns that the AIIB may not live up to internationally recognized environmental, labour and procurement standards,[98] China made great efforts to prove that the AIIB would rigorously adopt the best practices of established institutions such as the World Bank.[99] In February 2016, the AIIB established its own Environmental and Social Framework.[100] In practice, because most of the AIIB's projects are co-financed with the World Bank and the ADB, these projects also follow their environmental and social standards. This helps the AIIB to appease criticisms and attract more partners.[101]

All of these suggest that, during the AIIB's establishment, Beijing paid great attention to demonstrate its self-restraints and signal its commitment to further international cooperation. Pre-existing institutions and other states have been allowed to shape the AIIB's development. It is in China's interest to create and operate the AIIB in a transparent and open manner so as to alleviate external suspicions. An inclusive approach in turn facilitated the bank's smooth launch[102] The AIIB thus can be described as a multi-function device for Beijing. It reduces China's loss from the lack of voice in pre-existing institutions, allows China to make infrastructure investment where existing regimes cannot meet local demand, alerts established powers that Beijing has viable alternatives if pre-existing institutions remain unchanged, and demonstrates China's self-restraints to appease fears of Chinese domination. All of these serve to enhance Beijing's leverage in promoting faster and deeper reforms of international

---

[94]Nan Zhong and Xiao Cai, 'AIIB leads support for belt and road infrastructure projects', *China Daily*, (8 June 2016), available at: http://europe.chinadaily.com.cn/business/2016-06/08/content_25645174.htm (accessed 25 July 2017).

[95]Matthew Yglesias, 'How a Chinese Infrastructure Bank turned into a diplomatic fiasco for America', *Vox*, (1 April 2015), available at: http://www.vox.com/2015/4/1/8311921/asian-infrastructure-investment-bank (accessed 25 July 2017).

[96]'ADB, AIIB Sign MOU to strengthen cooperation for sustainable growth', *Asian Development Bank*, (2 March 2016), available at: https://www.adb.org/news/adb-aiib-sign-mou-strengthen-cooperation-sustainable-growth (accessed 25 July 2017).

[97]'Approved Projects', Asian Infrastructure Investment Bank, available at: https://www.aiib.org/en/projects/approved/ (accessed 6 January 2018).

[98]Robert Keatley, 'China's AIIB challenge: How should America respond?' *The National Interest*, (18 April 2015), available at: http://nationalinterest.org/feature/americas-big-strategic-blunder-not-joining-chinas-aiib-12666 (accessed 6 August 2017); Weiss, 'Asian Infrastructure Investment Bank'.

[99]'Why China is creating a new "World Bank" for Asia,' The Economist.

[100]'Environmental and social framework', Asian infrastructure Investment Bank, (22 February 2016), available at: http://www.aiib.org/uploadfile/2016/0226/20160226043633542.pdf (accessed 6 August 2017).

[101]Jane Perlez, 'Canada to join China-Led Bank, signaling readiness to bolster ties', *The New York Times*, (31 August 2016), available at: http://www.nytimes.com/2016/09/01/business/international/canada-china-aiib.html (accessed 6 August 2017).

[102]Daniel Bob et al., 'Asian Infrastructure Investment Bank: China as responsible stakeholder?', Sasakawa Peace Foundation USA, (7 August 2015), available at: http://spfusa.org/research/asian-infrastructure-investment-bank-china-as-responsible-stakeholder/ (accessed 6 August 2017).

financial governance structure, alongside many other political and economic interests under-lying the AIIB's creation.

Conclusion

As Ikenberry has suggested, 'China and other emerging great powers do not want to contest the basic rules and principles of the international order; they wish to gain more authority and leadership within it'.[103] In a partially globalized world with nuclear weapons and complex transnational interdependence, institutional contests have become a new form of great power competitions.[104] Through a bargaining framework, this article presents two innovative findings. First, the barrier to institutional reforms lies not only in the credibility of the challenger's threat but also in the commitment problem associated with rapid power shifts. Second, the creation of competitive multilateral regimes could help rising states simultaneously enhance the credibility of their threats and signal cooperative commitments to reassure other states. Both functions are indispensable for the success of the rising powers' advocacy for global institutional reform in the power transition process.

The AIIB's development testifies to the aforementioned mechanisms. As the world's second-largest economy, China believes it deserves more voice in global financial institutions. After Washington blocked Beijing's call for reform due to the strategic distrust of China's future policies, Beijing chose to create parallel institutions such as the AIIB. In the AIIB's inauguration and subsequent evolution, Beijing clearly signalled its self-restraints and commitment to multi-lateral cooperation, a gesture instrumental to reassuring other players and stimulating the reform of established multilateral regimes.

In this sense, the AIIB case gives us both a warning and a hope for understanding the current power shift and institutional change. The warning is that even when space of compromise exists between rising and established powers, mutual distrust could preclude a redistributive adaptation of the global economic governance structure. The good news is that the creation of parallel institutions and their rivalry with existing regimes does not necessarily lead to a strategic clash. If properly managed, a new institution can reveal not only the rising power's strength and resolve but also its self-restraints and commitment to multilateralism. The new institution thus helps induce incremental and peaceful reforms of the existing order. Even a so-called 'authoritarian' rising power like China could benefit from it. If international institutions imply an optimistic prospect of power transition for a declining hegemon, so do they for the rising powers.

Acknowledgments

The authors would like to thank Robert Keohane, G. John Ikenberry, Rosemary Foot, Xiaoyu Pu, Chuyu Liu, Jing Qian and colleagues of the Oxford-Princeton Global Leaders Fellowship Programme for their insightful suggestions on earlier drafts. The authors are also very grateful for anonymous reviewers' pertinent comments. The primary author can be reached by email at chenzhengpku@gmail.com.

Disclosure statement

No potential conflict of interest was reported by the authors.

---

[103]Ikenberry, 'The Future of the Liberal world order', pp. 56–57.
[104]Kai He, *Institutional Balancing in the Asia Pacific: Economic Interdependence and China's Rise* (New York: Routledge, 2009); He, 'Contested Regional Orders and Institutional Balancing in the Asia Pacific'.

Funding

This research is funded by the Oxford-Princeton Global Leaders Fellowship Programme [2016-2018].

6 China's Silk Road Economic Belt Initiative

Network and Influence Formation in Central Asia

Jeffrey Reeves

ABSTRACT

This article demonstrates that, rather than constituting a new model for Central Asian international relations, the SREB's real strategic value for China is as an organizational concept and as an influence multiplier. In recasting its Central Asian bilateral relations as part of the SREB engagement model, Beijing has overlaid a strategic-level concept to its otherwise disparate patterns of engagement. In so doing, the Xi administration has consolidated its multiple lines of efforts and the diverse Chinese-based actors—both state and private—into a grand narrative: one that serves the strategic purpose of integration. The Xi administration has used (and is using) this integration to expand its influence throughout the Central Asian region, both through its bilateral relations and through a SREB-resulting network of Central Asian states. In particular, one sees regular instances within China's SREB engagement where the Xi administration uses the initiative to reconstitute regional states' development priorities, interests and relations in ways that benefit China's overall strategic interests.

This article applies the international relations theory of relationalism to the study of China's SREB relations to demonstrate how the Xi administration has used the initiative to consolidate its state relations and how it has, in turn, leveraged these relations to expand its regional influence. In so doing, the article demonstrates the SREB's strategic value as an influence multiplier for China, in contrast to the Xi administration's claims that the initiative is a model for new Central Asian relations.

Since 2013, the Xi Jinping administration has presented the Silk Road Economic Belt (SREB) initiative to its Central Asian partner states as a new framework for engagement predicated on a five-path approach to cooperation and integration. Conceptually refined over subsequent years, senior Chinese leaders, Chinese ministries and Chinese overseas ambassadors have routinely stressed the initiative's innovative components, arguing, for instance, that the SREB is a paradigm-shifting approach to state relations that is more egalitarian, inclusive and responsive than the existing regional and/or international order. Such rhetoric reached a crescendo in 2017 at the China-hosted Belt and Road Forum (BRF), where President Xi identified the SREB as part of a regionally-based approach to redefine Asia's geopolitics and referenced the initiative with regard to China's growing interconnectivity in Central Asia.[1]

---

[1]'习近平在"一带一路"国际合作高峰论坛圆桌峰会上的开幕'['Xi Jinping opens roundtable discussion on "One Belt, One Road" at the International Cooperation Summit'], *Ministry of Foreign Affairs*, (15 May 2017), available at: http://www.fmprc.gov.cn/web/zyxw/t1461700.shtml (accessed 28 November 2018).

Examination of China's SREB engagement in Central Asia—as defined by China and its partner states—does not, however, reveal an innovative, disruptive approach to China's Central Asian relations. Much of what one sees within China's self-defined SREB engagement in Central Asia, rather, are projects that predate the initiative or patterns of state exchange that are independent from the larger strategic concept, such as trade, investment and/or security relations.[2] While the Xi administration has, to be certain, identified some major infrastructure development projects in Central Asia as wholly related to SREB engagement, actual investment in and construction of such projects remain largely unrealized and/or unfunded in 2017.[3] Applying the SREB as a framework for analysis of Sino–Central Asia relations, rather, one sees repeated attempts by China to employ the initiative as a catchall concept to rationalize engagement and to justify deeper state integration along traditional lines.

This article demonstrates that, rather than constituting a new model for Central Asian international relations, the SREB's real strategic value for China is as an organizational concept and as an influence multiplier. In recasting its Central Asian bilateral relations as part of the SREB engagement model, Beijing has overlaid a strategic-level concept to its otherwise disparate patterns of engagement. In so doing, the Xi administration has consolidated its multiple lines of efforts and the diverse Chinese-based actors—both state and private—into a grand narrative: one that serves the strategic purpose of integration. The Xi administration has used (and is using) this integration to expand its influence throughout the Central Asian region, both through its bilateral relations and through a SREB-resulting network of Central Asian states. In particular, one sees regular instances within China's SREB engagement where the Xi administration uses the initiative to reconstitute regional states' development priorities, interests and relations in ways that benefit China's overall strategic interests.

This article applies the international relations theory of relationalism to the study of China's SREB relations to demonstrate how the Xi administration has used the initiative to consolidate its state relations and how it has, in turn, leveraged these relations to expand its regional influence. In so doing, the article demonstrates the SREB's strategic value as an influence multiplier for China, in contrast to the Xi administration's claims that the initiative is a model for new Central Asian relations.

Relationalism, Networks and Influence in China's SREB Engagement

Relationalism identifies transactional interaction between states as the foundation of their bilateral relations. Contrasting sharply with substantialist theories such as neo-realism, which hold states as primitive and unitary actors, relationalism, rather, argues that state ties are the result of processes, observable at the local or micro-level.[4] These processes, or transactions, subsequently form the basis of state ties, provide the means for bilateral exchange, cooperation and interoperability, and allow for more accurate analysis of changes within state relations.[5] As such, relationalism is a bottom-up approach to understanding state engagement at the bilateral level, albeit with theoretical applications for systemic analysis, as outlined below.

Relationalism informs a methodological approach that employs processual analysis to outline transactional interaction between states. Specifically, relationalist methodology calls for the examination of the processes, configurations, projects and yoking within bilateral relations with the intent of 'mapping' bilateral linkages between states (outlined in Table 1).[6] In doing so, relationalism allows for better understanding of state relations, particularly across which sectors and under which parameters the relations take place. Processes that result in strong configurations between states' security sectors, for instance,

[2]Chen Xiangming, 'China and Central Asia: a significant new energy nexus', *European Financial Review* 4, (2013), pp. 38–42.
[3]Gabriel Wildau, 'China new "Silk Road" investment falls in 2016', *Financial Times*, (10 May 2017), available at: https://www.ft.com/content/156da902-354f-11e7-bce4-9023f8c0fd2e (accessed 28 November 2017).
[4]Patrick Thaddeus Jackson and Daniel H. Nexon, 'Relations before states: substance, process and the study of world politics', *European Journal of International Relations* 5(3), (1999), p. 301.
[5]Daniel H. Nexon, *The Struggle for Power in Early Modern Europe: Religious Conflict, Dynastic Empires, and International Change* (Princeton, NJ: Princeton University Press, 2009), pp. 25–26.
[6]Daniel H. Nexon and Thomas Wright, 'What's at stake in the American empire debate', *American Political Science Review* 101(2), (2007), p. 257.

Table 1. Relationalism: processes, configurations, projects and yoking.

Transaction	Description	Method
Processes	A set of occurrences that produce a change in the existing 'complexion of reality'. Processes are actions, typically undertaken and 'owned' by an actor, which result in a measurable outcome.	Examination of specific SREB interactions between China and its Central Asian partner state on a bilateral case-by-case basis. Identify 'sender' and 'receiver' within process to establish relational linkages. Focus is on micro-level outcomes.
Configurations	A pattern of relations and/or ties. Configurations are, in essence, an aggregation of processes.	Examination of patterns of SREB engagement. Studies as systems of meaning using interpretivist techniques. Focus is on macro-level outcomes resulting from micro-level processes.
Projects	Projects are configurations with actors, such as the individuals, institutions and/or the state. As such, they provide important insight into the nature of the state and the state's interactions. They are also the essential units for change within a system.	Examination of actors undertaking SREB engagement. Consideration of the actor(s) role, identity and agency.
Yoking	A process through which two different sites and/or projects infuse to become a single entity.	Examination of processes, configurations and projects to determine the extent of interconnectivity and/or dependence between states.

Source: Nexon and Wright, 'What's at stake in the American empire debate', p. 257.

demonstrate a pattern of engagement that prioritizes security cooperation. Configurations between states' economic sectors, conversely, suggest the states prioritize the development of economic ties over other types of engagement.

Relationalism's explanatory value is not, however, limited to mapping states' bilateral relations. Building on the foundations of processual analysis, for instance, relationalism outlines a robust account of how dominant states can consolidate dense bilateral relations into larger network structures, particularly when its diverse bilateral relations share enough commonalities to justify collectivization.[7] Specifically, relationalist theory argues that a dominant state can effect network formation through the expansion of bilateral processes to transnational linkages: a process called 'imperial brokering'. Dominant states can, in turn, use their network centrality to drive greater network interconnectivity through processes and configurations aimed at state integration, or yoking. The dominant state's network influence increases concurrent with its network centrality and the network's overall density.[8]

Relationalism accounts for dominant state influence development at both the bilateral and network levels. At the bilateral level, relationalism argues that dominant states gain influence through the establishment and maintenance of dense ties, particularly when the resulting ties are multi-sectoral and asymmetric.[9] Dominant states can leverage these ties to shape their subordinate state's domestic economic, political and security priorities through heterogeneous contracting, thereby effecting subordinate state interest transformation.[10] Interest transformation occurs when a dependent state aligns its interests with its dominant partner, whether unconsciously or purposefully, to the dominant state's benefit (not necessarily to the dependent state's detriment).[11] Notably, the denser the ties between a dominant and secondary state, the more influence the dominant state can exert over the secondary state's domestic and foreign policy-making process.

At the network level, dominant states can develop and effect influence through organization, direction and management of network state relations. Dominant states can use their centrality to establish 'specific rights and obligations' among network states with heterogeneous contracting, thereby gaining control over their intra-network identity and behavior.[12] Similarly, dominant states can use 'binding' strategies to consolidate state relations within the network, giving it the ability to create network 'insiders' and 'outsiders'. Centralized states can influence state network engagement through tactics such as 'divide and rule', which seeks network fragmentation, and 'brokering', which fosters network state engagement, albeit with the central state acting as an intermediary.[13] All such tactics result in varying degrees of dominant state influence over network state relations.

Relationalism informs a powerful framework for analysis of China's SREB engagement; one that provides a multi-sector, multi-level theoretical and methodological means to map its engagement in its totality and to determine areas where the SREB increases Chinese influence. Examination of the processes, configurations, projects and yoking attributed to SREB engagement, in particular, allows one to demonstrate China's use of the SREB as an organizing concept and to deconstruct the initiative's comprehensive engagement to understand more clearly where and how China uses the SREB to maximize its Central Asian influence at the bilateral level. This framework is a marked contrast to the majority of contemporary studies that either over-privilege the initiative's economic components or fixate on the initiative's strategic value through application of substantialist literature.

Relationalism's focus on network formation and network analysis also provides insight into the SREB's value as an overarching organizational concept for China's comprehensive Central Asian engagement.

---

[7]Emilie M. Hafner-Burton, Miles Kahler and Alexander H. Montgomery, 'Network analysis for international relations', *International Organization* 63, (2009), pp. 559–592.

[8]Barry Wellman and S. D. Berkowitz, *Social Structures: A Network Approach* (Cambridge: Cambridge University Press, 1988).

[9]David M. McCourt, 'Practice theory and relationalism as the new constructivism', *International Studies Quarterly* 60, (2016), pp. 475–485.

[10]Emily Erikson and Nicholas Occhiuto, 'Social network and macrosocial change', *Annual Review of Sociology* 43, (2017), pp. 229–248.

[11]François Dépelteau, 'Relational thinking: a critique of co-deterministic theories of structure and agency', *Sociological Theory* 26(1), (2008), pp. 51–73.

[12]Nexon and Wright, 'What's at stake in the American empire debate'.

[13]*Ibid*.

The theory informs a framework for expounding on China's bilateral, micro-level processual engagement to account for its larger regional-level outreach, specifically through the application of observed configurations (patterns of engagement) between the states that encourage multilateral, transnational engagement. Through this application of relationalism to the SREB's study, one gains a greater understanding of the initiative's strategic application as a network unifier as well as its interactive logic.

Relationalism's theory of state influence development also contributes to greater understanding of the Xi administration's strategic application of the SREB and its overall strategic value for Beijing. Specifically, the theory allows one to identify areas within China's bilateral relations where the Xi administration uses the SREB to develop influence and, subsequently, to effect interest transformation. Through processual analysis, in particular, one identifies instances within China's SREB relations where China gains influence over domestic priorities, policies and institutions. Similarly, one sees the Xi administration's use of the SREB to shape transnational ties between states, to establish regional, multilateral priorities and to facilitate a Central Asian SREB network identity based on material and normative conditions (themselves linked to SREB engagement).

The remaining article is divided into three parts. First, it employs processual analysis to study China's SREB engagement with its self-identified 'key' Central Asian partner states of Kazakhstan, Kyrgyzstan, Tajikistan, Turkmenistan and Uzbekistan, and to map the processes, configurations, projects and yoking taking place under the larger SREB framework. The article draws from Chinese official and semi-official statements to identify areas of SREB exchange, both with regard to new areas of engagement and past areas of engagement that the Xi administration has subsumed within the initiative's larger framework. Second, the article outlines areas where SREB engagement has led to multilateral and/or transnational linkages between China and its Central Asian partner states that contribute to a regional network structure. The article specifically looks at configurations to identify areas where SREB interaction transcends integration in purely bilateral terms to take on regional dimensions of interoperability and interconnectedness. Third, the article identifies areas of Chinese influence within its SREB model, within both its bilateral and network relations, to demonstrate the initiative's role as an influence multiplier for Beijing.

Processes, Configurations, Projects and Yoking in China's SREB Engagement

Kazakhstan

The Xi administration uses the SREB to define the primary components of its bilateral relationship with Kazakhstan and to align Kazakhstan's economic development priorities with its own.[14] With regard to the two states' economic relations, Chinese Vice Premier Zhang Gaoli and Kazakh Prime Minister Karim Masimov agreed in 2015 to align Kazakhstan's 'Path of Light' development strategy with the SREB's development priorities to ensure continued 'win–win' bilateral ties.[15] To encourage this policy linkage, President Xi Jinping personally guaranteed the SREB would contribute to Kazakhstan's economic development and forge interconnectedness between the states.[16] One sees this alignment clearly with regard to the two countries' financial sectors as China and Kazakhstan have agreed to deepen their existing currency swap agreements, to establish currency settlement mechanisms, to coordinate payment agreements, and to set up a Chinese–Kazakh Investment Fund, all within the SREB framework.[17] One sees similar alignment and interest transformation in China's use of the SREB to push for greater Chinese involvement in Kazakhstan's domestic infrastructure development. By linking China's provision of foreign direct investment (FDI) to SREB-related projects, such as the 400 hectare China Industrial

[14]Huang Wendi, '习近平访哈萨克斯坦 "一带一路" 再提速' ['Xi Jinping visits Kazakhstan to speed up the One Belt, One Road'], *Global Times*, (8 May 2015), available at: http://world.huanqiu.com/exclusive/2015-05/6377172.html (accessed 28 November 2017).
[15]'China, Kazakhstan agree to integrate growth strategies', *Xinhua*, (26 June 2015), available at: http://news.xinhuanet.com/english/2015-06/27/c_134359830.htm (accessed 28 November 2017).
[16]'China, Kazakhstan vow enhanced cooperation through Silk Road Initiative', *Xinhua*, (27 March 2015), available at: http://news.xinhuanet.com/english/2015-03/27/c_134103608.htm (accessed 28 November 2017).
[17]Chu Yin, '"一带一路"投资政治风险研究之哈萨克斯坦' ['One Belt, One Road investment and political risk research in Kazakhstan'], *China Net*, (19 March 2015), available at: http://opinion.china.com.cn/opinion_14_124814.html (accessed 28 November 2017).

Park near Kazakhstan's Aktau Port, the Xi administration has successfully co-opted Kazakh President Nazarbayev to support the initiative, indeed to pledge his administration's SREB alignment through streamlined approval processes and market access.[18]

The Xi administration also used the SREB initiative to inform the 'Chinese–Kazakh 2020 Long-term Plan for Economic Cooperation' agreement, through which both states committed to expand bilateral trade, to optimize their bilateral trade structure, and to increase the proportion of high value-added and high-tech products included in bilateral trade.[19] China has further identified SREB exchange as the rationale to further develop the Sino–Kazakh free trade area in Altynkol–Huoerguosi, which the Xi administration has called its SREB land gateway to Kazakhstan and Central Asia.[20] China has also called for an expansion of the Altynkol–Huoerguosi border crossing area under the SREB to facilitate cross-border trade, to update customs technology, and to expand infrastructure interconnectedness with Kazakhstan.[21]

The Xi administration has also used the SREB as a mechanism to establish and to expand political linkages with Kazakhstan. In general terms, the states have agreed to increase political coordination, to deepen political trust and to align strategic political interests under the SREB framework, both in support of their bilateral economic exchange and as a standalone effort to facilitate leadership relations. At the 8th Sino–Kazak Cooperative Committee in Astana in 2017, for example, First Deputy Prime Minister Askar Mamin and Vice Premier of the State Council Zhang Gaoli called for increased SREB engagement to enable greater bilateral political engagement and coordination. Askar and Zhang identified the SREB as a mechanism to drive bilateral policy coordination at the state and local levels, to enable economic integration, and to increase 'mutual trust'.[22] Presidents Xi and Nazarbayev further labeled the SREB as a tool to facilitate political integration, to establish high-level exchanges, to consolidate political trust, and to strengthen strategic coordination between China and Kazakhstan at the BRF in Beijing in 2017.[23] Indeed, President Nazarbayev declared that China had become a world 'leader' at the BRF and that Kazakhstan would work to integrate itself more into China's sphere of influence through SREB alignment.[24] More practically, one sees China's use of the SREB to establish political linkages between China's National People's Congress (NPC) and Kazakhstan's parliament. Zhang Dejiang, Chairman of the NPC's Standing Committee, described this process clearly during a 2016 meeting with the Chairman of Kazakhstan's Senate, Kassym-Jomart Tokayev, when he identified the SREB as a framework for legislative engagement, exchange and coordination.[25] Zhang specifically identified a SREB 'cycle' of engagement in which the initiative would lead to greater legislative linkages and these linkages, in turn, would enable greater political coordination on SREB-related development.

The Xi administration is also using the SREB framework to establish cultural, social and education linkages with Kazakhstan. In 2016, for instance, PRC Foreign Minister Wang Yi noted that the Xi

---

[18] 'First China industrial park to be built in Kazakhstan', *Xinhua*, (30 August 2014), available at: http://www.inform.kz/en/first-china-industrial-park-to-be-built-in-kazakhstan_a2692627 (accessed 28 November 2017).

[19] '中华人民共和国和哈萨赫斯坦共和国联合宣言' ['Joint Declaration between the People's Republic of China and Kazakhstan'], *Xinhua*, (19 May 2014), available at: http://news.xinhuanet.com/world/2014-05/19/c_1110761549.htm (accessed 28 November 2017).

[20] '打通"一带一路"上的金融大动脉' ['Open the One Belt, One Road's financial artery'], *Bank of China*, (21 July 2015), available at: http://www.boc.cn/aboutboc/ab8/201507/t20150721_5319635.html (accessed 28 November 2017).

[21] '中哈霍尔果斯国际边境合作中心即将迎来运营5周年' ['China–Kazakhstan Horgos International Border Cooperation Center is about to usher in the fifth anniversary of its operation'], *Xinhua*, (10 April 2017), available at: http://news.xinhuanet.com/silkroad/2017-04/10/c_129528339_7.htm (accessed 27 November 2017).

[22] '张高丽会见哈萨克斯坦总统纳扎尔巴耶夫并主持中哈合作委员会第八次会议' ['Zhang Gaoli meets with Kazakhstani President Nazarbayev and hosts eighth meeting of China–Kazakhstan Cooperation Committee'], *Xinhua*, (19 April 2017), available at: http://news.xinhuanet.com/politics/2017-04/19/c_129548405.htm (accessed 28 November 2017).

[23] '习近平会见哈萨克斯坦总统纳扎尔巴耶夫' ['Xi Jinping meets Kazakh President Nazarbayev'], *Ministry of Foreign Affairs*, (15 May 2017), available at: http://www.fmprc.gov.cn/ce/cedk/chn/zgwj/t1461424.htm (accessed 28 November 2017).

[24] '纳扎尔巴耶夫：中国成为促进国际合作的新"领头人"' ['Nazarbayev: China becomes the new leader in international cooperation'], *Kazinform*, (15 May 2017), available at: http://www.inform.kz/cn/article_a3026398 (accessed 28 November 2017).

[25] '张德江与哈萨克斯坦议会上院议长托卡耶夫举行会谈' ['Zhang Dejiang holds talks with Tokayev, Kazakhstan's upper house of parliament'], *Xinhua*, (7 December 2016), available at: http://www.npc.gov.cn/npc/xinwen/syxw/2016-12/07/content_2003106.htm (accessed 28 November 2017).

administration will use the SREB to facilitate people-to-people engagements and to increase public linkages and public trust.[26] The Chinese embassy in Astana has taken the primary role in such engagement, hosting joint events under the SREB framework aimed at artistic and athletic exchange, for instance.[27] The Xi administration has also used the SREB framework to establish social ties with Kazakhstan through cooperation on science and technology, such as its invitation to Kazakhstan's national space agency to provide an astronaut to undertake a mission on China's spacecraft.[28] With regard to education exchange, China's Ministry of Education established a Silk Road education fund for scholarships and to develop Chinese language learning centers in Kazakh schools to support bilateral relations and to educate students on the SREB.[29]

Lastly, the Xi administration has used the SREB to deepen security relations between China and Kazakhstan, both at the strategic and operational levels. The Xi administration has used the initiative to call for greater coordination between China's People's Liberation Army (PLA) and Kazakhstan's armed forces on peacekeeping and counter-terrorism. Senior leadership from both states have also identified the SREB as a vehicle for security coordination at the tactical level, particularly with regard to drug trafficking, weapons smuggling and border control. To support this local level security engagement, the Xi administration has proposed expanding SREB engagement to include coordination between the two states' respective Ministries of Justice.[30] China and Kazakhstan have also referenced the SREB with regard to cooperation on cyber security, information security, military-technology cooperation and the potential manufacturing of Chinese weapons in Kazakhstan.[31]

Kyrgyzstan

Kyrgyzstan's senior leadership were early proponents of the Xi administration's SREB, arguing as early as 2013 that engagement through the initiative could lead to greater integration between China's and Kyrgyzstan's economies, legislatures and societies.[32] The Xi administration built on this early enthusiasm to push forward with multi-focal SREB outreach aimed at ensuring bilateral alignment between the countries' economic, political and security priorities.[33] Indeed, the Xi administration used the prospect of greater bilateral SREB engagement in 2014 as the primary rationale to revise and deepen the Sino–Kyrgyz 2013 Comprehensive Strategic Partnership Agreement.[34]

---

[26] '王毅与哈萨克斯坦外长伊德里索夫举行会谈' ['Wang Yi holds talks with Kazakhstan Foreign Minister Idrissov'], *Ministry of Foreign Affairs*, (21 May 2016), available at: http://www.fmprc.gov.cn/web/wjbzhd/t1365364.shtml (accessed 28 November 2017).

[27] '"感知中国·哈萨克斯坦行"系列人文交流活动成功开幕' ['China and Kazakhstan successfully implement a series of humanities exchange'], *Ministry of Foreign Affairs*, (29 August 2016), available at: http://www.fmprc.gov.cn/web/zwbd_673032/gzhd_673042/t1392599.shtml (accessed 28 November 2017).

[28] 'Kazakh cosmonaut may fly on China's spacecraft', *Tengri News*, translated by the Open Source Enterprise (OSE), (23 June 2014). The OSE is a United States Government organization dedicated to open-source intelligence that was established by the Office of the Director of National Intelligence; 'Kazakh observers on military cooperation with China', *Kursiv.kz*, translated by the OSE, (24 September 2014).

[29] '驻阿拉木图总领事张伟在"丝绸之路：友谊与合作"中哈留学生招待会上的致辞' ['Almaty Consul General Zhang Wei's message to overseas studies on Silk Road friendship and cooperation'], *Ministry of Foreign Affairs*, (23 November 2016), available at: http://www.fmprc.gov.cn/web/wjdt_674879/zwbd_674895/t1415835.shtml (accessed 28 November 2017).

[30] '司法部部长：扩大交流加强合作为"丝绸之路经济带"建设提供法律服务和保障' ['Minister of Justice: expanding exchanges and enhancing cooperation to provide legal services and guarantees for the construction of "Silk Road Economic Belt"'], *Ministry of Justice*, (31 October 2016), available at: http://www.gov.cn/xinwen/2016-10/31/content_5126458.htm (accessed 28 November 2017).

[31] 'Kazakh president hails outcomes of China visit', *Kazinform Online*, translated by the OSE, (5 September 2016).

[32] '习近平会见吉尔吉斯斯坦议长叶延别科夫' ['Xi Jinping meets with Kyrgyz Speaker Asylbek Jeenbekov'], *Ministry of Foreign Affairs*, (11 September 2013), available at: http://www.fmprc.gov.cn/ce/cgbrsb/chn/zgxw/t1075668.htm (accessed 28 November 2017).

[33] '习近平同吉尔吉斯斯坦总统阿塔姆巴耶夫举行会谈，宣布中吉关系提升为战略伙伴关系' ['Xi Jinping holds talks with Kyrgyz President Atambayev to promote the Sino–Kyrgyzstan relations to a strategic partnership'], *Ministry of Foreign Affairs*, (11 September 2013), available at: http://www.fmprc.gov.cn/ce/cedk/chn/zgwj/t1075591.htm (accessed 28 November 2017).

[34] '华人民共和国和吉尔吉斯共和国关于进一步深化战略伙伴关系的联合宣言' ['Joint declaration of the People's Republic of China and the Kyrgyz Republic on further deepening strategic partnership'], *Xinhua*, (18 May 2014), available at: http://news.xinhuanet.com/world/2014-05/18/c_1110742415.htm (accessed 28 November 2017).

With regard to economic engagement, both the Xi and Atambayev administrations have identified the SREB as a coordination mechanism. In a 2014 speech to the Foreign Affairs Committee of Kyrgyzstan, for example, the Chinese Chargé D'affaires, Wu Changhong, called for both states to use the SREB to establish a 'Silk Road economic zone' based on bilateral trade, mutual investment and joint construction.[35] Kyrgyz President Atambayev agreed to link his economic development priorities to the SREB in 2014; a concession that took concrete form in 2015 when he approve previously disproved plans for Chinese construction of a Sino–Kyrgyz–Uzbek rail line which the Xi administration (retroactively) identified as a SREB priority.[36] Concurrently, Chinese senior leadership used the SREB framework to push for Sino–Kyrgyz cooperation on the construction of a north–south road linking Kyrgyzstan with Kazakhstan, a road encircling Kyrgyzstan's Lake Issyk Ku, highways from Bishkek to Tuer Ga and from Osh to Erkistan, a rail change station in Kyrgyzstan's Naryn Province, and a cross-border economic zone between Naryn and the Xinjiang Uygur Autonomous Region (XUAR).[37]

The Xi and Atambayev administrations have also agreed to employ the SREB framework to expand China's presence in Kyrgyzstan's energy sector. In 2015, for example, the Xi administration provided SREB funding to the Chinese firm Tebian Electric Apparatus (TBEA) to construct a 500 kV power transmission line in Kyrgyzstan, which runs from Datka to Kemin.[38] Chinese firms also received SREB funding to refurbish a thermal power plant in Bishkek and to construct an oil refinery in the state. The Xi administration has pledged an additional US$1.4 billion in SREB funding to construct a gas pipeline that will transit Kyrgyzstan and connect the country into a larger Central Asia gas infrastructure network.[39]

Beijing and Bishkek have also used the SREB framework to establish policy linkages. As early as 2013, both President Xi and President Atambayev identified the initiative as a tool for political integration between the two states' respective leadership and legislatures. Presidents Xi and Atambayev formalized this engagement in 2014, when they referenced the SREB in their joint-statement on deepening strategic relations, which included expanding legislative exchange, political alignment and strategic integration.[40] Chinese Ambassador to Kyrgyzstan, Qi Daoyu, specifically noted in 2016 that political interconnectivity and coordination is a primary goal of China's SREB engagement with Krgyzstan.[41] In a speech to Kyrgyzstan's diplomacy university, Qi also noted that SREB engagement between the two states has resulted in numerous high-level meetings between Presidents Xi and Atambayev, increased political trust between the two states, and policy coordination on foreign and regional affairs at the bilateral level and within multilateral forums, such as the United Nations and the Shanghai Cooperation Organization (SCO).[42]

35 '驻吉尔吉斯斯坦使馆临时代办吴长虹出席"丝绸之路沿线国家的共同发展与繁荣"国际研讨会' ['Wu Changhong, Charge d'affaires in Kyrgyzstan, attended the International Symposium on "Common development and prosperity of countries along the Silk Road"'], *Ministry of Foreign Affairs*, (12 February 2014), available at: http://www.fmprc.gov.cn/chn//pds/gjhdq/gj/yz/1206_13/1206x2/t1216141.htm (accessed 28 November 2017).
36 '吉尔吉斯斯坦总统：全力支持丝绸之路经济带建设' ['Kyrgyzstan President: all-out support for the Silk Road Economic Belt construction'], *The State Information Office of the People's Republic of China*, (29 December 2014), available at: http://www.scio.gov.cn/31773/35507/35510/35524/Document/1527562/1527562.htm (accessed 28 November 2017).
37 'China, Kyrgyzstan ink deals to cement pragmatic cooperation', *Xinhua*, (16 December 2015), available at: http://news.xinhuanet.com/english/2015-12/16/c_134924367.htm (accessed 28 November 2017).
38 'China Kyrgyzstan ties enriched by deepening economic ties', *Xinhua*, (2 November 2016), available at: http://news.xinhuanet.com/english/2016-11/02/c_135800737.htm (accessed 28 November 2017).
39 'Kyrgyzstan cheers rise in China's investment', *Global Times*, (3 November 2016), available at: http://www.globaltimes.cn/content/1015733.shtml (accessed 27 November 2017).
40 '中华人民共和国和吉尔吉斯共和国关于进一步深化战略伙伴关系的联合宣言' ['Joint declaration between the People's Republic of China and the Kyrgyz Republic on further deepening strategic partnership'], *Xinhua*, (18 May 2014), http://news.xinhuanet.com/world/2014-05/18/c_1110742415.htm (accessed 27 November 2017).
41 '驻吉尔吉斯斯坦大使齐大愚就吉总统阿塔姆巴耶夫对华进行国事访问并出席亚信峰会接受吉媒体书面采访', *Ministry of Foreign Affairs*, (14 May 2014), available at: http://www.fmprc.gov.cn/web/ziliao_674904/zt_674979/dnzt_674981/qtzt/ydyl_675049/zwbd_675055/t1156034.shtml (accessed 28 November 2017).
42 '驻吉尔吉斯斯坦大使齐大愚在吉外交学院演讲全文' ['Qi Dayuchi, Ambassador to Kyrgyzstan, to visit China and attend the conference on interaction and confidence-building measures in Asia'], *Ministry of Foreign Affairs*, (16 September 2014), available at: http://www.fmprc.gov.cn/web/gjhdq_676201/gj_676203/yz_676205/1206_676510/1206x2_676568/t1191592.shtml (accessed 28 November 2017).

China also uses the SREB framework to foster closer cultural and education linkages with Kyrgyzstan. The Chinese embassy in Bishkek regularly organizes SREB cultural presentations, for example, that high-light ancient Sino–Kyrgyz Silk Road ties.[43] In 2015, the Xi administration announced the establishment of a five-year SREB scholarship scheme to bring 1,500 Kyrgyz students to study in Chinese higher education institutes and the establishment/expansion of five Confucius Institutes in the country's predominant universities under the SREB framework. The Chinese embassy in Bishkek also identified the SREB as a mechanism for student exchange between the two countries' diplomatic universities; a move that the Xi administration believes will increase personal ties between the two countries' future leadership.[44]

SREB relations between China and Kyrgyzstan also include coordination of military, border security and police forces to act against the 'three forces' of terrorism, separatism and radicalism. Moreover, the SREB has become an important framework between the two states for security coordination, information sharing and joint training.[45]

Tajikistan

In 2014, President Xi published a signed letter in Tajikistan's *Khovar National News Agency*, the predominant state-run media outlet, exhorting China and Tajikistan to establish denser linkages between their economic, political, social and security sectors through SREB cooperation. President Xi also identified Sino–Tajik relations as crucial for the SREB's ultimate success and for wider Central Asian integration and development.[46] The letter preceded President Xi's first-ever official state travel to Tajikistan, where he met with Tajik President Emomali Rahmon and signed a joint declaration on furthering and deepening the two states' existing strategic partnership under the SREB framework.[47] China and Tajikistan formalized this agreement in 2015 by linking the SREB to Tajikistan's 'Three Strategic Goals' development plan and signing a memorandum of understanding (MOU) between China's National Development and Reform Commission (NDRC) and Tajikistan's Ministry of Economic Development and Trade to align the two states' national development goals through SREB engagement.[48]

Since 2014, China has used the SREB framework to expand Chinese investment in and construction of energy-related projects and transportation routes in Tajikistan. With regard to energy development, key SREB projects include the Chinese construction of and investment in the Number 2 Dushanbe thermal power plant, the D line pipeline, which will connect Tajikistan into a larger Central Asian gas and oil pipeline infrastructure system, the TBEA-constructed 500-kV South–North, the 220-kV Lolazor–Khatlon and 220-kV Khujand–Ayni power transmission lines, the Dong Ying Heli Investment and Development Co. Ltd construction of an oil refinery, and the Huaxin Cement Co., Ltd construction of a cement plant.[49] SREB-related transport projects include the Chinese funded and constructed Dushanbe–Khojand–Chanak

[43]'驻吉尔吉斯斯坦大使齐大愚出席中国爱乐乐团丝绸之路比什凯克巡演开幕式' ['Qi Dayu, Ambassador to Kyrgyzstan, attend the opening ceremony of the China Philharmonic Orchestra's Silk Road Bishkek tour'], *Ministry of Foreign Affairs*, (10 August 2015), available at: http://www.mfa.gov.cn/chn//pds/gjhdq/gj/yz/1206_13/1206x2/t1287778.htm (accessed 28 November 2017).

[44]'驻吉尔吉斯斯坦大使齐大愚在吉外交学院演讲全文' ['Qi Dayu, Ambassador to Kyrgyzstan, attend the opening ceremony of the China Philharmonic Orchestra's Silk Road Bishkek tour'], *Ministry of Foreign Affairs*, (16 September 2014), available at: http://www.fmprc.gov.cn/web/gjhdq_676201/gj_676203/yz_676205/1206_676548/1206x2_676568/t1191592.shtml (accessed 28 November 2017).

[45]*Ibid.*

[46]'习近平在塔吉克斯坦媒体发表署名文章' ['Xi Jinping published a signed article in Tajikistan media'], *Ministry of Foreign Affairs*, (7 June 2017), available at: http://www.fmprc.gov.cn/web/ziliao_674904/zt_674979/dnzt_674981/xzxzt/xzxcf0603_689862/zxxx_689864/t1468443.shtml (accessed 27 November 2017).

[47]'习近平同塔吉克斯坦总统拉赫蒙举行会谈 进一步发展和深化中塔战略伙伴关' ['Xi Jinping holds talks with Tajik President Rakhmon to further develop and deepen China–Tajik strategic partnerships'], *Ministry of Foreign Affairs*, (13 September 2014), available at: http://www.fmprc.gov.cn/ce/cedk/chn/zgwj/t1190870.htm (accessed 28 November 2017).

[48]'驻塔吉克斯坦大使岳斌接受塔"阿维斯塔"通讯社专访' ['Yue Bin, Ambassador of Tajikistan, accepts exclusive interview with Tower Avista News Agency'], *Ministry of Foreign Affairs*, (3 February 2016), available at: http://www.fmprc.gov.cn/web/dszlsjt_673036/t1337954.shtml (accessed 2 January 2018); '丝绸之路为塔吉克斯坦提供前所未有历史机遇' ['The Silk Road offers Tajikistan an unprecedented historic opportunity'], *Eurasia Trade Network*, (24 June 2015), available at: http://www.hebi.gov.cn/swj/741681/1164133/index.html (accessed 28 November 2017).

[49]'习近平为"一带一路"奔忙' ['Xin Jinping is One Belt, One Road hustling'], *Ministry of Commerce*, (23 December 2016), available at: http://fec.mofcom.gov.cn/article/fwydyl/zgzx/201612/20161202331370.shtml (accessed 28 November 2017).

highway and Dushanbe–Vahdat–Yovon railway.[50] China has also used the SREB initiative to drive greater financial integration with Tajikistan. The Xi administration used the initiative, for example, to expand and to finance the China Development Bank (CDB) in Tajikistan in order to provide small and medium loans to Tajik farmers and small business owners.[51] At the state level, the Xi administration has used the SREB to establish a currency swap mechanism with Tajikistan through the People's Bank of China (PBoC) and to provide the Rahmon administration with a direct line of credit for economic stabilization.[52] China's Exim Bank, the PBoC, the Agriculture Bank of China and the CDB have all issued concessional and non-concessional loans to the Tajik government to support the country's infrastructure development, such as rail, and to address issues related to poverty reduction through the SREB.[53]

China has also leveraged the SREB to expand political integration with Tajikistan, particularly with regard to leadership engagement, legislative exchange, and domestic and foreign policy alignment. In a 2016 speech to Tajikistan's National University, for example, China's Ambassador to Tajikistan, Yue Bin, identified the SREB as a mechanism for state-level integration, arguing that the initiative has increased interaction between Presidents Xi and Rahmon, enabled bilateral foreign policy alignment and greater integration and exchange between the two states' respective legislatures, and facilitated bilateral political trust.[54] The Xi administration also used the SREB to increase political exchange between China and Tajikistan which has, in turn, led to greater bilateral political integration. In 2015, for instance, Zhang Chunxian, Chinese Communist Party (CCP) secretary to the XUAR, travelled to Tajikistan to sign SREB agreements enabling coordination between the XUAR government and Dushanbe on matters including trade, investment, and counter-terrorism, counter-separatism and counter-radicalization.[55] China and Tajikistan also identified the SREB as a mechanism to streamline coordination between the two states' respective Ministries of Justice, particularly with regard to their 2015 mutual extradition treaty.[56] The Xi administration also employed the SREB framework to justify provision of political and diplomatic 'support' to the Rahmon administration when it held the SCO's rotating presidency in 2014.[57]

The Xi administration has also expanded cultural and education programs with Tajikistan under the SREB framework.[58] In 2015, for instance, the Chinese embassy in Dushanbe and the Tajik Ministry of Culture signed an MOU to expand cultural engagement under the SREB framework with a specific focus on their shared Silk Road past.[59] Such programs include a joint Chinese–Tajik 'Silk Road History' artistic project, an annual Chinese-embassy hosted New Year festival and an annual Silk Road Cultural

[50]'塔吉克斯坦外长：建丝绸之路经济带促塔中实现互利共' ['Tajikistan Foreign Minister: building a Silk Road Economic Belt and mutual benefit for the Tars Tower'], *The State Information Office of the People's Republic of China*, (24 July 2015), available at: http://www.scio.gov.cn/ztk/wh/slxy/31200/Document/1442228/1442228.htm (accessed 28 November 2017).
[51]'中国坚持互利共赢创新丝绸之路经济带金融合作' ['China adheres to mutually beneficial, win–win and innovative Silk Road Economic Belt, financial cooperation'], *State Council Web*, (26 June 2016), available at: http://www.gov.cn/xinwen/2014-06/26/content_2708714.htm (accessed 28 November 2017).
[52]'China, Tajikistan sign currency swap deal to bolster trade', *Xinhua*, (7 September 2015), available at: http://news.xinhuanet.com/english/2015-09/07/c_134598741.htm (accessed 28 November 2017).
[53]'China's share in investment in Tajikistan exceeds 70 per cent', *Ozodagon*, translated from Tajik by OSE, (30 January 2017).
[54]'驻塔吉克斯坦大使岳斌在塔吉克斯坦国立民族大学的讲演' ['Yue Bin, Ambassador of Tajikistan; gives speech to the National University of Tajikistan'], *Ministry of Foreign Affairs*, (6 April 2016), available at: http://www.fmprc.gov.cn/chn///gxh/tyb/zwbd/dszlsjt/t1353459.htm (accessed 28 November 2017).
[55]'Tajikistan, China's Xinjiang to deepen cooperation', *Xinhua*, (21 April 2015), available at: http://news.xinhuanet.com/english/2015-04/21/c_134171270.htm (accessed 28 November 2017).
[56]'China ratifies treaties with Tajikistan, Sri Lanka', *Xinhua*, (7 April 2016), available at: http://news.xinhuanet.com/english/2016-11/07/c_135812160.htm (accessed 28 November 2017).
[57]'Tajik President vows to expand cooperation with China', *Xinhua*, (1 August 2014), available at: http://www.360doc.com/content/14/0802/08/363711_398745921.shtml (accessed 28 November 2017).
[58]'驻塔吉克斯坦大使岳斌邀请塔文化部长奥鲁姆别克佐达做客使馆' ['Yue Bin, Ambassador of Tajikistan, invites Culture Minister to visit the embassy'], *Chinese Embassy, Tajikistan*, (14 June 2014), available at: http://tj.china-embassy.org/chn/sbgx/t1371969.htm (accessed 28 November 2017).
[59]'驻塔吉克斯坦大使岳斌到任拜会塔文化部长奥鲁姆别克佐达' ['Yue Bin, Ambassador of Tajikistan, holds the post of Chief Culture Minister'], *Chinese Embassy, Tajikistan*, (17 December 2015), available at: http://tj.china-embassy.org/chn/sbgx/t1325314.htm (accessed 28 November 2017).
[60]'驻塔吉克斯坦使馆与塔文化部共同举办"欢乐春节"音乐晚会' ['Embassy of Tajikistan and the Ministry of Culture co-host the "Happy Spring Festival" musical party'], *Chinese Embassy, Tajikistan*, (11 January 2017), available at: http://tj.china-embassy.org/chn/sbgx/t1430628.htm (accessed 28 November 2017).

Fair.[60] The Xi administration has also expanded access to Chinese language programs, both in Tajikistan and in China, for Tajik students under the SREB framework. The Chinese embassy in Tajikistan also leverages the SREB to facilitate science and technology education exchange between the two states, both through Chinese investment in Tajik education and through SREB scholarships aimed at Tajik youth.[61]

The Xi administration also aligns its security priorities with Tajikistan through the SREB framework. Both states have undertaken specific SREB alignment, for example, on counter-terrorism joint patrols, training, capacity building, information sharing and border security. Such alignment extends to security policy, as exemplified in a 2016 meeting between Minister of Public Security Guo Shengkun and Tajik Minister of Internal Affairs Rakhimzoda Ramazon Hamro, where the two men agreed to use the SREB as a framework to enhance law enforcement engagement and to transfer Chinese law enforcement technology and equipment to the Tajik police force.[62] SREB security engagement also extends to the two countries' militaries, particularly with reference to increased coordination and joint operations on counter-terrorism, counter-separatism and counter-radicalization related activities. In 2016, for example, the PLA agreed to equip and to train the Tajik military for security operations along the country's border with Afghanistan. The Xi administration further agreed to build border outposts for the Tajik forces to strengthen their forward defenses.[63] China and Tajikistan now also coordinate their law enforcement and military activities with regard to drug trafficking, weapons proliferation and transnational crime.[64] The Xi administration has identified all such security engagement as part of the SREB framework.[65]

Turkmenistan

SREB engagement between China and Turkmenistan has led to a series of bilateral economic agreements, including a five-year plan for economic development coordination and integration signed by both President Xi and President Berdymukhamedov in 2014.[66] Central to that agreement, which President Berdymukhamedov specifically identified as evidence of Sino–Turkmen SREB exchange, is the purposeful linkage of the two states' energy and transport sector development priorities.[67] To advance this coordination, Chinese Vice Premier Zhang Gaoli and President Berdymukhamedov outlined a plan for bilateral engagement on gas production and transportation, all within the SREB framework, in 2014.[68] The two senior leaders agreed for joint development of Turkmenistan's Amu River gas field, which will accelerate construction of Phase 2 of the country's massive Galkynysh gas field, and joint management of A, B and C lines of the China–Turkmen gas pipeline, which link both states into the larger Sino–Central Asian energy infrastructure web. Under the SREB framework, the states agreed to construct line D of the gas pipeline, which came online in 2016, and to discuss opportunities for further energy linkages in support of their energy relations.[69] The Xi administration has also pushed for joint rail development with Turkmenistan under the SREB framework. The China Railway Corporation's linkage of the China–Kazakh rail line into the Kazakh–Turkmen–Iran rail line, for example, has become

[61] '驻塔吉克斯坦大使岳斌会见塔科学与教育部长萨义德' ['Yue Bin, Tajikistan's ambassador, meets the Minister of Science and Education'], *Chinese Embassy, Tajikistan*, (31 December 2015), available at: http://tj.china-embassy.org/chn/sbgx/t1328939.htm (accessed 28 November 2017).

[62] 'China, Tajikistan pledge security cooperation', *Xinhua*, (25 February 2016), available at: http://news.xinhuanet.com/english/2016-02/26/c_135131612.htm (accessed 28 November 2017).

[63] 'China boosts Tajikistan ties, as Russian influence fades', *BBC*, (24 October 2016).

[64] 'Tajikistan, China discuss new cooperation mechanisms to maintain regional stability', *Interfax*, (28 October 2016).

[65] '习近平会见塔吉克斯坦总统拉赫蒙' ['Xi Jin meets with Tajik President Rakhmon'], *Ministry of Foreign Affairs*, (2 September 2015), available at: http://www.fmprc.gov.cn/web/zyxw/t1293285.shtml (accessed 28 November 2017).

[66] '中国土库曼斯坦签署友好合作条约' ['China and Turkmenistan signs friendly cooperation treaty'], *Hubei Ribao*, (13 May 2014), available at: http://news.163.com/14/0513/08/9S44U5EP00014AED.html (accessed 28 November 2017).

[67] 'China, Turkmenistan vow to develop strategic partnership', *Xinhua*, (12 May 2014), available at: http://english.mofcom.gov.cn/article/zt_cicasummit/news/201411/20141100801696.shtml (accessed 28 November 2017).

[68] 'China Turkmenistan cooperation consolidates Central Asian energy corridor', *Xinhua*, (28 August 2014), available at: https://www.naturalgasworld.com/xinhua-china-turkmenistan-cooperation-consolidates-central-asian-energy-corridor-13380 (accessed 28 November 2017).

[69] 'Turkmenistan, China say interested in closer energy ties', *Ministry of Foreign Affairs Press Service*, translated by the OSC, (14 June 2016).

a SREB showpiece development project; the project that links China directly to Turkmenistan and also creates a larger regional rail network which the Xi administration argues will expand regional and extra-regional interconnectivity.[70]

Sino–Turkmen SREB-directed political engagement has, arguably, proceeded even more rapidly than the two states' economic integration. Under the initiative's framework, Turkmenistan has signed provincial 'friendship' agreements with Shandong province, for instance, which have led to an expansion of bilateral delegation visits in support of SREB engagement.[71] Ashgabat has entered into similar arrangements with Gansu province, where representatives from both central and local governments now engage in regularized dialogues on joint development within the SREB framework.[72] In 2016, President Berdymukhamedov also met with the head of the CCP's International Liaison Department, Song Tao, to discuss ways the two states could deepen party and parliamentary exchange and coordination under the SREB framework.[73] Summarizing this political coordination in 2016, Chinese Ambassador to Turkmenistan, Sun Weidong, noted that SREB bilateral engagement has increased senior-level meetings, enabled strategic trust and established strategic alignment between Beijing and Ashgabat.[74] Sun also identified President Xi and President Berdymukhamedov's linkage of the SREB to Turkmenistan's 'Revival of the Ancient Silk Road' plan as an area of bilateral political engagement and political alignment.[75]

In their 2015 joint statement on strategic relations, Presidents Xi and Berdymukhamedov also identified the SREB as a conceptual means to formalize bilateral social activities, including cultural exchange days and art and cultural performances. The two leaders also agreed to use the SREB to expand shared access to their states' respective radio, television and film programming to increase social trust.[76] At the local level, the Chinese embassy in Ashgabat has established a 'Chinese cultural day' under the SREB framework, through which it hopes to raise local awareness of Chinese art and history and to forge ties with Turkmen artists and performers.[77] Presidents Xi and Berdymukhamedov have called for expanded education exchange, joint scientific research, joint vocational training and joint language training for young people as part of the two states' SREB relations. President Xi, in particular, has pledged SREB scholarship funding for Turkmen youth to travel to China for study and exchange.[78]

[70]'中国－哈萨克斯坦－土库曼斯坦－伊朗第一列火车试运行' ['China–Kazakh–Turkmen–Iran trial train operation'], *Chinese Embassy, Turkmenistan*, (15 February 2016), available at: http://tm.mofcom.gov.cn/article/jmxw/201602/20160201255557.shtml (accessed 28 November 2017).
[71]'土库曼斯坦积极参与一带一路战略构想' ['Turkmenistan's active participation in the strategic Belt and Road Initiative'], *Ministry of Commerce*, (11 September 2015), available at: http://cafiec.mofcom.gov.cn/article/c/201511/20151101158880.shtml (accessed 28 November 2017).
[72]'中国和土库曼斯坦讨论交通运输领域合作问题' ['China and Turkmenistan discuss transportation cooperation'], *Chinese Embassy, Turkmenistan*, (28 April 2015), available at: http://tm.mofcom.gov.cn/article/jmxw/201504/20150400954863.shtml (accessed 28 November 2017).
[73]'President of Turkmenistan receives the head of International Liaison Department of the Central Committee of the Communist Party of the People's Republic of China', *State News Agency of Turkmenistan*, (14 June 2016), available at: http://www.turkmenistan.gov.tm/_eng/?id=6013 (accessed 28 November 2017).
[74]'孙炜东大使出席《土库曼斯坦中立政策及国际实践：稳定、发展与合作新成果》研讨会' ['Ambassador Sun Weidong attends seminar on "Turkmenistan's neutral policy and international practice: new results in stability, development and cooperation"'], *Chinese Embassy, Turkmenistan*, (12 December 2016), available at: http://tm.china-embassy.org/chn/xwdt/t1423200.htm (accessed 28 November 2017).
[75]'孙炜东大使就土中立日暨新年接受土国家电视台采访' ['State television interview with Ambassador Sun Weidong on Turkmenistan Independence Day'], *Chinese Embassy, Turkmenistan*, (12 May 2016), available at: http://tm.china-embassy.org/chn/xwdt/t1421511.htm (accessed 28 November 2017).
[76]'中华人民共和国和土库曼斯坦关于建立战略伙伴关系的联合宣言' ['Joint declaration between the People's Republic of China and Turkmenistan on establishing a strategic partnership'], *State Council Information Office, People's Republic of China*, (23 July 2014), available at: http://www.scio.gov.cn/xwfbh/xwbfbh/wqfbh/2015/33608/xgzc33614/Document/1451854/1451854.htm (accessed 28 November 2017).
[77]'中国文化日活动在土库曼斯坦成功举行' ['Chinese Culture Day was successfully held in Turkmenistan'], *Chinese Embassy, Turkmenistan*, (8 August 2015), available at: http://tm.china-embassy.org/chn/ztgx/t1287407.htm (accessed 28 November 2017).
[78]'Joint declaration between the People's Republic of China and Turkmenistan on establishing a strategic partnership'], *State Council Information Office, People's Republic of China*.

Uzbekistan

The Xi administration has identified Uzbekistan as a key SREB partner and argued that its adherence to SREB engagement is essential for the initiative's overall success in Central Asia.[79] Since 2014, President Xi has used the SREB to establish denser linkages between the two states that would allow greater economic and policy coordination.[80] Both Uzbek President Islam Abduganiyevich Karimov, who passed away in 2016, and his successor, President Shavkat Mirziyoyev, pledged to use the SREB to expand Sino–Uzbek bilateral ties.[81] Indeed, China and Uzbekistan's senior leadership signed a SREB cooperation MOU in 2015, through which both states committed to SREB engagement across their respective economic, political, cultural/educational and security sectors.[82]

Central to the two states' SREB economic engagement is rail line development, construction of the Uzbek section (Line D) of the Sino–Central Asian gas pipeline and bilateral trade. With regard to rail development, the Xi administration retroactively identified ongoing rail projects in East Uzbekistan as core components of China's SREB engagement with Uzbekistan in 2014. President Xi specifically identified the China Railway Tunnel Group constructed Kamchiq tunnel—the longest in Central Asia—as a key SREB project. The tunnel links China directly to Uzbekistan via the country's Angren–Pap railway line.[83] Relatedly, the Xi administration also pledged SREB support to modernize Uzbekistan's Soviet-era rail system, widening the country's rail track gauge to regional standards so that it can serve as a regional hub for Chinese integration in Central Asia.

Beijing and Tashkent have also agreed to develop the Line C and D segments of the Sino–Central Asia gas pipeline in Uzbekistan under the SREB framework, a development that would integrate the country into the regional gas pipeline network. The states have also pledged to use the initiative to develop a special economic zone in Uzbekistan's Jizza city, which the China Development Bank will finance through a US$50 million concessional loan.[84] Chinese firms such as Huawei, PetroChina, Peng Sheng and ZTE have also driven SREB investment in the country and contributed to the development of Uzbekistan's telecommunications, information technology and energy industries.[85] As of 2016, China became Uzbekistan's largest source of foreign investment, an outcome President Xi directly attributed to SREB bilateral engagement in a signed letter in Uzbekistan's *Narodnoye Slove* newspaper.[86]

In 2014, the Xi administration pledged to use the SREB to help Uzbekistan improve its governance and state administration in line with China's own political development experience.[87] To this end, the states agreed to employ the SREB framework to expand political dialogue at all levels, to establish mechanisms to coordinate their foreign policies (particularly with regard to regional affairs), and to establish institutional linkages between China's National People's Congress (NPC) and Uzbekistan's Senate and Legislative Chamber.[88] Presidents Xi and Karimov also agreed to establish regular heads

---

[79]'驻乌兹别克斯坦大使孙立杰出席中乌丝绸之路经贸合作论坛' ['Sun Lijie, Ambassador to Uzbekistan, attended the China–Ukraine Silk Road Economic and Trade Cooperation Forum'], *Ministry of Foreign Affairs*, (16 March 2014), available at: http://www.kstq.gov.cn/xwpd/GZTQ/201403/00001891.html (accessed 28 November 2017).

[80]'习近平见乌兹别克斯坦总统：共建丝绸之路经济带' ['Xi Jinping meets Uzbekistan President: building a Silk Road Economic Belt'], *Xinhua*, (20 May 2014), available at: http://www.vtfunds.com/2014-05-20/164965921.html (accessed 28 November 2017).

[81]'在乌兹别克斯坦"遇见"丝绸之路' ['Meet the Silk Road in Uzbekistan'], *Global Times*, (25 June 2017), available at: http://www.yisou.sd.cn/lvyou/content/11024663.html (accessed 28 November 2017).

[82]'中国与乌兹别克斯坦签署共建"丝绸之路经济带"合作文件' ['China and Uzbekistan sign cooperation document on building "Silk Road Economic Belt"'], *Ministry of Commerce*, (17 June 2015), available at: http://www.mofcom.gov.cn/article/ae/ai/201506/20150601014939.shtml (accessed 28 November 2017).

[83]'Chinese company builds 500 m-dollar tunnel in Uzbek east', *Central Asian News Service*, translated by the OSE, (16 July 2014).

[84]'Uzbekistan, China to develop special economic zone in Jizzakh', *Gazette of Central Asia*, (26 January 2013), available at: http://gca.satrapia.com/+uzbekistan-china-to-develop-special-economic-zone-in-jizzakh+ (accessed 28 November 2017).

[85]'Belt and Road Initiative accelerates cooperation between China, Uzbekistan', *Xinhua*, (18 June 2016), available at: http://news.xinhuanet.com/english/2016-06/18/c_135447423.htm (accessed 27 November 2017).

[86]'Full text of Chinese president's signed article on Uzbek newspaper', *China Daily*, (22 June 2016), available at: http://www.chinadaily.com.cn/china/2016-06/22/content_25796225.htm (accessed 28 November 2017).

[87]'Xi Jinping, Uzbek President meet in Shanghai; underscore bilateral cooperation, economic ties', *Xinhua*, (20 May 2014), available at: http://www.fmprc.gov.cn/mfa_eng/topics_665678/yzxhxzyxrcshydscfh/t1158604.shtml (accessed 28 November 2017).

[88]'中华人民共和国和乌兹别克斯坦共和国联合宣言' ['Joint declaration between the People's Republic of China and Uzbekistan'], *Xinhua*, (20 August 2014), available at: http://news.xinhuanet.com/world/2014-00/20/c_1112111669.htm (accessed 28 November 2017).

of state meetings under the SREB's auspices—a policy that continues under President Mirziyoyev.[89] Sino–Uzbek SREB cooperation also formed the basis for the country's 2016 agreement to establish a Comprehensive Strategic Partnership. Indeed, both states specifically referenced SREB engagement as a key rational for formally expanding their existing political coordination and ties.[90] Similarly, the Xi and Mirziyoyev administrations referenced the SREB in their joint 2017 statement, in which both states committed to expand non-economic cooperation such as political exchange.[91]

The Xi administration has also used the SREB to effect 'people diplomacy' (民间外交) with Uzbekistan, particularly with regard to the countries' shared civilizations and common history. In 2017, for instance, Chinese ambassador to Uzbekistan, Sun Lijie, hosted a workshop in Tashkent, where he identified the SREB as an essential mechanism to deepen bilateral cultural exchange and to drive Central Asian regionalization. Sun credited the states' SREB relations with the establishment of such cultural events as the 'Oriental Rhythm' music festival, the Sino–Uzbek 'cultural week', the Sino–Uzbek 'film week' and the annual Chinese New Year celebration in Tashkent. Sun called for further bilateral SREB cultural align-ment though joint education, research and communication through the two countries' universities and non-governmental organizations.[92] Specific to the issue of education, the Chinese Embassy in Tashkent provided SREB-related funding for Chinese language learning in Uzbekistan's universities (through Confucius Centers) and secondary schools. As of 2016, China provided over 300 SREB scholarships to Uzbek students to study in Chinese universities.[93] In 2016, Ambassador Sun identified education as a means to develop Silk Road 'values' between the two states, aimed at deepening engagement, social trust and a shared community of common interest.[94]

SREB and Regional-Level Integration

In addition to its bilateral relations, the Xi administration also uses the SREB to drive regional-level integration between China and its Central Asian partners (and between the Central Asian states them-selves), both in material and ideational terms. One observes this tendency in patterns of behavior (configurations) that conflate SREB exchange with multilateral engagement and transnational state ties.[95] The Xi administration has propagated the concept of a SREB 'zone', for instance, through which it seeks to yoke Central Asian states together through an infrastructure web and a supranational system of economic and political alignment.[96] The Xi administration has funded and constructed transnational

89'孟建柱同阿齐莫夫举行中乌政府间合作委员会双方主席会晤' ['Meng Jianzhu holds presidents meetings with Azimov on China–Ukrainian Intergovernmental Cooperation Committee'], *Xinhua*, (28 April 2017), available at: http://news.xinhuanet.com/politics/2017-04/28/c_1120892107.htm (accessed 28 November 2017).

90'中华人民共和国和乌兹别克斯坦共和国联合声明' ['Joint statement between the People's Republic of China and the Republic of Uzbekistan'], *Xinhua*, (22 June 2016), available at: http://news.xinhuanet.com/world/2016-06/22/c_1119094471.htm (accessed 28 November 2017).

91'中华人民共和国和乌兹别克斯坦共和国关于进一步深化全面战略伙伴关系的联合声明' ['Joint statement of the People's Republic of China and Uzbekistan on further deepening the comprehensive strategic partnership'], *Ministry of Foreign Affairs*, (12 May 2017), available at: http://www.mfa.gov.cn/mfa_chn//ziliao_611306/1179_611310/t1461149.shtml (accessed 28 November 2017).

92'驻乌兹别克斯坦大使孙立杰在"民间外交在丝绸之路发展中的作用"圆桌会议上的致辞' ['Statement by Ambassador Sun Lijie to Uzbekistan at a round table on the role of civil diplomacy in the development of the Silk Road'], *Ministry of Foreign Affairs*, (25 January 2017), available at: http://www.mfa.gov.cn/web/dszlsjt_673036/t1433903.shtml (accessed 28 November 2017).

93'驻乌兹别克斯坦大使孙立杰接受"中国媒体丝路行"记者采访' ['Sun Lijie, ambassador to Uzbekistan, interviewed by reporters from China Silk Road'], *Ministry of Foreign Affairs*, (10 June 2014), available at: http://www.fmprc.gov.cn/web/ziliao_674904/zt_674979/dnzt_674981/qtzt/ydyl_675049/zwbd_675055/t1163870.shtml (accessed 28 November 2017).

94'驻乌兹别克斯坦大使孙立杰在"丝绸之路普世价值观与民族价值观：语言、教育、文化"学术研讨会上的发言' ['Statement by Sun Lijie, Ambassador of Uzbekistan, to the Symposium on "Universal values and ethnic values of the Silk Road: language, education and culture"'], *Ministry of Foreign Affairs*, (27 May 2016), available at: http://www.fmprc.gov.cn/web/gjhdq_676201/gj_676203/yz_676205/1206_677052/1206x2_677072/t1367133.shtml (accessed 28 November 2017).

95'与中国共建丝绸之路经济带：中亚国家一马当先' ['Building the Silk Road Economic Belt with China: Central Asian countries take the lead'], *State Council Information Office*, (26 February 2015), available at: http://www.scio.gov.cn/ztk/dtzt/2015/33995/34002/34016/Document/1463774/1463774.htm (accessed 28 November 2017).

96'习近平重回丝绸之路经济带首倡地 开启" 一带一路 " 新篇章', *Belt and Road Portal*, (6 June 2017), available at: https://www.yidaiyilu.gov.cn/xwzx/roll/15317.htm (accessed 28 November 2017).

rail, highways and gas pipelines (described in detail above) throughout Central Asia, for example, in support of the SREB zone, arguing that doing so increases Central Asian states' interconnectedness and interoperability. The Xi administration has also used the SREB zone concept to drive regional-level political consultation and alignment between China and its Central Asian partners, building on its bilateral SREB linkages to establish formal and informal multilateral mechanisms for policy integration.[97] Through this process, the Xi administration has framed the SREB as a mechanism for Central Asian unification structured around Chinese economic and political leadership.[98] The result is a more integrated Central Asia network based on SREB exchange and predicated on Chinese centrality.

The Xi administration has also used the SREB framework to co-opt existing multilateral forums, such as the Shanghai Cooperation Organization (SCO), and, in so doing, to redefine state engagement within those institutions. One sees the Xi administration's use of the SREB in this respect in its repeated calls for greater interoperability and policy alignment between SREB and SCO participating states.[99] This push for integration is clearest with regard to threat perception, security cooperation, security interoperability and joint training at the bilateral and multilateral levels.[100] Notably, the Xi administration's appeals for SREB/SCO policy and engagement alignment do not typically extend to greater Russian involvement, but rather focus on the desirability for expanded engagement between China, its Central Asian partners and the Central Asian states themselves. As such, one discerns that Beijing's appeal for policy alignment is more about influence maximization (on which more is written below) than about strengthening the SCO.

The Xi administration has also used the SREB to appeal for a Central Asian-based 'Silk Road Spirit' (丝路精神), a concept predicated on the multilateral acceptance that greater political, cultural and/or educational interconnectivity is desirable.[101] Central to this formulation is the Xi administration's contention that China and its Central Asian partners share a common historical identity they can draw on to justify and to advance SREB engagement. This historical identity includes shared cultural and ethnic linkages based on a (imagined) community of Silk Road traders, artists and peoples. The SREB's Silk Road Spirit has clear multilateral, regional-level applications as it appeals to a historical and contemporary identity predicated on transnational interconnectedness and interoperability. As such, the Silk Road Spirit provides a normative overlay to the SREB's more material aspects.

Relationalism and Chinese Influence in the SREB

One gains greater insight into the Xi administration's use of the SREB through application of a relationalist framework to its study. Through examination of the SREB's processes, for instance, one sees evidence that the Xi administration uses the SREB framework to justify increased multi-sector exchange with its bilateral partner states. Far from serving an entirely economic purpose, as many contemporary studies would suggest, processual analysis demonstrates the initiative's wide scope for engagement, including political, social and security exchange. One observes similar outcomes through consideration of configurations, or patterns, in China's SREB engagement. As demonstrated above, for instance, the Xi administration's SREB outreach results in configurations of economic, political, social and security exchange between China and each of its Central Asian partners, to varying degrees. One similarly

---

[97]Han Lu, '丝绸之路经济带在中亚的推进：成就与前景' ['Xi Jinping back to Silk Road Economic Belt Initiatives to start a new chapter of the "Belt and Road"'], *China Institute of International Studies*, (16 May 2017), available at: http://www.ciis.org.cn/gyzz/2017-05/16/content_9484045.htm (accessed 28 November 2017).

[98]'习近平：同中亚国家共建"一带一路"' ['Xi Jinping: building "the Belt and Road" with Central Asian countries'], *Caixin*, (23 June 2016), available at: http://www.caixin.com/2016-06-23/100957543.html (accessed 28 November 2017).

[99]'苏晓晖："一带一路"与上合组织互为动力' ['Su Xiaohui: "Belt and Road" and the SCO mutual drive'], *Belt and Road Portal*, (13 June 2017), available at: https://www.yidaiyilu.gov.cn/ghsl/gnzjgd/15985.htm (accessed 28 November 2017).

[100]'上合组织经贸合作势头良好 成员国积极推进与"一带一路"对接' ['The SCO Economic and Trade Cooperation member countries actively promote linkage with the Belt and Road Initiative'], *Belt and Road Portal*, (6 July 2017), available at: https://www.yidaiyilu.gov.cn/xwzx/hwxw/15431.htm (accessed 28 November 2017).

[101]'习近平：传承丝路精神' ['Xi Jinping: inheritance of Silk Road spirit'], *Xinhua*, (15 May 2016), available at: http://news.xinhuanet.com/politics/2017-05/16/c_1120982090.htm (accessed 28 November 2017).

observes a 'whole of government' application of the initiative through examination of SREB projects, as Chinese actors involved in SREB exchange range from state-owned organizations and Chinese embassies to Chinese artists, universities and student groups. Similarly, through the application of a relationalist framework, one sees the Xi administration's use of the SREB to effect yoking, both in material and ideational terms, through its joint development projects and through the alignment of its partner states' domestic policies with the SREB.

Further, relationalism provides a theoretical lens for determining how the Xi administration's SREB engagement results in Chinese influence. One sees clear examples of heterogeneous contracting in the Xi administration's SREB engagement, for example, where it gains influence over it partner states' domestic development priorities through purposeful alignment of the SREB's core concepts with their economic and political development programs. SREB heterogeneous contracting further enables the Xi administration to gain influence over its partner states' security priorities, to expand its 'Strategic Partnership' relations in Central Asia, and to facilitate local, state and regional level SREB linkages between state and non-state actors. Indeed, viewed in line with heterogeneous contracting, one sees that the SREB has become the Xi administration's primary tool to influence transformation in Central Asia, by which it uses incentives to bring its Central Asian partner states' domestic priorities in line with its own.

Relationalism also provides a theoretical foundation to understand China's use of the SREB to facilitate regional integration, as described above, and to identify avenues of Chinese influence development within the resulting network. One sees, for instance, the Xi administration's purposeful use of the SREB to effect physical interconnectivity at the regional level, which serves the purpose of linking its Central Asian partner states into a Sino-centric infrastructure web that forms the material foundation of a regionally-based network structure. The Xi administration also uses the SREB to drive policy alignment and to overlay a normative network component—the Silk Road Spirit—that further integrates China into Central Asia on its own ideological terms. The end result is greater Sino-centric regionalization, where China largely dictates the terms of bilateral and multilateral engagement while encouraging interdependence and interconnectivity between states.

There are examples of both binding and brokering in China's regional-level application of the SREB. The Xi administration uses the initiative, for example, to consolidate its engagement in Central Asia, both past and present, under a single unifying concept. In so doing, China binds its Central Asian partners into a regional structure predicated on Chinese interests and Chinese power, both of which are essential to realize for the structure's continued 'win–win' viability. While China's influence consolidation and development in Central Asia is not specific to the SREB—rather the result of continued engagement in the region since the 1990s—the Xi administration's initiative framing increases China's value among its partner states as it presents China as operating a regional grand strategy based on long-term logic. Coupled with the Xi administration's commitment to resource allocation through trade, security provisions and educational scholarships, the SREB allows China to present a more unified, coordinated approach than other great powers actors—such as Russia and the United States—operating in the region at the current time. The Xi administration has leveraged its increased SREB prestige to increase in network centrality in Central Asia.

Through this centrality, China has gained regional influence as a regional broker; one, in particular, with a comprehensive plan for regional development and enrichment that it formulates and controls. Through this position, China is able to create bilateral and multilateral conditions for Central Asian states' SREB engagement, thereby endowing itself with the ability to choose network 'insiders' and 'outsiders'. As such, Beijing is able to dictate, to an extent, the terms of its bilateral relations and state interaction at the regional level. Such centrality directly results in widespread influence of the self-propagating kind. As China increases its centrality through SREB brokering, its ability to broker, as such, becomes more acute.

Conclusion

The Xi administration's SREB initiative does not constitute as innovative a break from China's past patterns of foreign engagement in Central Asia as Beijing routinely claims. Rather, the concept provides an overarching framework for China's Central Asian engagements that is organizationally innovating and, as a result, strategically valuable. Specifically, Beijing has used the SREB to reconstitute its economic, political, security and social exchange with its Central Asian partners so as to construct a regional grand strategy through which it gains influence within its multilateral and bilateral relations. This construct applies to past patterns of engagement as well as future processes and projects identified as part of the SREB framework. Governments from Kazakhstan, Kyrgyzstan, Tajikistan, Turkmenistan and Uzbekistan have embraced the SREB as a means to justify greater engagement with China and to receive increased resource allocation through the scheme.

This understanding of the Xi administration's use of the SREB and of the initiative's potential to maximize Chinese influence becomes clearer through the application of a relationalist framework to China's Central Asia relations. The approach provides a theoretical and methodological framework for viewing China's SREB engagement in its totality, in contrast to other contemporary studies that take a more parochial approach. Relationalism also provides important insight into the SREB's function as an influence maximizer for the Xi administration and, as such, allows for a more detailed account of the initiative's strategic value for Beijing than currently available.

Disclosure statement

No potential conflict of interest was reported by the author.

7   The Domestic Politics of the Belt and Road Initiative and its Implications

Baogang He

ABSTRACT

Within the Belt and Road Initiative literature, as well as in the media more broadly, geopolitical and geostrategic analyses have largely undervalued a role for domestic politics analyses. This article seeks to redress this deficiency, and supplements geopolitical analyses with a domestic politics perspective. It brings back the centrality of domestic politics. The domestic politics approach pays attention to the influence of personal leadership on the BRI and focuses on the political mobilisation and control mechanisms of the BRI, their impact and the various entanglements of international relations and domestic politics.

In recent years, China's 'Belt and Road Initiative' (BRI) has become a topical subject within numerous disciplines, perhaps none more so than International Relations. The unprecedented scale and scope of the BRI is indicative of China's growing ambition and budding global pretensions. The nomenclature of belt and road refers to the overland corridors that will connect Western China with Europe via Central and South Asia (the Silk Road Economic Belt), and the maritime routes that are intended to link China's southern provinces to Southeast Asia and beyond (the twenty-first-century Maritime Silk Road).[1] While the Chinese government continues to attempt to frame the BRI purely in economic-opportunity 'win-win' terms, it has nevertheless elicited a wide range of geopolitical and geostrategic analyses. To date, however, geopolitical and geostrategic analyses have largely undervalued a role for domestic politics analyses.

The economic corridors and maritime nodes of BRI[2] connect China with developing and developed economies in a way that positions China at the world's economic centre-of-gravity.[3] The BRI is intended to perform the infrastructure-exporting function as a means to open 'new markets, generate demand for higher value-added Chinese goods and help ... China build globally competitive industries.'[4] In contrast to Japan in the 1980s, China's economic strength does not derive from technological leadership or regionalised production networks for consumer products[5] —rather, due to almost four decades of rapid domestic industrialisation on a massive scale, China's

---

[1]Peter Cai, *Understanding China's Belt and Road Initiative* (Sydney: Lowy Institute, 2017), p. 2.

[2]The six economic corridors of the BRI are the New Eurasian Land Bridge, and the economic corridors of China-Mongolia-Russia; China-Central Asia-West Asia; China-Indochina; China-Pakistan; and Bangladesh-China-India-Myanmar; as well as the maritime pivot points that link them. See Geoff Wade, 'China's "One Belt, One Road" initiative', *Parliament of Australia*, Parliamentary Library Briefing Book.

[3]Christopher K. Johnson, *President Xi Jinping's 'Belt and Road' Initiative* (Washington, D.C.: Centre for Strategic and International Studies, 2016), p. 2.

[4]Thomas Vien, Kevin Yan and Robin Blackburn, "The Grand Design of China's New Trade Routes," *Stratfor Worldview*, 24 June 2015, available at: https://worldview.stratfor.com/article/grand-design-chinas-new-trade-routes (accessed 24 August 2017)

[5]See Baogang He, *Contested Ideas of Regionalism in Asia* (London: Routledge, 2016).

comparative advantage lay in infrastructure development and construction. Dams, highways, electricity generation and high-speed rail are to contemporary China what televisions, computers and automobiles were to 1980s' Japan. By emphasising a complementarity between China's exportable know-how and the infrastructure needs of developing countries, the BRI presents an opportunity for the Chinese to utilise their vast foreign currency reserves (China held $1.2 trillion in bonds in August 2017) in an ostensibly magnanimous fashion.[6]

Of course, there is more to the BRI than the official economic narrative, and many analysts—especially in the West—remain wary of what they consider as Beijing's ulterior geopolitical and geostrategic motivations. Theresa Fallon deciphers the BRI as a Chinese attempt to consolidate previously distinct interests and initiatives—like the Asian Infrastructure and Investment Bank (AIIB) and 'March West'—together into 'one mega-foreign policy project.'[7] Indeed, it would be foolish to assume that China would *not* seek to expand its geopolitical influence commensurate to its rising economic clout—they are sides of the same coin.[8] Two factors in particular speak to the geopolitical and geostrategic logic of the BRI. First, many BRI routes conspicuously bypass the maritime chokepoints that China has hitherto (by necessity) relied upon American naval capability and benevolence to secure, with the China-Pakistan Economic Corridor's circumvention of the Malacca, Sunda and Lombok Straits, being a case in point.[9] Second, several BRI initiatives traverse regions of political volatility, meaning that security challenges remain significant, and their potential to incur costs high. The dearth of Chinese investment, and the ubiquity of state-owned enterprises (SOEs) involvement in such ventures,[10] again underlines the subordination of economic logic to political rationale with many BRI projects.

Within the BRI literature, as in the media more broadly, the above geo-economic and geopolitical arguments tend to dominate discussion. What has often been omitted from the BRI analyses, especially in the English-speaking world, is a comprehensive appraisal of the role that domestic Chinese politics plays in shaping BRI implementation except Hong Yu, Shichen Wang, Xinyi Yang and David A. Parker, Adrian Raftery, Jessica Batke and Matthias Stepan whose works have been cited throughout in this article. This article seeks to redress this deficiency. It supplements geopolitical analyses with a domestic politics perspective, examining the interaction between domestic politics and the BRI, while also taking into account the various entanglements of international relations and domestic politics.

The role of domestic politics has often been debated in the international relations literature. It is common practice to use domestic structure as a variable in explaining foreign policy. However, domestic structure itself stems from the pressures of international relations. Thus, Peter Gourevitch's thesis, in 'The Second Image Reversed,' focuses on how types of international regimes, institutions, coalitions, and policies, in particular those pertaining to international economics and military rivalry, shape domestic politics.[11] However, the debate on whether international relations determine domestic politics or the other way around is unproductive. Robert D. Putnam thus proposes a 'two-level games' method to study the entanglements of domestic and international politics, offering several insights concerning central decision-maker attempts to reconcile domestic and international imperatives, the paradox of strengthening their influence as decision-makers at home but weakening their international

[6]Michael D. Swaine, 'Chinese Views and Commentary on the "One Belt, One Road" Initiative', *China Leadership Monitor* 47, (2015), p. 3.
[7]Theresa Fallon, 'The New Silk Road: Xi Jinping's Grand Strategy for Eurasia', *American Foreign Policy Interests* 37, (2015), p. 140.
[8]Hong Yu, 'Motivation behind China's "One Belt, One Road" Initiatives and Establishment of the Asian Infrastructure Investment Bank', *Journal of Contemporary China* 26(105), (2017), p. 356.
[9]Vien, Yan and Blackburn, 'The Grand Design of China's New Trade Routes'.
[10]Kate Hannan and Stewart Firth, '"One Belt One Road": China's Trade and Investment in Pacific Island States', ISA Asia-Pacific Conference 2016 Hong Kong, *International Studies Association*, p. 11, available at: http://web.isanet.org/Web/Conferences/AP%20Hong%20Kong%202016/Archive/72aa134d-b73e-4a8d-9dcf-d9fc8adf9f96.pdf (accessed 19 July 2017).
[11]Peter Gourevitch, 'The Second Image Reversed. The International Sources of Domestic Politics', *International Organization* 32 (4), (1978), pp. 881–912.

bargaining position, and vice versa, and the strategic uses of uncertainty about domestic politics as a means to bargain in international negotiation.[12]

Located in the above intellectual context, this article brings back the centrality of domestic politics. The domestic politics approach pays attention to the influence of personal leadership on the BRI and focuses on the political mobilisation and control mechanisms of the BRI, their impact and the various entanglements of international relations and domestic politics. An understanding of the impact of Chinese personal leadership on the BRI and the BRI's mobilisation and control mechanism can help us to understand the interactive nature of international relations and domestic politics regarding the BRI. It can enrich geopolitics analysis and even highlight some intellectual blind spots of geopolitics analysis. Since the early reform period, the international system has shaped Chinese domestic players. Now, with the rise of China, it has become a turning point, at which Chinese domestic players start to shape the regional and/or international system and influence the domestic politics of the BRI recipient countries. It is therefore urgent that we study the interactive domestic politics of China and the BRI recipient counties, and the entanglements of domestic and international politics. While this article does not examine these interactive politics directly, it provides an opportunity for a more thorough examination of interactive politics, and it is hoped this article will prove a starting point for others to carry out such research.

The article has four sections. The first one provides an examination of the bearing of individual leadership on the BRI hegemonic project. The second investigates the CCP's organisational structure and decision-making processes vis-à-vis BRI, in particular the mobilisation of the BRI at the ministerial, provincial and SOE levels. The third section analyses China's management of dissent, both in its ability to exert control domestically, but also the attempts made to manage opposition extraterritorially. And the fourth discusses the impact that these domestic factors have had, considering a number of effects of the interactions and influences in the process of implementing the BRI. The article is based on a literature survey, interviews, and seven fieldworks in Australia, Malaysia, Bangladesh, Myanmar and China in 2016–2018.

Xi Jinping in command

While it is well known that in all political systems the role of political leaders is paramount, this is especially so in the authoritarian system in China, as embodied in and epitomised by Xi Jinping's command. The BRI is an ambitious project reflecting his ambitious style of leadership, his China Dream and his vision of new Sino-empire building.[13]

Xi launched the Silk Road Economic Belt and the twenty-first-century Maritime Silk Road in 2013. Before 2013, the Ministry of Foreign Affairs involved infrastructure diplomacy. In particular, in ASEAN countries, the central economic agencies proposed a Chinese version of the Marshall Plan to increase investment in overseas infrastructure, and Chinese security specialists proposed the 'China goes west' to rebalance maritime Asia and Eurasia continental diplomacy.[14] In this context, Johnson argues against the BRI as a grand scheme formulated by Xi, insisting it is the result of an evolutionary and ongoing internal Chinese foreign policy. According to this logic, while Xi's strategic vision will likely evolve or be altered once he is gone, elements of it are likely to persist.[15]

---

[12]Robert D. Putnam, 'Diplomacy and Domestic Politics: The Logic of Two-Level Games', *International Organization* 42(3), (1988), pp. 427–460.

[13]Please see Chinese expanded perceptions of region, Baogang He, 'Chinese Expanded Perceptions of the Region and Its Changing Attitudes toward the Indo-Pacific', *East Asia: An International Quarterly* 35, (2018), pp. 117–132.

[14]Wang Jisi, 'Toward West: China's Geostrategic Rebalance,' *Global Time*, 17 October 2012, available at: http://opinion.huanqiu.com/opinion_world/2012-10/3193760.html (accessed 9 April 2016).

[15]Johnson, *President Xi Jinping's 'Belt and Road' Initiative*, p. 3; Matt Ferchen, "How New and Crafty is China's 'New Economic Statecraft?' Carnegie-Tsinghua Center for Global Policy, 22 March 2016, available at: http://carnegieendowment.org/files/How_New_and_How_Crafty_is_Chinas_New_Economic_Statecraft_CTC_Web_Version.rd.pdf (accessed 14 July 2017).

While the BRI is indeed the product of an evolutionary and ongoing Chinese economic foreign policy, it is directly under the leadership of Xi, who has coordinated and centralised all efforts of different governmental agencies. The BRI adopts an ambitiously holistic approach that aggregates industry, investment, aid, trade, security and foreign policy. More a conceptual framework than a rigidly-defined label,[16] the BRI is what Tim Summers calls an 'omnibus programme' that 'support[s] a growing range of [different government level] policy goals, from the economic and commercial to the political and social.'[17] It has been applied to various infrastructure projects and investment initiatives—including those not strictly along the 'belt' or the 'road.'

Like Jiang Zemin's 'Theory of the Three Represents,' or Hu Jintao's 'Scientific Outlook on Development,' Xi has advocated 'BRI as the signature foreign policy theme of his leadership tenure and the practical embodiment of his "China Dream."'[18] In contrast to earlier pillars of Chinese strategy that prioritised *regional* Asian engagement and leadership—such as ASEAN Plus Three[19]— the BRI represents an expansion of Beijing's strategic imagination that extends *globally*. In this way, Xi Jinping's foreign policy vision can be conceived as the latter bookend to Deng Xiaoping's 'hide and bide' approach. Underpinning this shift is a desire to construct, both figuratively and literally, Beijing's own hybrid global production networks and trade routes. These developments, in aspiration and endeavour, signal a Chinese transformation from 'world factory' to 'world builder' and Chinese 'alternatives within or to international order.'[20]

The bearing of personal leadership on the BRI must be seen as a power game in Chinese politics. The BRI provided a unique opportunity for Xi to concentrate, extend, and legitimate his power. As a grand project, the BRI requires substantive power to achieve its goal, thus it has helped Xi to pick up the pace with which his concept of the 'China Dream' and the BRI are to be seen to have 'attained the status of party and state dogma.'[21] Xi Jinping's thoughts on neo-socialism with Chinese characteristics for the new age was written into the 19th Party Constitution in his second term. This is illustrative of his centralisation and consolidation of foreign policy-making power.[22]

The BRI enabled Xi to extend his power beyond the normal two terms limit set up by Deng Xiaoping. Early in 2012, Xi insisted on including phrasing that cited China's *long*-term struggle in the 18th Party Congress, implying that long-term leadership would ensure long-term policy stability in order to win the battle in a long-term struggle. The Official report of the 19th National Congress of the Chinese Communist Party mentions the BRI five times and offers further incentive for the General Secretary to spruik his leadership credentials and consolidate power.[23] The successful implementation of the long-term BRI project offers a strong justification to abandon the two-term rule, which was finally achieved in the Constitutional revision in March 2018.

More importantly, the BRI granted Xi greater external legitimacy when he was on the central stage of the BRI Summit in May 2017, attended by 29 heads of state and 60 representatives of international organisations. Following the Chinese traditional concept of legitimacy, such an attendance can be interpreted as a symbol of restoring the centrality of China's power. Arguably, this external perspective of legitimacy plays a more role than that of electoral democracy in the

[16]Adrian Raftery, 'Many Belts, Many Roads: How China's Provinces Will Tweak a Global Project,' *The Diplomat*, 4 February 2017, available at: http://thediplomat.com/2017/02/many-belts-many-roads-how-chinas-provinces-will-tweak-a-global-project/ (accessed 18 July 2017).

[17]Tim Summers, 'China's "New Silk Roads": sub-national regions and networks of global political economy', *Third World Quarterly* 37(9), (2016), p. 1639.

[18]Johnson, *President Xi Jinping's 'Belt and Road' Initiative*, p. v.

[19]Rosemary Foot, 'Chinese strategies in a US-hegemonic global order: accommodating and hedging', *International Affairs* 82(1), (2006), pp. 85–86.

[20]Summers, 'China's "New Silk Roads"', p. 1638.

[21]Willy Lam, 'Xi Jinping's Ideology and Statecraft', *Chinese Law and Government* 48(6), (2016), p. 409.

[22]Shichen Wang, 'Xi Jinping's Centralisation of Chinese Foreign Policy Decision-Making Power', *East Asian Policy* 9(2), (2017), pp. 34–42; Hong Yu, 'Motivation behind China', p. 356.

[23]Paul Haenle, 'Xi's Vision for China's Belt and Road Initiative,' *Carnegie-Tsinghua Center for Global Policy* 9 May 2017, available at: http://carnegietsinghua.org/2017/05/09/xi-s-vision-for-china-s-belt-and-road-initiative-pub-69890#5 (accessed 31 August 2017).

Chinese politics of legitimacy[24]; and this should be taken seriously to understand the politics of BRI in China.

Xi's BRI demonstrates intrinsically top-down, hierarchical processes whereby the leadership provides the strategic impetus, and the Party and State then work hard to implement it.[25] There is no equivalent of US congressional hearings or approval within the Chinese political system— such as the soliciting of congressional support required of President Truman to enact the Marshall Plan.[26] Compared to those of liberal democracies, China's foreign policy mechanisms can appear intricate and almost obscure, and lack transparency.[27] Yet this lack of transparency and public accountability should not be conflated with a lack of consultation, coordination or planning. With respect to the BRI, consultative behind-the-scenes dialogue would have been a primary reason for the interlude between the initial BRI announcements in 2013, and the next substantive statement a year later.[28]

Often the BRI is said to be a state-led project; more precisely, in the Chinese context, it is the Party that makes a final saying. The preponderance of Party members within the foreign policy-making apparatus demonstrates the Party's paramount role. That the People's Liberation Army (PLA) is an armed wing of the Party is an obvious manifestation of this.[29] Specific to the BRI, this preference for Party was observed during a period when Russia was concerned over China's penetration into what it saw as its traditional Central Asian 'sphere of influence.' To allay Russian concerns, Xi sent an emissary to meet Putin personally—his de facto chief of staff and Politburo member Li Zhanshu. This assigning of an apparatchik to what many would conventionally assume to be the role of a senior diplomat speaks volumes to 'Xi's party-centric approach to BRI.'[30]

The politics of BRI mobilisation

The impetus for the BRI is to mobilise all resources and coordinate activities politically, economically and financially and ideologically. It has developed in such a way that it is the largest-scale economic and strategic development in human history.

BRI leading small group

There is an identifiable body that wields considerable influence in matters of foreign policy decision-making—namely the relevant Leading Small Groups (LSGs). More broadly, LSGs play an advisory role, 'functioning both as coordination mechanisms for different state and Party interests, and as bodies to implement central directives.'[31] It is ad hoc in origin, and varies in influence according to the ranks of their commissioning body and senior member.[32] This is pertinent in the case of foreign policy LSGs, who are all headed, directly or by proxy, by Xi Jinping.[33] The LSG for

[24]Regarding legitimacy issue, see Baogang He, 'Legitimacy in Deng's Era in China: A Critical Re-appraisal', *Journal of Communist Studies and Transition Politics* 7(1), (1991), pp. 20–45; Baogang He, 'Legitimation and Democratization in a Transitional China', *Journal of Communist Studies and Transition Politics* 12(3), (1996), pp. 315–342.
[25]David Arase, 'China's Two Silk Roads Initiative: What it Means for Southeast Asia', *Southeast Asian Affairs* (2015), p. 26.
[26]Diane B. Kunz, 'The Marshall Plan Reconsidered: A Complex of Motives', *Foreign Affairs* 76(3), (1997), pp. 166–167.
[27]Hong Yu, 'Motivation behind China', p. 355.
[28]Regarding the long tradition of Confucian consultation and its impact on Chinese politics, see Baogang He, 'Deliberative Culture and Politics: The Persistence of Authoritarian Deliberation in China', *Political Theory* 42(1), (2014), pp. 58–81.
[29]Linda Jakobson and Ryan Manuel, 'How are Foreign Policy Decisions Made in China?', *Asia and the Pacific Policy* Studies 3(1), (2016), p. 99.
[30]Johnson, *President Xi Jinping's 'Belt and Road' Initiative*, p. 24.
[31]Jakobson and Manuel, 'How are Foreign Policy Decisions Made in China?', p. 101.
[32]For an informative interactive graph of LSGs and their Party and State members, see Jessica Batke and Matthias Stepan, 'Party, State and Individual Leaders: The Who's Who of China's Leading Small Groups,' *Mercator Institute for China Studies*, available at: https://www.merics.org/en/merics-analysis/china-mapping/the-whos-who-of-chinas-leading-small-groups/ (accessed 30 August 2017).
[33]Jakobson and Manuel, 'How are Foreign Policy Decisions Made in China?', p. 101.

Advancing the Development of the Belt and Road Initiative (hereafter BRI LSG), created in 2015 to oversee, coordinate and implement BRI, is no exception.[34]

It is noteworthy that of the five BRI LSG members, only one, State Councillor Yang Jiechi, is directly involved in foreign policy, being tasked with the management of BRI-related foreign suspicions and diplomatic tensions.[35] Heading the group, and with a focus on industry and finance, was senior Politburo member and Executive Vice Premier Zhang Gaoli. Vice Premier Wang Yang oversees trade and commercial engagement; politburo member Wang Huning assumes his familiar Public Relations role in crafting and integrating the overall BRI message; and Yang Jing is in charge of party-state BRI coordination.[36] Currently this group is under a reshuffle. Yang Jing is no longer a member after he faced a corruption charge in 2018. Vice Premier Han Zheng is now the head of the BRI LGS.

The BRI LSG coordinates the different primary interests of a diversity of state organisations and aims to address the criticism of the lack of an effective leadership structure, or its absence of a unified strategy.[37] It can be seen to project an image of global Chinese economic accomplishment and prestige domestically, that in turn delivers satisfaction to the populace, and insures against regime instability. The office of BRI's LSG is located in the National Development and Reform Commission (NDRC).

The Ministerial Mobilisation

At the Ministerial level, the NDRC, the Ministry of Foreign Affairs, and the Ministry of Commerce serve as the core mobilisation bodies for BRI—reflected not only by their co-leading role of the BRI, signifying the importance ascribed to BRI.[38] In 2015 three organisations jointly released an authoritative vision and action plan document.[39]

As is to be expected with an initiative of the magnitude of BRI, its successful realisation will require a comprehensive approach that spans multiple ministries. Due to different ministerial specialisations, interests and functions, BRI mobilisation is not a uniform action. Instead, each ministry has a BRI action plan tailored to meet specific, relevant objectives. For instance, the Ministry of Culture's action plan prioritises the improvement of cultural exchange and co-operation mechanisms, the promotion of BRI as a cultural exchange 'brand,' and the cultivation of cultural industry and trade along the BRI routes.[40] Likewise, the Ministry of Education's 2016 action plan commissions ten overseas science research institutions, and around five-hundred BRI think-tanks and research centres. It also establishes a Belt and Road Scholarship committed to sponsoring fifty-thousand BRI-partner state students to study in China by 2021, as well as a reciprocal seventy five hundred Chinese students to study in BRI countries by 2019.[41] Countless protocols, agreements, memoranda of understanding and other documents have also been signed between Chinese

---

[34]Xinyi Yang and David A. Parker, 'Buckling Down: How Beijing is Implementing its "One Belt, One Road" Vision,' *Centre for Strategic and International Studies*, CogitAsia Blog, 7 May 2015, available at: https://www.cogitasia.com/buckling-down-how-beijing-is-implementing-its-one-belt-one-road-vision/ (accessed 29 August 2017).

[35]Richard Q. Turcsanyi, 'BRI's Older Brother: Lessons Learned from the China-CEE 16 + 1 Platform,' *IAPS Dialogue*, 19 July 2017, available at: https://iapsdialogue.org/2017/07/19/BRIs-elder-brother-lessons-learned-from-the-china-cee-161-platform/ (accessed 27 July 2017).

[36]Johnson, *President Xi Jinping's 'Belt and Road' Initiative*, p. 19.

[37]Hong Yu, 'Motivation behind China', p. 363.

[38]Johnson, *President Xi Jinping's 'Belt and Road' Initiative*, p. 19.

[39]'Vision and Actions on Jointly Building Silk Road Economic Belt and 21st-Century Maritime Silk Road,' *Ministry of Foreign Affairs of the People's Republic of China*, 28 March 2015, available at: http://www.fmprc.gov.cn/mfa_eng/zxxx_662805/t1249618.shtml (accessed 31 August 2017).

[40]"Ministry of Culture's Action Plan for Belt and Road Cultural Development (2016–2020)," *HKDTC Research*, 28 December 2016, available at: http://china-trade-research.hktdc.com/business-news/article/The-Belt-and-Road-Initiative/Ministry-of-Culture-s-Action-Plan-for-Belt-and-Road-Cultural-Development-2016-2020/obor/en/1/1X000000/1X0A9K2A.htm (accessed 31 August 2017).

[41]'China's new scholarship to sponsor students from Belt and Road Initiative nations,' *Xinhua News*, 11 August 2017, available at: http://news.xinhuanet.com/english/2016-08/11/c_135587410.htm (accessed 31 August 2017).

Ministries and official foreign entities.[42] A very important institute in this regard has been the International Liaison Department of Chinese Communist Party of China that has coordinated international think tanks, and organised the CCP-World Political Parties Dialogue Summit in Beijing in 2017 (30 November–3 December), which was attended by approximately 300 parties from 120 countries.

Provincial Mobilisation

Perhaps the most interesting dynamics of BRI mobilisation occurs at a provincial level, especially given the perceptible disparity between the extant, and initially enunciated roles of particular provinces. One of the founding motivations for the BRI was the need to consolidate China's west and south-western provinces; the idea being to make them new engines of economic growth that could stimulate the next phase of Chinese development.[43] The BRI is hoped to finally deliver on Beijing's 'western development strategy'—an initiative commenced in 1999 that has generated few tangible results, despite significant fiscal injections, state-directed investment and preferential policies. Other factors considered by Beijing as consequences of poverty and underdevelopment, like the enduring Uighur separatist movement in Xinjiang, also provide impetus for the BRI.[44] Hence, the official designation of target provinces: Xinjiang as 'a core area on the Silk Road Economic Belt,' Fujian as 'a core area of the twenty-first-century Maritime Silk Road,' Guanxi as 'an important gateway connecting' the Belt and Road, and Yuanan as 'a pivot of China's opening-up to South and Southeast Asia.'[45]

As it has materialised, however, it has become clear that BRI has deviated in practice from the original plan. First, of the abovementioned provinces, only Fujian rated among the top five in a study that indexed BRI provincial participation rates. Xinjiang, conversely, has hitherto played a minor role and is yet to live up to expectations. Second, after being initially overlooked, China's wealthier eastern coastal provinces lobbied for, and were successful in securing inclusion within the larger BRI framework.[46] This point relates to the third, namely, the deliberate and sufficiently ambiguous official language of the BRI that affords provincial-level officials 'interpretative leniency' in implementing policy. As with departmental priorities, each province has different needs and objectives, and longstanding moribund or underfunded local projects with dubious connections to improving trade connectivity are often 'lumped under the BRI banner.'[47] While this utilisation of local policy frameworks and practices may well increase the chances of successful BRI implementation,[48] it will nevertheless produce a BRI *distinct* to that originally envisaged by the central leadership.

The case of Guangdong Province is illustrative in this respect. Between 2003 and 2007, the Province contributed more than fourteen per cent to China's total GDP; its crucial role as a maritime node likewise reflected in 2012 through its generation of over a fifth of China's total maritime production.[49] Having attained this success as a designated 'special economic zone' during

---

[42]For a comprehensive list, see 'List of Deliverables of the Belt and Road Forum for International Cooperation,' *China Daily Europe*, 16 May 2017, available at: http://europe.chinadaily.com.cn/china/2017-05/16/content_29359530.htm (accessed 31 August 2017).

[43]Shashi Tharoor, 'China's Silk Road Revival—and the Fears It Stirs—Are Deeply Rooted in the Country's History', *New Perspectives Quarterly* 32(1), (2015), p. 19.

[44]Cai, *Understanding China's Belt and Road Initiative*, pp. 6–7.

[45]'Vision and Actions on Jointly Building Silk Road Economic Belt and 21st-Century Maritime Silk Road,' *National Development Reform Commission, People's Republic of China*, 28 March 2015, available at: http://en.ndrc.gov.cn/newsrelease/201503/t20150330_669367.html (accessed 20 April 2018).

[46]François Godement et al., '"One Belt, One Road": China's Great Leap Outward', *European Council on Foreign Relations China Analysis*, (2015), p. 10.

[47]Raftery, 'Many Belts, Many Roads'; Johnson, *President Xi Jinping's 'Belt and Road' Initiative*, p. 23.

[48]Summers, 'China's "New Silk Roads"', p. 1634.

[49]Sumie Yoshikawa, 'China's Maritime Silk Road Initiative and Local Government', *Journal of Contemporary East Asia Studies* 5(2), (2016), p. 85.

China's reform and opening-up, the provincial government was understandably keen to replicate it under the auspices of the BRI. Accordingly, the Guangdong party standing committee formulated a BRI implementation and participation plan that was endorsed by the BRI's LSG in June 2015.[50] Guangdong has since been at the vanguard of BRI promotion,[51] ranking first in the provincial BRI participation index. It has demonstrated innovation in organising international fora, and establishing city-to-country links with Pacific Island states, as well as replicating a Singaporean scheme of hosting and training officials and professionals from BRI participant countries.[52] Guangdong's existing infrastructure, and its prior experience as an engine of Chinese growth, has enabled it to adeptly exploit the opportunities afforded by the BRI. For local actors, geopolitical objectives might not be their primary consideration; however, the way in which each city in Guangdong province is designated to link to one individual country in the Pacific, does have geo-political consequences.

The rivalry between provinces is a driving force for China's evolving BRI project, making it much bigger in scope. The grandiosity of the BRI—more specifically, the large sums of funding it makes accessible—has incited competition between 'provinces aiming to justify Silk Road-related projects, or to attract more investment to their areas.'[53] This intensifying provincial competition for preferential BRI policies—such as Yunnan and Guangxi's competing claims to be China's gateway to Southeast Asia[54]—again emphasises the sub-national dimension of BRI.[55] A caveat is appropriate here, in that it is still relatively early days for an initiative projected to continue for decades—there is, of course, plenty of time to pass before BRI could be genuinely judged a success or failure. Nevertheless, the above clearly demonstrates how provincial level Chinese politics can impact upon centrally-led government programs and policy, underscoring the deficiencies of analyses that depict China as a unitary actor.

The SOE Mobilisation

Another type of BRI mobilisation occurs at the SOE level, and is characterised by a twin dynamic of rationale and utility. On the one hand, China's 'new normal' of single-digit economic growth presents an overcapacity challenge to several 'smokestack industries' configured to the old growth model—industries typically associated with Chinese SOEs.[56] This conundrum forms part of the *economic rationale* for the BRI, which is intended to unlock other, non-domestic avenues of consumption by way of addressing regional infrastructural deficits. In emanating from China, this supply-based, 'build it and they will come'[57] approach differs to the original Silk Route, which instead arose organically from regional demand.[58]

On the other hand, given the instability and risk synonymous with many BRI-participant countries and regions, private Chinese companies are unwilling to assume what they deem an unacceptable burden. Answerable to the State (and in many cases the Party), SOEs thus have a *political utility*—and can be leveraged by government as the proverbial tip of the BRI spear, often in pursuit of non- or semi-economic objectives. The problem with this variety of 'going global' is that in subordinating fiscal logic to geopolitical calculation, China could end up negating the very

[50]'Guangdong's Implementation Plan for Participating in the Belt and Road Initiative,' *Guandong News*, 24 June 2015, available at: http://www.newsgd.com/gdnews/content/2015-06/04/content_125729632.htm (accessed 1 September 2017).
[51]'Belt and Road Initiative injects new impetus into Guangdong,' *Xinhua News*, 26 May 2017, available at: http://www.chinadaily.com.cn/business/2017-05/26/content_29510763.htm. (accessed 1 September 2017).
[52]The interview with Guangdong's think tank in August 2017.
[53]Summers, 'China's "New Silk Roads"', p. 1634.
[54]Hong Yu, 'Motivation behind China', p. 363.
[55]Summers, 'China's "New Silk Roads"', p. 1631.
[56]Alvin Cheng-Hin Lim, 'Africa and China's 21st Century Maritime Silk Road', *The Asia-Pacific Journal* 13(10:1), (2015), p. 3; Gabriel Wildau, 'China's state-owned zombie economy,' *Financial Times*, 1 March 2016, available at: https://www.ft.com/content/253d7eb0-ca6c-11e5-84df-70594b99fc47 (accessed 1 September 2017).
[57]Joshua Eisenman and Devin T. Stewart, 'China's New Silk Road is Getting Muddy,' *Foreign Policy*, 9 January 2017, available at: http://foreignpolicy.com/2017/01/09/chinas-new-silk-road-is-getting-muddy/ (accessed 1 September 2017).
[58]Godement *et al.*, 'One Belt, One Road', p. 13.

economic benefits the BRI was ostensibly intended to confer. The China Export-Import Bank, established with a mandate and model that 'cover[ed] costs, without necessarily making a profit'[59] is a noteworthy manifestation of this. It also ties into the long-running debate as to the profitability and efficiency of China's SOEs,[60] more specifically, whether or not it is wise to continue investing in low-return and high risk projects.[61] This is especially pertinent given that private companies had a return on assets over double that of SOEs in 2014.[62] Commercial Chinese banks, concerned by the financial viability of BRI projects, have tended to be much more stringent in their lending—making only perfunctory contributions aimed at appeasing the Government.[63]

China does derive benefits from using SOEs in this way. Following the devaluation of the renminbi in 2015, brought on by the Shanghai and Shenzhen stock market fiasco, there were large outward flows of capital from China. Beijing responded by imposing stricter capital regulations, and scrutinising large private foreign transactions. The logic behind this move has been surmised as follows: 'State-owned assets, whether in China or abroad, are still state assets. But when private entrepreneurs take their money out, it's gone. It's no longer something that China can benefit from or the Chinese government can get a handle on.'[64] Put another way, the intrinsic value of SOEs is that they are controllable entities that can be relied upon to toe the State and Party line—they can be deployed with effect overseas to implement China's 'global pork-barrelling.'[65] This is not to say economic logic is completely disregarded—SOEs could not all operate indefinitely at-a-loss—but to highlight the role political considerations play in their deployment and utilisation.

Take for example the China COSCO Shipping Group. With the world's fourth largest container fleet, and projected 2020 status as the foremost global terminal operator, COSCO has been a major BRI player. Its 2009 concession agreement to control port Piraeus in Greece has been held up as an example of how BRI should be implemented.[66] For the Greeks, the deal has contributed over half-a-billion US dollars in tax and income, creating 2000 local jobs. Similarly, the port has climbed from the ninety-third to the thirty-ninth port in the world in terms of container capacity.[67] For Beijing, such success is advantageous in that it burnishes the credentials of the BRI, and by extension, China itself. But for the SOE involved, this political success has not materialised economically. During 2011 and 2012, COSCO lost 10 billion and 9 billion yuan, respectively; between 2013 and 2015 it remained profitable only through government subsidies and the sale of shares and assets, and in 2016 it again posted a 10 billion yuan loss.[68] Yet despite this, as of mid-2017 COSCO had either secured, or was poised to commit to new BRI-related investments in Kazakhstan, Spain, the Netherlands, Hong Kong, Greece and the United Arab Emirates—many of them 'large-scale investments [that] could further hurt ... [COSCOs] financial health.'[69]

[59]Vivien Foster et al, Building Bridges: China's Growing Role as Infrastructure Financier for Sub-Saharan Africa (Washington DC: The International Bank for Reconstruction and Development, 2009), p. 55.

[60]Gao Xu, 'State-owned enterprises in China: How profitable are they?' The World Bank: East Asia and Pacific on the Rise, 3 February 2010, available at: http://blogs.worldbank.org/eastasiapacific/state-owned-enterprises-in-china-how-profitable-are-they (accessed 1 September 2017).

[61]Godement et al., 'One Belt, One Road', p. 2.

[62]Wildau, 'China's state-owned zombie economy'.

[63]Peter Cai, Understanding China's Belt and Road Initiative (Sydney: Lowy Institute, 2017), p. 14.

[64]Wade Shepard, 'Xi Jinping To China's Private Sector: Go Home, The New Silk Road Is Not For You,' Forbes, 25 July 2017, available at: https://www.forbes.com/sites/wadeshepard/2017/07/25/xi-jinping-to-chinas-private-sector-go-home-the-belt-and-road-is-not-for-you/#794829ee17fb (accessed 1 September 2017).

[65]Scott Cendrowski, 'Inside China's Global Spending Spree,' Fortune, 12 December 2016, available at: http://fortune.com/china-belt-road-investment/ (accessed 23 July 2018).

[66]Wade Shepard, 'These 8 Companies Are Bringing The "New Silk Road" To Life,' Forbes, 12 March 2017, available at: https://www.forbes.com/sites/wadeshepard/2017/03/12/8-new-silk-road-companies-that-you-can-invest-in/#36a8711f4db9 (accessed 2 September 2017).

[67]Susanna Su, 'Risky Business: Financing "One Belt, One Road",' Foreign Brief, 23 August 2016, available at: https://www.foreignbrief.com/asia-pacific/china/risky-business-china-standard-obor-financing-model-unpacked/ (accessed 23 July 2018)

[68]Sun Lizhao and Song Shiqing, 'COSCO Returns to Profit as Shippers Survive Year Adrift,' Caixin Global, 8 July 2017, available at: http://www.caixinglobal.com/2017-07-08/101112091.html (accessed 2 September 2017).

[69]Daisuke Harashima, 'Cosco leading China's "Belt and Road" drive,' Nikkei Asian Review, July 15, 23 July 2017, 2018, available at: https://asia.nikkei.com/Business/AC/Cosco-leading-China-s-Belt-and-Road-drive (accessed 23 June 2018).

This trade-off between politics and profitability has long been a defining characteristic of China's brand of state capitalism. By default, China's SOE investment decisions are subject to political considerations, given that the Party derives its legitimacy from the delivery of sustained economic prosperity.[70] Indeed, despite the supposed failure of state-led economies at 'the end of history,'[71] state management of the Chinese economy remains endemic, with it playing various initiating, leading, dictating, coordinating and negotiating roles. According to Bremmer, the costs of state capitalism include increased production expenditures and added market inefficiencies, as well as high-level corruption.[72] The benefits, at least from the perspective of the State, stem from the transferral of 'increasingly large levers of economic power and influence to [a] central authority.'[73] This allows the State to steer the country's economic course via mechanisms that either direct SOEs, or coerce or persuade private enterprises to acquiesce to government directives.[74] The growing popularity of the 'Beijing Consensus,' stemming from the contrasting trajectories of stuttering liberal market economies and China's tenacious state-economic model post-2008, suggest that other states see merit in this approach.[75]

The politics of managing dissent

Managing domestic control

The above mobilisation strategies and channels generate serious problems which are liable to domestic criticism. To ensure the success of the BRI and that the leader's vision be implemented, the Party/State has established control mechanisms to deal with the domestic criticism of the state-led project. Control mechanisms deal with ideas and dissidents, while mobilisation is about resources. Both are the two sides of one 'BRI coin.'

Beijing's management of domestic BRI dissent is not dissimilar from its approach to intramural opposition more generally. For one, the Chinese State has focused on controlling and shaping the BRI discourse. Kejin Zhao argues that China's leaders place a lot of emphasis on their discursive power, predominantly as a means to 'cast as illegitimate the "China Threat Theory,"'[76] and project a more amenable image of China internationally. Given that China is a one-party state that lacks electoral accountability, it has a vested interest in shaping and controlling the BRI discourse, especially considering the centrality of the BRI to President Xi's overarching strategy.

One particularly blunt example of this tactic was the moratorium on academic conferences pertaining to the BRI in China prior to the official May 2017 summit—a development experienced firsthand by this author. This is characteristic of the Chinese government's attempts to delineate the parameters of acceptable BRI academic enquiry. For instance, the Government's standardisation of terminology—essentially proscribing the usage of 'strategy' and replacing it with 'initiative'—is intended to downplay the geopolitical implications of, and accentuate the investment opportunities afforded by the BRI.[77] Advance screenings of international conference papers to ensure they toe the Party line; mandatory approval procedures required for international academic activities; the 'Great Firewall's' blocking of Google Scholar[78]; the restrictive access to official Chinese investment, loan and aid data; and the propensity for delegated, rather than independently formulated BRI-related studies—generally in the

[70]Ian Bremmer, 'State Capitalism Comes of Age', *Foreign Affairs* (2009), p. 44.
[71]Francis Fukiyama in Li Xing and Timothy M. Shaw, 'The Political Economy of Chinese State Capitalism', *Journal of China and International Relations* 1(1), (2013), pp. 89–90.
[72]Bremmer, 'State Capitalism Comes of Age', p. 45.
[73]Bremmer, 'State Capitalism Comes of Age', p. 40.
[74]Li and Shaw, 'The Political Economy of Chinese State Capitalism', p. 103.
[75]Li and Shaw, 'The Political Economy of Chinese State Capitalism', p. 89.
[76]Kejin Zhao, 'China's Rise and Its Discursive Power Strategy', *Chinese Political Science Review* (2016), p. 7.
[77]*Xinhua News*, 'A List of words to be banned or carefully used in News Report (July 2017),' available at: http://bianji.org/news/2017/04/5682.html (accessed 18 April 2018)
[78]Hannah Beech, 'China's Great Firewall is Harming Innovation, Scholars Say,' *Time*, 2 June 2016, available at: http://time.com/4354665/china-great-firewall-innovation-online-censorship/ (accessed 12 September 2017).

form of policy papers instead of critical enquiry—are all examples of the constraints imposed on Chinese scholars by central and local authorities.

Aside from frustrating academics, these measures coalesce to essentially stifle or pre-empt domestic critique of the BRI. For the Party-State, this façade creates the outward perception of a unified Chinese voice in support of the BRI—one which proffers political utility. But an approach that punishes or precludes constructive criticism inevitably runs the risk of institutionalising a 'yes-men' culture of groupthink. Xi's crackdown on corruption, and the pervading sense that it is simultaneously a political purge, no doubt amplifies this dynamic.[79] As a result, significant issues with, or challenges to the BRI that provoke vigorous debates externally—such as the question of how developing countries will pay back their accrued BRI debts, or criticisms of CPECs transparency and economic feasibility—are either rarely heard within the Chinese echo-chamber, or dismissed outright as disinformation.[80] Yet, despite it being anathema to critical scholarship—with its dearth of accessible, accurate information and data, its scarcity of veritable social science-based research, and its near absence of criticism and ideational innovation—China's state monopolisation of the BRI narrative nevertheless succeeds as an effective domestic dissent management strategy. Managing extraterritorial opposition, however, is a different problem that requires different solutions.

Managing external dissent

Just as Japan confronted the anti-Japan protests in the 1980s in Southeast Asia, China has encountered hostility toward Chinese-funded and operated projects. In Kyrgyzstan, in 2012, over two-hundred Chinese workers were forced to flee after a local protest over workplace mistreatment and environmental degradation at the Taldy-Bulak Levoberezhnyi gold field turned violent.[81] A concession from the Papua New Guinea government, allowing China's Metallurgical Corporation to develop a marine industrial zone on public land near its majority-owned Ramu nickel mine, similarly sparked local riots.[82] The relative impotency of China's dissent management outside of a domestic milieu can be confirmed by the following two events. First, the Myitsone hydropower project in Myanmar in 2011 was suspended due to the projects unpopularity during the country's nascent democratisation, and Thein Sein's subsequent acquiescence to public opinion.[83] Second, the Rajapakse government lost 2015 election in Sri Lanka, and the ensuing diplomatic uncertainty in Beijing over the successor administration's intentions to preserve close ties with China, or initiate more congenial relations with India, Japan and the West.[84] Compounding this, from Beijing's viewpoint, is the invocation of 'China' by local opposition parties as a proxy criticism levelled at incumbent authorities—especially when such grievances are not directly attributable to Chinese malfeasance.[85]

This constitutes a challenge to the successful implementation of the BRI, and poses a profound dilemma. As a grand, signature scheme, China has an obvious interest in securing the longevity and success of BRI-related achievements as a matter of national prestige. At the same time, there is an obligation on the part of Beijing to safeguard Chinese companies and

[79]Chris Zhang, 'Where Is China's Corruption Crackdown?' The Diplomat, 21 July 2017, available at: http://thediplomat.com/2017/07/where-is-chinas-corruption-crackdown/ (accessed 12 September 2017).

[80]Abdur Rehman Shah, 'China's Trouble with Pakistan's Turbulent Democracy,' The Diplomat, 7 January 2017, available at: http://thediplomat.com/2017/01/chinas-trouble-with-pakistans-turbulent-democracy/ (accessed 13 September 2017).

[81]Friedrich Wu, Vidhya Logendran and Wan Tin Wai, 'A Double-Edged Sword: The risks to China's Silk Road Economic Belt', The International Economy, (2015), pp. 69–91.

[82]Hannan and Firth, 'One Belt One Road', p. 12.

[83]Hong Yu, 'Motivation behind China', p. 367; Rachel Harvey, 'Burma dam: Work halted on divisive Myitsone project,' BBC News, 30 September 2011, available at: http://www.bbc.com/news/world-asia-pacific-15121801 (accessed 12 September 2017).

[84]Kadira Pethiyagoda, 'What's driving China's New Silk Road, and how should the West respond?' Brookings: Order From Chaos Blog, 17 May 2017, available at: https://www.brookings.edu/blog/order-from-chaos/2017/05/17/whats-driving-chinas-new-silk-road-and-how-should-the-west-respond/ (accessed 18 July 2017)

[85]Godement et al., 'One Belt, One Road', p. 12.

their interests. But the mechanisms to achieving these ends remain elusive.[86] That is not to say that China has been sedentary in the face of such problems, as its attempts to influence Pakistani public opinion through training its journalists in the People's University of China and the purchase of dubious local media 'reports.' Recently, the Party-state has offered research grants for Chinese scholars to carry out studies on how to improve China's soft power in the BRI recipient countries.

An incremental shift in Chinese strategy is already underway. China has stressed the non-interference principle for decades. However, on 9 December 2017, Wang Yi, the Minister of Foreign Affairs, suggested that China should explore a sort of 'constructive intervention with Chinese characteristics.' On 5 March 2018, Wang Yi specified three normative conditions for constructive intervention: peaceful dialogue and consultation against the use of force; legitimate intervention without internal interference; and constructive intervention based on an objective and fair position.[87] While it remains to be seen whether this new policy constitutes a substantial dilution of the non-interference,' the challenge[s] of political engineering may [prove] far greater than mechanical engineering.'[88] Chinese planners have hitherto failed to fully comprehend and consider local dynamics and regional politics, let alone decisively influence them.[89]

The impact of the Chinese politics

Politics of Name

It would have been much better for China to adopt a more common term of connectivity, which would cover road, air, maritime, internet and many other channels or nodes at both regional and global levels. This would increase common understanding, reduce ideational resistance to China's BRI, facilitate the China-ASEAN connectivity, and avoid subject interpretations of the Belt and Road such as where historically the Silk Road has implied an unstable and insecure road with high risks.' One Belt One Road' arose from a need in the Chinese authoritarian system's official discourse to brand itself. Later in 2017, the government standardised the term as the 'Belt and Road Initiative,' forbidding the use of the term 'Belt and Road Strategy' to reduce suspicion and resistance. The proposal for the replacement of 'Belt and Road Strategy' with 'Belt and Road Initiative' came from the Center for China and Globalization (CCG) think tank whose members are largely returned scholars and professional experts from the USA and Europe. They submitted a policy brief to Zhao Gaolin who approved the proposal in 2017. It should be noted that CCG had its own agenda to promote closer integration with the West and avoid confrontation.

Politics of Pleasing

One noteworthy corollary in the domestic sphere has been the emergence of a 'politics of pleasing' among Party and State officials. Amid the crowded and hierarchic Chinese bureau-cracy, myriad 'commissions, ministries and state administrative and regulatory bodies' compete for the patronage of higher-ranked entities or individuals.[90] Seeking to curry favour or expedite career advancement, subordinates have engaged in dubious practices such as inflating provin-cial economic statistics,[91] retroactively rebranding successful projects as BRI, and aggrandising BRI accomplishments. In this sense, the 'politics of pleasing' is somewhat analogous to moral

---

[86]Ge in Godement *et al.*, 'One Belt, One Road', p. 12.

[87]Pang Zhongyin, 'New Age, New diplomacy and New Principle,' *Huaxia Daily*, 13 March 2018.

[88]Hongying Wang, 'A Deeper look at China's "Going Out" Policy"', *Centre for International Governance Innovation*, Commentary, March 2016, p. 3.

[89]Godement *et al.*, 'One Belt, One Road', p. 4.

[90]Jakobson and Manuel, 'How are Foreign Policy Decisions Made in China?' p. 103.

[91]Massoud Hayoun, 'Once again, China has been cooking the books,' *Pacific Standard*, 14 June 2017, available at. https://psmag.com/economics/china-has-been-cooking-the-books (accessed 13 September 2017).

hazard. The Chinese State's 'pathological obsession with quantitative targets and indicators as make-or-break criteria for judging officials,' is not novel, with overstated crop figures having exacerbated a crippling famine during the 'Great Leap Forward.'[92] Given the sheer scale of BRI, however, the 'politics of pleasing' poses a correspondingly higher risk, at least fiscally.

Acknowledging this problem, the Chinese government has recently sought to stamp out such conduct, purportedly amending the review mechanisms for official performance by reducing 'excessive emphasis on economic indicators.'[93] The fact this issue was addressed suggests that there is a genuine appetite in Beijing for more transparent and accurate reportage, at least in the economic space—though its efficacy remains to be seen.

Politics of Centralisation

The BRI involves different players from different ministerial institutions with different focuses and demands. Often there is contestation within state institutions in China. To overcome this kind of problem grand coordination is often required, which, in turn, draws on its centralised power. Moreover, infrastructure projects need the government's guarantee and stability. In short, management of gigantic BRI projects further strengthen the Chinese authoritarian system. If China were to democratise overnight, it is likely that its citizens would have ended all BRI commitments, especially projects with dubious fiscal benefits.

In some ways, China's rapid economic rise is reminiscent of Japanese and South Korean development experiences, insofar as it has 'buil[t] on a strong authoritarian leadership and an elite bureaucracy [to] pursu[e] developmentally oriented policies, including the direct role of the state in governing the market.'[94] Indeed, China has long demonstrated an ability to adapt and adopt 'worldwide development experiences without abandoning its own policy-making sovereignty as to when, where and how to adopt foreign ideas.'[95] However, the emergence of market-economy dynamics in China has brought with it neither political pluralism, nor a diminishing of state embeddedness within economic decision-making.[96] In this regard, China may prove the exception to Bernard and Ravenhill's observation that state-capitalism tends to lose its prefix over time. Japan, Taiwan and Korea have engendered a diffusion that 'undermine[d] the state-centric notions of the product cycle approach, which link[ed] the production of specific products with "national" stages of development.'[97] Being underwritten by infrastructure construction rather than exportable consumer goods—Chinese state-centric development policies and strategy appear less susceptible to this 'diffusion.' It seems that the role of the state has become well entrenched: 'Chinese capitalism is on a strong but flexible leash. The leash can be tightened by the top leadership any time as political and economic needs arise.'[98]

Politics of Regime Affinity

During the late 1940s and early 1950s, America predominantly targeted their investments at diplomatically friendly countries, such as Britain, France, and the Netherlands, as well as neutral,

[92]Hayoun, 'Once again, China has been cooking the books.'
[93]'China will not tolerate fake economic data,' *China Daily*, 25 April 2017, available at: http://www.chinadaily.com.cn/business/2017-04/25/content_29073511.htm (accessed 13 September 2017).
[94]Li and Shaw, 'The Political Economy of Chinese State Capitalism', p. 103.
[95]IBID, p. 103.
[96]IBID, p. 106.
[97]Mitchell Bernard and John Ravenhill, 'Beyond Product Cycles and Flying Geese: Regionalization, Hierarchy, and the Industrialization of East Asia', *World Politics* 47(2), (1995), p. 187.
[98]Jamie Peck and Jun Zhang, 'A variety of capitalism ... with Chinese characteristics?' *Journal of Economic Geography* 13(3), (2013), p. 371.

geostrategic countries like West Germany and Turkey.[99] China has executed the BRI in much the same way, with long-time friend Pakistan hosting the initiative's flagship corridor in CPEC, and nonaligned, but geostrategic states such as Russia and Indonesia also receiving a considerable proportion of BRI investment.[100] This trend is confirmed by Chinese evaluations of the top five BRI participant countries—Russia, Kazakhstan, Thailand, Pakistan and Indonesia.[101] In contrast, American alliance countries like Australia and Japan have resisted the BRI just as the East European countries resisted the Marshal plan in the past. One possible reason, among many, is the effect of regime affinity. Obviously, mobilisation strategies and channels have had the effect of creating fear and resistance in western democratic countries, but in contrast, state-led mobilisation has offered favourable terms and conditions for the ruling elites who have welcomed China's BRI project. Furthermore, it is likely that democratic societies will oppose the control mechanisms of the BRI, compared to authoritarian regimes who are less concerned about these control mechanisms since they organise their societies in a similar way.

Enabling and Inhibiting Functions

China's top-down mobilisations and control mechanisms have both enabling and inhibiting functions. Where they 'enable' many great projects, China's investment model does confer certain benefits. Low levels of executive constraints mean that investments and interests can be pursued through privileged access to leadership—with economic objectives being susceptible to political and diplomatic leverage. Indeed, Chinese aid can seem indistinguishable from investment, due to the often unclear divisions between state and non-state entities.[102] In Kazakhstan in 2013, for example, Beijing successfully lobbied Astana to purchase and then on-sell a stake in the Kashagan oil project to the China National Petroleum Corporation—blocking India's Oil and Natural Gas Corp's bid in the process.[103] Regarding high-risk and high-return projects, SOEs are at the vanguard of economic statecraft. Statistics reveal that since 2012 SOEs have increased investment from two to ten times in high-risk areas.[104] The hierarchic channelling of national resources, and the state monopolisation of the BRI discourse, are similarly effective in this regard.

China's top-down mobilisations and control mechanisms have inhibiting effects, politically motivated lending in high-risk locales runs the risk of creating 'roads to nowhere.'[105] The vast sums being funnelled into the BRI, in addition to its persistently lax accountability mechanisms, make for a configuration that is particularly susceptible to corruption, ineptitude and political instability. Between 2005 and 2014, twenty-five per cent of all Chinese projects abroad failed. Cumulatively, these thirty-two ventures cost over fifty-six billion US dollars—nearly a quarter of China's foreign investment total over that period.[106]

---

[99]Roy Gardner, 'The Marshall Plan Fifty Years Later: Three What-Ifs and a When', in *The Marshall Plan: Fifty Years After* ed. Martin Schain (New York: Palgrave Macmillan, 2001), p. 120.

[100]Hong Kong Trade Development Council, 'China Takes Global Number Two Outward FDI Slot: Hong Kong Remains the Preferred Service Platform,' *HKTDC Research*, 11 November 2016, available at: http://hkmb.hktdc.com/en/1X0A804W/hktdc-research/China-Takes-Global-Number-Two-Outward-FDI-Slot-Hong-Kong-Remains-the-Preferred-Service-Platform (accessed 13 September 2017).

[101]National Information Centre, 'An Evaluation Report of the Cooperation with the BRI Recipient Countries (2016)', available at: http://www.sic.gov.cn/archiver/SIC/UpFile/Files/Default/20170531100246569274.pdf (accessed 18 April 2018).

[102]Denise E. Zheng, 'China's Use of Soft Power in the Developing World: Strategic intentions and implications for the United States', in Carola McGiffert, ed., *Chinese Soft Power and its Implications for the United States*, (Washington D.C.: Centre for Strategic and International Studies, 2009), p. 3.

[103]Wu, Logendran and Wai, 'A Double-Edged Sword', p. 69.

[104]Li Jiang, 'China's BRI Should Avoid to be Big Gamble,' *Financial Times (Chinese Online version)*, 23 June 2017, available at: https://www.boxun.com/news/gb/china/2017/06/201706231744.shtml (accessed 8 August 2018).

[105]Nadège Rolland, 'All aboard the Belt and Road Initiative? Not so fast...,' *Lowy Interpreter*, 7 June 2017, available at: https://www.lowyinstitute.org/the-interpreter/all-aboard-belt-and-road-initiative-not-so-fast (accessed 14 September 2017).

[106]Wang Yongzhong and Li Xicheng, 'Characteristics and Risks of Chinese Investment among the BRI Recipient Countries', *Chinese Social Science Research Network*, p. 8, available at: http://www.cssn.cn/jjx/jjx_gzf/201511/W020151130796447771290.pdf (accessed 14 April 2018).

Distinct disadvantages thus emanate from the centralisation dynamics of China's authoritarian investment model. They reveal how the economic and political stimuli of the BRI are not always complementary, and can in fact be mutually exclusive. Put another way, if adjudged on short- to medium-term political benefit, the contemporary authoritarian investment model may appear to trump its democratic counterpart. But given this political utility often comes at the cost of fiscal robustness and worthwhile return-on-investment—the BRI's economic feasibility, and, by extension, its longer-term political practicality, appear suspect. In contrast, the Marshall Plan, modelled on democratic investment, achieved parallel geostrategic and economic objectives within a remarkably short period.[107]

Politics of Assessment

It is difficult to provide an objective and comprehensive assessment of the outcome of the BRI. A starting problem is the lack of true information; a follow-up problem is the politics involved. Even if projects are economic failures, they can be said to be a 'success' since it is easy to claim that they have achieved their strategic or political task. Assessments of BRI are contingent upon the criteria of conflictive economics and geopolitical goals. Although the two are *both* necessary to understanding BRI, they can nevertheless be difficult to reconcile with one another, given their oft-contradictory underlying priorities. What works to enhance China's regional diplomatic influence may not be conducive to sustainable economic development—despite official statements to the contrary.

Conclusion

This article has focused on three aspects of Chinese domestic politics—individual leadership, a variety of political mobilisation strategies and channels, and control mechanisms. All point out a set of the serious problems associated with the BRI including its 'politics of pleasing,' its lack of transparency and information, its tendency to strengthen authoritarianism, its self-reinforcing assessment, and many more, casting doubt over the claims to date of its great success.

The BRI is permeated by underlying and interrelated tensions that derive from China's domestic political dynamics. One such dilemma is that between the size of the BRI and the limited ability of governance through control and mobilisation—the latter inevitably puts a huge burden on the Chinese bureaucracy. This dilemma is indicative of a duality in the BRI's operationalisation which is *simultaneously hierarchical and plural with local flexibility*. Such an approach is considered necessary to a functional Chinese bureaucracy, but that makes it no less paradoxical. Consequently, in a phenomenon somewhat akin to 'mission creep,' BRI designs have proven susceptible to implementative alteration at the provincial level. Cumulatively, these tensions comprise a dilemma that stems from managing an endeavour so vast, and pose challenges to President Xi's signature initiative.

The domestic politics analysis developed by this article constitutes a starting point to explore the convergent or divergent interests of ruling elites in China and the BRI recipient countries. The BRI mobilisation and control mechanisms can also help us to understand how it engenders regional and global trepidation and deference. Thus, this intellectual approach offers a basis to study the interaction of the domestic politics of two or more countries regarding the BRI. Essentially, given its transnational character, the successful implementation of the BRI program 'depends upon active cooperation from others. China cannot realise it on its own.'[108] This is only achievable 'if China focus[es] on consultation to avoid perceptions of unilateralism, and give states with a stake in BRI a

---

[107]Kunz, 'The Marshall Plan Reconsidered', pp. 162–163.
[108]Peter Ferdinand, 'Westward ho the China dream and "one belt, one road": Chinese foreign policy under Xi Jinping', *International Affairs* 92(4), (2016), p. 956.

sense of ownership.'[109] However, as the analysis of the politics of naming demonstrates, China needs ownership of its initiative for its domestic consumption.

The implementation of the BRI falls under personalised politics and is likely to strengthen authoritarian rule through state capitalism. Irrespective of the initiatives future achievements (or lack thereof), its already felt influence will have substantial implications. There are myriad prognostications vis-à-vis China's prospective global power and its potential implications. Yet without the benefit of hindsight, we cannot know what impact the BRI will have—especially given it is still in a preliminary phase. What does seem inevitable, however, is that the BRI will have lasting geo-economic, geopolitical and even geo-cultural ramifications. Nevertheless, Chinese political institutions currently lack any mechanism to correct potential mistakes committed by its top leaders. One may wonder whether the BRI poses a nightmare for China if it opens a great strategic hole which sucks away China's money or falls into a sort of Chinese geopolitical overstretching as empires did in history.

Acknowledgements

The author would like to thank Matthew Clark, Suisheng Zhao, Kai He, Pradeep Taneja, Chengxin Pan, and Tim Winter for their constructive comments and suggestions; and Tom Barber and Matt Hood for their research assistance.

Disclosure statement

No potential conflict of interest was reported by the author.

---

[109]Hong Yu, 'Motivation behind China', pp. 367–368.

8   Overseas Port Investment Policy for China's Central and Local Governments in the Belt and Road Initiative

Jihong Chen, Yijie Fei, Paul Tae-Woo Lee and Xuezong Tao

ABSTRACT

The Belt and Road Initiative (BRI) is a national strategy proposed by China to strengthen globalization and regional economic integration, connecting the country to the world. The BRI will drive China's ports to expand connectivity through construction and operation along the '21st-Century Maritime Silk Road (MSR)'. At the same time, port governance involves central, provincial and local governments engaging in overseas investment and financing in the context of the BRI. Under the double-level governance of the central and local governments, discrepancies, disjointed actions and gaps inevitably arise between the policies launched by the central and local governments. This article evaluates 14 major coastal ports operating with state-level support and overseas investment. 11 evaluation indexes are determined from the existing development conditions of ports and the economic strength of port cities. Fuzzy clustering method is applied to evaluate and classify the development of the coastal ports in China and to develop a reasonable implementation mode of the 'going global strategy' of the ports. Consequently, it would help policymakers and stakeholders in China deal with the rivalry of provincial governments, alleviate overseas investment risks and strengthen the foreign port chain management along the MSR.

Introduction

The government officially issued the *Vision and Actions on Jointly Building Silk Road Economic Belt and 21st-Century Maritime Silk Road* in March 2015.[1] It aims to connect China to the world by sea and by land by developing corridors in tandem with infrastructure development and enhancing international trade capacity and economic cooperation among the countries along the 'Belt and Road (B&R)'. Through the '21st-Century Maritime Silk Road (MSR)', China's coastal ports are playing an important role in promoting the country's foreign trade competitiveness as an important node of international logistics. President Xi Jinping described a port as an 'important pivot point' and an 'important hub' in a number of international occasions to show their importance.[2]

China's ports are actively responding to the Belt and Road Initiative (BRI) and are stepping up efforts seeking development and cooperation opportunities with ports along the B&R. China has become the No 1 country in terms of ports, and is home to 14 of the top 20 ports in the world in terms of cargo

---

[1] Haitang Qiu, 'Shouquan fabu: tuidong gongjian sichouzhilu jingjidai he 21shijie haishang sichouzhilu de yuanjing yu xingdong', ['The vision and action to promote the construction of the Silk Road Economic Belt and the Maritime Silk Road in twenty-first Century'], *www.xinhuanet.com*, 8 June 2015, translation, available at: http://news.xinhuanet.com/gangao/2015-06/08/c_127890670.htm (accessed 21 October 2017).

[2] Mengmeng Dai and Jingdong Wang, 'Shuxie xinshiji haishang sichouzhilu xinpianzhang', ['Writing a new chapter of the maritime Silk Road in the new century'], *People's Daily*, 6 June 2017, translation, http://news.cctv.com/2017/07/06/ARTI7ZELOBdb3IVbnzwipi6Z170706.shtml. (accessed 21 October 2017).

throughput and container throughput.[3] The B&R construction has become one of key elements of infrastructures attracting global investment. Data from the Ministry of Commerce show that Chinese enterprises invested a total of 14.53 billion US dollars in countries along the B&R in 2016. As of the end of 2016, Chinese enterprises set up 56 inchoate cooperation zones in countries along the B&R, with the accumulated investment totaling 18.55 billion US dollars.[4] China has invested in ports and terminals in 23 countries and regions along the B&R, with the annual amount exceeding 10 billion US dollars.[5] Chinese investors used to focus more on maritime enterprises and terminal operation. With their investment in leasing and constructing foreign ports answering the call of the BRI, Chinese port enterprises have made more solid strides in 'going global' along the MSR.[6] Such port investment will enjoy favorable benefits and returns by improving port connectivity and establishing supply chain network for the nation's economy.[7] For example, Shanghai Port has taken a lead in 'going global' by connecting China to the world and developing its port alliance in foreign ports. For instance, the port in 2015 won the bid for running terminals at the Haifa New Port in Israel for 25 years starting from 2021.[8] At the call of the BRI, many coastal ports in China are trying to tap into the global market and seek to develop investment opportunities for expanding port connectivity along the Maritime Silk Road. However, national preferential policies alone are not enough to promote the 'going global strategy' because enterprises need to possess sound conditions and orderly prioritized investment policies. Not all ports are as powerful as Shanghai Port; ports are in different locations with their different capacities and local urban economic strengths. For this reason, major coastal ports in China have to formulate reasonably prioritized development plans based on 11 variables (see Section 3 in this article), including their port characteristics and economic environment to promote the 'going global strategy' steadily.[9]

To manage this, the 'going global strategy' of Chinese coastal ports has been proposed. The ports cover Shanghai, Tianjin, Ningbo-Zhoushan, Guangzhou, Shenzhen, Zhanjiang, Shantou, Qingdao, Yantai, Dalian, Fuzhou, Xiamen, Quanzhou and Haikou as key gateways providing support to the 'going global strategy' along the B&R, and the proposal regards these port cities as nodes to co-build a smooth, safe and efficient transportation passage. The 14 ports try to actively promote the 'going global strategy', and respond to China's BRI (See Figure 1). However, their conditions and the strengths of their cities are diverse. Considering these factors, the ports are required to develop their 'going global strategy' in a rational and orderly manner based on their own development status. There is also the matter of which port will 'go global' first. This is related to governance issue because several stakeholders, including central, provincial and local governments, engage in overseas investment and financing in the context of the BRI, and some seaports will be connected to dry ports in the country.[10] In addition, a study on the priority of China's overseas port investment is critical to avoid waste of national resources and provide a

---

[3]United Nations Conference on Trade And Development (UNCTAD), 1995–2015, Review of Maritime Transport, available at: http://unctad.org/en/Pages/Publications/Review-of-Maritime-Transport-(Series).aspx (accessed 17 July 2018).
[4]'Yidaiyilu zhi gangkou daguan', ['Grand view on ports in the Belt and Road Initiative'], *Shipping Exchange Bulletin*, 26 July 2017, translation, available at: http://www.chinaports.com/portlspnews/553038F9A2FD7616E0530101007F2EC9/view (accessed 21 October 2017).
[5]'Haiwai gangkou beihou de zhongguo ziben: yinian touzi chao 200yi meiyuan', ['Chinese capital behind overseas ports: over $20 billion a year'], *www.people.com.cn*, 9 October 2017, translation, available at: http://www.ssfcn.com/detailed.asp?id=623848 (accessed 21 October 2017).
[6]Xiaoyi Wang, 'Yidaiyilu dailai gangkou fazhan xinjiyu', ['New opportunities for ports brought from The Belt and Road Initiative'], *People's Daily*, 8 August 2017, translation, available at: http://news.163.com/17/0808/03/CR9LHI0300018AOP.html (accessed 21 October 2017).
[7]'Yidaiyilu zhi gangkou daguan', ['Grand view on ports in the Belt and Road Initiative'], *Shipping Exchange Bulletin*, 26 July 2017, translation, available at: http://www.chinaports.com/portlspnews/553038F9A2FD7616E0530101007F2EC9/view (accessed 21 October 2017).
[8]'Shanggang jituan zhongbiao yiselie haifaxingang 25nian matou jingyingquan', ['SIPG won the right to operate 25 years of Wharf in Haifa, Israel'], *www.stcn.com*, 27 March 2015, translation, available at: http://finance.eastmoney.com/news/1354,20150327491020914.html (accessed 21 October 2017).
[9]Shasha Tang and Jian Hao, "Zouchuqu' xuyao qiye you zhengque de zhanlue he celue', ['"Going out" requires enterprises to have the right strategy and policy'], *http://jjsb.cet.com.cn*, 20 May 2015, translation, available at: http://finance.eastmoney.com/news/1371,20150520508170211.html (accessed 21 October 2017).
[10]Hairui Wei, Zhaohan Sheng and Paul Tae-Woo Lee, 'The role of dry port in hub and spoke network under Belt and Road Initiative', *Maritime Policy & Management* 45(3), (2018), pp. 370–387.

sound guideline to mitigate conflicts between the central government and the provincial government and among the provincial governments. This article analyzes the 14 ports to investigate priority reference of the ports for implementing the 'going global strategy', applying fuzzy clustering method, which draws indices to show which port has investment priority of the ports to go global along the MSR.

The rest of the article is organized in this following manner: Section 2 conducts a literature review and draws research gaps. Section 3 describes the linkage between Chinese domestic ports and international ports. In Section 4, the fuzzy clustering method is discussed to explore priority index system to show, which ports will 'go global' first in a quantitative manner. Section 5 analyzes priority of 'going global' of the 14 key ports along the MSR based on the indices drawn by the fuzzy clustering method and discusses the test results and their implications. Section 6 deals with discrepancy and conflicts between provincial/local and central governments for port development based on the test results. Section 7 concludes this article.

Figure 1. Key ports under the 'going global strategy' along the '21st-century maritime silk road'.

Literature review

The governance of ports along with investment in global maritime transportation has long been a focus of the international shipping community. A number of previous studies have addressed the correlation of world maritime transportation, and a summary of such academic work is presented below. Much existing academic research focuses on concepts, theories, and models of governance.

Port governance is influenced by entity of investment, e.g., private sector or public (central and local government) sector or private/public joint sector. Port development in the U.K. was led by the private sector based on the belief that its benefits will be borne by port users in the context of invisible market function. Therefore, ports are often considered as commercial entities, which are required in recovering their full costs from the users. Hence, ports ought to be self-sufficient, and the pricing strategy is commercial- or profit-oriented. This development approach belongs to the Anglo Saxon Doctrine. Countries in the European continent, on the other hand, view the ports as the region's social infrastructure, hence assesses their value in terms of their contribution to regional economic development, rather than in terms of profitability. Given the public good nature of ports, the local and central governments provide a strong argument in favor of partially subsidizing port infrastructure. This is called the (Continental) European Doctrine. Different scholars arrived at decisions on port governance models from different perspectives. Observing that among the global top 25 container ports, the number of top ports in Asia increased dramatically from 2 in the top 25 in 1970 to 15 in 2010, while in North America that figure fell from 7 to 3 and in Europe from 14 to 5 over the same period, Lee and Flynn attributed the Asian success to a newly proposed doctrine, the so-called 'Asian Port Doctrine (APD)'.[11] They said that Asian port development, in particular China and Korea, is based on peculiar governance and investment model, where central governments play a leading role in constructing infrastructure and consequently, and govern ports as public utilities. But as briefly described above, the Anglo-Saxon Doctrine relies on market functions, so the private sector is responsible for port construction, with users bearing the costs.

Lee and Lam highlighted that central governments in Asia, such as China, Korea, and Singapore, played a key role in port infrastructure investment because port infrastructure is regarded as social overhead capital like highways and railways and contributes to lowering logistics costs.[12] Therefore, port governance in those countries is influenced by the central governments, although the degree of their influence is changing over the years.

Thanks to China's central government's role in developing transportation infrastructure over the past two decades, transportation network and connectivity have significantly improved, both within China and between China and other countries.[13] This connectivity is closely related to corridor developments in the B&R. Unlike connectivity by railways and highways across the nations, the development of maritime transport routes in association with port connectivity expansion along the MSR does not face 'juridico-political framework'.[14] However, this article needs to understand port governance and port integration in the context of the 'going global strategy' because infrastructure, superstructure, and operations have been gradually decentralizing from central government to provincial and local authorities. In other words, a decentralization process is taking place in the industry in the country where inter-port integration has been emerging, for example, Ningbo-Zhoushan Port. This movement initiated by the central government is changing governance from the central government-province structure to the central government-province-port/city. This will be further discussed in Section 5.

No consensus on the theoretical system on port governance in tandem with port investment has been reached among researchers yet. Baltazar and Brooks applied the contingency theory to their port governance research. In the case studies of Canadian ports, they held that the Canadian government authorized external private sector for port governance was an advisable management model.[15] Debrie et al. sorted out the port governance model reforms and studied the relationship between the global trend and port embed ability.[16] Daamen and Vries, Parola et al pointed out that the sustainable governance model of ports was restricted by the urbanization process and environmental policies.[17] Monios et al.

[11]Paul Tae-Woo Lee and Matthew Flynn, 'Charting A New Paradigm of Container Port Development Policy: The Asian Doctrine', *Transport Reviews* 31(6), (2011), pp. 791–806.
[12]Paul Tae-Woo Lee and Jasmine Siu Lee Lam, 'A review of port devolution and governance models with compound eyes approach', *Transport Reviews* 37(4), (2017), pp. 507–520.
[13]Yu Qin, 'China's Transport Infrastructure Investment: Past, Present, and Future', *Asian Economic Policy Review* 11(2), (2016), pp. 199–217.
[14]Claude Comtois, Brian Slack and Gunnar K. Sletmo, 'Political issues in inland waterways port development: prospects for regionalization', *Transport Policy* 4(4), (1997), pp. 251–265.
[15]Ramon Baltazar and Mary R. Brooks, 'Port governance, devolution and the matching framework: a configuration theory approach', *Research in Transportation Economics* 17, (2006), pp. 379–403.
[16]Jean Debrie, Valérie Lavaud-Letilleul and Francesco Parola, 'Shaping port governance: the territorial trajectories of reform', *Journal of Transport Geography* 27, (2013), pp. 56–65.
[17]Tom A. Daamen and Isabelle Vries, 'Governing the European port–city interface: institutional impacts on spatial projects between city and port', *Journal of Transport Geography* 27, (2013), pp. 4–13, Francesco Parola and Salvatore Maugeri, 'Origin and taxonomy of conflicts in seaports: Towards a research agenda', *Research in Transportation Business & Management* 8, (2013), pp. 114–122.

and Brooks stressed the importance of inland terminal investment in port management which helped to concentrate the inland logistic markets. Lam et al. pointed out that amid the fierce competition, it is necessary to promote overall governance at the port cluster layer to achieve collaborated configuration of resources among ports in a region. Wanke and Carlos, and Laxe et al. as well as Verhoeven, were active promoters of the port governance model featuring public–private partnerships (PPP) between Brazilian public port authorities and private terminals.[18] The PPP model is typical to expand port capacity in association with port pricing model. This is being developed in Asian ports, including China. Many scholars asserted the port governance model in the future, including lowering down entry barriers, introducing inter-port competition and labor reforms, limiting existing political interference, reducing economic interference, setting scientific pricing mechanisms for ports, attracting shipping alliances to call at the ports, and establishing global supply chains for ports.[19]

Song and Yeo, on the other hand, used the ranking process to identify the competitiveness of container ports in China, including Hong Kong, and indicated the significance of port governance.[20] A key research field of governance is the innovation of port governance models and system setup. Specifically, the focus of innovation may vary. De Martino et al. tried to apply the logistics innovation theory to seaport governance, while Acciaro et al. enabled port governance models to evolve toward sustainability from the energy technology innovation perspective.[21] Both logistics and energy technology innovations are dedicated to effective implementation of port governance model reform.[22] Literature on establishment of port governance systems can be roughly divided into the following opinions: institutional elements can well impact ports' governance levels and logistic capacity. But in the long term, the institutional impact on port governance is diminishing. Different ports are pursuing common governance models and the original port governance models need to be re-evaluated.[23]

Foreign capital from terminal operators combined with local governments and port authorities in container terminal operation are gradually moving into practice in China.[24] This is a motivation for provincial and local governments to accelerate the 'going global strategy'. In addition, the BRI has triggered global port network developments along the MSR with a long-term port lease such as Darwin Port in Australia and Hambantota Port in Sri Lanka and

[18]Jason Monios and Gordon Wilmsmeier, 'The role of intermodal transport in port regionalisation', *Transport Policy* 30, (2013), pp. 161–172; Mary R. Brooks, 'The governance structure of ports', *Review of Network Economics* 3(2), (2014), pp. 168–183; Jasmine Siu Lee Lam, Adolf K.Y. Ng and Xiaowen Fu, 'Stakeholder management for establishing sustainable regional port governance', *Research in Transportation Business & Management* 8, (2013), pp. 30–38; Peter F. Wanke and Carlos Pestana Barros, 'Public-private partnerships and scale efficiency in Brazilian ports: Evidence from two-stage DEA analysis', *Socio-Economic Planning Sciences* 51, (2015), pp. 13–22; Fernando González Laxe, Maria Jesus Freire Seoane and Carlos Pais Montes, 'Maritime degree, centrality and vulnerability: port hierarchies and emerging areas in containerized transport (2008–2010)', *Journal of Transport Geography* 24, (2012), pp. 33–44; Patrick Verhoeven, 'A review of port authority functions: towards a renaissance?', *Maritime Policy & Management* 37(3), (2010), pp. 247–270.
[19]Adolf K.Y. Ng and Girish C. Gujar, 'Government policies, efficiency and competitiveness: The case of dry ports in India', *Transport Policy* 16(5), (2009), pp. 232–239; Athanasios A. Pallis, 'Whither port strategy? Theory and practice in conflict', *Research in Transportation Economics* 21, (2007), pp. 343–382; Christophe Theys, Theo E. Notteboom, Athanasios A. Pallis and Peter W. De Langen, 'The economics behind the awarding of terminals in seaports: Towards a research agenda', *Research in Transportation Economics* 27(1), (2010), pp. 37–50; Roy Van Den Berg, Peter W. De Langen and Paul C.J. Van Zuijlen, 'Revisiting port pricing; a proposal for seven port pricing principles', *WMU Journal of Maritime Affairs* 16(2), (2017), pp. 1–18; Theo E. Notteboom, Francesco Parola, Giovanni Satta and Athanasios A. Pallis, 'The relationship between port choice and terminal involvement of alliance members in container shipping', *Journal of Transport Geography* 64, (2017), pp. 158–173; Adolf K.Y. Ng and John Liu, *Port-focal logistics and global supply chains*, (Berlin: *Springer, 2014*), pp. 58–77.
[20]Dong-Wook Song and Ki-Tae Yeo, 'A competitive analysis of Chinese container ports using the analytic hierarchy process', *Maritime Economics & Logistics* 6(1), (2004), pp. 34–52.
[21]Marcella De Martino, Luisa Errichiello, Alessandra Marasco and Alfonso Morvillo, 'Logistics innovation in seaports: An inter-organizational perspective', *Research in Transportation Business & Management* 8, (2013), pp. 123–133; Michele Acciaro, Hilda Ghiara and Maria Inés Cusano, 'Energy management in seaports: A new role for port authorities', *Energy Policy* 71, (2014), pp. 4–12.
[22]Mary R. Brooks and Athanasios A. Pallis, 'Assessing port governance models: process and performance components', *Maritime Policy & Management* 35(4), (2008), pp. 411–432.
[23]James J. Wang, Adolf Koi-Yu Ng and Daniel Olivier, 'Port governance in China: a review of policies in an era of internationalizing port management practices', *Transport Policy* 11(3), (2004), pp. 237–250.
[24]Daniel Olivier, 'Private entry and emerging partnerships in container terminal operations: evidence from Asia', *Maritime Economics & Logistics* 7(2), (2005), pp. 87–115.

purchasing shares of Piraeus Port in Greece. These developments will contribute to integrating Chinese coastal ports into a global port logistic network and strengthening the functions of ports in the supply value chain.[25] In this regard, it is worth noting a newly proposed 'New Maritime Silk Road'. Literature on BRI showed the following aspects of change in transport and logistics landscape[26]:

- development of inland-inter regional rail and highway corridors and city clustering in China;
- connectivity of economic corridors to the Indian Ocean and East Sea in association with dry ports in China;
- development of sea-river combined transport and sea-railway/highway;
- development of free trade economic zones along inland road corridors and in ports;
- structural changes in maritime cargo flow and shipping network in association with corridor developments and intermodal network; and
- alignment of participating countries' transport and logistics development along the B&R.

The above aspects provide an insight into how to implement the 'going global strategy', reflecting the current supply chain and future plan of Chinese coastal ports as well as the comprehensive economic and geographical characteristics of the port cities.[27] Meanwhile, Chinese coastal ports need to pay attention to new port governance structures from the perspective of new systems in China.[28] Because they are related to infrastructure investment, port financing through PPP and port efficiency and competitive edge.[29] Notteboom and Yang enumerated key factors influencing the container port system in China, such as the 'Go West' strategy, BRI, introduction of modern corporate governance principles, and free-trade zones, and argued that the above factors have accelerated 'port integration and co-operation and tried to attract foreign investments to Chinese ports with an internationalization of Chinese port-related companies through investments in foreign ports'.[30]

Relevant literature so far has centered on theories, models, philosophy of port governance. Therefore, research setting up an evaluation system and conducting quantitative studies on investment priority of ports going abroad is scanty. In particular, there is no study on port investment priority among Chinese coastal ports which are competitively 'going global' along the MSR. This article aims to fill the research gaps, achieving three goals: the first goal is to set up an index system for evaluating the priority of port investment under the 'going global strategy' in the context of the BRI; the second one is to provide a quantitative tool to draw priority index of port development applying the fuzzy clustering method; and the third one is to develop decision-making references for policymakers and stakeholders for their port development under the 'going global strategy' as well as investment planning along the MSR.

[25]Theo E. Notteboom and Jean-Paul Rodrigue, 'Port regionalization: towards a new phase in port development', *Maritime Policy & Management* 32(3), (2005), pp. 297–313.

[26]Paul Tae-Woo Lee, Zhi-Hua Hu, Sang-Jeong Lee, Kyoung-Suk Choi and Sung-Ho Shin, 'Research trends and agenda on the Belt and Road (B&R) initiative with a focus on maritime transport', *Maritime Policy & Management* 45(3), (2018), pp. 282–300.

[27]Kevin Cullinane, Yahui Teng and Teng-Fei Wang, 'Port competition between Shanghai and Ningbo', *Maritime Policy & Management* 32(4), (2005), pp. 331–346; Olaf Merk, 'The competitiveness of global port-cities: synthesis report', *OECD Regional Development Working Papers*, available at: http://www.oecd.org/cfe/regional-policy/oecdport-citiesprogramme.htm, (accessed on 21 October 2017).

[28]Qiang Zhang, Harry Geerlings, Abdel El Makhloufi and Shun Chen, 'Who governs and what is governed in port governance: A review study', *Transport Policy* 64, (2018), pp. 51–60.

[29]World Bank. (2014). Public–private partnerships: Reference guide version 2.0. Working Paper no. 90384, World Bank and PPIAF.

[30]Theo Notteboom and Zhongzhen Yang, 'Port governance in China since 2004: institutional layering and the growing impact of broader policies', *Research in Transportation Business & Management* 22, (2017), pp. 184–200.

Linkage between Chinese domestic ports and international ports

Cooperation between Chinese and international ports

An international port, as a node in the global logistics network, has played a vital role in building and developing marine transport corridors. About 65% of overseas terminals established by Chinese port enterprises are located along the '21st Century Maritime Silk Road'. Guided by the 'going global strategy', Chinese ports' overseas investment projects are not only conducive to building international shipping pivots along the B&R to boost China's foreign trade, but also help strengthen international cooperation and division of labor to extend ports' industry chains. Chinese port constructors are the earliest overseas investors. For example, China Communications Construction Company Limited built the Gwadar Deep-water Port in Pakistan in 2002 to fuel port construction along the '21st Century Maritime Silk Road'. Except for China Merchants Port Holdings Company Limited and COSCO Shipping Ports Limited, domestic terminal operators in China, such as Shanghai International Port Group, Port of Qingdao Group and Guangxi Beibu Gulf International Port Group, have just begun to put the 'going global strategy' onto their agenda. Their 'going global strategy' focuses on exporting terminal operation technologies and management experience and acquiring terminal operation rights. At present, the strategy of Chinese port enterprises is primarily carried out in three ways: merger and acquisition (M&A), joint venture, and leasing.[31]

Chinese port enterprises have accumulated some experience in overseas investment and port construction. Two global terminal operators as the first-tier group in the country—China Merchants Port Holdings Company Limited and COSCO Shipping Ports Limited—have succeeded in improving their capabilities of merger and acquisition and operation and management of port terminals. Shanghai International Port Group as one of the second-tier port enterprises is a quasi-terminal operator whose development potential cannot be underestimated. The third-tier enterprises in China mainly rely on domestic homeports to serve overseas upstream and downstream terminal companies. For example, Port of Yantai Group serves its homeport and cooperates with several large domestic and foreign port groups to jointly invest in building the Port of Boke in Guinea, enjoying full management over the port's terminal business. Chinese port enterprises' investment in overseas ports has been demonstrating potential growth. The status quo of ports' 'going global' is shown in Table 1.

Macro control and governance of ports' 'Going Global Strategy' advocated by the central and local governments

Against the background of the BRI, Chinese ports continue to evolve toward 'going global' and internationalization, and reach out to countries along the B&R through cooperation with ports in those countries. The Chinese government put forward the BRI and proposed to focus on port infrastructure, land-water combined transport and port cooperation, increase seagoing routes and liner frequency, and strengthen cooperation in maritime logistics information in accordance with the vision and plan of the BRI. This will not only activate and expand port trade and cooperation between China and the countries along the route, but will also encourage major coastal ports in China to step up overseas investment and construction and strive to become new international shipping centers and transit hubs. Ports play a pivotal and pioneering role in the joint effort of building the B&R. President Xi Jinping has described ports as 'important pivots' and 'important hubs' on many international occasions to highlight their importance in the BRI. As a carrier of global trade flow, ports have increasingly become a kernel of regional economic development, and

---

[31]As an M&A case, in 2013 China Merchants Port Holdings Company Limited acquired 49% stocks of Terminal Link, a subsidiary of CMA CGM, bringing the number of ports under its operation and management to more than a dozen on major global routes. The case of joint venture is the MCKIP project of Guangxi Beibu Gulf International Port Group in Malaysia in 2013. Leasing case shows that In 2013, Shanghai International Port Group won the bid for the 25-year franchise of Israel Haifa Bayport starting from 2021.

Table 1. Overseas investment and operation of Chinese port enterprises

Port Enterprises	Year	Terminal Projects	Investment
COSCO Shipping Ports Limited	2001	Port of Long Beach in the U.S.	Stake of 51%
	2003	Pasir Panjang Terminal in Brazil	Stake of 49%
	2004	Port of Antwerp in Belgium	Stake of 25%
	2005	Port of Naples in Italy	Stake of 46.25%
	2006	Port of Rotterdam in the Netherlands	Joint construction
	2007	Container terminal of Port Said (East) in Egypt	Stake of 20% in the Suez Canal Container Terminal
	2008	SSA Terminals in the U.S.	Stake of 33.33%
	2009	Terminal expansion of Piraeus Port in Greece	35-Year franchise of Container Terminal 2# and 3#
	2012	Taiwan Kao Ming Container Terminal in China	Stake of 30%
	2015	Port of Busan in South Korea	Stake of 20%
	2015	Kumport Terminal in Turkey	Stake of 26%
	2016	Reefer Terminal S.P.A in Italy	Stake of 40%
	2016	Abu Dhabi Khalifa Port in the U.A.E.	Stake of 90%
	2016	Euromax Terminal in the Netherlands	Stake of 47.5%
	2016	Piraeus Port in Greece	Stake of 67%
	2016	Cosco-PSA Terminal in Singapore	Joint venture
	2017	Zeebrugge Terminal in Belgium	Stake of 100%
	2017	Noatum Port in Spain	Stake of 51%
China Merchants Port Holdings Company Limited	2008	VICP in Vietnam	Stake of 49%
	2010	Port of Hambantota in Sri Lanka	Stake of 64.98% together with China Harbor Engineering Corporation (CHEC)
	2010	Vung Tau Container Terminal in Vietnam	Stake of 49%
	2010	TICT in Nigeria	Stake of 28.5%
	2011	CICT in Sri Lanka	Stake of 85%
	2012	Togo Container Terminal	Stake of 50%
	2013	Djibouti Container Terminal	Stake of 23.5%
	2013	Terminal Link	Stake of 49%
	2013	Comprehensive development project of Bagamoyo Port in Tanzania	Investment of 10 US billion dollars
	2014	Zarubino Port in Russia	Joint construction
	2014	Newcastle Port in Australia	Stake of 50%
	2015	Kumport Terminal in Turkey	Stake of 26%
	2015	Kyaukpyu Port in Myanmar	Build-operate-transfer (BOT) project
	2017	TCP in Brazil	Stake of 90%
	2017	Hambantota Port in Sri Lanka	Stake of 85%
China Communications Construction Company Limited	2002	Gwadar Deep-water Port in Pakistan	Providing 75% of port construction funds and obtaining operating rights in 2013
	2013	New Container Berth at Port Sudan	Providing assistance in construction
	2014	Mauritania Friendship Port Construction Project	–
	Commenced in 2014	Walvis Bay Container Terminal in Namibia	Providing assistance in construction
China Harbour Engineering Corporation (CHEC)	Commenced in 2013	Colombo South Harbor Container Terminal in Sri Lanka	–
	Commenced in 2014	International Bulk Cargo Terminal of Port Qasim in Pakistan	–
	Commenced in 2014	New harbor in Abaco Island in the Bahamas	–
	Signed in 2014	Southern Port of Ashdod in Israel	–
	2015	Port of Ain Sukhna in Egypt	–
China Road & Bridge Corporation	Commenced in 2014	Mauritania Friendship Port Expansion Project	Providing assistance in construction
Shanghai International Port Group	2010	Zeebrugge Terminal in Belgium	Stake of 25%
	2015	Haifa Bayport in Israel	25-year franchise from 2021 onwards

(Continued)

Table 1. (Continued).

Port Enterprises	Year	Terminal Projects	Investment
Qingdao Port Group	2011	Maday Island Terminal, Kyaukpyu Port in Myanmar	Signed China-Myanmar Oil Pipeline and Oil Terminal Operation Strategic Framework Agreement with PetroChina
	2016	Vado Port in Italy	Acquisition
Guangxi Beibu Gulf International Port Group	2013	MCKIP in Malaysia	Joint construction
	2013	Kuantan Port in Malaysia	Joint construction
	2015	Kuantan Port in Malaysia	Stake of 40%
	2017	Muara Port in Brunei	Joint construction
Port of Yantai Group	2015	Port of Boke in Guinea	Stake of 10%
Dalian Port Group	2016	DMP and Djibouti Free Trade Zone	Joint construction
Shenzhen Yantian Port Group and Rizhao Port Group	2016	Melaka Gateway Port in Malaysia	Joint construction
Hebei Port Group	2016	Jambi Industrial Park Port in Indonesia	–

Source: Annual Report of COSCO Shipping Ports Limited, Annual Report of China Merchants Port Holdings Company Limited, 'Belt and Road' Initiative and Interactive Development of China's Shipping Industry by Zhen Hong, Shanghai Pujiang Education Press, 2016.

remain a major driver of global city growth. To become new international shipping centers, Chinese ports must forge ahead in an orderly and steady manner, instead of rushing out. Generally, ports that 'go global' are required to possess comprehensive capabilities for development. Investment and cooperation with ports along the MSR not only depend on the development and comprehensive competitiveness of Chinese ports, but also on the economic strength of the cities where these ports are located.

With regard to the governance over investment and cooperation with ports along the B&R, the central government and local governments have distinct focuses in terms of governance models and methods due to China's port management system reform. Since the central government initiated the port system reform in 1998, local governments have played an increasingly important role in operation and management of ports, resulting in intense competition in different regions and surging investment. But the situation lacks effective control. Both the central government and local governments back ports' 'going global strategy', but they take different governance models and methods. The central government looks at national interests and introduces macro-governance policies on investment in and cooperation with ports along the B&R, while local governments are responsible for governing the international cooperation of local port enterprises.

Therefore, under the double-level governance of the central and local governments, discrepancies inevitably arise between the policies launched by the central and local governments. Local governments often think more about parochial interests, and favor huge investments and large scales in 'going global'. They blindly follow the trend and compete fiercely with other domestic investors in overseas ports. In contrast, the central government hopes that port enterprises can steadily implement the strategy based on their own strengths and effective internal cooperation, and achieve reasonable allocation of resources. Therefore, it becomes essential and critical to build a well-designed governance framework and system for Chinese ports' investment and cooperation, which is an important objective of this study. Through analysis and research of the 'going global' strength of China's major ports, this article aims to determine a rational and robust policy framework for Chinese ports' overseas investment and cooperation, so as to provide government departments and port stakeholders effective decision-making methods and tools to govern overseas investment, enable the central government to offer constructive advice and strategies for foreign investment by ports, and guide local governments in governing international cooperation of ports. As a result, the 'Going Global Strategy' of Chinese ports can be better aligned with the national strategy of the'21st Century Maritime Silk Road' in a sustainable and robust way.

Methodology

Priority index of a port development

The priority index of ports to 'Go Global' along the MSR discussed in this article starts from two dimensions: the ports' own conditions and the economic situations of the port city, as shown in Figure 2. Specifically, a port's development conditions involve, among others, cargo throughput, container throughput, berth length, number of berths and number of machineries at the port. The economic indicators of a port city include the annual gross product, the annual gross product of the secondary industries, the annual gross product of the tertiary industries, the urban area, permanent population and import and export trade volumes of the port city. The priority evaluation index of a port is represented by $A_i (i = 1, 2, \ldots, 10)$, where A_1 stands for the cargo throughput of the port (10,000 tonnes), A_2 stands for the container throughput of the port (10,000 TEUs), A_3 stands for the berth length (km), A_4 stands for the number of berths, and A_5 stands for the number of machineries at the port. A_6 represents the city's annual gross product (100 million yuan), A_7 represents the annual gross product of the secondary industries (100 million yuan), A_8 represents the annual gross product of the tertiary industries (100 million yuan), A_9 represents the urban area (sq km), A_{10} represents the permanent population in the city (10,000 people), and A_{11} represents the import and export trade volume of the city (100 million yuan). Detailed explanations are provided below:

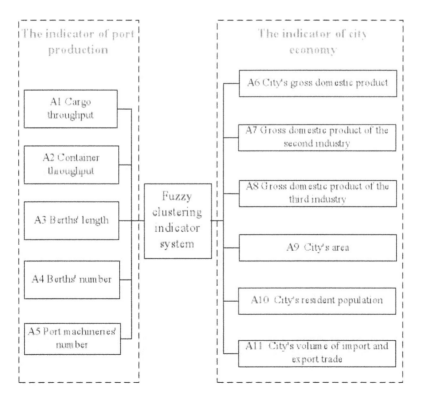

Figure 2. Variables of development priority of ports in fuzzy clustering index system.

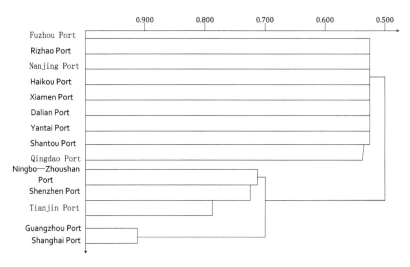

Figure 3. Dynamic cluster graph for port priority development.

A1 and **A2**, cargo throughput and container throughput of the port, indicate the current scale of the port, given the fact the throughput is the most direct manifestation of a port's development scale and fundamental conditions. Of the two, the cargo throughput uses 10,000 tonnes as the unit, being an important quantitative indicator reflecting the port's scale and service level, and indicating the local construction and development status. The container throughput uses 10,000 TEUs as the unit, being an important indicator of the port scale.

A3, berth length at a port, refers to the actual length of berths for docking ships and shows the production infrastructure levels. It can also indicate the size of vessels allowed to dock at the port. Larger ships generally choose to call at ports with sufficient cargo sources, wide shipping routes and complete port facilities. **A4**, the number of berths at a port, refers to the number of berths that are able to dock ships and complete cargo loading and unloading operations. The more berths a port owns, the more frequent the port is called at by ships. This article can say the number of berths impacts the port scale to a large extent.

Sufficient machineries (**A5**) can meet the requirements for high-intensity port production operations. It is an indicator of the port's productivity. The number of machineries impacts the labor intensity and cargo throughput capacity of a port and reflects the fundamental conditions of a port.

The annual gross product indicator of **A6** of a city reflects the total value of all products produced by the city within a period of time. It is used to evaluate the overall economic development status of a city. The annual gross product of the secondary industries, **A7**, refers to the result of industry-related activities by all units or factories in a region, measured by the actual product prices. The annual gross product of the tertiary industries, **A8**, refers to the result of service-related activities by all units in a region, measured by the actual product prices. They are all indicators of a city's economy. Sound economic conditions are conducive to promoting the maritime shipping demands of a port. Therefore, they are included in the fuzzy clustering indicator system for prioritizing 'going global' of ports.

A9, the urban area, directly impacts the division of land use. It is an indicator of urban land scale. Sufficient land areas are the foundation for port development. The larger the area allocated to ports, the more space for port plans to meet the city's development demands.

A10, urban population, refers to the population that has close relationships with urban activities. It is an indicator reflecting a city's economic potentials. Urban population constitutes the major part of a city. The larger the urban population is, the larger the consumption potential of the city is. Consequently, the larger the demands for both goods and shipping services are. This sequence will boost the city's economic development and the demands for maritime shipping at the port.

A11, the import and export trade volume of a city, is used to observe the overall scale of a city in its foreign trade. It signals the existing economic and trade structures. The larger the import and export trade volume, the more foreign-trade-oriented the city's economy, and the more favorable for the city to implement the 'going global' development policies.

Fuzzy clustering model

The fuzzy clustering analysis model is a method that calculates the fuzzy similar distances between samples based on the similarity or dissimilarity of objective things, and then conducts dynamic clustering based on different threshold value λ. The fuzzy clustering process is a branch of the clustering analysis method. It expands the value range of membership and enables data categorization after standardizing data of different units. This method boasts sound clustering effects and data-processing capabilities, and is easy to apply. These features make it suitable for dividing the 'going global' priority of ports based on the 11 indicators of varied units in this example. The fuzzy clustering method is comprised of four steps as described in Appendix 1.

Case study

Data collection and organization

Data in this article are from *China Ports Yearbook 2016, China City Yearbook 2016* and databases of the National Bureau of Statistics of China. The original data matrix of the total 11 categorized indicators for prioritizing port development for 'going global strategy' is shown in Table 2.

Application of the prioritizing method of port development to 'going global strategy'

Translate the original data in Table 2 with the Formula (1) in Appendix 1 and measure the standard deviation, and the original data can be standardized. The standardized data matrix is shown in Table 3.

Use the similarity coefficient method, that is, Formula (2) in Appendix 1, to process values in the matrix to within the [−1 to 1] range.

$$\begin{pmatrix}
1.000 & 0.587 & 0.410 & 0.839 & 0.447 & -0.848 & -0.408 & -0.085 & -0.285 & -0.472 & -1.000 & -0.234 & -0.781 & -0.612 \\
0.587 & 1.000 & 0.038 & 0.169 & 0.174 & -0.272 & -0.100 & 0.017 & -0.028 & -0.201 & -0.314 & -0.038 & -0.234 & -0.159 \\
0.410 & 0.038 & 1.000 & 0.060 & -0.280 & -0.342 & 0.012 & 0.077 & 0.072 & -0.229 & -0.306 & -0.121 & -0.120 & -0.088 \\
0.839 & 0.169 & 0.060 & 1.000 & 0.292 & -0.339 & -0.214 & -0.051 & -0.158 & -0.204 & -0.379 & -0.115 & -0.322 & -0.266 \\
0.447 & 0.174 & -0.280 & 0.292 & 1.000 & -0.110 & -0.184 & -0.031 & -0.121 & -0.030 & -0.149 & -0.033 & -0.182 & -0.180 \\
-0.848 & -0.272 & -0.342 & -0.339 & -0.110 & 1.000 & 0.119 & -0.028 & 0.041 & 0.254 & 0.442 & 0.131 & 0.306 & 0.227 \\
-0.408 & -0.100 & 0.012 & -0.214 & -0.184 & 0.119 & 1.000 & 0.019 & 0.090 & 0.055 & 0.143 & 0.032 & 0.123 & 0.156 \\
-0.085 & 0.017 & 0.077 & -0.051 & -0.031 & -0.028 & 0.019 & 1.000 & 0.050 & -0.017 & -0.011 & -0.038 & 0.018 & 0.012 \\
-0.285 & -0.028 & 0.072 & -0.158 & -0.121 & 0.041 & 0.090 & 0.050 & 1.000 & 0.012 & 0.071 & 0.002 & 0.082 & 0.087 \\
-0.472 & -0.201 & -0.229 & -0.204 & -0.030 & 0.254 & 0.055 & -0.017 & 0.012 & 1.000 & 0.277 & 0.036 & 0.202 & 0.084 \\
-1.000 & -0.314 & -0.306 & -0.379 & -0.149 & 0.442 & 0.143 & -0.011 & 0.071 & 0.277 & 1.000 & 0.127 & 0.355 & 0.253 \\
-0.234 & -0.038 & -0.121 & -0.115 & -0.033 & 0.131 & 0.032 & -0.038 & 0.002 & 0.036 & 0.127 & 1.000 & 0.075 & 0.084 \\
-0.781 & -0.234 & -0.120 & -0.322 & -0.182 & 0.306 & 0.123 & 0.018 & 0.082 & 0.202 & 0.355 & 0.075 & 1.000 & 0.182 \\
-0.612 & -0.159 & -0.088 & -0.266 & -0.180 & 0.227 & 0.156 & 0.012 & 0.087 & 0.084 & 0.253 & 0.084 & 0.182 & 1.000
\end{pmatrix}$$

Use Formula (3) in Appendix 1 to process values to within the [0–1] range to work out the fuzzy similarity matrix R.

Table 2. Original data matrix

Port	A1	A2	A3	A4	A5	A6	A7	A8	A9	A10	A11
Shanghai	64906.000	3654.000	126.900	1300.000	3256.000	24964.990	7991.000	17022.630	8359.120	2415.270	28000.000
Tianjin	54051.000	1411.000	38.729	173.000	1184.000	16538.190	7704.220	8625.150	11946.000	1547.000	7513.970
Ningbo-Zhoushan	88929.000	2063.000	86.790	1054.000	843.000	8011.500	2497.350	2382.140	21014.120	347.300	7768.740
Guangzhou	50053.000	1762.490	38.467	769.000	1305.000	18100.410	4495.100	9498.600	7434.400	1350.110	63600.000
Shenzhen	21706.000	2420.450	16.943	172.000	1172.000	17502.990	6296.850	8198.140	1991.640	1137.890	27516.000
Shantou	5181.000	117.860	9.627	87.000	152.000	1850.000	812.060	656.070	2064.420	555.210	610.136
Yantai	25163.000	245.000	29.857	186.000	977.000	6446.080	1433.200	1093.570	13851.500	701.410	3278.175
Qingdao	48453.000	1744.000	28.335	121.000	756.000	9300.070	2433.380	2645.780	11282.000	909.700	8972.600
Dalian	41482.000	945.000	27.318	120.000	739.000	7731.600	2228.210	2583.270	13237.000	676.680	3476.400
Xiamen	21023.000	918.000	12.152	159.000	1213.000	3466.010	1434.790	1557.380	1699.390	386.000	5169.500
Haikou	9204.210	127.100	2.772	21.000	47.000	1161.280	217.030	629.510	3134.840	222.300	868.600
Nanjing	21454.000	294.000	36.274	346.000	277.000	9720.770	3450.580	4356.560	6597.000	821.610	3500.478
Rizhao	33707.000	281.000	15.606	62.000	331.000	1670.800	704.750	390.740	5359.000	295.950	997.837
Fuzhou	13967.230	242.820	23.687	171.000	197.000	5618.100	850.110	1438.240	12000.000	750.000	2065.500

Table 3. Standardized data matrix

Port	A1	A2	A3	A4	A5	A6	A7	A8	A9	A10	A11
Shanghai	1.284	2.423	2.866	2.485	3.035	2.225	1.966	2.734	−0.039	2.707	0.973
Tianjin	0.807	0.245	0.109	−0.428	0.378	1.018	1.852	0.921	0.622	1.191	−0.247
Ningbo-Zhoushan	2.339	0.878	1.612	1.849	−0.059	−0.204	−0.215	−0.428	2.291	−0.905	−0.232
Guangzhou	0.632	0.586	0.101	1.112	0.533	1.241	0.578	1.109	−0.209	0.847	3.093
Shenzhen	−0.613	1.225	−0.572	−0.431	0.363	1.156	1.293	0.828	−1.211	0.476	0.944
Shantou	−1.339	−1.011	−0.801	−0.650	−0.945	−1.086	−0.884	−0.801	−1.198	−0.542	−0.659
Yantai	−0.461	−0.887	−0.169	−0.394	0.113	−0.428	−0.638	−0.706	0.973	−0.287	−0.500
Qingdao	0.562	0.568	−0.216	−0.562	−0.171	−0.019	−0.241	−0.371	0.499	0.077	−0.160
Dalian	0.256	−0.208	−0.248	−0.565	−0.193	−0.244	−0.322	−0.384	0.859	−0.330	−0.488
Xiamen	−0.643	−0.234	−0.722	−0.464	0.415	−0.855	−0.637	−0.606	−1.265	−0.838	−0.387
Haikou	−1.162	−1.002	−1.015	−0.821	−1.080	−1.185	−1.120	−0.806	−1.001	−1.124	−0.643
Nanjing	−0.624	−0.840	0.032	0.019	−0.785	0.041	0.163	−0.001	−0.363	−0.077	−0.486
Rizhao	−0.086	−0.852	−0.614	−0.715	−0.716	−1.112	−0.927	−0.858	−0.591	−0.995	−0.636
Fuzhou	−0.953	−0.890	−0.361	−0.433	−0.888	−0.547	−0.869	−0.632	0.632	−0.202	−0.572

$$
\begin{pmatrix}
1.000 & 0.794 & 0.705 & 0.919 & 0.724 & 0.076 & 0.294 & 0.458 & 0.358 & 0.264 & 0.000 & 0.383 & 0.110 & 0.194 \\
0.794 & 1.000 & 0.519 & 0.585 & 0.587 & 0.364 & 0.450 & 0.508 & 0.486 & 0.399 & 0.343 & 0.481 & 0.383 & 0.420 \\
0.705 & 0.519 & 1.000 & 0.530 & 0.360 & 0.329 & 0.506 & 0.539 & 0.536 & 0.385 & 0.347 & 0.440 & 0.440 & 0.456 \\
0.919 & 0.585 & 0.530 & 1.000 & 0.646 & 0.330 & 0.393 & 0.475 & 0.421 & 0.398 & 0.310 & 0.442 & 0.339 & 0.367 \\
0.724 & 0.587 & 0.360 & 0.646 & 1.000 & 0.445 & 0.408 & 0.485 & 0.439 & 0.485 & 0.426 & 0.483 & 0.409 & 0.410 \\
0.076 & 0.364 & 0.329 & 0.330 & 0.445 & 1.000 & 0.559 & 0.486 & 0.521 & 0.627 & 0.721 & 0.566 & 0.653 & 0.614 \\
0.296 & 0.450 & 0.506 & 0.393 & 0.408 & 0.559 & 1.000 & 0.510 & 0.545 & 0.528 & 0.571 & 0.516 & 0.561 & 0.578 \\
0.458 & 0.508 & 0.539 & 0.475 & 0.485 & 0.486 & 0.510 & 1.000 & 0.525 & 0.492 & 0.495 & 0.481 & 0.509 & 0.506 \\
0.358 & 0.486 & 0.536 & 0.421 & 0.439 & 0.521 & 0.545 & 0.525 & 1.000 & 0.506 & 0.535 & 0.501 & 0.541 & 0.544 \\
0.264 & 0.399 & 0.385 & 0.398 & 0.485 & 0.627 & 0.528 & 0.492 & 0.506 & 1.000 & 0.638 & 0.518 & 0.601 & 0.542 \\
0.000 & 0.343 & 0.347 & 0.310 & 0.426 & 0.721 & 0.571 & 0.495 & 0.535 & 0.638 & 1.000 & 0.563 & 0.678 & 0.626 \\
0.383 & 0.481 & 0.440 & 0.442 & 0.483 & 0.566 & 0.516 & 0.481 & 0.501 & 0.518 & 0.563 & 1.000 & 0.537 & 0.542 \\
0.110 & 0.383 & 0.440 & 0.339 & 0.409 & 0.653 & 0.561 & 0.509 & 0.541 & 0.601 & 0.678 & 0.537 & 1.000 & 0.591 \\
0.194 & 0.420 & 0.456 & 0.367 & 0.410 & 0.614 & 0.578 & 0.506 & 0.544 & 0.542 & 0.626 & 0.542 & 0.591 & 1.000
\end{pmatrix}
$$

Use the convolution method (4) in Appendix 1 to process the fuzzy similarity matrix R, that is, work out the transitive closure $t(R)$ using the quadratic: $R \to R^2 \to R^4 \to R^8$, and $R^8 \circ R^8 = R^8$. This article can obtain the fuzzy equivalence matrix $t(R) = R^8 = R^*$, as shown below:

$$
\begin{pmatrix}
1.000 & 0.794 & 0.705 & 0.919 & 0.724 & 0.536 & 0.536 & 0.539 & 0.536 & 0.536 & 0.536 & 0.536 & 0.536 & 0.536 \\
0.764 & 1.000 & 0.705 & 0.794 & 0.724 & 0.536 & 0.536 & 0.539 & 0.536 & 0.536 & 0.536 & 0.536 & 0.536 & 0.536 \\
0.705 & 0.705 & 1.000 & 0.705 & 0.705 & 0.536 & 0.536 & 0.539 & 0.536 & 0.536 & 0.536 & 0.536 & 0.536 & 0.536 \\
0.919 & 0.794 & 0.705 & 1.000 & 0.724 & 0.536 & 0.536 & 0.539 & 0.536 & 0.536 & 0.536 & 0.536 & 0.536 & 0.536 \\
0.724 & 0.724 & 0.705 & 0.724 & 1.000 & 0.536 & 0.536 & 0.539 & 0.536 & 0.536 & 0.536 & 0.536 & 0.536 & 0.536 \\
0.536 & 0.536 & 0.536 & 0.536 & 0.536 & 1.000 & 0.578 & 0.536 & 0.545 & 0.638 & 0.721 & 0.566 & 0.678 & 0.626 \\
0.536 & 0.536 & 0.536 & 0.536 & 0.536 & 0.578 & 1.000 & 0.536 & 0.545 & 0.578 & 0.578 & 0.566 & 0.578 & 0.578 \\
0.539 & 0.539 & 0.539 & 0.539 & 0.539 & 0.536 & 0.536 & 1.000 & 0.536 & 0.536 & 0.536 & 0.536 & 0.536 & 0.536 \\
0.536 & 0.536 & 0.536 & 0.536 & 0.536 & 0.545 & 0.545 & 0.536 & 1.000 & 0.545 & 0.545 & 0.545 & 0.545 & 0.545 \\
0.536 & 0.536 & 0.536 & 0.536 & 0.536 & 0.638 & 0.578 & 0.536 & 0.545 & 1.000 & 0.638 & 0.566 & 0.638 & 0.626 \\
0.536 & 0.536 & 0.536 & 0.536 & 0.536 & 0.721 & 0.578 & 0.536 & 0.545 & 0.638 & 1.000 & 0.566 & 0.678 & 0.626 \\
0.536 & 0.536 & 0.536 & 0.536 & 0.536 & 0.566 & 0.566 & 0.536 & 0.545 & 0.566 & 0.566 & 1.000 & 0.566 & 0.566 \\
0.536 & 0.536 & 0.536 & 0.536 & 0.536 & 0.678 & 0.578 & 0.536 & 0.545 & 0.638 & 0.678 & 0.566 & 1.000 & 0.626 \\
0.536 & 0.536 & 0.536 & 0.536 & 0.536 & 0.626 & 0.578 & 0.536 & 0.545 & 0.626 & 0.626 & 0.566 & 0.626 & 1.000
\end{pmatrix}
$$

Fetch different λ-cut matrixes in the fuzzy equivalence matrix. For example, when $\lambda = 0.919$, this article can get the corresponding λ-cut matrix:

When $\lambda = 0.919$, China's 14 ports can be categorized into three priority groups:

The first priority group for the 'going global strategy' is {Shanghai, Guangzhou}.

The second priority group is {Tianjin, Shenzhen, Ningbo-Zhoushan}.

The third priority group is {Qingdao, Shantou, Yantai, Dalian, Xiamen, Haikou, Nanjing, Rizhao, Fuzhou}.

Based on different $\lambda(0 \leq \lambda \leq 1)$ values, namely, from small to large, 0.536, 0.539, 0.705, 0.724, 0.794 and 0.919, this article can get different priority groups for ports 'going global' along the MSR which constitute the following dynamic clustering graph.

Analysis of calculation results and suggestions

This article chooses $\lambda = 0.919$ as the basis and categorizes China's 14 ports into three priority groups (see Figure 3):

The first group is {Shanghai, Guangzhou}.

The second is {Tianjin, Shenzhen, Ningbo-Zhoushan}.

The third is {Qingdao, Shantou, Yantai, Dalian, Xiamen, Haikou, Nanjing, Rizhao, Fuzhou}.

Drawing reference from the above categorization method, the following strategies can be adopted for prioritizing port development under the 'going global strategy' along the MSR.

Strategy for ports in the first priority group: Shanghai, Guangzhou

The test results show that Shanghai and Guangzhou ports belong to the first priority group. It means that the first priority to promote the 'going global strategy' goes to the two ports because they enjoy sound port scales and outstanding economic and foreign trade foundations. Shanghai Port, as the largest container port in the world, owns advanced and dense shipping routes. It took the lead in 2015 to win the bid for running the Haifa New Port terminals in Israel for 25 years starting from 2021. Shanghai Port will leverage its long years of port management experience, management techniques and long-term friendly partnerships with many shipping companies to build Haifa New Port into the hub of the Mediterranean region. In addition, Shanghai has implemented free trade zones and harvested rich experience in innovations and breakthroughs in the shipping system. The 'going global strategy' can bring the advanced experience of Shanghai Port to foreign markets to roll out overseas warehousing logistics as well as overseas processing logistics, and to develop bonded warehouses and establish supporting international shipping services. Shanghai ranks first in eight indicators among the total 11. For this reason, Shanghai Port has obvious advantages in the 'going global strategy', and plays a leading and exemplary role in this respect. Guangzhou Port marks an important node in the Pearl River Delta port cluster. This cluster is backed by a hinterland boasting advanced processing and manufacturing industries, and is industry-wise and economically complementary with areas along the B&R. In view of this, it has advantages in developing transshipment, containerized transport and other container shipping logistic services based on its geographical and industrial features and building itself into a logistic service hub with container shipping as the center and serving the MSR. The foreign trade imports and exports of Guangzhou city were as high as 6.36 trillion yuan in 2015, more than double that of Shanghai, the runner-up on this indicator. These data dramatically improve the ranking of Guangzhou Port on the priority list of ports for 'going global'. In addition, *The Paper*, a newspaper, recently reported that Guangzhou and Dongguan cities in Guangdong province have signed a cooperation agreement to accelerate port resource integration, and integrate Guangzhou-Dongguan ports into one.[32] The regional integration of ports is expected to greatly elevate the overall scale and fundamental conditions of Guangzhou Port and curb excessive inter-port competition in the adjacent regions and differences between the local governments. This move toward port integration is good for the Chinese industry to efficiently implement the 'going global strategy'. Another case of this inter-port integration can be found in the second priority group.

---

[32]Xiaoyi Wang, 'Guangdong gangkou ziyuan zhenghe: Guangzhou, Dongguan dazao zuhegang, jinyibu rongru dawanqu', ['The integration of Guangdong port resources: Guangzhou, Dongguan to build a portfolio into the Bay Area'], 20 October 2017, translation, http://www.thepaper.cn, available at: http://news.163.com/17/1020/17/D177UEIT000187VE.html (accessed on 21 October 2017).

Strategy for ports in the second priority group: Tianjin, Shenzhen, Ningbo-Zhoushan

The test results show that ports of Tianjin, Shenzhen, Ningbo-Zhoushan fall into the second priority. These ports are also world-class. Their comprehensive strength is not as good as that of ports in the first group. However, they boast a big potential for 'going global' along the MSR. The advantage of Tianjin Port lies in its advanced sea-railway combined transportation, which is connected to major land bridges. This makes Tianjin an important port connecting the B&R, which means it has the potential to become a land-sea combined transportation hub serving the Far East and the B&R. Considering its superior geographical location as the maritime portal of Beijing, Tianjin and Hebei areas, and the nearest easternmost point of the Eurasian Continental Bridge, Tianjin Port undoubtedly gains an upper hand in the BRI. Shenzhen Port is an important component in the Pearl River Delta port cluster and has a hinterland with advanced processing and manufacturing industries. From its establishment to the year of 2017, Shenzhen Port has built friendly partnerships with 22 world-renowned ports, including the Port of Hamburg in Germany, the Port of Colombo in Sri Lanka, and Port of Zeebrugge in Belgium. However, owing to the limited land area of Shenzhen city, Shenzhen Port may face difficulties in further expanding its capacity. The Ningbo-Zhoushan Port (NZP) is in advantageous position in leading cargo throughput thanks to the merging synergy effects. The NZP Group released the 2016 annual statement, showing that the port recorded an accumulated container throughput of 21.56 million TEUs, rising by 4.5% year-on-year, the growth rate being the highest among the top five ports in the world.[33] In addition, its urban area is the largest among the 14 ports. The two merged ports are necessary to capture cargoes from their hinterland by investing in port construction and by speeding up regional integration in Zhejiang province. These actions will contribute to attracting neighboring cities to join the integration tide so that its cargo shipping and container throughput can be amplified. The five ports in the first and second priority groups have their own advantages and are all ready to launch the 'going global strategy'. The $0.900 < \lambda < 1.000$ of the first priority group is higher than the $0.700 < \lambda < 0.800$ of the second group, implying the former has a higher priority for 'going global' along the MSR than the latter.

The purpose of port regionalization resides in the qualitative improvement and quantitative expansion of the port system at home.

Strategy for ports in the third priority group: Qingdao, Shantou, Yantai, Dalian, Xiamen, Haikou, Nanjing, Rizhao, Fuzhou

The ports in the third group have strong motivation to steadily promote the 'going global strategy', though they still have to close the gap in terms of port scale or urban economic strength, and lag behind large domestic ports. They are still in the cultivation phase, pursuing a higher container throughput. Qingdao, Yantai, Dalian, and Rizhao ports are all in the Bohai-Rim port cluster. Dalian Port, an international shipping center, in Northeast Asia, works with Qingdao Port in Shandong province to invest efforts in transforming themselves into container trunk ports and improving their container throughput capacities. Ports of smaller scales such as Yantai and Rizhao ports in Shandong province can jointly pursue staggered development to avoid face-to-face competition with Qingdao Port for container sources. They can try to build themselves into professional ports for natural gas, iron ore, grain and other staple bulk cargoes. Nanjing Port in the Yangtze River Delta port cluster is useful to actively respond to the 'Yangtze River Strategy' of Shanghai Port and, as a container feeder port of Shanghai Port, promote the water-water transfer business in the lower reaches of Yangtze River. Xiamen and Fuzhou ports in the southeast coastal port cluster may resort to staggered development, namely the Xiamen cruise port and Fuzhou bulk cargo port, while

---

[33]Xiaoyi Wang, 'Niu! 2016nian Ningbo-Zhoushangang jizhuangxiang tuntuliang zengfu ju quanqiu wudagang zhishou', ['In 2016, Ningbo-Zhoushan port container's throughput growth ranked first in the world's five largest ports'], http://www.cnnb.com.cn, 13 January 2017, translation, available at: http://money.163.com/17/0113/18/CAMBLDBP002580S6.html (accessed 21 October 2017).

striving to elevate their respective container throughputs. Haikou Port in the Pearl River Delta is necessary to accelerate port integration in the island and to integrate the industrial logistics at Yangpu Port in the northwest of the island and the cruise services at Sanya Port in the south of the island to further grow the port's strength in the island. Shantou Port must also pursue a higher container throughput to further its strength. The nine ports in the third priority group are under-developed compared with the ports in the first and second groups, but they are close to each other and no more refined division can be made among them. Some ports in this third priority group can enter the second group after a period of fast development, and win the chance for 'going global', while others may remain in the third group, and even be overtaken by ports below them.

Discrepancy between provincial/local and central governments for port developments

The actual port development in China does not match the three-tier rankings. As Table 1 shows the third-tier ports in Qingdao, Yantai, Dalian have put the 'going global strategy' onto their agenda in recent years. As of March 2018, China has 8 out of top 20 container ports in the world, except Hong Kong, in which the central government does not have investment. Such remarkable port development led by the local governments has contributed to eco-nomic growth. But it has also exposed negative externalities, such as deteriorating efficiency of port performance, misallocation of national resources and excessive inter-port competition among provinces sharing the same hinterland, and unequal development between a port and a city. To cope with those problems, the central government issued a notice to implement the pilot reform of regional port integration development on 5 March 2015. As a result, the central government and Zhejiang province government jointly approved the master plan of Ningbo-Zhoushan Port (NZP) for 2014–2030 as an exemplary port integration project. Following the plan, NZP Group was launched in September 2015, co-transferring 100% state-owned equity and assets between Ningbo Port Group and Zhoushan Port Group. This implies that NZP Group has become physically and legally integrated in terms of operation and investment and governance of the NZP and now both decentralization and centralization mode co-exist in the port.[34] This inter-port integration among operators and authorities in the two neighboring ports, i.e. Ningbo and Zhoushan, having the same hinterland for container cargoes, is a remarkable case, although it is too early to judge its performance and success. NZP belongs to the second priority group. The NZP has Yangtze River-Sea combined policy under the central government development agenda. This article assumes that NZP will take advantage of the 'going global strategy' in tandem with BRI. Although Tianjin Port belongs to the same group as NZP, from the geo-economic-political viewpoint and the indicators of port connectivity and cargo throughput, the port lags behind NZP. Despite that, the port city government tries to exercise its decentralized power in moving toward the 'going global strategy'. In doing so, BRI tends to be used by provincial and local governments to recklessly justify their port expansion.

Therefore, the test results in the article help policymakers of the central government find a sound threshold to prioritize China's overseas port investment between the ports in the second priority group and Qingdao, Shantou, Yantai, Dalian, Xiamen, Haikou, Nanjing, Rizhao, Fuzhou in the third group. Consequently, the country could save national as well as provincial resources, mitigating conflicts with the central and the provincial governments.

---

[34]Shiyuan Zheng and Rudy R. Negenborn, 'Centralization or decentralization: A comparative analysis of port regulation modes', *Transportation Research Part E*. 69, (2014), pp. 21–40.

Conclusion

The 'Belt and Road Initiative (BRI)' aims to connect China to Asia, Africa, and Europe and with nearby oceans and establish and enhance partnerships between countries along the routes. In this regard, the BRI will further promote China's port connectivity under the 'going global strategy', taking part in global port construction and operation. However, not all ports are capable of implementing this strategy with their current position and economic strength. Therefore, they need to weigh their own development scales and fundamental conditions as well as the foreign trade situations of the port cities comprehensively. Having considered this situation, this article has chosen 14 coastal ports to prioritize port development indexes to implement the 'going global strategy', and categories the ports into three priority groups, applying the fuzzy clustering method in an effective and objective manner. The test results show that the first priority group contains ports of {Shanghai, Guangzhou}, the second one includes ports of {Tianjin, Shenzhen, Ningbo-Zhoushan}, and the third covers ports of {Qingdao, Shantou, Yantai, Dalian, Xiamen, Haikou, Nanjing, Rizhao, Fuzhou}.

However, from a domestic perspective, under the double-level governance of the central and local governments, discrepancies, disjointed actions and gaps inevitably arise between the policies launched by the central and local governments. Local governments often think more about parochial interests and favor huge investments without considering their positions in a national strategy. Recent changes in Chinese port governance system in association with growing influences of provincial and local governments in port investment and operation have motivated some ports/cities to follow the 'going global strategy' without sound evaluation of risk and profitability. In addition, China's overseas port investment requires huge capital and complex series of undertaking along the MSR where several provincial and local governments and private sectors will participate in the investment process. Therefore, this article highlights the priority assessment of port development, offers corresponding countermeasures against enthusiasm of the provincial and local governments scrambling for port expansion and overseas port investment, and suggests that ports/cities 'go global' according to their varied scales and fundamental conditions. These countermeasures can avoid waste of national and regional resources, help not only policymakers implement the 'going global strategy' based on the identified priority but also the Chinese port industry achieve its sustainable development in the context of the BRI.

Acknowledgments

The authors acknowledge the commentators at the BRI workshop held at Ocean College of Zhejiang University in Zhoushan, China, on December 1-2, 2016, and Professor Baogang He for their constructive comments to improve this article. This research was supported by the National Natural Science Foundation of China (Grant No. 51409157; 71603162), the Program of Humanities and Social Science of the Ministry of Education of China (14YJC630008), Shanghai Pujiang Program (17PJC053), and Shanghai Science & Technology Committee Research Project (15590501700 and 17040501700).

Conflict of Interests:

The authors declare that there is no conflict of interests regarding the publication of this paper.

Funding

This research was supported by the National Natural Science Foundation of China (Grant Nos. 51879156;51409157; 71603162), the Program of Humanities and Social Science of the Ministry of Education of China(14YJC630008), Shanghai Pujiang Program (17PJC053), and Shanghai Science & Technology Committee Research Project (15590501700 and 17040501700).

Appendix 1. Four Steps of Fuzzy Clustering Method

Step 1: Define the data matrix. This article supposes $U = \{x_1, x_2, \ldots, x_n\}$ is the collection of n ports, and each port has m corresponding indicators impacting port development and core competitiveness. The collection of the m indicators is represented by $x_i = \{x_{i1}, x_{i2}, \ldots, x_{im}\}(i = 1, 2, \ldots, n)$. This article can thereby work out the original data matrix $X = \{x_{ik}\}$ of the port, where $i = 1, 2, \ldots, n; k = 1, 2, \ldots, m$.

$$\begin{pmatrix} x_{11} & x_{12} & \cdots & x_{1m} \\ x_{21} & x_{22} & \cdots & x_{2m} \\ \cdots & \cdots & \cdots & \cdots \\ x_{n1} & x_{n2} & \cdots & x_{nm} \end{pmatrix}$$

Step 2: Standardize data. It is impossible to guarantee that the m indicators selected are of the same unit in actual problem-solving process. The article needs to standardize the data to facilitate effective accumulation and comparison of indicators of varied units. The first standard deviation conversion is shown as follows:

$$x'_{ik} = \frac{x_{ik} - \bar{x}_k}{S_k} (i = 1, 2, \ldots, n; k = 1, 2, \ldots, m) \tag{1}$$

Specifically, $\bar{x}_k = \frac{1}{n}\sum_{i=1}^{n} x_{ik}$, and $S_k = \sqrt{\frac{1}{n}\sum_{i=1}^{n}(x_{ik} - \bar{x}_k)^2}$.

Step 3: Establish the fuzzy similarity matrix. Although data have been standardized, the result x'_{ik} is not necessarily within the range of $[0, 1]$. According to the fuzzy matrix requirements, this article needs to compress the data to within the $[0, 1]$ range and suppose $U = \{x_1, x_2, \ldots, x_n\}$, and $x_i = \{x_{i1}, x_{i2}, \ldots, x_{im}\}$, the similarity coefficient can be determined by using the traditional clustering method and this article also establishes a fuzzy similarity matrix. The similarity between x_i and x_j is represented by $r_{ij} = R(x_i, x_j)$ which can adopt the scalar product method in the similarity coefficient method:

$$r_{ij} = \begin{cases} 1, i = j \\ \frac{1}{M}\sum_{k=1}^{m} x'_{ik} \cdot x'_{jk}, i \neq j \end{cases} \tag{2}$$

Specifically, $M = \max(\sum_{k=1}^{m} x'_{ik} \cdot x'_{jk})$.

Obviously, $|r_{ij}| \in [0, 1]$. If r_{ij} is negative, this article can further convert the r'_{ij} value to within the $[0, 1]$ range. Make

$$r'_{ij} = \frac{r_{ij} + 1}{2} \tag{3}$$

Step 4. Use the transitive closure method to get the fuzzy equivalence matrix. The calibrated fuzzy matrix is a fuzzy similarity matrix R and not necessarily a fuzzy equivalence one. For the convenience of categorization, this article needs to transform R to a fuzzy equivalence matrix R^*. There is a theorem as follows: Suppose $R \in \mu_{n \times n}$ is the fuzzy similarity matrix. There exists a least natural number $k(k \leq n)$ that enables the transitive closure $t(R) = R^k$. For any natural number q that is bigger than k, it is always true that $R^q = R^k$. At this point, $t(R)$ is the fuzzy equivalence matrix. This fuzzy matrix multiplication is also called fuzzy matrix synthesis. The formulas are: if $A = (a_{ij})m \times s$ and $B = (b_{ij})s \times n$, this article says the fuzzy matrix $A \circ B = (c_{ij})m \times n$ is the synthesis of matrix A and matrix B, where

$$c_{ij} = \vee_{k=1}^{s}(a_{ij} \wedge b_{ij}) \tag{4}$$

After the transitive closure $t(R)$ is calculated with the above quadratic, the result $t(R) = R^*$ is the desired fuzzy equivalence matrix R^*, that is, $t(R) = R^*$. Clustering different threshold values λ and setting different λ values based on the fuzzy equivalence matrix R^*, the corresponding clustering result and the dynamic cluster graph can be obtained with the λ threshold values decreasing.

9 Regional Responses to China's Maritime Silk Road Initiative in Southeast Asia

Shaofeng Chen

ABSTRACT

Southeast Asia has sat atop China's Maritime Silk Road Initiative (MSRI). By and large, most Southeast Asian countries hailed China's MSRI, but their responses to it have some variances. The article aims to analyze why they have differing responses. It contends that the primary determinant is changing domestic politics, specifically, ruling elites' policy priority, degree of trust of China, leaders' ideology and preference, and social response. While rejecting the impact of trade imbalance and outward foreign direct investment (FDI) from China, the influence of the South China Sea dispute and America's Asia policy have been partially verified.

Introduction

The Belt and Road Initiative (BRI), which is composed of the land-based 'New Silk Road Economic Belt' and the oceangoing '21st Century Maritime Silk Road Initiative' (MSRI), has become China's overarching development plan and foreign strategy. Since its debut it has riveted world-wide attention. A host of works focus on China's motivations,[1] challenges,[2] impact on some country or region,[3] and so forth. Whether the BRI can succeed or not, however, is contingent not only on China's own capacity, but also on other countries' responses. As President Xi Jinping underscores, 'The programs of development (BRI) will be open and inclusive, not exclusive. They will not be a solo for China but a real chorus comprising all countries along the routes.'[4]

As China's contiguous neighbors with close economic ties, Southeast Asian (SEA) countries not only pertain to China's national and economic security, but also act as an important testing ground for the MSRI and a bridge to other regions, thus crucial to China's MSRI. Although some studies have

---

[1]See, for example, Jean-Marc F. Blanchard and Colin Flint, 'The geopolitics of China's Maritime Silk Road Initiative', *Geopolitics* 22(2), (2017), pp. 223–245; Hong Yu, 'Motivation behind China's "One Belt, One Road" initiatives and establishment of the Asian Infrastructure Investment Bank', *Journal of Contemporary China* 26(105), (2017), pp. 353–368; Simeon Djankov and Sean Miner, eds, *China's Belt and Road Initiative Motives, Scope, and Challenges*, PIIE (Peterson Institute for International Economics) Briefing 16(2), (2016).

[2]See, for example, Jean-Marc F. Blanchard, 'Probing China's twenty-first-century Maritime Silk Road Initiative (MSRI): an examination of MSRI narratives', *Geopolitics* 22(2), (2017), pp. 246–268.

[3]See, for example, Shuaihua Wallace Cheng, 'China's New Silk Road: implications for the US', *Yale Global*, (28 May 2015), available at: http://yaleglobal.yale.edu/content/chinas-new-silk-road-implications-us (accessed 31 October 2017); Enright, Scott & Associates Limited, Prepared for Tekes, *One Belt One Road: Insights for Finland*, Team Finland Future Watch Report (January 2016), available at: https://www.tekes.fi/globalassets/julkaisut/future_watch_report_one_belt_one_road__insights_for_finland.pdf (accessed 31 October 2017).

[4]'China unveils action plan on Belt and Road Initiative', *Xinhua* (28 March 2015), available at: http://news.xinhuanet.com/english/2015-03/28/c_134105372.htm (accessed 31 October 2017).

delved into its implications on SEA,[5] insufficient analysis has been done on SEA countries' responses to the MSRI. This article thus aims to address how SEA countries respond to China's MSRI and why they support it with varying degrees.

In the next section, the author elaborates on the research framework, followed by measurement of SEA countries' support for China's MSRI. The fourth and fifth sections analyze the influence of some variables, particularly domestic politics, on SEA countries' support for the MSRI. Finally, the conclusion discusses the implications of the findings.

Explaining Different Responses From SEA Countries: a Research Framework

Why have SEA countries responded differently? Understandably, their response falls within the purview of overall bilateral relations with China. This article poses the following hypotheses:

Hypothesis 1: Countries enjoying trade surplus with China are more willing to embrace China's MSRI; conversely, countries having trade deficits are less willing.

'Mercantilism never really went away.'[6] Central to mercantilism is the view that the best avenue for countries to become prosperous is to maximize exports while reducing imports. In effect, many countries prefer trade surplus while being averse to trade deficits, which more often than not sows a seed of frictions between countries. This article thus puts forth the above hypothesis.

Hypothesis 2: Countries having more FDI inflows from China are more supportive of the MSRI; conversely, countries having less are less supportive.

FDI inflows have brought capital, technology and know-how, which are crucial to economic development. Studies have found that FDI has a considerable positive effect on host country economic growth thanks to technology spillovers and/or capital buildup.[7] As the MSRI involves massive FDI flows, most SEA countries should have a strong interest to join. This article thus hypothesizes that countries receiving more FDI inflows from China are more supportive considering that they have already hit a sweet spot.

Hypothesis 3: Countries having no territorial disputes with China are more supportive for China's MSRI; conversely, countries having territorial disputes are less supportive.

The territorial dispute over the South China Sea (SCS) has soured China's relations with SEA claimant states. It has not only heightened the risk of conflict, but has also eroded trust among them. Hence, claimant states including Vietnam, the Philippines, Brunei, Malaysia and Indonesia, are liable to suspecting China's strategic intent behind the MSRI.

Hypothesis 4: The US policy towards the SEA is another variable that has a strong impact on SEA countries' responses. When Washington actively engages in Asia, SEA countries are in a better position in dealing with China; but when the US remains aloof from Asia, they may face more difficulties turning down Chinese offers.

Hypothesis 5: Changing domestic politics lead to changing a country's attitude towards the MSRI.

There are many different categories of domestic politics used to analyze how a country behaves in the international sphere, such as two-level games, state strength, bureaucratic politics, domestic coalition,

---

[5]See, for example, David Arase, 'China's two Silk Roads Initiative: what it means for Southeast Asia', *Southeast Asian Affairs* 2015, (2015), pp. 25–45; Hong Yu, 'China's Belt and Road Initiative and its implications for Southeast Asia', *Asia Policy* no. 24, (2017), pp. 117–122.
[6]Dani Rodrik, 'In truth, mercantilism never really went away', *The National*, (11 January 2013), available at: https://www.thenational.ae/business/in-truth-mercantilism-never-really-went-away-1.281703 (accessed 31 October 2017).
[7]V. N. Balasubramanyam, M. Salisu and David Sapsford, 'Foreign direct investment and growth in EP and IS countries', *The Economic Journal* 106(434), (1996), pp. 92–105; E. Borensztein, J. De Gregoriob and J W. Lee, 'How does foreign direct investment affect economic growth?', *Journal of International Economics* 45(1), (1998), pp. 115–135.

etc. This article will explain why SEA countries have differing responses, primarily from three domestic politics factors: regime type, elite legitimation and influence of public opinion.

Hypothesis 5a: More undemocratic countries tend to be more supportive than democratic ones.

As an authoritarian regime, China's MSRI should be more easily accepted by undemocratic countries, where the leaders have the final say. In contrast, more democratic countries will be less supportive as the governments face greater opposition.

Hypothesis 5b: Ruling elites in countries prioritizing wealth creation are more supportive relative to those in countries prioritizing security enhancement.

According to Kuik Cheng-Chwee, a small state's response to a rising power is largely motivated by 'an internal process of regime legitimation in which the ruling elite evaluate—and then utilize—the opportunities and challenges of the rising power for their ultimate goal of consolidating their authority to govern at home'.[8] Akin to the theory of omnibalancing,[9] elite legitimation is built on the premise that the top priority for leaders of developing countries is to try to stay in power. To that end, both theories believe leaders of developing countries need to take account of both external threat and internal challenge.

The impact of a rising power on a small state often encompasses two aspects: one is the prospect of wealth creation. Often associated with a rising power is its burgeoning economy, from which the small state is very likely to reap benefits through expanding exports and outward FDI. The other aspect is security ramifications. Growing economic prowess often will prompt the rising power to build up the military. Consequently, the small state is concerned about whether the rising power may break regional order and pose a security threat to it, particularly those recalcitrant neighbors having interest conflicts. In the face of a rising power, leaders of small states have to calculate its implications for their regime legitimation.

The diversified political systems in SEA countries imply that their legitimacy may derive from different sources, but whatever system they are, it is the government's basic obligations to improve people's lives and safeguard national sovereignty. The two goals, however, are sometimes incompatible, or pursuing one may be detrimental to the other in the long run. Hence, in instances when the ruling elites prioritize wealth growth, they are more willing to support China's MSRI, but if they prioritize security enhancement, they will be more reluctant.

Hypothesis 5c: Countries with a higher degree of trust in China are more supportive of China's MSRI; conversely, countries with a low degree of trust are more indifferent.

Trust is considered an immediate antecedent of cooperation,[10] whereas lack of trust constitutes a roadblock to both domestic and international cooperation.[11] The diversified political systems imply that the space for public participation on policy responses to the MSRI varies in different countries. Democratic institutions, in general, allow for more public participation in the policy process relative to autocratic institutions, but even in the latter, strong opposition from the public may still hold back the government's involvement in the MSRI.

---

[8]Kuik Cheng-Chwee, 'The essence of hedging: Malaysia and Singapore's response to a rising China', *Contemporary Southeast Asia* 30(2), (2008), pp. 159–185.
[9]Omnibalancing is a theory aiming to account for why leaders of developing countries have particular alignment behaviors. See, Steven David, 'Explaining Third World alignment', *World Politics* 43(2), (1991), pp. 233–256.
[10]K. G. Smith, S. J. Carroll and S. J. Ashford, 'Intra- and interorganizational cooperation: toward a research agenda', *The Academy of Management Journal* 38(1), (1995), pp. 7–23; C. Obodia, 'Cross-border interfirm cooperation: the influence of the performance context', *International Marketing Review* 25(6), (2008), pp. 634–650.
[11]L. Danik and M. Lewandowska, 'Motives and barriers in the field of cooperation between companies', *Journal of Economics & Management* 14, (2013), pp. 21–34.

Different behavior patterns may arise hinging upon their different calculations on the pros and cons of the MSRI for consolidating their ruling status. International relations theorists posit that small states tend to balance against big powers or bandwagon when handling relations with big powers.[12] There are different balancing strategies. One includes hard balancing, denoting that a small state tries to enhance military capabilities or build alliances in order to countervail a big power. The other is soft balancing, meaning that small states seek to 'develop diplomatic coalitions or ententes with one another' to balance a big power.[13] Bandwagoning is a strategy wherein a small state chooses to expand its economic gains by aligning itself with the big power, or makes concession to it so as to stay safe from being attacked.[14] In reality, some small states try taking a middle line by walking between the lines of great powers' rivalries so as to gain benefits from both sides, which is called hedging. Van Jackson defines hedging as a strategy of 'pursuing opposing or contradictory actions as a means of minimizing or mitigating downside risks associated with one or the other action'.[15] It is utilized to cope with uncertainties stemming from big powers' unpredictable behaviors. Unlike bandwagoning, which contains no defiant component, hedging normally carries deferential and defiant elements.

Measurement of SEA Countries' Responses to China's MSRI

Most SEA countries long for greater financial support from China to help them develop infrastructure, while Singapore is keen on schemes which contribute to trade and investment liberalization. Meanwhile, as they hold different concerns about the MSRI, their support varies to different extents.

The author draws on two types of indicators to gauge the degree of SEA countries' support for the MSRI and assign them different values. These indicators are applied to measure their support since 2013 when the MSRI was unveiled. The first indicators are on gesture. As they are nominal and less important, the value being assigned will be smaller than indicators on actions. First, if the top power-holder of a country voiced support for the MSRI, the country is assigned a 1; if not, it is given a 0. Second, if the top power-holder attended the 2017 BRI Summit in Beijing, the country is assigned a 1; if not, it is given a 0. Third, if a country joined to issue the Joint Declaration on Lancang–Mekong cooperation (LMC) in production capacity, it is assigned a 1; if not, it is given a 0.

The other types of indicators are on action. These indicators are much more important in that they are the concrete results of the BRI. First, if a country has signed an intergovernmental cooperation document linking China's MSRI to its development program, it is assigned a 3; if a country expressed such an intent either in any leadership meeting or joint statement, it gets a 1; if none of the above are true, it gets a 0. Thus far, Cambodia and Laos have signed bilateral cooperation plans to jointly build the Belt and Road, while Malaysia, Myanmar and Singapore have inked memoranda of understanding (MoU) on Belt and Road cooperation with China.[16] Except for the Philippines, other Southeast Asian countries have expressed their willingness to integrate their development plans with China's MSRI.

Second, if a country allows China to help set up any industrial park or special economic zone in its territory or it helps China in this regard, the country receives a 3; if not, it gets a 0. So far China has built the Saysettha Development Zone in Laos, and industrial parks in Cambodia, Indonesia, Malaysia, Vietnam and Thailand. Both sides have agreed to build an industrial park in the Philippines while the Brunei–Guangxi Economic Corridor is under construction. Singapore has helped China to build the Suzhou Industrial Park, Tianjin Eco-city and Chongqing Connectivity Initiative.[17]

---

[12]Kenneth Waltz, *Theory of International Politics* (Reading, MA: Addison-Wesley, 1979).
[13]T. V. Paul, 'Soft balancing in the age of US primacy', *International Security* 30(1), (2005), pp. 46–71.
[14]Randall L. Schweller, 'Bandwagoning for profit: bringing the revisionist state back in', *International Security* 19(1), (1994), pp. 72–107; Stephen M. Walt, *The Origins of Alliance* (New York: Cornell University Press, 1990).
[15]Van Jackson, 'Power, trust, and network complexity: three logics of hedging in Asian security', *International Relations of the Asia–Pacific* 14(3), (2014), p. 333.
[16]China's Ministry of Foreign Affairs, 'Full text: list of deliverables of the Belt and Road Forum for International Cooperation', (16 May 2017), available at: http://www.fmprc.gov.cn/web/zyxw/t1461873.shtml (accessed 31 October 2017).
[17]Chong Koh Ping, 'Singapore, China ink pacts on Suzhou Industrial Park, Tianjin Eco-city and other bilateral projects', *The Straits Times*, (27 February 2017), available at: www.straitstimes.com/asia/east-asia/singapore-china-ink-pacts-on-suzhou-industrial-park-tianjin-eco-city-and-other (accessed 20 July 2017).

Third, another important indicator showing a country's support for the MSRI is the number of significant projects under construction or being completed as scheduled in a SEA country. Beijing has considered these projects as evidence of considerable progress of the BRI. Each project will be given a 3. The list of such projects is in light of official recognition by the Chinese government, including the China–Laos Railway, China–Myanmar Railway, China–Myanmar Oil & Gas Pipelines, China–Malaysia Kuantan Industrial Park, Jakarta–Bandung High-speed Rail, China–Thailand Railway, Railway in Southern Malaysia, Malaysia's East Coast Rail Line and the Cambodian Sihanoukville Special Economic Zone.[18]

Fourth, correspondingly, if any of the above-mentioned significant projects have been postponed, the country receives −3 in view of the fact that it remains skeptical about Chinese projects; if not, it gets a 0. The China–Thailand Railway, China–Myanmar Railway and Jakarta–Bandung High-speed Rail have all been postponed.

Fifth, a country that has signed the BRI Financing Guidance Principle receives a 1;[19] if not, it is given a 0.

Sixth, a country being a founding member of the Asian Infrastructure Investment Bank (AIIB) is assigned a 3; if not, it is given a 0.

Seventh, a foreign direct investment (FDI) score will be calculated to gauge SEA countries' support. Developing countries in general embrace FDI as it is a major catalyst to development.[20] However, as FDI may cause potential drawbacks for host economies, restrictive measures remain in many SEA countries.[21] Hence, the FDI flows to some extent can reflect SEA countries' support for the MSRI. The FDI score is a composite indicator, composed of the ranking of Chinese total FDI during 2013–2015 and the percentage of Chinese FDI in the recipient country's total FDI during 2013–2015. If China sits atop in the host country's FDI, it receives a 3; if China is the second largest investor, it gets a 2; if China is the third largest, it gets a 1; but if China is not in the top three, it is given a 0. If the percentage of China's FDI is more than 30% of the total FDI of the host country, it is assigned a 3; if the percentage ranges between 15% and 30%, it receives a 2; if it is between 5% and 15%, it gets a 1; if the percentage is lower than 5%, it is given a 0. The FDI score is the total of the above two parts (see Table 1). Since the data since 2016 are missing, the author only can conjecture the FDI scores in the Philippines after Duert and in Vietnam after the 12th Party Congress. Both have been assigned 1 and 4, respectively, based on 0 under Aquino and 2 before the Congress in Vietnam, in view of the fact that China's FDI into the Philippines and Vietnam increased 47% and 113% in 2016, respectively.

Therefore, the higher the score a country receives, the more supportive it is of the MSRI.[22] Based on their scores (see Table 2), the SEA countries can be categorized into three tiers. As shown in Table 3, with a total value larger than 20, Tier 1 countries including Cambodia, Laos and Malaysia are most supportive of China's MSRI, whereas Tier 3 countries, including Vietnam before the 12th Party Congress and the Philippines under Aquino III, were the least supportive. Other than Vietnam after the 12th Party Congress and the Philippines under Duterte, Thailand, Brunei, Indonesia, Myanmar and Singapore are grouped as Tier 2 countries conditionally supporting the MSRI with strong reservations.

---

[18]The list of these significant projects can be found at: Zhongguo Yi Dai Yi Lu Wang [Belt and Road Portal], "'Yi Dai Yi Lu" guoji hezuo zhongda gongcheng xiangmu pandian' ['An inventory of the significant international projects of the "Belt and Road Initiative"'], (4 February 2017), available at: https://www.yidaiyilu.gov.cn/qyfc/xmal/2475.htm (accessed 31 October 2017); 'Tujie: "Yi Dai Yi Lu" guoji hezuo zhongda gongcheng xiangmu pandian' ['Graph illustration: an inventory of the significant international projects of the "Belt and Road Initiative"'], Renmin Wang [People's Daily Online], (14 May 2017), available at: http://politics.people.com.cn/n1/2017/0504/c1001-29253733.html (accessed 31 October 2017).

[19]Recognizing that financial integration is an important underpinning for implementing the BRI, the Guiding Principles aim to build a long-term, stable, sustainable financing system that is well-placed to manage risks, support channeling of financial resources to serve the real economy of countries and regions involved, and so on. See Ministry of Finance of China, 'Guiding Principles on Financing the Development of the Belt and Road', (16 May 2017), available at: https://eng.yidaiyilu.gov.cn/zchj/qwfb/13757.htm (accessed 31 October 2017).

[20]OECD, Foreign direct investment for development: maximizing benefits, minimizing costs, OECD Report (2002).

[21]Darryl Jarvis, Shaofeng Chen and Tan Tek Boon, 'ASEAN investment liberalization: progress, regress or stumbling bloc?', in Julien Chaisse and Philippe Gugler, eds, Expansion of Trade and FDI in Asia: Strategic and Policy Challenges (London: Routledge 2008), pp. 138–185.

[22]It is worth noting that Singapore's support may be underestimated given Singapore has less demand for Chinese investments.

Table 1. Flows of inward foreign direct investment (FDI) by host country and source country.

Host country	Source country	(in US$ million)				Ranking	% in host country's total IFDI	FDI score
		2013	2014	2015	2013–2015			
Brunei	World	725.47	568.18	171.32	1,464.97			
	China	8.52	−3.28	3.92	9.16	5	0.63%	0
	France	3.01	3.31	8.88	15.2	4		
	Germany	15.20	8.12	5.17	28.49	3		
	India	0.00	0.00	0.00	0			
	Japan	15.81	26.58	−37.26	5.13			
	Singapore	−11.85	48.94	49.13	86.22	2		
	UK	430.43	300.55	43.26	774.24	1		
	US	−5.34	−38.82	−7.06	−51.22			
Cambodia	World	1,274.90	1,726.53	1,700.97	4,702.4			
	China	286.75	553.89	537.68	1,378.32	1	29.31%	5
	France	30.92	18.41	18.27	67.6			
	Germany	−24.81	8.49	7.45	−8.87			
	India	6.14	3.28	0.48	9.9			
	Japan	38.52	84.91	52.50	175.93			
	Singapore	83.68	60.83	51.54	196.05			
	UK	115.99	46.68	110.76	273.43	2		
	US	33.87	50.33	40.65	124.85	3		
Indonesia	World	18,443.84	21,810.42	16,916.79	57,171.05			
	China	590.78	1,068.21	321.89	1,980.88	3	3.46%	1
	France	452.54	−158.32	61.07	355.29			
	Germany	−1,333.80	−354.20	−720.64	−2,408.64			
	India	8.21	3.10	37.81	49.12			
	Japan	5,556.95	5,792.61	4,459.59	15,809.15	2		
	Singapore	9,257.89	12,090.08	9,242.27	30,590.24	1		
	UK	925.84	764.44	−125.18	1,565.1	4		
	US	1,063.93	−1,098.14	606.33	572.12	5		
Lao PDR	World	426.67	913.24	1,079.15	2,419.06			
	China	0.00	614.26	665.09	1,279.35	1	52.89%	6
	France	0.00	0.00	7.67	7.67			
	Germany	0.00	0.00	0.02	0.02			
	India	0.00	0.90	2.46	3.36			
	Japan	0.00	2.10	75.81	77.91	2		
	Singapore	0.00	1.49	0.14	1.63			
	UK	0.00	3.02	12.04	15.06	3		
	US	0.00	0.21	8.93	9.14			
Malaysia	World	12,297.38	10,875.31	11,289.60	34,462.29			
	China	133.13	302.21	275.25	710.59	6	2.06%	0
	France	104.47	453.10	298.08	855.65	4		
	Germany	−145.17	326.66	−264.29	−82.8			
	India	−24.78	6.70	−8.03	−26.11			
	Japan	2,635.93	669.96	2,519.45	5,825.34	1	16.90%	
	Singapore	1,788.08	2,162.01	1,862.88	5,812.97	2		
	UK	155.55	20.25	567.42	743.22	5		
	US	227.00	−520.13	1,436.21	1,143.08	3		
Myanmar	World	2,620.90	946.22	2,824.48	6,391.6			
	China	792.60	70.54	52.44	915.58	2	14.32%	4
	France	202.30	0.00	117.18	319.48	3		
	Germany	0.00	0.00	4.07	4.07			
	India	7.30	0.74	8.07	16.11			
	Japan	36.00	37.72	95.05	168.77	4		
	Singapore	654.80	578.52	1,562.60	2,795.92	1	43.74%	
	UK	68.90	28.28	70.49	167.67	5		
	US	0.00	0.00	0.00	0			

(Continued)

Table 1. (*Continued*).

Host country	Source country	2013	2014	2015	2013–2015	Ranking	% in host country's total IFDI	FDI score
					(in US$ million)			
Philippines	World	3,859.79	5,814.57	5,724.22	15,398.58			
	China	6.00	46.61	59.02	111.63	5	0.72%	0
	France	1.12	62.01	−414.92	−351.79			
	Germany	21.51	60.91	67.67	150.09	4		
	India	−0.05	−2.78	330.59	327.76	3		
	Japan	437.51	408.15	473.31	1,318.97	2		
	Singapore	−138.04	151.02	40.14	53.12			
	UK	−8.89	−220.23	166.48	−62.64			
	US	−653.23	2,307.05	2,023.22	3,677.04	1	23.88%	
Singapore	World	60,379.60	74,420.30	61,284.80	196,084.7			
	China	2,729.90	4,206.60	5,658.60	12,595.1	3	6.42%	2
	France	178.60	2,466.50	876.60	3,521.7			
	Germany	597.70	−140.10	1,186.80	1,644.4			
	India	2,043.10	653.40	1,139.50	3,836			
	Japan	2,737.00	4,433.60	4,727.40	11,898	4		
	Singapore	0.00	0.00	0.00	0			
	UK	3,336.50	6,544.30	5,009.80	14,890.6	2		
	US	5,582.20	13,446.40	8,390.20	27,418.8	1	13.98%	
Thailand	World	15,935.96	3,720.21	8,027.49	27,683.66			
	China	938.86	−81.77	305.47	1,162.56	3	4.20%	1
	France	104.66	−104.24	−200.68	−200.26			
	Germany	182.27	84.49	84.04	350.8			
	India	59.89	−78.29	1.11	−17.29			
	Japan	10,927.21	3,280.61	4,238.60	18,446.42	1	66.63%	
	Singapore	−132.11	−1,071.21	1,459.86	256.54			
	UK	634.40	−49.85	8.27	592.82			
	US	857.17	471.09	1,029.49	2,357.75	2		
Viet Nam	World	8,900.00	9,200.08	11,800.00	29,900.08			
	China	948.16	209.56	381.01	1,538.73	3	5.15%	2
	France	28.87	20.06	50.83	99.76			
	Germany	48.00	73.27	38.51	159.78			
	India	1.14	18.89	72.08	92.11			
	Japan	2,365.24	969.18	954.96	4,289.38	1	14.35%	
	Singapore	1,801.09	1,219.52	638.48	3,659.09	2		
	UK	77.25	146.00	658.92	882.17			
	US	51.64	130.54	118.08	300.26			

Source: ASEAN Secretariat, 'Flows of inward foreign direct investment (FDI) by host country and source country', available at: https://data.aseanstats.org/fdi_by_country.php (accessed 15 July 2017).

Economic Variables, SCS and American Policy and SEA Support for the MSRI

Trade Imbalance

China's trade with ASEAN has continued to surge. Since 2009, China has been ASEAN's largest trading partner, while ASEAN has been the third-largest partner of China since 2011. The start of the China–ASEAN FTA has further enhanced their economic ties. Bilaterally, China has become the largest trading partner of Malaysia, Singapore, Indonesia, Thailand, Vietnam, Myanmar and Cambodia. However, China's trade with ASEAN members tends to be more imbalanced. In 2015, they all had trade deficits except Singapore. Vietnam's trade deficit with China even hit US$32.9 billion (see Table 4). Using degree of support[23] and total trade imbalance data during 2008–2015 respectively, the author calculates their correlation coefficients and the outcomes are 0.296 ($p = 0.407$) and 0.098 ($p = 0.787$), respectively, showing that they have no correlation. Then the author calculates the correlation coefficient between degree of support and total bilateral trade during 2006–2015; the result is −0.258 ($p = 0.472$) and −0.342

[23] There are two sets of data, one including the Philippines and Vietnam before 2016, and the other including the two countries in 2016, similarly hereinafter.

Table 2. Degree of support of China's MSRI by SEA countries.

Country	Indicators on gesture				Indicators on action						
	Voiced support	Attended summit	Joint declaration on LMC in production capacity	Sign any inter-governmental cooperation document linking China's MSRI to their development program or express such a willingness	Set up any industrial park or special economic zone	Significant project under construction	Significant project postponed	Sign BRI Financing Guidance Principle	FDI score	Founding member of AIIB	Total values
Brunei	1	0	0	1	3				0	3	8
Cambodia	1	1	1	3	3	3		1	5	3	21
Indonesia	1	1	0	1	3	3	−3	1	1	3	11
Laos	1	1	1	3	3	3		1	6	3	22
Myanmar	1	1	1	3		6	−3	1	4	3	17
Malaysia	1	1	1	3	3	9		1	0	3	21
Philippine Aquino III	0	0	0	0					0	3	3
Duterte	1	1	0	0	3				1	3	9
Singapore	1	0	0	3	3				2	3	12
Thailand	1	0	1	1	3	3	−3	1	1	3	11
Vietnam Before the 12th Party Congress	0	0	0	0	3				2	3	8
After the 12th Party Congress	1	1	1	1	3				4	3	14

Table 3. Response of SEA countries to China's MSRI.

Degree of support	Countries	
Strongly support	Tier 1: Cambodia, Laos, Malaysia	
Conditionally support with strong reservation	Tier 2: Brunei, Indonesia, Myanmar, Singapore, Thailand	
Swing state	Tier 2: Conditionally support with strong reservation	Vietnam after the 12th Party Congress, the Philippines under Duterte
	Tier 3: Least support	Vietnam before the 12th Party Congress, the Philippines under Aquino III

w($p = 0.333$), indicating the two variables have no significant correlation in statistics. Hence, Hypothesis 1 cannot be verified. The results show that trade imbalance does not seem to be a determinant affecting the responses of the SEA countries to the MSRI, in spite of the fact that it is a grave concern for them.

FDI Inflows

This article uses data of total FDI inflows to each SEA country from China during 2010–2016 (see Table 5), and SEA support for the MSRI data to calculate their correlation, but the FDI score value needs to be scrapped from the support data in order to avoid the homogeneity problem. The outcome is 0.002 ($p = 0.995$), indicating they have no correlation in statistics. This implies that a larger magnitude of FDI from China does not necessarily solicit stronger support from SEA countries. It is noteworthy that many Chinese FDIs into SEA countries are routed through Singapore, which distorts their correlations.

Territorial Dispute

The SCS dispute is an irritant adversely affecting some ASEAN states' responses to China's MSRI, but it is not a decisive dividing line. At one end are countries such as Vietnam before the 12 Party Congress and the Philippines under Aquino III. Both were very skeptical about China's MSRI, worrying that band-wagoning with the MSRI might cause them to be entrapped by Beijing and undermine their territorial claims over the SCS. Thanks to the Scarborough Shoal standoff in the mid-2012, Aquino III adopted a more assertive posture towards China to the extent that it relinquished the way of resolving disputes through dialogue and brought the case to the Permanent Court of Arbitration in the Hague. Consequently, its relations with China went into a tailspin and were locked for years in a bitter territorial dispute. To counterbalance China, the Philippines greatly reinforced strategic alignments with the US and Japan. Through the Enhanced Defense Cooperation Agreement signed in 2014, US military forces came back after being booted out of the country in the early 1990s. Aquino III also solicited support from Japan and South Korea, both of which promised to deliver ten coastguard ships, and two FA-50 fighter jets respectively. In contrast, he was skeptical about China's MSRI, correlating the latter with China's claim over the SCS. 'To date, there's been little or no explanation of how China's "One Belt, One Road" pan-regional infrastructure concept fits into China's territorial claims to the entire South China Sea under its "Nine-Dotted Line". He even openly argued that 'China may use its financial prowess to extract territorial concessions from its neighbors'.[24]

Some Vietnamese are concerned that China's MSRI might change the status quo of the SCS where Hanoi occupies the largest number of islands and reefs. Vietnam is hesitant to build the Trans-Asia railway because it worries that more Chinese goods would flood into its market. Pham Sy Thanh, director at the Vietnam Institute for Economic Research and Policy, described China's MSRI as 'infrastructure traps', arguing that once those plans related to China's MSRI were executed, they would hinder Vietnam's infrastructure development, in that 'Beijing's plan to set up a massive regional transport network to and

[24]Richard Javad Heydarian, 'The Philippines' dilemma on China's new infrastructure bank', *The Diplomat*, (9 July 2015), available at: https://thediplomat.com/2015/07/the-philippines-dilemma-on-chinas-new-infrastructure-bank/ (accessed 31 October 2017).

Table 4. China's trade with ASEAN countries.

						(Million US$)					
		2006	2007	2008	2009	2010	2011	2012	2013	2014	2015
Brunei	Export	174.4	201.0	38.8	291.3	584.6	515.4	289.4	156.4	97.1	94.9
	Import	119.9	157.5	173.3	143.4	171.0	219.5	294.5	406.4	357.7	377.0
	Trade balance	54.4	43.5	−134.5	147.9	413.6	295.9	−5.1	−249.9	−260.6	−282.1
Cambodia	Export	13.1	10.3	12.9	16.4	64.4	152.8	178.0	274.4	356.6	427.6
	Import	515.5	653.3	933.4	881.4	1,153.6	1,733.6	3,354.6	2,992.1	7,457.3	4,035.2
	Trade balance	−502.4	−642.5	−920.5	−865.0	−1,089.2	−1,580.8	−3,176.6	−2,717.7	−7,100.7	−3,607.6
Indonesia	Export	8,343.6	8,896.7	11,636.5	11,499.3	15,692.6	22,941.0	21,659.5	22,601.5	17,605.9	15,046.4
	Import	6,636.9	8,616.5	15,247.2	14,002.2	16,949.4	26,212.2	29,385.8	29,849.5	30,624.3	23,551.5
	Trade balance	1,706.7	280.2	−3,610.7	−2,502.8	−1,256.7	−3,271.2	−7,726.3	−7,248.0	−1,3018.4	−8,505.0
Laos	Export	0.5	35.1	15.3	2.9	94.9	70.8	97.7	363.4	709.9	751.9
	Import	23.2	42.8	131.4	96.4	164.1	353.2	463.5	511.2	465.9	1,000.8
	Trade balance	−22.6	−7.7	−116.2	−93.5	−69.2	−282.4	−365.7	−147.8	244.0	−248.9
Malaysia	Export	1,1390.6	1,5443.0	18,422.0	19,066.7	24,894.9	30,245.5	28,753.9	30,719.3	28,171.8	25,976.0
	Import	15,543.1	18,897.2	18,646.0	17,200.6	20,668.1	24,676.9	29,732.9	33,723.9	35,314.1	33,121.5
	Trade balance	−4,152.6	−3,454.2	−224.0	1,866.1	4,226.8	5,568.6	−979.0	−3,004.6	−7,142.3	−7,145.5
Myanmar	Export	133.2	475.0	499.1	474.7	507.5	15,15.3	1,382.9	3,053.1	4,035.4	4,830.8
	Import	396.8	564.2	671.5	781.5	1,130.3	2,303.7	2,496.6	3,662.5	5,026.8	6,432.3
	Trade balance	−263.6	−89.2	−172.4	−306.8	−622.8	−788.4	−1,113.7	−609.5	−991.4	−1,601.5
Philippines	Export	4,627.7	5,749.9	5,466.9	2,929.7	5,701.5	6,102.3	6,159.1	6,582.6	8,467.4	6,393.1
	Import	3,647.4	4,001.2	4,249.7	4,035.6	4,933.9	6,382.1	7,136.4	8,554.1	10,472.2	11,493.9
	Trade balance	980.3	1,748.6	1,217.2	−1,105.9	767.6	−279.9	−977.3	−1,971.5	−2,004.8	−5,100.8
Singapore	Export	26,471.7	28,924.6	31,080.8	26,302.5	45,914.2	42,656.4	43,949.7	48,350.8	51,469.0	47,702.1
	Import	27,185.0	31,908.1	33,754.8	25,927.4	33,654.2	37,977.6	39,189.1	43,680.2	44,374.0	42,104.6
	Trade balance	−713.4	−2,983.5	−2,674.0	375.2	12,260.0	4,678.8	4,760.6	4,670.6	7,095.0	5,597.4
Thailand	Export	10,840.3	14,872.5	15,930.9	16,123.8	17,706.8	27,402.4	26,899.7	27,238.2	25,084.4	16,380.9
	Import	13,577.6	16,183.6	19,936.2	17,028.9	18,905.2	22,893.5	28,832.1	37,718.5	38,498.3	39,839.7
	Trade balance	−2,737.3	−1,311.0	−4,005.3	−905.1	−1,198.4	4,508.9	−1,932.4	−10,480.2	−13,413.9	−23,458.9
Viet Nam	Export	3,015.1	3,336.4	4,491.5	4,885.3	7,308.8	11,126.6	12,344.3	13,205.8	14,851.6	16,645.7
	Import	7,305.5	12,148.3	15,545.4	16,500.1	20,018.8	24,593.7	28,618.3	36,864.5	43,721.2	49,558.2
	Trade balance	−4,290.4	−8,811.5	−11,053.9	−11,614.8	−12,710.0	−13,467.1	−16,274.0	−23,658.7	−28,869.7	−32,912.6

Source: ASEAN stats, available at: https://data.aseanstats.org/trade.php (accessed 20 July 2017).

Table 5. Flows of inward foreign direct investment.

	(in US$ million)							
	2010	2011	2012	2013	2014	2015	2016	2010–2016
Brunei	0.01	0.00	0.00	0.00	0.00	0.00	0.00	0.01
Cambodia	126.94	179.68	367.76	286.75	553.89	537.68	501.54	2,554.24
Indonesia	353.57	214.88	335.09	590.78	1,068.21	323.54	298.19	3,184.26
Laos	45.57	278.32	0.00	0.00	614.26	665.09	709.98	2,313.22
Malaysia	−6.45	−15.28	33.70	94.16	302.21	275.25	883.16	1,566.75
Myanmar	1,520.90	670.60	482.20	792.60	70.54	52.44	205.48	3,794.76
Philippines	0.19	−4.11	−1.61	6.00	46.61	59.02	19.55	125.65
Singapore	699.30	5,462.50	6,162.60	2,696.20	3,401.30	3,812.70	5,367.60	27,602.2
Thailand	633.43	20.92	598.46	938.86	−81.77	305.47	255.61	2,670.98
Viet Nam	115.14	382.60	190.03	948.16	209.56	381.01	969.44	3,195.94

Source: ASEAN stats, available at: https://data.aseanstats.org/fdi_by_country.php (accessed 20 July 2017).

from China will make what Vietnam is building, including many deep-sea ports, across the country be obsolete.'[25] Moreover, Vietnam has constantly made every attempt to seek external powers like the US and Japan to counterbalance China. As a Vietnamese scholar argues,

> So, for this initiative, I think Vietnam's policy makes it quite pragmatic as long as this initiative does not bear any negative implications for Vietnamese sovereignty in the South China Sea and its national interests in the South China Sea.[26]

At the other end of the line are countries such as Malaysia, which has not flinched despite the SCS dispute. Malaysian Transport Minister Liow Tiong Lai said, 'The Malaysian government believes that the new maritime silk road and the Trans-Asian railway will be instrumental in expanding the economy and would present new opportunities to many countries especially ASEAN'.[27] In fact, Malaysia is not only very supportive of China's MSRI but also active in promoting it through a series of meetings and conferences.[28]

Equally worth noting is that no claimant state will rescind their claims in the SCS even if they benefit from the MSRI. The SCS dispute, however, is hanging like a sword of Damocles over China. If not well handled, it might jeopardize China's security environment and even its rise.

America's Policy

America has strong influence globally, including on SEA. With the rise of China, Beijing's influence in Asia is growing. When both meet in this region, geopolitical tussles between them have often been thrown into the spotlight. SEA has been pinpointed as 'the decisive territory, on the future of which hangs the outcome of a great contest for influence in Asia'.[29] When the two elephants fight, the grass suffers; but if they make love, it is still the grass that suffers. As Graham points out,

---

[25]Thoai Tran, 'China's transport infrastructure initiative to have bad impact on Vietnam's plan: expert', *Tuoi Tre News*, (29 September 2015), available at: http://tuoitrenews.vn/business/30678/chinas-transport-infrastructure-initiative-to-have-bad-impact-on-viet-nams-plan-expert (accessed 31 October 2017).

[26]Le Hong Hiep, 'China's Maritime Silk Road and ASEAN connectivity: a Vietnamese perspective', presented at a symposium on 'The Belt and Road Initiative and Its Implications for Cambodia', co-hosted by the Royal University of Phnom Penh and the Embassy of China in Cambodia on 21–22 December 2015, Symposium Proceedings, (28 April 2016), p. 101.

[27]'China's "Belt and Road" initiative presents new opportunities to ASEAN: Malaysian official', *Xinhua*, (15 December 2015), available at: http://news.xinhuanet.com/english/2015-12/15/c_134919693.htm (accessed 31 October 2017).

[28]Prashanth Parameswaran, 'China, Malaysia mull dispute resolution for "Belt and Road" countries', *The Diplomat*, (20 September 2016), available at: https://thediplomat.com/2016/09/china-malaysia-mull-dispute-resolution-for-belt-and-road-countries/ (accessed 31 October 2017).

[29]In Nicholas Kitchen, ed., *The New Geopolitics of Southeast Asia* (London: LSE IDEAS, 2012), p. 21.

Even among Southeast Asian states that evince support for a revitalized US presence as a hedge against China's strategic intentions and rapidly growing capabilities, anxiety is felt about a downward spiral ensuing in US–China relations augmenting their own security dilemma.[30]

An optimal scenario is to have sporadic tensions with limits. With that, they have more opportunities to capitalize on the rise of China and the pivot of America.

American policy towards SEA, however, has its own cycle. Alice Ba portrays ASEAN's perceptions of the US policy towards it as swinging between the extremes of over-militarization and 'systemic neglect'.[31] During the George Bush administration, initially they were concerned whether the US would open a 'second front' against terrorism in SEA, but eventually they found SEA was far from the center of its chessboard, hallmarked by the absence of American leaders at successive meetings of the ASEAN Regional Forum. SEA countries hailed Obama's rebalancing to Asia, but they had worries of over-militarization of that policy given that 60% of fleets would be stationed in the Pacific. Such a military realignment was likely to heighten tensions in Asia. After Trump took office, he started to put his 'Make America Great Again' into force. His approach to attaining that goal is to put 'America First' on all issues, leaving many SEA countries to cast doubt on whether the US will maintain its strategic commitments abroad.

The American policy cycle has a great impact on SEA countries' responses to the MSRI. First, they will size up Washington's attitude towards China's BRI and incorporate it into their responses. Second, considering the asymmetric relationship with China, SEA countries might be absorbed into Beijing's orbit without America's strong presence in Asia. Conversely, they will have more guts and leverage in dealing with China with the US pivoting to Asia. Third, the American rebalancing means more military presence and more financial assistance from Washington. More importantly, it will spark fiercer competition among big powers, which would furnish them with more leverage to deal with China. In practice, after rebalancing to Asia had begun, Asia witnessed a wave of heightened tensions over the SCS, such as the Scarborough Shoal standoff in 2012, the China–Vietnamese skirmish over the oil rig and the anti-China riots in Vietnam in 2014, culminating in the Court's Arbitration in 2016.[32] It is difficult to conclude that it was the US policy that hastened regional instability, but its impact should not be ignored.

Trump's Asia policy remains unclear despite the reassurance of continuing commitment by several of his Cabinet.[33] As Rapp-Hooper presciently put it, 'Given Trump's devotion to unpredictability, he might not craft such a strategy at all: he could instead pick and choose from a neo-Jacksonian, unilateralist buffet, deciding what "America first" means as circumstances change'.[34] Although Trump's emphasis of building a 'free and open Indo-Pacific' contributes to allaying concerns about US retrenchment, the transactional approach and hard-line economic nationalism that he showcased during his Asia tour may estrange SEA countries from Washington. According to Pew's survey, the global median percentage of people holding a favorable view of the US sharply dropped to 49% from 64% recorded across the same countries in the final years of the Obama administration.[35] The survey on confidence in the American president in Indonesia, Vietnam and the Philippines declined from 64, 71 and 94% in 2015 to 23, 58 and 69% in 2017, respectively.[36] This partially exhibited SEA countries' declining confidence in the US. Recognizing the limits of US power, some SEA countries 'are beginning to revise their strategic

[30]Euan Graham, 'Southeast Asia in the US rebalance: perceptions from a divided region', *Contemporary Southeast Asia* 35(3), (2013) pp. 305–332.

[31]Alice Ba, 'Systemic neglect? A reconsideration of US–Southeast Asia policy', *Contemporary Southeast Asia* 31(3), (2009), pp. 368–398.

[32]Peter van Ham, Francesco Saverio Montesano and Frans Paul van der Putten, 'A South China Sea conflict: implications for European security', *Clingendael Report* (March 2016), p. 7, available at: https://www.clingendael.org/sites/default/files/pdfs/Clingendael%20 Report%20South%20China%20Sea.pdf (accessed 20 November 2017).

[33]Zakir Hussain, 'America cannot disengage itself from Asia: PM Lee', *Straits Times*, (26 October 2017), available at: http://www. straitstimes.com/world/united-states/america-cannot-disengage-itself-from-asia-pm-lee (accessed 20 October 2017).

[34]Mira Rapp-Hooper, 'Deciphering Trump's Asia policy', *Foreign Affairs*, (22 November 2016), available at: https://www.foreignaffairs. com/articles/asia/2016-11-22/deciphering-trumps-asia-policy (accessed 20 November 2017).

[35]Richard Wike *et al.*, 'Globally, more name US than China as world's leading economic power', Pew Research Center (13 July 2017), available at: http://www.pewglobal.org/2017/07/13/more-name-u-s-than-china-as-worlds-leading-economic-power/ (accessed 31 October 2017).

[36]Pew Research Center, 'Build your own chart: tracking US favorability and confidence in the US president, 2002 to 2017', (26 June 2017), available at: http://www.pewglobal.org/interactives/us-image/ (accessed 31 October 2017).

[37]James Guild, 'How the US is losing to China in Southeast Asia', *The Diplomat*, (23 October 2017), available at: https://thediplomat. com/2017/10/how-the-us-is-losing-to-china-in-southeast-asia/ (accessed 31 October 2017).

Table 6. Democracy index and degree of support.

	2014		2016	
	Overall score	Degree of support	Overall score	Degree of support
Cambodia	21	4.78	4.27	21
Indonesia	11	6.95	6.97	11
Laos	22	2.21	2.37	22
Myanmar	17	3.05	4.2	17
Malaysia	21	6.49	6.54	21
Philippine	3	6.77	6.94	9
Singapore	12	6.03	6.38	12
Thailand	11	5.39	4.92	11
Vietnam	11	3.41	3.38	14
Correlation coefficient				
	−0.413 ($p = 0.269$)		−0.551 ($p = 0.124$)	

Source: The Economist Intelligence Unit, 'Democracy index 2016' and 'Democracy index 2014'.

calculus accordingly'.[37] They are more proactive in endorsing China's MSRI compared with their attitudes before 2016.

Domestic Politics and SEA Support for the MSRI

Regime Type

The author uses the democracy index compiled by the *Economist* to measure regime type, and analyzes its correlation with SEA countries' support for the MSRI. The data on Brunei are unavailable. As shown in Table 6, their correlation coefficient was −0.413 ($p = 0.269$) and −0.551 ($p = 0.124$) in 2014 and 2016, respectively, showing the two variables have no significant correlation.

Policy Priority for Elite Legitimation

In some SEA countries, there is often a debate regarding whether they should prioritize economic interests or geopolitical/security concerns when responding to China's MSRI. Typical are those SEA countries having a territorial dispute with China. Countries prioritizing economic interests are more supportive than those prioritizing security concerns.

As the most underdeveloped countries, Cambodia and Laos are most concerned about getting out of poverty. Laos, for example, is striving hard to divorce from the least developed countries by 2020. To that end, faster development of infrastructure is indispensible. The Lao government has formulated a plan for turning Laos from a 'landlocked country' to a 'land-lined country'.[38] Hence, the accruement of wealth has become an overarching source for elite legitimation. Although Laos is a de facto protectorate of Vietnam, it is fully aware that only China can help build the infrastructure it needs. Likewise, embracing an objective of turning Malaysia into a high-income country by 2020, Malaysia views China's MSRI very positively despite some concerns. Najib told President Xi, 'Your vision of a comprehensive strategic partnership, One Belt One Road, and Maritime Silk Road has not only been accepted, but implemented'.[39]

In contrast, as mentioned previously, Tier 3 countries including Vietnam before the 12th Party Congress and the Philippines under Aquino III were skeptical about the MSRI as they worried that joining it might undermine their territorial claims over the SCS.

---

[38]Somsack Pongkhao, 'Laos supports China's "One Belt, One Road" initiative', *Vientiane Times*, (22 September 2015), available at: http://www.asianews.network/content/laos-supports-chinas-one-belt-one-road-initiative-992 (accessed 6 July 2017).

[39]Lokman Mansor, 'PM Najib meets President Xi, says China visit has been "extremely successful"', *New Straits Times*, (3 November 2016), available at: https://www.nst.com.my/news/2016/11/185724/pm-najib-meets-president-xi-says-china-visit-has-been-extremely-successful (accessed 31 October 2017).

Tier 2 countries face a dilemma when deciding whether they should bolster the MSRI. For example, Indonesia tends to perceive the MSRI as an opportunity for realizing its economic potential. President Joko Widodo said, 'Indonesia supports discussing the connection of China's MSRI with Indonesia's Global Maritime Axis vision, and is willing to deepen cooperation with China in trade, investment, finance, infrastructure and other areas'.[40] Indonesia particularly greets Chinese investment in infrastructure, hoping it would help strengthen its maritime connectivity infrastructure. On the other hand, Indonesia is suspicious of 'Xi's vision of Asia's future with China as its hub, and with Chinese-led institutions playing an ever bigger role in Asian economies'.[41] Some have contended that the MSRI was part of China's strategy to expand its influence in the region. Bantarto Bandoro at the Indonesian Defense University claimed, 'This is part of China's race with the US for influence in the region. Indonesia should remain very alert about this', and 'Indonesia should not allow itself to be used by China to persuade other ASEAN members to cooperate'. A recent dispute surrounding Chinese boats fishing at the Natuna Islands has eroded Indonesian trust in China. Widodo made it clear that Indonesia would not accept China's territorial claims. He even visited the disputed area to claim sovereignty. Consequently, it seems that Indonesia has further shied away from the prospective implementation of the MSRI.[42]

Likewise, Thailand has to balance between big powers. On one side is the US, its ally, and Japan, its largest FDI contributor; on the other side is China, the largest trading partner with which Thailand has traditionally maintained friendly relations. To revitalize the domestic economy, the ruling junta has mapped out a plan to develop domestic infrastructure and turn Thailand into a hub of manufacturing, logistics and training in the SEA region. China's MSRI has been considered conducive to this goal. In his Beijing visit in 2014, Prime Minister Prayuth Chan-o-cha vowed that Thailand was willing to facilitate collaboration with China in agriculture and railways and promote regional connectivity by building the BRI. However, to avoid annoying the US and Japan, Thailand has played a balancing game, as typified by the high-speed railway case. While signing a MoU with China to build a railway from Bangkok to Nong Khai in 2014, it made an offer to Japan to build the 635-kilometre high-speed railway from Bangkok to Chiang Mai, a 319-kilometre railway from Bangkok to Laem Chabang and a 225-kilometre railway from Bangkok to Sa Kaeo.

Trust/Public Opinion

Societal trust of another country is a lubricant that can facilitate inter-state cooperation; conversely, lack of trust may dampen bilateral cooperation even if the government agrees to join the MSRI. In reality, SEA countries have different degrees of trust in China. Compared with Vietnam and the Philippines, Malaysia has a higher level of trust in China, so it tends to perceive the MSRI as a good opportunity to accrue wealth (see Table 7).

Countries in Tier 2 tend to have contradictory views of the MSRI. While expecting to gain more benefit from it, they have moderate trust in China. Hence, they are more reluctant to over-rely on China, worrying that such an over-reliance might undermine their sovereignty or strategic interests. In response, they resort to a hedging strategy, trying to harvest the low-hanging fruits while jealously guarding against their sovereignty and bringing other big powers in. Indonesia is a typical example. While granting China the contract to develop its first high-speed railway linking Jakarta to Bandung, Indonesia has awarded two contracts to Japan to construct a mass rapid transit (MRT) system in Jakarta

---

[40]'China, Indonesia to deepen cooperation in trade, finance', *Xinhua*, (2 September 2016), available at: http://news.xinhuanet.com/english/2016-09/02/c_135655127.htm (accessed 6 July 2017).

[41]'Where all Silk Roads lead', *The Economist*, (11 April 2015), available at: https://www.economist.com/news/china/21648039-through-fog-hazy-slogans-contours-chinas-vision-asia-emerge-where-all-silk-roads (accessed 31 October 2017).

[42]Patrick Mendis and Daniel Balazs, 'President Xi's Silk Road conundrum', *China–US Focus*, (24 October 2016), available at: http://www.chinausfocus.com/finance-economy/president-xis-silk-road-conundrum (accessed 31 October 2017).

[43]See Le Hong Hiep, 'China's Maritime Silk Road and ASEAN connectivity', see note 26, p. 98.

Table 7. How Asians rate China, Japan and the US.

| | Favorable views of | | | | |
| | China | | Japan | US | |
Survey year	2014	2017	2014	2014	2017
Views in:	%	%	%	%	
Indonesia	66	55	77	59	48
Malaysia	74		75	51	
Philippines	38	55	80	92	78
Thailand	72		81	73	
Vietnam	16	10	77	76	84

Source: Compiled by the author according to data from the Pew Research Center.

and its largest coal-fired power plant in North Java. Indonesia granted the project to China largely because 'the Chinese offer to Indonesia was too good to decline and the Indonesian government could not resist because what impressed me is that they promised to build 150 km express railway within only three years that is really impressive.'[43]

Swing states in Tier 3 have low trust in China and hold inconsistent or even conflicting views of the MSRI resulting from regime change. At one extreme, when their elites prioritized security enhancement for legitimation, they took a hard balancing strategy, resisting the MSRI, endeavoring to have military buildup and even aligning with other powers to contain China. Hence they were less keen to join the MSRI; at the other extreme, they acted like countries in Tier 2. To counterbalance China, Vietnam is revving up efforts to heighten military cooperation with other powers. President Rodrigo Duterte prefers to change the confrontational policy adopted by Aquino III, but the policy adjustment by no means implies that the Philippines will repeal its alliance with Washington. Through this policy change, the Philippines would be in a better position to maximize its national interests. At present, both Vietnam and the Philippines tend to show some support for China's MSRI, but should their relations with China change tack due to a skirmish over the SCS dispute, or if they have not received what they expect from China, they may turn their back on China's MSRI. As data on trust in some SEA countries on China are unavailable, this article uses their concerns about the MSRI as a proxy.

With varying attitudes towards the MSRI, SEA countries have different concerns. These concerns, if unresolved, may affect their trust in China's MSRI. It is worth noting that the nature of concerns of countries in different tiers is distinct. What Cambodia and Laos are concerned about is largely of a low-politics nature, such as quality of Chinese products, project management, etc. SEA countries in other tiers have similar concerns, but the major ones are of a high-politics nature. For instance, Singapore and the Philippines are more concerned about whether overreliance on China could undermine their security relations with other big powers; Indonesia and Myanmar have misgivings over whether their sovereignty independence would be under threat, while Vietnam and the Philippines worry about whether their participation in the MSRI would provide China with leverage which could be zeroed in on the territorial dispute. 'OBOR might be China's grand strategy to create a core-to-periphery structure of connectivity—Beijing as the hub and other countries the spokes of the system—of which smaller countries have to compromise on their interests.'[44] Such a typical argument is prevalent in some countries. Apparently, the concerns of Tier 1 countries are less grave than those of Tier 3 states, which are almost synonymous with low trust.

[44]Cheunboran Chanborey, 'China's Maritime Silk Road and ASEAN connectivity: regional politico-economic perspectives', presented at a symposium on 'The Belt and Road Initiative and Its Implications for Cambodia', p. 89.

Other Domestic Politics Factors and SEA Support for the MSRI

Other domestic political factors in SEA countries also hold sway in their responses to China's MSRI: first, the leaders' ideology and preferences often have a strong impact on the country's foreign strategy, as evidenced by Cambodia, Malaysia, and the present Vietnamese and Philippine governments. Cambodia's strong support for the MSRI is largely a decision by Cambodian Prime Minister Hun Sen as he sees this as a means of bringing economic development and a guarantor for Cambodian security amid tension with Thailand and influence from Vietnam.[45] In receiving Chinese Minister of Commerce Gao Hucheng's visit, Hun Sen said that Cambodia would coordinate and cooperate with China's MSRI and incorporate it with Cambodia's platforms.[46]

Duterte is another case that has showcased the style of a strongman. Starkly different from his predecessor, Duterte tends to develop more balanced diplomatic relations with other countries rather than being too reliant on the US. While choosing China for his first state visit, Duterte tried to extend an olive branch to China. He has not insisted that the Hague ruling be implemented. Since his visit, the bilateral relationship has started a new chapter. Duterte expressed his wish that the Philippines wanted to join in China's MSRI. In particular, he expected that China would provide the Philippines with necessary capital to help it build infrastructure.[47] By contrast, Duterte was very unhappy towards Washington's criticism of his campaign against illegal drugs. Meanwhile, it is worth noting that the Duterte cabinet is not monolithic. Many bureaucrats are pro-America. As a result, policy discrepancies are inevitable. For instance, Philippine Defense Secretary Delfin Lorenzana made an accusation that Chinese vessels were likely to enter its waters illegally to conduct survey missions in the Benham Rise in March 2017, but Duterte responded that he had authorized the entry of these Chinese vessels.[48] Then he made a sudden reversal. On 6 April 2017, Duterte told reporters he would visit the island of Pagasa (Thitu) to raise the flag there, and build a barracks for servicemen operating in the area.[49]

Second, within SEA countries, there is often such a line of contention regarding whether they should be more pro-China or pro-US/Japan. Vietnam stands out in this case. Anti-China sentiment was much stronger when Nguyen Tan Dung (NTD) was the Prime Minister. In the context of the American 'rebalancing to Asia', how to deal with China and the US had eventually become a fault line splitting the Vietnamese leadership, which had been divided into pro-China northerners, led by General Secretary Nguyen Phu Trong (NPT), and pro-America southerners, led by NTD. The faction winning the internal struggle had the decisive influence on Vietnamese foreign policies. Before the 12th Party Congress in Vietnam in January 2016, NTD had widely been considered the most influential figure. Under his tenure, NTD was more inclined to weave closer ties with Washington and take a strong position towards China. For instance, he pushed hard to let Vietnam join the TPP, and proposed closer military cooperation with Washington. In May 2014, Vietnam dispatched its armed vessels to interrupt rigging activities by a Chinese oil platform in the Paracel Islands, and an anti-China riot swept Vietnam. To provoke protest against China, NTD sent a message to the civilians, saying that 'the Prime Minister calls and asks every Vietnamese to carry forward the patriotic spirit and defend the sacred sovereignty of the state in legal

[45]Pou Sothirak, 'Sino–Cambodia relations in the context of the "One Belt and One Road" initiative', presented at a symposium on 'The Belt and Road Initiative and Its Implications for Cambodia', p. 38.

[46]Ven Rathavong, 'Cambodia, China talk business', *Khmer Times*, (2 August 2016), available at: http://www.khmertimeskh.com/news/27926/cambodia--china-talk-business/ (accessed 6 July 2017).

[47]Yibing Qi and Zhi Li, 'Feilvbing Zongtong Fanghua, Zhongguo changkai damen zhu "poubing"' ['Filipino President visiting China and China opened its door to help "break ice"'], *Zhongguowang* (official website of the Chinese Central government), (19 October 2016), available at: http://www.china.com.cn/news/world/2016-10/19/content_39518972.htm (accessed 6 July 2017).

[48]'Philippine officials: Chinese ships spotted near coast "very concerning"', *Reuters*, (11 March 2017) available at: https://uk.news.yahoo.com/philippine-officials-chinese-ships-spotted-012700254.html (accessed 31 October 2017).

[49]Manuel Mogato, 'Duterte considering visiting South China Sea island', *Reuters*, (6 April 2017), available at: https://www.usnews.com/news/world/articles/2017-04-06/philippines-duterte-plans-to-visit-disputed-south-china-sea-island (accessed 31 October 2017).

[50]Bian Yizu, 'Yuenan Zhengtan Jubian: Qinmeipai Ruan Jinyong weihe chuju' ['Radical change in Vietnamese politics: why pro-America Ruan Jinyong was out?'], *Fenghuang Jujiao* [*Phoenix Focus*] 267, (26 January 2016), available at: http://news.ifeng.com/a/20160126/47243184_0.shtml (accessed 6 July 2017).

[51]'Party chief Nguyen Phu Trong meets with his Chinese counterpart in Beijing', *Vietnam Net*, (13 January 2017), available at: http://english.vietnamnet.vn/fms/government/171149/party-chief-nguyen-phu-trong-meets-with-his-chinese-counterpart-in-beijing.html (accessed 31 October 2017).

actions'.[50] Hence, Vietnam seemed to resist the MSRI before 2016. NTD's resignation in January 2016 opened a new window. After being re-elected as the General Secretary, NPT chose China for his first state visit. During his visit, both leaders emphasized, 'Vietnam and China will enhance partnership in improving production capacity and strengthening the connection between the "Two Corridors, One Economic Belt" and "One Belt, One Road" initiatives to match the demand, benefit and development strategy of each country'.[51] In addition, Vietnam has been involved in the Lancang–Mekong Cooperation mechanism. However, Vietnam has not yet committed to any 'Belt and Road' transportation infrastructure megaproject, neither has it mapped out any plan to construct the trans-Asian Railway. Moreover, the policy division resulting from leadership change should not be exaggerated. It takes time to watch considering that NTD had many supporters in the VCP's Politburo, and this small adjustment may also be caused by their concentration on power transition and uncertainties from the Trump Administration.

Thanks to the evolving regional order in Asia, Singapore has to grapple with the relations with big powers. For decades, Singapore has been hedging, adopting an economically pro-China and militarily pro-US strategy. However, fearing being isolated, Singapore eventually found itself in a more intricate position since the Trump Administration tends to be more inward-looking while its relations with China soured. Beijing was displeased with Singapore's military ties with Taiwan, and vocal support for the ruling over the SCS by an international tribunal.[52] Within Singapore, debates arose concerning its foreign policy, culminating in a spat between two veteran diplomats, Kishore Mahbubani and Bilahari Kausikan.[53] To some extent, this has reflected two opposing views on how to engage with China and whether Singapore should change tack in its constant pro-Washington policy. In realizing its economic future is hitched to China's wagon, Singapore has decided to mend its ties with Beijing, eagerly jumping on the bandwagon of China's BRI. At the same time, Singapore strives hard to keep America more engaged in Asia.

Third, strong social resistance may constitute a stumbling block for a government to embrace the MSRI. The MSRI has provided a golden opportunity for Myanmar to promote its development, but when it comes to implementation, Myanmar has strong concerns that it may do harm to its security interests; and its society remains highly vigilant against the Chinese's likely growing influence in this country. After all, many Burmese still have bad memories about China's unconditional support for the previous military junta, which has generated negative political and public sentiments toward Beijing.

Therefore, domestic politics have played a significant role in determining the SEA countries' responses to the MSRI. Specifically, their attitudes may change because of power struggles, a change of ruling parties and leaders, and state–societal antagonism. It is widely believed that Malaysia's strong support for the MSRI under Prime Minister Datuk Seri Najib Razak might be reversed if he lost the up-coming general election.[54] Currently, the opposition party led by Ex-Prime Minister Mahathir Mohamad has harshly criticized Najib for his policies 'destabilizing the country and threatening the party's nearly six-decade stretch of uninterrupted governance', including his rapprochement with Chinese investments.[55]

[52]Tan Zhi Xin, 'Singapore's big balancing act: the US vs China', *ASEAN Today*, (24 December 2016), available at: https://www.asean-today.com/2016/12/singapores-big-balancing-act-the-us-vs-china/ (accessed 26 October 2017).
[53]Regarding their debates, see Kishore Mahbubani, 'Qatar: big lessons from a small country', *The Straits Times*, (1 July 2017), available at: http://www.straitstimes.com/opinion/qatar-big-lessons-from-a-small-country (accessed 31 October 2017); Bilahari Kausikan, 'Singapore cannot be cowed by size', *The Straits Times*, (3 July 2017), available at: http://www.straitstimes.com/opinion/singapore-cannot-be-cowed-by-size (accessed 31 October 2017).
[54]Author's interview with Hee Kong Yong, Shanghai (19 November 2016), and with Lai Menn Tatt, Beijing (2 July 2017).
[55]Thomas Fuller and Louise Story, 'Power struggle in Malaysia pits former premier against yet another protégé', *New York Times*, (17 June 2015), available at: https://www.nytimes.com/2015/06/10/world/asia/malaysia-prime-minister-najib-razak-mahathir-mohamad.html (accessed 20 October 2017).

Conclusion

This article aims to account for why SEA countries show different degrees of support for China's MSRI. In the spectrum of SEA countries' responses to China's MSRI, Cambodia, Laos and Malaysia are strongly supportive of China's MSRI. Thailand, Brunei, Singapore, Indonesia and Myanmar have rendered conditional support. They are more suspicious, worrying that joining with China is likely to jeopardize their independent sovereignty or geostrategic interests. Vietnam and the Philippines are two swing states. Sometimes they have some interest in joining, but sometimes they are resistant, much hinging upon the leadership.

The authors' analyses show that the hypotheses of trade imbalance and FDI inflows cannot be verified; the SCS dispute adversely affects some SEA countries' support for the MSRI, but it is not a decisive dividing line, neither will they back down from their territorial claim notwithstanding any gains that may arise by joining the MSRI; America's policy towards SEA is an important exogenous variable in the sense that stronger US involvement in Asia will provide more leverage, with which SEA countries are in a more advantageous position in dealing with China.

It is found that the different responses from SEA countries are largely determined by their domestic politics. Specifically, ruling elites in countries prioritizing wealth creation are more supportive relative to those in countries prioritizing security enhancement; SEA countries with a higher degree of trust in China are more supportive of China's MSRI; their leaders' ideology and preference, power struggle and social reactions also have a pronounced impact.

The policy implications are clear. China confronts considerable challenges in its effort to win SEA countries' hearts through the MSRI considering some SEA countries remain vigilant and suspicious. The SCS dispute may not be a decisive dividing line, but it has deeply intertwined with domestic politics in SEA countries and America's Asia policy. If China wants to make this initiative a success, it should change its way of paying little attention to engage with opposition parties, NGOs and civil society organizations.[56] In particular, China should redouble efforts to clear away concerns and improve trust in SEA, and strive for more support from the US.

Thus far, there are only two swing states—Vietnam and the Philippines—both of which seem to have adjusted their policies towards the MSRI. With more regime changes in other SEA countries in the future, it is very likely that more swing states will emerge.

When making the above judgment, it is worth noting that SEA countries' responses to China's MSRI are undergoing changes. These changes may result either from a change in domestic politics, rising nationalism within each country, and/or from ups and downs of strategic rivalry among big powers.

Acknowledgements

The author is grateful to Jean-Marc F. Blanchard, Zhao Suisheng, Donald Emmerson, Tan Mullins and Thomas Fingar for their very constructive comments and suggestions. Thanks also go to Erin McKay for her excellent editing work.

Disclosure statement

No potential conflict of interest was reported by the author.

---

[56]See Pou Sothirak, 'Sino–Cambodia relations in the context of the "One Belt and One Road" initiative', see note 45.

10 The Political Economy of a Rising China in Southeast Asia

Malaysia's Response to the Belt and Road Initiative

Hong Liu and Guanie Lim ⓘD

ABSTRACT

Disputing research that depicts weak states getting overwhelmed by China's financial might, this article argues that the political elites in a relatively weak and small state such as Malaysia are adept in engaging with a rising China to advance key projects, furthering their own agenda. In the case of Malaysia, the eventual outcome of this interaction is dependent on three key conditions: fulfilment of Malaysia's longstanding pro-ethnic Malay policy, a mutual vision between the state and federal authorities, and advancement of geopolitical interests for both Malaysia and China. The article puts forward a typology illustrating various possible outcomes to examine the interconnections between key players at a time of Chinese ascendancy.

The Belt and Road Initiative from a Southeast Asian perspective

In 2013, Chinese President Xi Jinping announced a pair of initiatives, which aims to restructure the economies spanning Europe and Asia. The 'Silk Road Economic Belt' was announced in September 2013 in Kazakhstan as a program to connect China to Europe by land, with routes interlinking relevant countries. A month later, in Indonesia, President Xi announced the '21st Century Maritime Silk Road', a maritime development initiative targeting the ports of Southeast Asia, South Asia, the Middle East, East Africa, and the Mediterranean. These two Silk Road programs collectively form the 'Belt and Road Initiative' (BRI). It has become China's foremost diplomatic and economic strategy in engaging with neighbouring countries and beyond since 2013. The investment associated with the BRI has surpassed US$1 trillion and will continue to define China's relationship with the world.[1]

Although BRI is a China-driven strategy, unlike other national plans (such as developing the Western regions or *Xibu Dakaifa*) that fall within the domestic political economy of China, its operation and success (or failure) depends fundamentally upon the engagement with and response from countries alongside the BRI nations (numbering more than 60). Existing studies on BRI has focused almost exclusively on China's interests and strategies, giving little attention to the responses of small states, such as those from Southeast Asia.[2] Echoing Blanchard and Mohan Malik, this article reaffirms the critical role that Southeast Asia plays in the BRI for it is one of the most critical areas making up the 21st Century Maritime Silk Road.[3] It goes beyond a macro-level

---

[1] Peter Ferdinand, 'Westward Ho—the China dream and "One Belt, One Road": Chinese foreign policy under Xi Jinping', *International Affairs* 92(4), (2016), pp. 941–957.

[2] See, for example, Zhangxi Cheng and Ian Taylor, *China's Aid to Africa: Does Friendship Really Matter?* (Oxford: Routledge, 2017).

[3] Jean-Marc F. Blanchard, 'China's Maritime Silk Road Initiative (MSRI) and Southeast Asia: a Chinese "pond" not "lake" in the works', *Journal of Contemporary China* 27(111), (2017), pp. 329–343; J. Mohan Malik, 'Myanmar's role in China's Maritime Silk Road Initiative', *Journal of Contemporary China* 27(111), (2017), pp. 362–378.

analysis, employing a meso-scale perspective to take into account diverse economic, political, ethnic interests, and more importantly, the fluid interplay among these factors.

A Southeast Asian perspective

Malaysia is a good case study to unravel the BRI in Southeast Asia because of several reasons. First, it is one of the founding members of the Association of Southeast Asian Nations (ASEAN), a multilateral platform established in 1967 to promote regional integration and cooperation. Second, as China's strategic ally, Malaysia enjoys a special relationship with China when then Prime Minister Tun Abdul Razak established diplomatic ties with Beijing in 1974. The bilateral relationship has blossomed under successive Prime Ministers, especially former Prime Minister Najib Razak (in office from 2009 to May 2018). Thirdly, Malaysia's ethnic Chinese minority (about 25% of the population) has long played a key role in advancing bi-lateral trade and investment, in spite of a state-sanctioned affirmative action policy limiting ethnic Chinese participation in various activities.[4] Thanks to their economic success, the ethnic Chinese have often been portrayed as a bogeyman by some politicians representing the ethnic Malay population (roughly 65% of the population).[5] At a time of China rising, the financially powerful (yet politically weak) ethnic Chinese across Southeast Asia have also been viewed as a conduit in fostering China-Southeast Asia economic ties.[6] This makes the community influential agents to decipher whether Beijing's engagement with them represents a new mode of transnational governance.[7]

With the above as a backdrop, this article addresses the following questions: What are the key elements of the BRI in the context of the Southeast Asian political economy? How do business groups from China (both state-owned and private) undertake their operations in Southeast Asia (in general) and Malaysia (in particular)? Moreover, how do different forces in Malaysia (ruling coalition, opposition bloc, and civil society) react to the BRI, and what are their key stakes in engaging (or disengaging) with China? What are the impacts, if any, of the complex meshing of such forces on Malaysia's domestic politics and Beijing's regional politico-economic engagement? What implications can be drawn from Malaysia for a better understanding of the BRI, especially the huge opportunities that come with the initiative and its operational constraints?

This article unpacks these questions by analysing three of the most prominent BRI projects in Malaysia: East Coast Rail Link (ECRL), Bandar Malaysia, and Forest City. ECRL is orchestrated by the China Communications Construction Company (CCCC), a state-owned enterprise (SOE), with strong endorsement by Najib and several Chief Ministers. Bandar Malaysia was jointly developed by China Railway Engineering Corporation (CREC), another SOE, and parties aligned with Najib. Forest City, on the other hand, is driven by Country Garden (a private firm), in partnership with the Sultan of Johor, reflecting a rising trend of wealthy Chinese private firms venturing abroad. The article argues that domestic players in these projects are astute in co-opting their Chinese counterparts to advance their own goals. Their eventual success is dependent on three conditions: fulfilment of Malaysia's pro-ethnic Malay agenda, a common development goal between the state and federal authorities, and advancement of geopolitical interests for both Malaysia and China. As will be detailed later, ECRL's modest success (at least until the recently concluded general election in May 2018 which saw the Najib administration losing to the opposition bloc), Bandar Malaysia's failure,

[4]James Chin, 'The Malaysian Chinese dilemma: the Never Ending Policy (NEP)', *Chinese Southern Diaspora Studies* 3, (2009), pp. 167–182.
[5]Joan Nelson, 'Political Challenges in Economic Upgrading: Malaysia Compared with South Korea and Taiwan', in *Malaysia's Development Challenges: Graduating from the Middle*, eds. Hal Hill, Siew Yean Tham, and Haji Mat Zin Ragayah (Oxford: Routledge, 2012), pp. 43–62.
[6]Caroline Hau, 'Becoming "Chinese"—but what "Chinese"?—in Southeast Asia', *The Asia-Pacific Journal: Japan Focus* 10(26), (2012), pp. 1–36; Hong Liu, 'Opportunities and anxieties for the Chinese diaspora in Southeast Asia', *Current History: A Journal of Contemporary World Affairs* 115(784), (2016), pp. 311–317.
[7]Hong Liu and Els van Dongen, 'China's diaspora policies as a new mode of transnational governance', *Journal of Contemporary China* 25(102), (2016), pp. 805–821.

and Forest City's arrested development underline the need to be wary of societal contestation within the BRI recipient state as well as Beijing's geopolitical goals.

Data for this article were obtained from personal interviews with individuals who have been directly involved in China's economic engagement with Malaysia. The interviews were conducted from May 2016 to May 2017 in China, Malaysia, and Singapore, focusing on two main topics: the overall business approach of the Chinese firms and their interactions with important domestic stakeholders. It was supplemented by information gathered from two public forums (March and May 2017, respectively, in Singapore) voicing views on Chinese investment in Malaysia. To enhance the robustness of the primary data, they are cross validated with newspaper essays, published reports, and company websites in the English, Chinese and Malay languages. In certain cases, materials from personal blogs were retrieved to explore views candidly expressed but seldom heard, although they are handled with caution, given their limitations. The use of these sources of information allowed for data verification and triangulation, resulting in a clearer reading of the situation from multiple perspectives. Given the sensitive nature of the issues discussed (e.g. ethnic relations and business-state interactions), all interviewees were promised confidentiality.

The next section examines the literature on the internationalization of China. It identifies the gap in knowledge, especially the tendency to (over)focus on Chinese actors and the lack of perspectives from Southeast Asia. The third section provides a wider context by analysing the political economy of Malaysia with respect to China's growing influences in the nation. The fourth section puts forth a conceptual framework hypothesizing various possible outcomes to better analyse how Malaysia (and other states) respond to the BRI. It then focuses on the progress of the aforementioned projects (ECRL, Bandar Malaysia, and Forest City). The article then discusses interconnections between key players in the BRI recipient state and unpacks the manners in which domestic stakeholders utilize Chinese capital to further their own agendas. The last section concludes with a summary of the main arguments and suggests avenues for future research.

Studies on the Belt and Road Initiative: a critique

There has been a growing body of research analysing the motivations and impacts of China in its overseas expansion. Such studies tend to view actors within China as the major (if not, sole) variable behind China's foreign direct investment (FDI). First, much of the debate has pinpointed the Chinese state as the primary determinant undergirding the BRI.[8] These studies emphasize policies that extend China's global reach. Callahan postulates that Beijing is utilizing new policies and institutions related to the BRI to construct a 'new regional order', weaving specific countries into a Sino-centric 'community of shared destiny'.[9] Beeson argues that China's recent moves are presenting a formidable challenge to its immediate neighbours.[10] He contends that China is adept at exploiting rifts between key Southeast Asian countries, complicating efforts to develop a common position vis-à-vis China and successfully undermining solidarity within the region.

Second, the state-centric perspective has been augmented by other studies on the multitude of actors shaping China's economy. They posit that the BRI is also driven by other Chinese players such as the SOEs, private firms, and less well-capitalized Chinese entrepreneurs. To ensure access to overseas energy supply, Beijing has been utilizing diplomatic instruments and policy banks to help its national firms—primarily the SOEs—tap into the oil and gas fields of Russia-Central Asia, Middle

[8]See, for example, Mark Beeson, 'Can ASEAN cope with China?', *Journal of Current Southeast Asian Affairs* 35(1), (2016), pp. 5–28; William Callahan, 'China's "Asia Dream": the Belt Road Initiative and the new regional order', *Asian Journal of Comparative Politics* 1(3), (2016), pp. 226–243; Hong Yu, 'Motivation behind China's "One Belt, One Road" initiatives and establishment of the Asian Infrastructure Investment Bank', *Journal of Contemporary China* 26(105), (2017), pp. 353–368; Weifeng Zhou and Mario Esteban, 'Beyond balancing: China's approach towards the Belt and Road Initiative', *Journal of Contemporary China* 27(112), (2018), pp. 487–501.
[9]Callahan, 'China's "Asia Dream": The Belt Road Initiative and the new regional order'.
[10]Beeson, 'Can ASEAN cope with China?'.

East-North Africa, and South America.[11] In agriculture, small-scale Chinese family farms have most actively expanded westward into Tajikistan, reacting much faster than the SOEs.[12]

These two strands of work, while insightful, tend to understand Chinese outward expansion mainly from the perspective of the Chinese actors, giving little attention to the responses formulated by players in the BRI recipient states who, as will be demonstrated later, harbour their own agendas in their engagement (or disengagement) with China. Without a more explicit analysis on the relevant state and non-state actors from the recipient state, the reality of the initiative is likely obscure. In Nepal, studies were conducted to unpack the manners in which Nepalese elites utilize Chinese capital and expertise to finance badly needed infrastructure. Such research illustrates how small and weak states like Nepal can advance projects of state formation and national security through a significant degree of elite agency, exploiting the geopolitical manoeuvring between its two large neighbours—China and India.[13]

Focusing on Chinese corporate expansion into Southeast Asia, Lim problematizes the concept that the Chinese state is the most important, if not the only, variable in explaining the outward investment of Chinese firms.[14] He argues that firm strategies are influenced by a broad range of actors, especially those in the host economies, which collectively shape global production and dictate value capture. Using examples from the automobile and electronics sectors, he shows that only those Chinese firms adept at managing a variety of complex factors are successful in their overseas expansion. Drawing lessons from recent BRI projects in Myanmar, scholars are increasingly aware of the need to pay attention to societal contestation within the BRI recipient states and how it potentially leads to a more contested outcome, just like how Myanmar in 2011 stunned global audiences by unilaterally suspending the construction of the Myitsone Dam, China's largest hydropower project abroad then. The suspension is primarily a product of the complex socio-historical evolution of Myanmar and the resistance strategy deployed by social actors at various geographical scales such as the Kachin nationalists and Lower Myanmar's activists.[15] These stakeholders—who do not normally collaborate because of competing interests—projected the construction of the Myitsone dam as a common external enemy. Such an alliance eventually built a cross-ethnic and cross-state solidarity that was strong enough to pressure Naypyidaw to suspend the project.[16]

Such research is sparse compared to more 'popular' literature about Chinese overseas investment under the themes of 'colonialism' and 'imperialism'. This body of literature mainly draws on case studies of Chinese firms operating in Africa, and (to a lesser extent) South America. It commonly highlights Beijing's opaque state–SOE nexus, no-strings-attached stance on human rights, and the poor corporate governance of the Chinese firms.[17] The situation is exacerbated by these countries' weak organizational capacity of civil society and poor institutional setting.[18] Most of these works remain relatively nascent, transitioning somewhat slowly from broad-brush approaches to more critical and nuanced research.

Therefore, a perspective from Southeast Asia is imperative to decipher the on-the-ground intricacies of the BRI. Indeed, the region's political economy, socio-cultural landscapes, and

[11]Monique Taylor, *The Chinese State, Oil and Energy Security* (New York: Palgrave Macmillan, 2014).

[12]Irna Hofman, 'Politics or profits along the "Silk Road": what drives Chinese farms in Tajikistan and helps them thrive?', *Eurasian Geography and Economics* 57(3), (2016), pp. 457–481.

[13]Galen Murton, Austin Lord, and Robert Beazley, '"A handshake across the Himalayas:" Chinese investment, hydropower development, and state formation in Nepal', *Eurasian Geography and Economics* 57(3), (2016), pp. 403–432.

[14]Guanie Lim, 'China's "Going Out" strategy in Southeast Asia: case studies of the automobile and electronics sectors', *China: An International Journal* 15(4), (2017), pp. 157–178.

[15]Laur Kiik, 'Nationalism and anti-ethno-politics: why "Chinese development" failed at Myanmar's Myitsone Dam', *Eurasian Geography and Economics* 57(3), (2016), pp. 374–402.

[16]Ibid.

[17]Henry Sanderson and Michael Forsythe, *China's Superbank: Debt, Oil and Influence—How China Development Bank is Rewriting the Rules of Finance* (Singapore: Wiley, 2013).

[18]Cheng and Taylor, *China's Aid to Africa: Does Friendship Really Matter?*

developmental trajectories are fairly good representatives of the developing world.[19] This article's analysis of infrastructure development in Malaysia, Southeast Asia's fourth-largest economy, aims to redress the knowledge gap pertaining to the BRI. It also highlights the socioeconomic intricacies embedded within the BRI recipient country. It reveals how key domestic political actors have remoulded the initiative, thus challenging the China-centric angle that is hitherto dominant in the literature.

The political economy of Malaysia: ethnicity and state–federal contestation

Malaysia has successfully transformed its previously commodities-driven economy into a middle-income economy since independence in 1957. Like the other newly industrialized economies (NIEs) of Asia, it has done so by maintaining a relatively open stance towards foreign trade and invest-ment and utilizing its low labour cost advantage.[20] This model of economic development, however, has come under considerable stress as Malaysia has become less appealing in the eyes of interna-tional investors following the emergence of a newer cohort of NIEs such as Vietnam and Indonesia. In particular, Malaysia's decades-old affirmative action policy, designed to redistribute income along ethnic lines, has become a stumbling block for investors.[21] The New Economic Policy (NEP) has also alienated a significant portion of the country's ethnic minorities. Its ethnocentric nature has been exploited by the pro-Malay United Malays National Organisation (UMNO), who frequently projects the financially powerful ethnic Chinese minority as a bogeyman of the Malay community.-[22] If anything, the pro-Malay agenda has strengthened in recent years, in light of the failure of the UMNO-led ruling coalition to secure its customary two-third parliamentary majority over the last two decades.[23] Pandering more forcefully to the ethnic Malays, UMNO's goal is to capture enough votes from the ethnic Malay-heavy rural constituencies to overcome its loss of the (predominantly non-Malay and anti-establishment) urban seats.[24]

As Malaysia finds it increasingly difficult to attract FDI from its 'traditional' sources (i.e. the industrialized western countries, Singapore, and Japan), policymakers are forced to seek alternative investments. China has thus emerged as an attractive FDI contributor, especially since the formula-tion of the BRI. The latest governmental statistics show that China became Malaysia's largest investor in 2016, contributing an investment totalling US$1.6 billion (equivalent to 17.5% of the country's total FDI inflow).[25] Chinese FDI has eclipsed those from the Netherlands (11.7% of inward FDI), Germany (9.5% of inward FDI), UK (9.5% of inward FDI), Korea (8.0% of inward FDI) and Singapore (7.7% of inward FDI). Chinese investment is especially noticeable in large-scale, capital-intensive infrastructure projects. In certain cases, Malaysian Chinese business people have become useful middlemen in attracting mainland Chinese investment, mobilizing their knowledge about

---

[19]Cf. Gary Hawes and Hong Liu, 'Explaining the dynamics of the Southeast Asian political economy: state, society, and the search for economic growth', *World Politics* 45(4), (1993), pp. 629–660; Erik Kuhonta, Dan Slater, and Tuong Vu, eds., *Southeast Asia in Political Science: Theory, Region, and Qualitative Analysis* (Stanford: Stanford University Press, 2008).

[20]Hal Hill, Siew Yean Tham, and Ragayah Haji Mat Zin, 'Malaysia: a success story stuck in the middle?', *The World Economy* 35 (12), (2012), pp. 1687–1711.

[21]Formally known as the New Economic Policy (NEP), which was imposed following racial riots in 1969, the policy provides preferential treatment to the *Bumiputera* (essentially Malay) population in almost all features of the economy such as employment opportunities and home ownership. Despite its lopsided nature, the NEP has arguably preserved the rule of the United Malays National Organisation (UMNO), its chief architect and the hegemon within the ruling administration, from August 1957 to the recently concluded May 2018 general election. See Chin, 'The Malaysian Chinese dilemma: the Never Ending Policy (NEP)'.

[22]Nelson, 'Political Challenges in Economic Upgrading: Malaysia Compared with South Korea and Taiwan'.

[23]James Chin, 'Malaysia: heading for Sharia domination?', *The Round Table* 105(6), (2016), pp. 737–739.

[24]The party's failure to garner support from the ethnic minorities was not damaging, at least until the 2000s, as Malaysia's relatively high growth rate in the post-independence decades was sufficient to sway the opinions of a large enough portion of the citizenry (both Malays and non-Malays). However, since the early 2000s, a slowing economy and more intense competition from other NIEs have placed significant strain on this dynamic.

[25]MIDA, *Malaysia Investment Performance Report: Strengthening the Growth Momentum* (Kuala Lumpur: Malaysian Investment Development Authority, 2016).

China and the domestic market as well as their intimate relationship with the ethnic Malay-dominated state institutions and government-linked corporations (GLCs).[26]

The optimistic view on the Chinese business community has to be moderated with the politico-economic reality. More prosaically, Chinese firms almost always conform to the NEP in their cross-border investment. Studies show that Chinese capital has largely collaborated with the ethnic Malay-led GLCs rather than Malaysia's ethnic Chinese firms, particularly in the more-regulated industries (such as infrastructure and automobile manufacturing).[27] The success of Huawei and Zhongxing Telecommunication Equipment Corporation (ZTE) in their Malaysian ventures is not dependent on forging ties with the ethnic Chinese firms; rather, they benefit from strong compliance with the NEP. Huawei especially is adept at conducting technical and societal programs (e.g. flood relief efforts in ethnic Malay-heavy constituencies) that are widely perceived to benefit ethnic Malay stakeholders.[28]

Notwithstanding the lopsided nature of the NEP, one also needs to consider the state–federal ties. While responsibilities and revenue sources are geared strongly towards the federal government, Malaysia's 13 states still enjoy some autonomy in matters such as land use, local public services, and religious affairs.[29] Nine of these states are led by ethnic Malay hereditary monarchies (also known as Sultanates). Under Malaysia's unique form of constitutional monarchy, the Sultans assume largely a ceremonial role, with executive power in the hands of the respective Chief Ministers (the heads of government).[30] While the Sultans are generally popular amongst the citizenry (especially the Malays), there were some high profile instances where the Sultans came up against the federal government.[31]

As Malaysia's second most populous state, Johor's relationship with the federal government is further complicated by the 2006 inception of Iskandar Malaysia, a 9,300-acre special economic zone bordering Singapore. Although Johor, the country's southernmost state, stands to benefit from the success of Iskandar Malaysia, the project is viewed as an encroachment into Johor's land use, a sphere traditionally under the remit of the Johor government.[32] Furthermore, it is driven primarily by the federal government, with only limited autonomy provided to its Johorean counterpart. The dominance of the federal government vis-à-vis the Johor administration is in turn undergirded by the former's preoccupation to distribute economic growth across the country. Johor's proximity to Singapore means that there are concerns about the shift of Malaysia's centre of gravity from Kuala Lumpur to the neighbouring city-state (and Johor, to a smaller extent). This also implies that there must be some federal oversight and monitoring mechanism in place whenever major projects (such as Iskandar Malaysia) are undertaken in Johor.[33]

Conceptual framework: entanglement of international politics and domestic forces

Synthesizing the above literature, this article aims to account simultaneously for the interaction of international and domestic factors by presenting a tentative framework to analyse how Malaysian

---

[26]Teck Ghee Lim, 'Abdullah Badawi, the NECC and the Corporate Equity Issue: View from a Personal Connection', in *Awakening: The Abdullah Badawi Years in Malaysia*, eds. Bridget Welsh and James Chin (Petaling Jaya: Strategic Information and Research Development Centre, 2013), pp. 457–480.

[27]Guanie Lim, 'China's investments in Malaysia: choosing the "right" partners', *International Journal of China Studies* 6(1), (2015), pp. 1–30.

[28]Ran Li and Kee-Cheok Cheong, 'Huawei and ZTE in Malaysia: the localisation of Chinese transnational enterprises', *Journal of Contemporary Asia* 47(5), (2017), pp. 752–773.

[29]Three other smaller territories are governed directly by the federal administrators.

[30]The Sultans are known to exercise their influence on the state administration, sometimes incurring the wrath of the politicians. See David Seth Jones, 'Resolving the constitutional question of the Malaysian king and rulers', *Asian Journal of Political Science* 3(1), (1995), pp. 13–31.

[31]Ibid.

[32]Keng Khoon Ng and Guanie Lim, 'Beneath the veneer: The political economy of housing in Iskandar Malaysia, Johor', *Trends in Southeast Asia* 3(12), (2017), pp. 1–28.

[33]Ibid.

Table 1. Alignment of interests between China and the Belt and Road Initiative recipient states.

Project/analytical dimension	Intertwining of domestic ethno-political agenda with Chinese objectives	State–federal contestation	Convergence of China–Malaysia geopolitical goals
East Coast Rail Link	High	Low	High
Bandar Malaysia	Moderate	Low	Low
Forest City	Low	High	Low

actors respond to China (see Table 1). The constructs are theoretical ideal-types and serve primarily as heuristic devices, yet they potentially contribute to a better understanding of how domestic actors engage with their Chinese counterparts. Examining the interplay involving domestic ethno-political goals and Chinese interests, state–federal contestation, and convergence of geopolitical goals, Table 1 isolates and examines *three* of the *most crucial variables* undergirding the BRI. It is *only* when these *three variables* are *properly addressed* that the projects *can be rolled out successfully*. This *three-tiered analysis* is useful to incorporate motivations from multiple interest groups, particularly in countries operating on a federal government structure (such as Malaysia), with political power often apportioned unevenly between the central and local administrative units.

As detailed previously, ECRL, Bandar Malaysia, and Forest City are chosen because they are three of the most important BRI projects in the country. In addition to their massive capital outlay, these three projects are selected because of the differing characteristics of their proponents and the power relations involved. ECRL and Bandar Malaysia are to be constructed by large Chinese SOEs, with support from Beijing and Putrajaya (especially Najib). Country Garden, a private firm, has instead cooperated with the Sultan of Johor. Because of the pervasive influence of the Sultan, Forest City cannot be classified as a traditional private-private collaboration. Table 1 hypothesizes that ECRL has been implemented expeditiously because it simultaneously fulfils the NEP directive, minimizes state–federal contestation, and advances the geopolitical aims of both China and Malaysia. By contrast, the collapse of Bandar Malaysia, even in the absence of state–federal conflict, is attributable to its moderate conformance to the NEP and the lack of convergence between Chinese and Malaysian geopolitical goals. Notwithstanding the clout of the Sultan, Forest City has failed to make a lasting impact because it neither promotes noticeable pro-Malay policies nor the geopolitical ambitions of both China and Malaysia. Johor's thorny ties with the central government has also undermined Forest City.

China in Malaysia: three case studies

East Coast Rail Link: remoulding regional geopolitics through China

With state-owned CCCC as the main contractor and with 85% of the construction cost financed by soft loans from Beijing, ECRL was lauded by Najib for its potential to better connect the relatively backward east coast states (Pahang [Najib's home state], Terengganu, and Kelantan) to Selangor, the country's most prosperous state. The improved connectivity (for passengers and freight) is expected to bridge the economic divide between both regions, a chronic issue since the British colonial era. Valued at a sum of US$18.2 billion, ECRL has been fast-tracked by the government to commence construction in July 2017 rather than in late 2017 as initially expected.[34] ECRL has also been given top priority by CCCC. The SOE believes that ECRL, currently the largest railway project in Southeast Asia, will create demonstration effects that would advance its business prospects in Southeast Asia as well as other countries involved in the BRI. Liu Qitao, Director of CCCC,

---

[34]Lin Say Tee, 'Flushed with Construction Jobs,' *The Star*, 11 March 2017 https://www.thestar.com.my/business/business-news/2017/03/11/flushed-with-construction-jobs/ (accessed 10 January 2018).

emphasizes that ECRL's success (or failure) will directly impact how other BRI recipient countries view and approach the initiative.[35]

The 600 km mega project boasts a strong pro-Malay undertone as almost the entire stretch of the railway passes through the three ethnic Malay-heavy states of Pahang, Terengganu, and Kelantan. Their importance to UMNO has increased further following UMNO's concerted attempt to promote an even stronger ethnic Malay agenda (vis-à-vis other ethnic groups).[36] One of UMNO's major moves was to forge an alliance with the Malaysian Islamic Party (PAS), its traditional rival in the rural east coast states. To attract more votes from the ethnic Malays (especially those from the rural constituencies), both parties have come together to advance a more hardline version of the already biased NEP. In the ground-breaking ceremony of ECRL, Najib, flanked by the Chief Ministers of the three east coast states, argued that ECRL is a 'game changer' and 'mindset changer' for the people along the railway route. He also promised that the economies of UMNO- and PAS-governed Pahang, Terengganu, and Kelantan would experience an additional annual growth of 1.5% when the project is completed as high value-added economic activities in sectors such as agriculture and tourism are stimulated.[37] The Terengganu Chief Minister, Ahmad Razif Abdul Rahman, was especially bullish about the project, stating that it would 'speed up the modernisation of the state' and 'transform Terengganu towards a first-class region to work and live in'.[38] His focus, as well as that of Najib, on the potential economic benefits of ECRL is reflective of Malaysian politics. UMNO, as the most dominant party of the governing coalition, has traditionally relied on its ability to develop the economy in securing its political legitimacy. The Chief Minister of opposition-governed Selangor was not present at this function, although the overall mood of Selangor is not to oppose ECRL, but to pressure the federal government to be more forthcoming with the public on the project's cost and financing. Nevertheless, Selangor is the smallest beneficiary of ECRL as only about 17km of the railway is planned within its territory.[39]

Another notable aspect of ECRL is its geopolitical dimension. Upon completion, it will connect Pahang's Kuantan Port (jointly managed by a Malaysian conglomerate and Guangxi Beibu Gulf International Port Group, an SOE) to the bustling Port Klang on the west coast. This potential land bridge could provide a 'significant resolution' to China's over-reliance on the Strait of Malacca, what it calls the 'Malacca Dilemma'.[40] To put things into perspective, about 80% of current Chinese energy needs pass through this narrow waterway. This new network will create alternative trade routes, but with significant Chinese involvement as China now has a direct interest in both the Kuantan Port and ECRL itself. The project could also negatively impact Singapore's stature as the leading shipping and commercial centre of Southeast Asia. While a combined sea and land route via Kuantan Port and ECRL is estimated to cost more (in bulk cargo per tonne) than the existing sea route via Singapore, the travel time can be shortened by 30 h (18% reduction from current levels).[41] The shorter travel time is useful for the movement of time-sensitive goods such as exotic food and biomedical products. Furthermore, the trade routes will help Malaysia bring back the highly valuable indirect trade between itself and China. Currently,

---

[35]Xinhua, 'Malaixiya Donghaiantielu Xiangmukaigong Zhilichengwei Shifangongcheng,' ['East Coast Rail Link to Become a Model Project'] *Xinhua Silk Road*, 14 August 2017 http://silkroad.news.cn/Company/Cases/ppjs/45238.shtml (accessed 10 January 2018).

[36]See Chin, 'Malaysia: Heading for Sharia domination?'.

[37]Abdul Halim Hadi, 'ECRL Bawa Limpahan Ekonomi Menyeluruh,' ['ECRL to Bring in Widespread Economic Benefits'] *Utusan Online*, 17 November 2017 http://www.utusan.com.my/berita/nasional/ecrl-bawa-limpahan-ekonomi-menyeluruh-1.554274 (accessed 21 January 2018).

[38]Adrian David, 'ECRL Set to Boost Terengganu Transformation Plan,' *New Straits Times*, 10 August 2017, https://www.nst.com.my/news/nation/2017/08/266293/ecrl-set-boost-terengganu-transformation-plan (accessed 10 January 2018).

[39]'Three Questionable Areas of East Coast Rail Line (ECRL),' *Blog Page of Yeo Bee Yin*, last modified 2 April 2017, http://www.yeobeeyin.com/2017/04/three-questionable-areas-of-east-coast.html (accessed 10 January 2018).

[40]Leslie Lopez, 'Malaysia's East Coast Rail Line Touted as a Game Changer,' *Straits Times*, 22 December 2016, http://www.straitstimes.com/asia/se-asia/malaysias-east-coast-rail-line-touted-as-a-game-changer (accessed 10 January 2018).

[41]Lopez, 'Malaysia's East Coast Rail Line Touted as a Game Changer'.

China–Malaysia indirect trade, estimated at about US$66.2 billion per year, is conducted mainly through the Port of Singapore.[42]

Bandar Malaysia: merging state capital with state capital

The second case illustrates intriguing linkages between a Chinese SOE and 1MDB, a Malaysian centrally controlled-GLC. Bandar Malaysia is a 197-ha mixed development project in the heart of Kuala Lumpur, encompassing both residential and commercial properties. Its main proponent is 1MBD, a GLC associated with Najib.[43] Bandar Malaysia's most important selling point is its strategic location and transit-oriented outlook. It would serve as Southeast Asia's premier transportation hub, housing the terminus of the proposed Kuala Lumpur–Singapore high-speed rail (HSR) project, providing railway linkage to several major airports in the region. Additionally, Bandar Malaysia will link up with the ambitious Pan-ASEAN Rail Transit to Bangkok and beyond. The entire project is expected to attract a total investment of US$53.0 billion over 20–25 years.[44]

As Kuala Lumpur is governed directly by the federal government and 1MDB is a centrally-controlled GLC, there is no need to navigate the complicated interests between different layers of governments, unlike the two other China–Malaysia projects. For 1MDB, it roped in a China–Malaysia consortium in December 2015, selling 60% of its stake in Bandar Malaysia to the latter.[45] The consortium is in turn 60%-owned by CREC, one of China's largest SOEs, with Malaysia's Iskandar Waterfront Holdings (IWH) holding the remaining 40% equity.[46] It is noteworthy that CREC's investment into the venture took place merely months after the *Wall Street Journal* reported that nearly US$700 million was deposited into what are allegedly the personal bank accounts of Najib.[47] The money is alleged to have moved through government agencies, banks, and companies linked to 1MDB before ending up in Najib's personal accounts. Najib had served as Chairman of 1MDB's Board of Advisors until the entire board was dissolved in May 2016. A comprehensive report was tabled after a probe into alleged graft and mismanagement at the 1MDB. In January 2016, the newly installed Attorney General of Malaysia cleared Najib of corruption charges pertaining to such allegations.[48] For CREC, this seemingly risky decision goes against conventional economic rationale. CREC even announced the establishment of its Asia Pacific regional headquarters in Bandar Malaysia, three months after its participation in the project. Its partner, IWH, was quick to highlight Bandar Malaysia as the latest example of how the BRI generates mutual benefits for both countries. According to IWH, Bandar Malaysia can serve as a platform for aspiring Chinese firms to enter the Malaysian as well as the wider Southeast Asian markets. IWH also stated that Malaysian firms, especially the small and medium enterprises (SMEs), stand to benefit from the potential influx of Chinese capital and technology.

Nevertheless, the investment drew immediate flak from the public. Liew Chin Tiong, a vocal member of the opposition bloc, argued that CREC's investment is tantamount to bailing out the

---

[42]Wah Foon Ho, 'China Projects to Hit Singapore,' *The Star*, 15 January 2017 http://www.thestar.com.my/news/nation/2017/01/15/china-projects-to-hit-singapore-the-giant-republics-aggressive-investments-in-ports-and-rail-links-i/ (accessed 10 January 2018).

[43]William Case, 'Stress testing leadership in Malaysia: the 1MDB scandal and Najib Tun Razak', *The Pacific Review* 30(5), (2017), pp. 633–654.

[44]Trinna Leong, 'Chinese Govt Firm to Invest $2.7b in Bandar Malaysia,' *Straits Times*, 22 March 2016, http://www.straitstimes.com/asia/chinese-govt-firm-to-invest-27b-in-bandar-malaysia (accessed 10 January 2018).

[45]Ibid.

[46]IWH, in which low profile ethnic Chinese businessman Lim Kang Hoo owns 60% of its equity and another GLC the remaining 40%, is one of Malaysia's more successful examples of public-private partnership in recent times.

[47]Tom Wright and Simon Clark, 'Investigators Believe Money Flowed to Malaysian Leader Najib's Accounts amid 1MDB Probe,' *Wall Street Journal*, 2 July 2015 https://www.wsj.com/articles/SB10130211234592774869404581083700187014570 (accessed 26 March 2018).

[48]Since taking over Putrajaya, the new administration has reinvestigated Najib's involvement in 1MDB. On 4 July 2018, Najib was charged in court with three counts of criminal breach of trust. See Channel NewsAsia, 'Former Malaysian PM Najib Razak Charged with Criminal Breach of Trust in 1MDB Probe,' *Channel NewsAsia*, 4 July 2018 https://www.channelnewsasia.com/news/asia/najib-razak-charged-in-court-1mdb-criminal-breach-of-trust-10497402 (accessed 4 July 2018).

beleaguered 1MDB.[49] Implying that bailouts usually come with conditions, Liew even wagered that a China-led consortium would be awarded the proposed Kuala Lumpur–Singapore HSR. Liew asked if such a bailout would lead to a compromise in the country's long-held neutrality in the face of China–US rivalry in Southeast Asia. While 1MDB was quick to stress that CREC's involvement in the project was not in any way linked to the eventual award of the Kuala Lumpur–Singapore HSR, several reports have seemingly nullified its claim. For instance, a report notes the 'many differences in the detailed terms' between officers from China and Malaysia.[50] One of the largest stumbling blocks is China pressuring Malaysia that it 'must try its best' to help China win the proposed HSR project, in which Japanese firms are also interested. Other major disagreements centred on the ownership and operation of the HSR terminus, and the design and concept of Bandar Malaysia.[51] According to Ho, the Malaysians 'could not agree to proposals that the HSR terminus be owned by China', as this will be 'against national interest'.[52]

These discrepancies weaken 1MDB's promise to further Malaysian interest. They especially jeopardize the livelihood of the ethnic Malay populace that GLCs like 1MDB are supposed to protect. Facing such pressures, 1MDB had to abort the deal with the CREC consortium. Indeed, it was withdrawn a few days before Najib was due to attend the inaugural BRI summit in Beijing in May 2017. As if to underline his stance, Najib courted Dalian Wanda, one of China's largest private firms, as a replacement for the consortium during the same visit. While Dalian Wanda eventually pulled out of the project because of financial difficulties and some political pressure from Beijing, Bandar Malaysia remains popular amongst other investors. At least two Japanese conglomerates, Mitsui and Daiwa, have submitted bids to take over the project.[53] Najib's bold move, while primarily driven by 1MDB's lack of relevance to the ethnic Malays as well as the geopolitical complications of excessive Chinese influence in Bandar Malaysia, is also buttressed by the (at least threefold) appreciation in value of the land beneath Bandar Malaysia and the project itself. The appreciation is largely due to a radically restructured 1MDB, clearer master plan, and already-formalized tax incentive package for Bandar Malaysia.[54]

Forest city: embedding transnational Chinese capital into local politics

The third example is Forest City, a project driven by Country Garden. The firm was listed on the Hong Kong Stock Exchange in 2007 and was worth US$20 billion as of May 2017. Country Garden selected Malaysia as its first overseas market to enter into, launching the Danga Bay project in 2012 before embarking on the significantly more ambitious Forest City in the following year. While the firm has also invested into other foreign economies, Malaysia remains its most important market.[55] Located near the Malaysia-Singapore Second Link, Forest City is the project closest to Singapore within Iskandar Malaysia. While still at an early phase of development, it eventually will take the form of four manmade islands sprawled over

[49]Malay Mail Online, 'DAP MP: China Firms Sure to Win KL-Singapore Rail Job after Role in 1MDB Turnaround,' *Malay Mail Online*, 1 January 2016 http://www.themalaymailonline.com/malaysia/article/dap-mp-china-firms-sure-to-win-kl-singapore-rail-job-after-role-in-1mdb-tur (accessed 26 March 2018).

[50]Wah Foon Ho, 'Rescue Bandar Malaysia or Face Fallout,' *The Star*, 5 May 2017, http://www.thestar.com.my/news/nation/2017/05/05/rescue-bandar-malaysia-or-face-fallout-buyers-of-project-failed-to-meet-payment-obligations-says-fin/ (accessed 10 January 2018).

[51]Sumisha Naidu, 'Capital Controls, High-Speed Rail behind Collapse of Bandar Malaysia Deal?' *Channel NewsAsia*, 6 May 2017 http://www.channelnewsasia.com/news/business/capital-controls-high-speed-rail-behind-collapse-of-bandar-8823716 (accessed 25 March 2018).

[52]Ho, 'Rescue Bandar Malaysia or Face Fallout'. The new federal administration has suspended the HSR project in late May 2018, citing cost concerns.

[53]TODAY, 'Tokyo Joins Beijing in Race for Bandar Malaysia Development,' *TODAY*, 20 July 2017, http://www.todayonline.com/world/asia/tokyo-joins-beijing-race-bandar-malaysia-development (accessed 25 June 2018).

[54]Public forum, Singapore, 25 May 2017.

[55]Country Garden, *2016 Annual Report* (Hong Kong: Country Garden, 2017).

1,386 ha of land. With a projected total investment of US$58.0 billion, it is envisioned to house 700,000 people over the next 20 years.[56]

Country Garden has established a 60/40 joint venture for the development of Forest City. It owns 60% stake in the project while Esplanade Danga 88 Private Limited holds the remaining 40%. The parties behind Esplanade Danga 88 are the Sultan of Johor (64.4% stake), the Johor state government investment arm (20% stake), and Daing Malek Daing Rahman, a member of the Royal Court of Advisers to the Johor Royal Court (15.6%).[57] Country Garden's choice of joint venture partner is within expectations, considering the receptive outlook of the Johor royalty towards business.[58] The Sultan has endorsed the increasing presence of Chinese FDI in Johor: 'The Chinese investors have the confidence and foresight to believe that their money is well spent... If the Chinese are prepared to invest here, why should it be an issue?'[59]

The Sultan is widely acknowledged to enjoy a good relationship with Yeung Kwok Keung, Country Garden's Chairman. In March 2017, Yeung was conferred by the former as a Dato' (a traditional ethnic Malay honorific title commonly used in Malaysia). According to Country Garden, Yeung was conferred the title for his 'outstanding contribution to the economic development of Johor and industrial collaboration between China and Malaysia'.[60] The Sultan viewed the development of Forest City as a watershed event: 'Today, the state's history has entered a new phase. At this special occasion, let us join hands to witness and promote the great friendship between Malaysia and China'.[61] More specifically, Country Garden asserts that Forest City's 'informal diplomacy' has facilitated communication between Chinese and Malaysian firms, underlining its commitment to the BRI. *The People's Daily* also reports the conferment event 'as an award to the BRI project'.[62]

Forest City's scale has not gone unnoticed and has become a contentious political issue. Mahathir Mohamad, Malaysia's longest-serving Prime Minister (1981–2003) and leader of the opposition bloc, has openly criticized the development. Mahathir harps on two interrelated issues—the outflow of capital and jobs to Chinese firms and the influx of Chinese immigrants. Mahathir's outcry over the potentially large numbers of Chinese immigrants into Forest City has become a nationwide political issue. On 6 January 2017, in his widely read blog, *Chedet*, Mahathir claimed that:

[W]e cannot allow thousands of acres to be owned, developed and settled by foreigners. If we do that literally they would become foreign enclaves... We are going to see large chunks of Malaysia being developed by the foreign buyers and being occupied by them.

He also tapped into Malaysia's decades-old ethnocentric politics by alleging that the Chinese citizens brought in through Forest City would be given identity cards, enabling them to vote in general elections and reshape Malaysia's political setting.[63] Mahathir's politicization of Forest City is

[56]A planned population increase of 700,000 (mostly from China) is almost equivalent to 20% of the entire population of Johor in 2016 (3.6 million).
[57]Nigel Aw, 'Royal Businesses—Who is Daing A Malek?' *Malaysiakini*, 18 July 2014 http://www.malaysiakini.com/news/269133 (accessed 26 June 2018).
[58]Straits Times, '10 Things to Know about the Sultan of Johor,' *Straits Times*, 20 March 2015 http://www.straitstimes.com/asia/se-asia/10-things-to-know-about-the-sultan-of-johor (accessed 26 June 2018).
[59]Chun Wai Wong and Nelson Benjamin, 'Johor Sultan: Singaporeans will Live in Johor and Work in Singapore,' *AsiaOne*, 19 March 2015 http://www.asiaone.com/singapore/johor-sultan-singaporeans-will-live-johor-and-work-singapore (accessed 26 June 2018).
[60]Country Garden, 'Country Garden's IECs Reopened after Upgrading,' *PR Newswire*, 20 March 2017 http://www.prnewswire.com/news-releases/country-gardens-iecs-reopened-after-upgrading-300426007.html (accessed 8 June 2017).
[61]Ibid.; 'China-Based Property Developer Country Garden Inks Agreement for Pacificview's New Project Forest City in Malaysia,' *PR Newswire*, 15 March 2017 http://www.prnewswire.com/news-releases/china-based-property-developer-country-garden-inks-agreement-for-pacificviews-new-project-forest-city-in-malaysia-300423871.html (accessed 8 June 2017).
[62]The People's Daily, '"Yidaiyilu" Xiangmu Huo Baojiang: Biguiyuan Senlinchengshi Chancheng Ronghe Erciqianyue," ["Belt and Road' Project Praised: Country Garden Inks Second Phase Agreement for Forest City"] *The People's Daily*, 13 March 2017 http://house.people.com.cn/n1/2017/0313/c164220-29141345.html (accessed 5 December 2017). This view of linking the Forest City project with the BRI emerged repeatedly in the authors' interviews with the key management personnel of the project (Singapore, May and July, 2016; Beijing, September, 2016).
[63]TODAY, 'Johor Sultan Slams Dr Mahathir for Playing "Politics of Fear and Race,"' *TODAY*, 16 January 2017 http://www.todayonline.com/world/asia/johor-sultan-says-had-enough-dr-mahathirs-fearmongering-over-chinese-investors (accessed 26 June 2018).

driven by the political agenda of his newly established *Parti Pribumi Bersatu Malaysia* (known simply as Bersatu).[64] Like the long-ruling UMNO, its electoral strategy depends largely on securing votes from the ethnic Malay populace, especially those from the rural heartlands. Mahathir's attacks on Forest City and its Chinese investors (and the Sultan of Johor, by extension) is seen as a tool to gain traction with these voters as the primarily conservative rural ethnic Malay remain wary of ethnic Chinese Malaysians and their links (whether real or imagined) with a rising China.[65]

For Mahathir, Johor is of crucial significance as the state has been chosen as the base of Bersatu. By campaigning against the 'Chinese-ness' of Forest City and categorizing those involved as 'selling out the Malays', the party is hoping to win elections in Johor, the birthplace and stronghold of UMNO.[66] Indeed, merely days after the blog posting, the Sultan of Johor, in an interview, responded: '...Mahathir has gone too far with his twisting of the issue... creating fear, using race, just to fulfil his political motives'.[67] The Sultan explained that Johor cannot be choosy with whom it does business with. As if to underline the Sultan's stand, Forest City was then hit by China's latest round of capital controls, implemented in March 2017 to directly curb the outflow of funds and to stabilize the exchange rate of the Chinese Yuan (CNY). According to the *Global Times*, an influential Beijing-controlled newspaper, the capital controls are necessary to stop Chinese companies from irrational foreign investment.[68] The sectors most scrutinized are real estate, cultural, and entertainment, implying that projects such as Forest City are no longer encouraged by Beijing. To further stem capital outflows, the Chinese government banned its citizens from converting CNY into other currencies for overseas property purchases. For Country Garden, it has since closed down all its Forest City sales centres in China and pledged to refund buyers who made down- payments on properties at Forest City but are no longer able to transfer the rest of the payment out of China.[69]

To prop up its hitherto China-heavy consumer base, it has been forced to market the project to clients from other economies. Sales galleries have been launched (or are being launched) in the Philippines, Indonesia, Vietnam, Thailand, Taiwan, and Dubai.[70] Nevertheless, a senior executive revealed that Country Garden faces substantial difficulties in marketing to non-Chinese consumers as its sales staffs are only experienced in selling to buyers from China. They have hardly sold to overseas buyers and can only converse in the Mandarin language, limiting their utility. It is also revealed that their sales plan remains *zhongguo* flavour (China-centric), with little attention paid to the aspirations of the target consumers.[71]

In short, the confluence of Malaysia's political struggle and China's financial curbs caught Country Garden by surprise, hampering Forest City's construction and sales efforts. In the meantime, a recent poll in Johor indicated that 29% of the survey subjects were unhappy with the influx of Chinese investment which was thought to have contributed to rising property prices in the state. The intertwining of politics and business through the example of Country Garden, therefore, highlights the precarious challenges of Chinese investments in a politically charged, multi-ethnic society such as Malaysia.[72]

---

[64]Mustafa Izzuddin, 'The Real Reason Malaysia's Mahathir is Taking on the Sultan of Johor,' *South China Morning Post*, 22 January 2017 http://www.scmp.com/week-asia/politics/article/2064002/real-reason-malaysias-mahathir-taking-sultan-johor (accessed 26 June 2018).

[65]Ibid.

[66]Bhavan Jaipragas, 'Mahathir versus the Sultan: How Chinese Investment could Sway Malaysian Election,' *South China Morning Post*, 18 January 2017 http://www.scmp.com/week-asia/politics/article/2063111/mahathir-versus-sultan-how-chinese-invest ment-could-sway (accessed 25 June 2018).

[67]Chun Wai Wong and Nelson Benjamin, 'Johor Ruler Slams Dr M over Chinese Investment Comments,' *The Star*, 16 January 2017 http://www.thestar.com.my/news/nation/2017/01/16/political-spin-angers-sultan-johor-ruler-slams-dr-m-over-chinese-investment-comments/ (accessed 25 June 2018).

[68]Cong Wang, '"Irrational" Overseas Investments Stop,' *Global Times*, 31 July 2017 http://www.globaltimes.cn/content/1058921.shtml (accessed 10 January 2018).

[69]Malaysiakini, 'Laporan: Pemaju Forest City Tutup Pusat Jualan di China,' ['Report: Forest City Developer Closes Sale Centers in China'] *Malaysiakini*, 10 March 2017 https://www.malaysiakini.com/news/375209 (accessed 21 January 2018).

[70]Ibid.

[71]Interview, Johor Bahru, 7 May 2017.

[72]Kok Leong Chan, 'Tak Percaya, Tak Rasa Kesan Buat Penduduk Johor Tolak China, Raikan Singapura,' ['Distrust, Disconnect Cause Johoreans to Spurn China, Embrace Singapore'] *The Malaysian Insight*, 23 February 2018 https://www.themalaysian insight.com/bahasa/s/39338/ (accessed 26 February 2018).

Discussion: politics in command

The experience of CCCC, CREC, and Country Garden reveals several points. First, the decades-old NEP remains a key variable. Despite some criticisms from opposition lawmakers, ECRL was viewed positively by the leadership of the three ethnic Malay-dominated states of Pahang, Terengganu, and Kelantan. Its proposed linkage to several hitherto economically backward towns and villages dovetailed well with UMNO's strategy to more aggressively capture votes from the ethnic Malays, especially those from the rural constituencies. The pro-Malay agenda is not too evident in Bandar Malaysia and Forest City. While CREC joined forces with two formidable domestic partners in IWH (40%-owned by a GLC) and 1MDB (a GLC), the reality is that 1MDB (and Najib) has been dogged by a series of high-profile controversies, diminishing the appeal of Bandar Malaysia to the citizenry (especially the ethnic Malays).

For Forest City, it is essentially a private venture undertaken by the Johor Sultan in conjunction with Country Garden, another private firm. While Country Garden also labelled Forest City as a BRI-related project, it is *not* a project driven by the Chinese and/or Malaysian authorities, although their endorsement was readily available, evidenced by the site visits of Najib and the Chinese ambassador to Malaysia on two separate occasions. Forest City does not emphasize very strongly any pro-Malay policies as it is envisioned to welcome foreign capital and expertise. Therefore, it has come under heavy criticisms from several quarters, especially Mahathir. His strategy of targeting ethnic Malay votes from the Malay heartlands of Johor, a traditional UMNO stronghold, further necessitates the need to heighten the 'Chinese-ness' of Forest City and associate the Chinese property investors with the domestic ethnic Chinese populace. Mahathir's moves are designed to tap into the fears of the conservative ethnic Malays who often view Malaysians of ethnic Chinese descent as a 'fifth wheel'.

The contrasting fates of the three China–Malaysia projects show that the NEP has intertwined itself with China's interests. Thus, projects without a clear conformance to the NEP (whether real or imagined) are unlikely to receive mass support. This consideration reaffirms Li and Cheong's and Lim's postulation that the NEP and the need to pander to the ethnic Malay voters will likely weigh heavily onto any major policies by the political leadership, including how receptive it can be to BRI projects.[73] For the ethnic Chinese business community of Malaysia in general, they have not been offered opportunities to take part in high profile projects such as ECRL and Forest City. In the event that they are, they are expected to function as a 'bridesmaid' to the GLCs and even the political elites, much like how IWH has behaved in Bandar Malaysia. This finding both strengthens and weakens Hau's and Liu's assessment on the ethnic Chinese.[74] On one hand, the ethnic Chinese are appreciated for their business know-how and ties to Chinese firms, the GLCs, and politically powerful ethnic Malay politicians. Yet, Malaysia's political nuances mean that ethnic Chinese firms such as IWH have to incorporate the wishes of their ethnic Malay partners and those of the Chinese investors into the BRI projects, in addition to their own commercial calculus. While they want to take part in the BRI, they are not as well-endowed as the GLCs because the latter enjoys state patronage and access to favoured projects. Notwithstanding the collapse of Bandar Malaysia, interviews with other prominent ethnic Chinese businessmen suggests that the ethnic Chinese firms are aware of the delicate situation that they are in, and have since readjusted their business models and broadened their political networks to better accommodate the new political economic situation. If anything, their tentative optimism, captured in the excited tone of the Chairman of a prominent ethnic Chinese firm, on the prospect of more BRI projects entering Malaysia underscores their sensitivity to the ever-changing dynamics between both countries.[75]

---

[73]Li and Cheong, 'Huawei and ZTE in Malaysia: The localisation of Chinese transnational enterprises'; Lim, 'China's investments in Malaysia: Choosing the "right" partners'.

[74]Hau, 'Becoming "Chinese"—but what "Chinese"?—in Southeast Asia'; Liu, 'Opportunities and anxieties for the Chinese diaspora in Southeast Asia'. See also Hong Liu and Yishu Zhou, 'New Chinese Capitalism and the ASEAN Economic Community', in *The Sociology of Chinese Capitalism in Southeast Asia*, ed. Yos Santasombat (New York: Palgrave Macmillan, (2019), pp.55 73.).

[75]Interview, Beijing, 31 October 2016.

Second, it is important to analyse the state–federal contestation undergirding these projects. For ECRL, this contestation is mostly subdued across the four states (three on the east coast and one on the west) it is to traverse through. While these states enjoy some autonomy, especially on land matters, their governments have not opposed ECRL, except that of opposition-governed Selangor. As illustrated in the previous section, the Selangor Chief Minister is relatively receptive to the project, notwithstanding some of his colleagues' concerns on its cost and financing terms. Indeed, the Chief Ministers of the three east coast states have welcomed the project as most of the railway will be located in their states. While it helps the federal government that the three Chief Ministers are either UMNO members (Pahang and Terengganu) or are aligned to it (Kelantan), another key factor is the manner in which Najib, in his capacity as the head of the federal government, has projected ECRL as a crucial cog in the development trajectory of both Malaysia and the east coast states. In particular, he has promised to more forcefully reduce the socio-economic gap between the east coast and the wealthier west coast of Peninsular Malaysia.

For Bandar Malaysia, state–federal contestation is absent as the project takes place exclusively in Kuala Lumpur, the country's de facto economic capital. While not needing to consult governments at the state level is helpful in advancing the project, this factor per se is insufficient to sustain Bandar Malaysia, as the next paragraph will illustrate (in addition to the previous paragraph's argument). The state–federal rivalry is most obvious in Forest City. Its extreme south location seems to have exacerbated the already uneasy ties between Johor and Putrajaya. The federal government, cognizant of the need to spread out economic growth across all of its states, has traditionally been wary about the southward movement of the country's economic clout. Forest City's emergence, coupled with the vibrancy of the rest of Iskandar Malaysia, could lead to a situation where the tail (Forest City and Johor) wags the dog (the entire country). More broadly, this observation reflects the experience of other developing economies lacking cohesive institutions to mediate differences between the central government and the local ones.

Thirdly, one needs to scrutinize the geopolitical dimension of these BRI projects. This issue is most clearly reflected in ECRL. Connecting the Kuantan Port on the east coast of Peninsular Malaysia to the bustling Port Klang on the west coast, it could resolve China's perennial 'Malacca Dilemma'. The new routes opened up by ECRL will also offer Malaysia a window of opportunity to bypass Singapore. The geopolitical undertone for Bandar Malaysia is just as salient. CREC has seemingly forwarded its interest as well as that of the Chinese state by securing a stake in one of Malaysia's largest infrastructure projects in recent years. In addition, Bandar Malaysia was considered a prized BRI project because of its position as the terminus of the proposed Kuala Lumpur–Singapore HSR and a key node of the mooted Pan-ASEAN Rail Transit network, both of which are poised to be landmark infrastructure projects within Southeast Asia. Yet, subsequent reports show that the terms demanded by the Chinese (such as the request for a leeway in the bidding of the HSR project) were not acceptable to the Malaysian bureaucracy. The timing of the project's abortion, merely days before the inaugural BRI Summit in Beijing in May 2017, also implies that the Malaysian leadership was in no mood to 'save China's face'. Buoyed by at least a tripling of Bandar Malaysia's original value, Najib attempted to secure a new partner in the form of Dalian Wanda during the BRI Summit. Although Dalian Wanda scrapped its bid for Bandar Malaysia, the project is still sought after by several well-capitalized investors.

Forest City's status as a private venture means that it is mostly devoid of geopolitical power. Despite claims of Forest City fostering China–Malaysia ties in its 'informal diplomacy' and the Sultan's cordial ties with Country Garden, the reality is that Malaysia's bilateral relationship is the purview of the federal government. Country Garden's alliance with the Sultan of Johor does not negate the fact that he remains a ceremonial figure, albeit with some degree of political influence. For Beijing, Forest City represents the type of 'irrational investment' that it is curbing through capital controls. It is thus unlikely for Country Garden to receive concrete support from Beijing, at least in the near to medium term.

The geopolitical agenda of the three China–Malaysia projects can be interpreted along two interrelated dimensions. The first dimension relates to the agency of small states (such as Malaysia) in attracting and even rejecting (or at least, circumscribing) Chinese capital to meet domestic geopolitical expectations. Malaysia's experience underlines the relative inability of China in imposing its will on its BRI partners. Yet, there is also a justified concern that Malaysia is creeping towards China's sphere of influence, especially with regard to ECRL. While it is too early to label it a 'new regional order' or a new Sino-centric 'community of shared destiny', this finding does demonstrate China's capacity in exploiting the weaknesses of various Southeast Asian countries through a series of diplomacy moves combined with aid and investment packages.

Conclusion

This article has demonstrated the complicated manners in which the BRI has taken shape in Malaysia. Despite their wealth and technical expertise, Chinese firms cannot forge ahead without understanding the needs of the Malaysian stakeholders. In short, BRI projects require the cooperation (or at the very least, non-hindrance) of these players. The article has underlined the value of looking beyond large-scale geopolitical shifts and conventional literature that depicts the BRI under sweeping, uncritical themes. ECRL's partial success, Bandar Malaysia's collapse, and Forest City's arrested development shows that the BRI's success (or failure) is dependent on three key conditions: fulfilment of Malaysia's longstanding pro-ethnic Malay policy, a mutual vision between the state and federal authorities, and advancement of geopolitical interests for both China and Malaysia.

As if to underline this article's central argument, UMNO and its allies were voted out in the most recent general election on 9 May 2018. While there were several reasons leading to its rejection, the disquiet surrounding the Najib administration's management of the BRI ranks as one of the more prominent factors. Although Mahathir has stopped short of cooling ties with Beijing since assuming the Prime Ministership for the second time, it must be noted that he actively critiqued large-scale projects like Forest City and the Kuala Lumpur–Singapore HSR. Mahathir's success at mobilizing electoral support further underlines how the debates and controversies surrounding the BRI have meshed and interacted with Malaysia's complex, multi-layered politics, indirectly inducing regime change. Indeed, during his official visit to China in August 2018, Mahathir announced that ECRL would be 'deferred until such time we can afford, and maybe we can reduce the cost also if we do it differently'.[76] Mahathir's decision to shelf ECRL (and the HSR which was cancelled merely weeks after he took over Putrajaya) is widely interpreted as a cost-cutting measure, but probably its more important goal is to shrink (or at least, delegitimize) the economic base of the Najib clique. This further reinforces our argument that the BRI recipient country has its own political and economic goals that may not be in-line with the BRI objectives and when the divergence emerges, the former tends to assume a bigger role in determining the outcome. More practically, ECRL's shelving does not negate the fact that despite losing Putrajaya, UMNO and PAS have reinforced their grip on the state assemblies of the three east coast states, in addition to defeating most of Mahathir's allies vying for federal seats there. To preserve his legitimacy, Mahathir cannot afford to alienate the voters from these states. Mahathir must have also realized that the expeditiousness in which the previous federal and state authorities implemented the project implies that some segments of the Malay-heavy constituencies can (and have already) tap into ECRL's spillover effects.

What then are the region-wide implications of these case studies? Thus far, Malaysian actors have seemingly captured economic benefits from China while preserving some level of

---

[76]Sui Noi Goh, "East Coast Rail Link and Pipeline Projects with China to be Deferred: Malaysian PM Mahathir," Straits Times, August 21, 2010, accessed August 22, 2018, https://www.straitstimes.com/asia/se-asia/east-coast-rail-link-and-pipeline-pro jects-with-china-cancelled-says-malaysian-pm.

independence in the face of gigantic BRI projects. The point is that the BRI is still relatively nascent and smaller states in the region certainly possess sufficient autonomy to hold and even bolster their positions. It is hoped that the framework put forth in this article as well as its arguments will contribute to the further explorations of the ways through which other Southeast Asian states have responded to the BRI and the latter's intertwining with the local political economy.

Acknowledgements

The authors thank Baogang He, Suisheng Zhao, Kai He, and David Hundt for their constructive comments on earlier versions of this manuscript.

Disclosure statement

No potential conflict of interest was reported by the authors. The authors are responsible for all interpretations and any remaining errors in this article.

Funding

This work was supported by the Singapore Ministry of Education AcRF Tier 2 Grant [grant number MOE2016-T2-02-87]; Lien Foundation; and Nanyang Centre for Public Administration's Lien Research Programme on the Belt and Road Initiative.

ORCID

Guanie Lim 🆔 http://orcid.org/0000-0001-9083-8883

11   Myanmar's Role in China's Maritime Silk Road Initiative

J. Mohan Malik

ABSTRACT

This article argues that the origins and theoretical underpinnings of Xi Jinping's Belt and Road Initiative can actually be traced back to the mid-1980s, that is, almost three decades before the official media unveiled the Maritime Silk Road Initiative (MSRI). It examines the changing role of Myanmar in China's grand strategy in general and in MSRI in particular by undertaking an investigation of trade and investment relations. This analysis of the geo-economic and geo-strategic implications of MSRI is undertaken in order to offer a prognosis of benefits and costs for Myanmar. Both the extent and the limits of MSRI are illustrated in Myanmar. It ends with a discussion of possible roadblocks, detours, cracks and fault lines along the Maritime Silk Road.

Myanmar/Burma is the second-largest country in Southeast Asia and is located at the juncture of Southeast and South Asia. Given its resources, natural endowments and strategic location bordering China and India, Myanmar finds itself at the center of political wrangling between major powers. While India's culture and religion have influenced the Burmese way of life over the centuries, China has traditionally exerted geopolitical and strategic pressure on Myanmar. As Tin Maung Maung Than notes: 'Geopolitical ramifications for modern Burma have been overwhelmingly determined by bilateral relations with China', which date back to the early Pyu kingdoms of the ninth century AD.[1] Myanmar suffers from centrifugal tendencies. Since independence in 1948, successive governments have battled around the country's periphery with ethnic separatist movements and communist insurgencies, some of which received direct support from Beijing. Post-independence, Myanmar has 'accommodated China as its "senior" in a *paukphaw* (kinsmen) relationship', and avoided taking actions inimical to China's interests.[2]

Transition From Military Rule to Democracy

The three decades of the 'Burmese road to socialism' during the Cold War turned the region's once most prosperous country into an economic basket case. In 1990, the State Law and Order Restoration Council (SLORC) presided over an election that the opposition National League for Democracy (NLD) won by a landslide but was not allowed to take office. Instead, the military junta placed the opposition leader Aung San Suu Kyi under house arrest and arrested thousands of NLD supporters, after which the West imposed economic sanctions. Faced with international isolation and domestic unrest, the military

---

[1] Tin Maung Maung Than, 'Myanmar: Myanmar-ness and realism in historical perspective', in Ken Booth and Russell Trood, eds, *Strategic Cultures in the Asia–Pacific Region* (New York: St. Martin's Press, 1999), p. 166.

[2] *Ibid.*

junta turned to China for survival. Myanmar urgently needed foreign exchange, capital equipment and technical expertise to prevent the collapse of its ailing economy.[3] At this point, Chinese interests conveniently synchronized with a range of the military regime's major concerns and the junta in Rangoon moved to establish closer ties with the Chinese communist regime, which had found itself in a similar predicament following the Tiananmen massacre in June 1989, this beginning Myanmar's slide into China's embrace. During 1988–2013, Beijing stepped in with liberal economic assistance, cheap loans, trade, investment, energy deals, and military and diplomatic support. Nearly 60% of Myanmar's weapons imports came from China, and Chinese firms contributed to 42% of the country's total foreign direct investment (FDI) (some US$33.67 billion). Between 2008 and 2011, China promised approximately US$13 billion in infrastructure investments and also became its largest donor country.[4] In return, China gained access to Myanmar's rich natural resources and moved closer to gaining a strategic passage from southwest China to the Bay of Bengal—its 'long-held ambition to create a proxy west coast and turn Myanmar into "China's California"'.[5]

However, China's growing footprint in Myanmar aroused popular resentment, social unrest and complaints about environmental degradation, insufficient compensation for expropriated land and the use of Chinese labor. With tens of thousands of Chinese moving south of the border, many feared the country was at risk of becoming just another Chinese province.[6] By the early 2000s, Myanmar's nationalist leaders, extremely sensitive about the country's sovereignty and suspicious of Beijing's geopolitical intentions, began expressing concern over Chinese economic domination and illegal immigration. In 2008, the military began a gradual process of limited political reform which culminated in a general election in November 2010, and the formation of a quasi-civilian government. The turning point came when President Thein Sein suspended several large Chinese investment projects in September 2011, including the US$3.6 billion Myitsone Dam in the north on the Irrawaddy River and the Letpadaung copper mine, following protests over environmental concerns. The Myitsone megadam, designed to supply 90% of its electricity to China, was seen as emblematic of China's economic dominance. The cancellation in July 2014 of China Railway Engineering Corporation's (CREC) proposed US$20 billion railway project, that was to connect China's southern Yunnan province with Myanmar's Rakhine western coast, soured bilateral relations. These decisions clearly sought to distance Naypyitaw from Beijing and indicated the new government's desire to diversify its diplomatic and economic relations and help Myanmar shed its pariah status.

Beijing looked on with some trepidation as the democratization process gathered momentum after 2011. The victory of Suu Kyi's party, the NLD, in the historic November 2015 election marked the logical conclusion of this process, with a civilian government assuming power after five decades, even though the military retains control of several key ministries. Despite media speculation on the new civilian government's pro-West tilt, Myanmar's geopolitical position and Beijing's clout as its biggest investor and trading partner, coupled with its links to Myanmar's ethnic groups, dictated that Suu Kyi's domestic priorities of economic development and making peace with insurgents could not be achieved by antagonizing the superpower on its doorstep. Not surprisingly, Suu Kyi chose to visit China first to reassure Beijing of close friendly ties and her government reopened the controversial Letpadaung copper mine to address concerns of Chinese investors.[7] Then came her visits to India, Thailand, the United States (US), Japan and the European Union (EU). This showed a prioritization of seeking good relations

---

[3]Bertil Lintner, 'Burma: centrifugal forces', *Far Eastern Economic Review*, (27 February 1992), p. 16.

[4]Jonathan T. Chow and Leif-Eric Easley, 'Rebalancing not pivoting: Myanmar's reforms and relations with Washington and Beijing', *PacNet#68*, (8 September 2016), available at: http://thediplomat.com/2017/05/a-new-chapter-in-myanmar-vatican-relations (accessed 10 September 2016).

[5]Tom Miller, *China's Asian Dream* (London: Zed Books, 2017), p. 128. The term 'China's California' is used by Thant Myint-U in 'Asia's new great game', *Foreign Policy*, (12 September 2011), available at: http://foreignpolicy.com/2011/09/12/asias-new-great-game (accessed 11 October 2015).

[6]'High mountains, distant emperors', *The Economist*, (23 April 2016), available at: https://www.economist.com/news/asia/21697287-aung-san-suu-kyi-extends-wary-welcome-china-tries-regain-lost-influence-high-mountains (accessed 24 April 2016).

[7]Evan Rees, 'Myanmar cannot ignore China', *Stratfor.com*, (25 November 2015), available at: https://www.stratfor.com/analysis/myanmar-cannot-ignore-china (accessed 25 November 2015).

with neighbors over distant powers to achieve the goals of domestic stability, economic growth and a more balanced foreign policy.

Myanmar: The Origins of China's Maritime Silk Road Initiative (MSRI)

Conventional wisdom holds that Chinese President Xi Jinping launched the Silk Road Economic Belt (丝绸之路经济带) during his visit to Kazakhstan in September 2013 and subsequently expanded the initiative to include the 21st Century Maritime Silk Road (21世纪海上丝绸之路) in October 2013 to promote greater connectivity between China and the Association of Southeast Asian Nations (ASEAN).[8] First referred to as 'One Belt One Road' (一带一路, OBOR), and now as 'the Belt and Road initiative' (BRI), the project seeks to build transportation infrastructure routes for trade and commerce from Asia to Africa and Europe. In reality, the signature foreign policy initiative of the Xi administration is certainly not as new as it is made out to be, nor is it a 'start-up' from scratch, but builds upon pre-existing or decades-old tangentially related economic programs and expands or repackages several ongoing or planned projects.[9]

This author argues that the conceptual origins of Beijing's Belt and Road initiative can actually be traced back to the mid-1980s, nearly three decades before the MSRI was officially unveiled.[10] Pan Qi, a former vice-minister of communications, penned an article in the *Beijing Review* of 2 September 1985 entitled 'Opening to the Southwest: An Expert Opinion' wherein he outlined the significance of Myanmar's geo-strategic location for China's economic growth. This article expressed the desire of Chinese economic planners to reopen the old Burma Road to link up the poorer inland provinces, such as Yunnan, which lagged behind the booming coastal provinces, with the fast growing economies of Southeast and South Asia. Beijing sought an overland route through Myanmar to a port from which it could export cheap consumer goods to mainland Southeast Asia, India and other developing countries farther afield. Such an outlet would reduce transport time for some of China's trade and help avoid the Malacca Strait choke point in the event of a conflict. Both geo-economic and geo-strategic calculations lay behind China's courting of Myanmar's military regime.

Over the last two decades, several Chinese multinational corporations (MNCs) have signed deals to engage in hydropower, mining, infrastructure, and oil and gas projects in Myanmar. Then in the early 2000s, first as part of the 'Great Western Development' strategy under President Jiang Zemin, and then as part of its 'March West' strategy under President Hu Jintao, Beijing embarked upon plans for spending hundreds of billions to build trade and economic corridors via pipelines, highways and railway networks with Central, Southwest and Southeast Asia to help develop China's underdeveloped central and western regions and to help Chinese companies go global.[11] All infrastructure projects on the drawing board or already under construction, such as the planned 1,350 km railway through Laos and Myanmar to Thailand, the China–Pakistan economic corridor (CPEC), the Bangladesh–China–India–Myanmar (BCIM) road network, and an energy corridor through Myanmar were co-opted into the new scheme by officials scrambling to peg their plans to Xi's all-encompassing horizon. For example, the BCIM corridor, conceived *before* the BRI, and the US$500 million China–ASEAN Maritime Cooperation Fund, established two years *before* the announcement of the MSRI, now constitute important parts of the MSRI.

[8]'Speech by Chinese President Xi Jinping to Indonesian Parliament', ASEAN–China Centre, 3 October 2013, available at: http://www.asean-china-center.org/english/2013-10/03/c_133062675.htm (accessed 7 October 2016).

[9]Raffaello Pantucci, 'How new is the "Belt and Road"?', *CPI Analysis*, (7 October 2016), available at: https://cpianalysis.org/2016/10/07/how-new-is-the-belt-and-road (accessed 7 October 2016).

[10]This was decades before Wang Jisi published his piece '"Marching westwards": the rebalancing of China's geostrategy', *Huanqiu Shibao*, (17 October 2012), p. 3.

[11]The concept of 'west' was stretched to anything beyond China's booming cities on the eastern seaboard. See Yun Sun, 'March west', *Brookings.blog*, (31 January 2013), available at: http://www.brookings.edu/blogs/up-front/posts/2013/01/31-china-us-sun (accessed 14 February 2013), Zhu Ningzhu, 'China to Pave Way for Maritime Silk Road', *Xinhua.net*, (11 October 2013), available at: http://news.xinhuanet.com/english/china/2013-10/11/c_132790018.htm (accessed 20 September 2014).

MSRI: The Economic Dimension and China–Myanmar Ties

For China today, economics is strategy. Money has now replaced Maoism as the tool for gaining influence. Bandwagoning with an economic juggernaut has always transformed the fortune of nations. In trade and commerce, nations do not pick sides but play all sides. For conflict-torn countries with autocratic regimes that cannot get funding from global financial institutions, China's aid and investment comes in handy. Being part of the Chinese sphere of influence may well be a small price to pay for economic success. Many countries may not trust China, but they depend on it for their own growth. In terms of cold, hard cash, China clearly trumps the West and Japan. For countries that want to build factories, schools, roads and ports, Chinese capital and engineering prowess is a godsend. China's cash-rich state-owned enterprises (SOEs), backed by the China Development Bank and other government institutions, have established a reputation for delivering big infrastructure projects quickly and without delays caused by environmental or human rights concerns.

Chinese leaders and official media, therefore, stress the economic dimension of the MSRI insofar as it can accelerate economic growth in less developed regions. This initiative was unveiled in the aftermath of an investment boom in China that ended in vast overproduction and overcapacity, particularly in the steel, machinery and construction material sectors, thereby necessitating the need to find new export markets abroad. With a domestic market slowdown and rising wages in China, Beijing now wants to export the surplus steel, cement, workers and engineers—and earn greater returns on investments. This requires the building of railroads, ports and trade corridors to link manufacturing centers in China with markets and natural resources around the world. These spokes or arteries would bring in raw materials and energy resources while exporting Chinese manufactured goods to those regions and beyond—a sort of Beijing style 'hub-and-spokes economic system in Eurasia' as a riposte to Washington's 'hub-and-spokes security system'. China's status as the world's second-largest economy, the world's largest goods trader and the world's largest holder of foreign exchange reserves provides a strong foundation for Chinese companies to extend their investment overseas. Beijing has promised hundreds of billions of dollars in funds for investment in Southeast Asia alone. Money matters and development requires investment. Many coastal states are courting Beijing to leverage Chinese financial and technical prowess (e.g. in creating artificial islands via dredging on a scale and speed that is unmatched). To finance this infrastructure network, Beijing has launched the US$40 billion Silk Road Fund and the US$100 billion Asia Infrastructure Investment Bank (AIIB). The disbursement of large amounts of money as loans and aid for countries participating in MSRI will enhance China's economic and diplomatic influence.

Most MSRI projects are linked by their proximity and utility to diversify, insulate and secure China's resource and trade access. China's FDI is now going to countries along the Silk Road: in 2015, China's total investment of US$145.67 billion overtook Japan's US$128.65 billion, and was second only to the US FDI of US$299.96 billion.[12] Official Chinese reports disclosed that more than 100 SOEs had established branches in countries participating in OBOR by the end of 2016. Reports indicate that more than 1,400 contracted projects were signed with nations along the Silk Road for a mix of high-speed rail, road construction, electricity upgrades, port development and coal power plants.[13]

Several connectivity projects have been unveiled to link China's underdeveloped and land-locked western region to open seas in the Indian Ocean and Gulf of Thailand for human, goods and energy transportation. The key to the success of the MSRI lies in future cooperation on connectivity and the new initiative of the Lancang–Mekong Cooperation framework that will also boost the AIIB's role in the triangular nexus of Asia's three largest Buddhist nations (Myanmar, Thailand and China).[14] The goal of connectivity inherent to the Silk Road initiative is also in sync with similar regional initiatives, such as the ASEAN plans for connectivity, the BCIM and India's plans for physical connectivity. The completion

---

[12]'Silk Road project sees Chinese overseas investment reach record levels', *SputnikNews.com*, (9 September 2016), available at: https://sputniknews.com/world/20160922/1045604165/silk-road-china-investment.html (accessed 10 September 2016).

[13]'Our bulldozers, our rules', *The Economist*, (30 June 2016), p. 5.

[14]Kavi Chongkittavorn, 'Emerging nexus of Myanmar–Thailand–China', *The Nation*, (22 August 2016), available at: http://www.strait-stimes.com/asia/se-asia/emerging-nexus-of-myanmar-thailand-china-the-nation-columnist (accessed 30 August 2016).

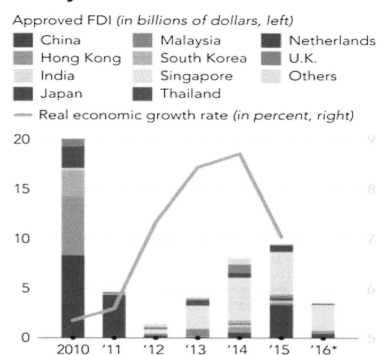

Figure 1. Key investment, growth metrics for Myanmar.

of the Asia Highway connecting Thailand and India via Myanmar in 2015 ties Myanmar to the more dynamic Thai economy. Myanmar and Thailand have also agreed on establishing a special economic zone between the Thai border town of Mae Sot and Myanmar's Myawaddy. This connectivity will be further enhanced by links to a planned deep-sea port in Dawei in Myanmar. As Thailand moves up the economic value chain, it should offload some production lines to Myanmar.[15] Mainland Southeast Asia is a key hub for China's MSRI to develop transportation networks to both South and Southeast Asia and to move manufacturing offshore to low cost producers such as Myanmar, Laos, Cambodia and Bangladesh. In contrast with maritime Southeast Asian states at odds with Beijing over the SCS disputes, countries like Laos, Cambodia, Myanmar and Thailand have welcomed the MSRI. The importance attached to the railway projects through Laos and Thailand 'reflects a strategic reorientation in China's policy toward mainland Southeast Asia'.[16]

---

[15]Information here is based on Rees, 'Myanmar cannot ignore China'.
[16]Yun Sun, 'China's strategic focus on mainland Southeast Asia', CogitAsia.com, (22 December 2013), available at: http://cogitasia. com/chinas-strategic-focus-on-mainland-southeast-asia (accessed 29 August 2016).

Figure 2. Myanmar-China relations: High mountains, distant emperors. Source: The Economist, Apr 23rd 2016. https://www.economist.com/news/asia/21697287-aung-san-suu-kyi-extends-wary-welcome-china-tries-regain-lost-influence-high-mountains.

China–Myanmar Economic Bonds

China's economic slowdown coupled with Myanmar's attempts to diversify its partners notwithstanding, China is still the most important player in Myanmar's economy and trade, and is likely to remain so. In December 2015, Myanmar's parliament approved plans to develop a deep-sea port, industrial zone, logistics hub and other facilities in Kyaukpyu—all by Chinese companies. China's size, proximity, economic complementarity and familiarity with the country work to Beijing's advantage. During 1988–2016, China's direct investment of US$18.53 billion, poured into nearly 130 projects in Myanmar, dwarfed all other countries; the EU was second with under US$6 billion over the same period. Figure 1 shows major investors in Myanmar while the map in Figure 2 shows the location of some of China's major investment projects in the country.[17]

Beijing has indicated a willingness to be flexible on loans and pricing to enmesh Myanmar in China's regional economic network provided its government 'remains friendly and cooperative'.[18] With its new role as a mediator in peace talks between rival ethnic groups and governments, Beijing is also better placed to tailor investment projects to bring peace to insurgency-hit impoverished areas. According to Song Qingrun,

[17]Aaron Balshan, 'Why the US shouldn't have lifted sanctions on Myanmar', The Diplomat, (3 October 2016), available at: http://thediplomat.com/2016/10/why-the-us-shouldnt-have-lifted-sanctions-on-myanmar (accessed 4 October 2016). Some estimates put Chinese investment around US$10 billion until 2009 and around US$12.5 billion between 2009 and 2012.

[18]Yun Sun, 'Aung San Suu Kyi's visit to Beijing', Security Risks Asia, (19 August 2016), available at: http://www.security-risks.com/security-trends-south-asia/myanmar/aung-san-suu-kyis-visit-to-beijing-recalibrating-myanmars-china-policy-6500.html (accessed 25 August 2016).

Table 1. Major Chinese MNCs and key projects in Myanmar.

Industry	PRC Company	Project	Status
Hydropower	China Power Investments Corporation (CPIC)	Mytisone Dam	Suspended 2011
	China Power Investments Corporation (CPIC)	Dams on Irrawaddy	Under construction/in operation
	China Three Gorges Corporation	Salween River	Suspended
Electric power	State Grid Corporation of China	Mandalay region	Operational
Hydroelectric	Sinohydro Corporation	Tarpein	Operational
Coal-fired power stations	China National Heavy Machinery Corporation (CHMC)	Tigyit (Shan state)	Operational
Mining	NORINCO	Mwetaung Nickel mine	Exploration
	NORINCO/Wanbao Mining Co.	Letpadaung copper mine	Suspended 2012 Under construction 2014
	China Non-ferrous Metal (CNMC)	Tagaung Nickel mine	Operational
	NORINCO	Mwetaung Nickel mine	Exploration
Telecom	China Mobile		Operational
Oil & gas	China National Offshore Oil Corporation	Oil exploration	Operational
	China National Petroleum Corporation (CNPC)	Myanmar–China gas pipeline, refineries	Operational
	Petro China	Kyaukphyu–Kunming oil pipeline	Operational
Railway	China Railway Engineering Corporation (CREC)	Kunming–Kyaukphyu railway	Suspended 2014
Infrastructure	CITIC Group China Harbor Engineering Company China Merchants Holdings	Kyaukphyu SEZ & Port	Under construction

China is the largest source of FDI, with investment agreements worth $25.4 billion signed between China (Hong Kong included) and Myanmar in the first 7 months of the year [2016], accounting for 40% of the total FDI to Myanmar, and 3.5 times the combined FDI from the US, EU and Japan.[19]

Other estimates of China's FDI in Myanmar as of August 2016 put it at 28.13% of total foreign investment, while India made up a mere 1.14%.

In 2014, China accounted for 42.7% of Myanmar's imports by value and 65.2% of its exports. Myanmar's next-largest partner, Thailand, is overshadowed by China in comparison, accounting for 19.3% of Myanmar's imports and 16.4% of its exports. In the fiscal year 2014–2015, China made up one-third of Myanmar's total trade volume, which stood at US$29.16 billion.[20] However, official economic data do not account for the trade in narcotics, black market timber, minerals, jade and Chinese shell companies operated by smugglers in Myanmar.

Myanmar's government earns billions of dollars from oil and gas pipelines, owned by China National Petroleum Corporation (CNPC), that bring gas from offshore Shwe gas platforms in the Bay of Bengal, and oil shipped to the Myanmarese coast from the Middle East, into the hinterlands of Yunnan.[21] The pipelines, the construction of a deep-sea port near Sittwe in Rakhine state where the two pipelines start from and the Kyaukphyu Special Economic Zone (SEZ) are indicative of how China is using infrastructure development within Myanmar to promote its energy and maritime security by lessening reliance on

[19]Song Qingrun, 'Benign engagement between Myanmar, China and the United States', China–US Focus, (6 September 2016), available at: http://m.chinausfocus.com/article/4869.html (accessed 20 September 2016).
[20]'Myanmar looks to China to increase foreign direct investment', Oxford Business, (28 September 2016), available at: http://www.oxfordbusinessgroup.com/news/myanmar-looks-china-increase-foreign-direct-investment (accessed 4 October 2016).
[21]Cao Siyi and Shan Jie, 'Sino–Myanmar oil pipeline launch a good signal: experts', Global Times, (28 March 2017), available at: http://www.globaltimes.cn/content/1039861.shtml (accessed 30 March 2017).

maritime transportation through the Malacca Straits.[22] Beijing has not given up on the railway line project, and work on the Kunming–Kyaukphyu railway line on China's side of the border has already been completed. China is also investing heavily in regional transportation networks. A railway link between Kunming and the Laotian capital Vientiane is now under construction. To meet Myanmar's growing energy needs, China Power Investments Corporation (CPIC) has proposed spending US$20 billion on a series of dams along the upper reaches of Burma's sacred heartland river, the Irrawaddy. In addition, Guangdong Zhenrong Energy plans to build a US$3 billion oil refinery further south in Dawei, near the border with Thailand. Table 1 provides a list of major Chinese projects in Myanmar.

Although Beijing retains considerable commercial and strategic influence, Myanmar is no longer a poor pariah nation. Now, Naypyitaw has other suitors that Beijing must contend and compete with. It cannot simply buy support by bribing generals. Foreign capital is pouring in: Singapore, Malaysia, Thailand and Vietnam ranked among the top five investors in 2013–2014 in Myanmar, and China's US$2.8 billion investment in 2016–2017 was down by nearly US$500 million compared with the previous year.[23] Myanmar aims to achieve US$6 billion in annual FDI between 2017 and 2020, raising the target to US$8 billion from 2021 through to 2030. For fiscal year 2015–2016, Myanmar received a record US$9.5 billion in FDI.[24] Global players are jostling for a slice of the huge infrastructure market, estimated to top US$130 billion. With the lifting of decades-old sanctions in October 2016, American power suppliers APR Energy and Convalt Energy have offered to build power plants. Thailand's largest construction company, Italian–Thai Development, is going to build a liquefied natural gas (LNG) plant in Dawei while PTT, a Thai state-owned oil and gas company, will construct a LNG plant in Kanbauk in the southeastern Tanintharyi region.

While China's CITIC is constructing a large deep-water port in Kyaukpyu, India's Essar Group in January 2017 completed the construction of a new port at the mouth of the Kaladan River that links the western city of Sittwe and northeastern India. According to one commentary,

> The Indian achievement pips to the post a Chinese endeavor to create a deep-sea berthing infrastructure and an SEZ further down the Rakhine coast at Kyaukphyu. The two investments are inevitably being seen as the Asian competitors' attempt to expand their spheres of naval influence in the Indian Ocean region, as in the case of Gwadar in Pakistan and Chabahar in Iran being built by China and India, respectively.[25]

Nonetheless, India's assistance under different categories of US$1.75 billion is easily dwarfed by that of Japan's. In November 2016, Tokyo stepped forward with a whopping US$7.7 billion aid over the next five years, making it the biggest donor.[26] Japanese investment and official development assistance (ODA) has been the driving force behind the development of Burma's first SEZ at Thilawa port near Rangoon and it is contributing significantly to transportation and electricity projects. Japanese ODA and low-interest, long-term yen loans come with considerably better terms than most Chinese investments. Myanmar is keen to attract Japanese, Korean and other investment into its railway modernization plans (e.g. the Mandalay–Yangon line) and in the US$14 billion Kyaukphyu SEZ being built by China's CITIC Group.[27]

---

[22]P. S. Ramya, 'China's Myanmar conundrum', *The Diplomat*, (22 April 2015), available at: http://thediplomat.com/2015/04/chinas-myanmar-conundrum (accessed 25 August 2016).

[23]'China's investment in Myanmar declines in 2016–2017 fiscal year', *Xinhuanet.com*, (8 March 2017), available at: http://english.mofcom.gov.cn/article/counselorsreport/asiareport/201703/20170302529763.shtml (accessed 10 March 2017).

[24]'Myanmar looks to China to increase foreign direct investment', *Oxford Business*.

[25]'Construction of the sea port is the first phase of an integrated $500-million project being funded by a long-term interest-free loan provided by India', see Ashis Ray, 'Kolkata–Mizoram trade route to open via Myanmar', *The Hindu*, (10 December 2016), available at: http://www.thehindu.com/news/international/Kolkata-Mizoram-trade-route-to-open-via-Myanmar/article16790655.ece (accessed 15 January 2017).

[26]*Ibid*.

[27]Phyo Wai, 'The Myanmar–China dilemma', *Eleven*, (8 March 2017), available at: http://www.elevenmyanmar.com/opinion/8220 (accessed 15 March 2017); Motokazu Matsui, 'Myanmar's great infrastructure race kicks off', *Nikkei Asian Review*, (11 January 2017), available at: http://asia.nikkei.com/Politics-Economy/Economy/Myanmar-s-great-infrastructure-race-kicks-off (accessed 15 January 2017).

MSRI: the Geo-Strategic Dimension and China–Myanmar Relations

Economic expansion creates overseas interests, fuels grandiose geopolitical ambitions and inevitably leads to military expansion. The colonization of Asia, Africa and Latin America by industrializing European powers in the eighteenth and nineteenth centuries was driven by the search for natural resources to fuel industrialization, markets to dump manufactured goods and bases (coaling stations) to protect both. These three variables—resources, markets and bases (RMB)—usually go together. Trade, markets, resource extraction, and port and infrastructure development are also now major ingredients of China's foreign policy. As in the past, the 'new' great game is essentially about having pliant and friendly regimes in resource supplier nations and ensuring access to ports for sea lane safety. Not surprisingly, parallels are being drawn between China's BRI and Lenin's theory of 'imperialism as the highest form of capitalism'. Both are indeed driven by capitalist surpluses in search of overseas RMB which bring them into competition and/or conflict with other overproducing capitalist societies in quests for their own RMB.[28] There is no denying that MSRI has a strong economic agenda, but it blends geopolitical and strategic objectives as well. The BRI points to China pursuing a foreign policy that seeks to simultaneously secure its continental and maritime interests via dominance of the Eurasian heartland and exploitation of its natural resources for its future economic growth, and development of a powerful navy. It shows the influence of nineteenth-century geopolitical thinker Halford Mackinder and maritime strategist Alfred Thayer Mahan.

Given the strategic importance of Myanmar's role in China's maritime strategy, Chinese strategists since the early 1990s have been questioning India's view of its status in the Indian Ocean, seeing India 'as the main party [which will be] affected by China's naval surges into the Indian Ocean in the next century'.[29] In 1993, director of the Chinese Academy of Military Sciences General Zhao Nanqi reportedly said that 'we are not prepared to let the Indian Ocean become India's Ocean'.[30] As early as in 1991, one Chinese analyst, Hua Di, remarked that 'China cannot claim to be a truly global superpower unless it has the capability to dominate two oceans, the Pacific and the Indian Ocean'.[31] This strategic debate coincided with China's emergence as an importer of Middle Eastern oil in 1993. Furthermore, nearly 80% of China's trade is carried by sea through the Strait of Malacca, the Indian Ocean and the Suez Canal, and the predominance of the Indian and American navies along these sea lanes was viewed as a threat to Chinese security. Arguing that China's SLOCs are subject to military blockades or interruption in the East and South China seas, Chinese defense planners began stressing the need for 'a route from Yunnan to Rangoon [as] an important transport line for goods and materials'.[32] Beijing's moves into Myanmar in the 1990s were thus a manifestation of a long-term Chinese strategic objective—an opening to the Bay of Bengal/Andaman Sea via China's southwest frontier.

Since China has significant advantages over its Asian neighbors in terms of geography, military and economic power, infrastructure diplomacy could redefine and reinforce relations with its neighbors. The author argues that China is building an empire of 'exclusive economic enclaves' (EEEs) that would give Beijing strategic influence. China's goal in its foreign relations is not usually conquest or direct control, but freedom of action, economic dominance and diplomatic influence through coercive presence. Beijing's growing might has strengthened the hold of traditional notions of hegemony, cultural supremacy and tributary relationships whereby patronage, protection and trading privileges are dispensed to countries in return for their obeisance. Some Chinese officials joke about buying off smaller countries instead of invading them. Through its economic stranglehold over Cambodia, Beijing

---

[28]See Charles Clover and Lucy Hornby, 'China's great game: road to a new empire', *Financial Times*, (12 October 2015), p. 1; Walter Mead, 'Xi wants foreign support for One Belt One Road', *The American Interest*, (26 May 2016), available at: http://www.the-american-interest.com/2016/05/26/xi-wants-foreign-support-for-one-belt-one-road (accessed 30 September 2016).

[29]Yossef Bodansky, 'PRC revives military threat to Taiwan as a prelude to wider expansion', *Defense & Foreign Affairs Strategic Policy* (July–August 1995), p. 11.

[30]General Zhao quoted in *Time*, (10 May 1993), p. 39; PTI, 'China's plan to build up navy', *Hindustan Times*, (13 January 1993), p. 14.

[31]Hua Di's remarks at a seminar at the Australian National University, Canberra, in May 1991. Also see 'Beijing expands its navy', *Inside China Mainland* [Taiwan], (April 1993), p. 67.

[32]See Chu et al., 'China's national security in the year 2000', cited in Larry M. Wortzel, 'China pursues traditional great-power status', *Orbis* 38(2), (1994), p. 164.

has come to hold an effective veto in ASEAN. With its infrastructure development and export-oriented industrial strategy, China is creating economic interdependencies that will constrain others from making policy choices that run counter to China's interests. Despite geopolitical frictions, Beijing has also used its economic muscle to draw countries such as Myanmar, the Philippines, Malaysia, Thailand and Sri Lanka into its orbit of influence. Many recipients of Chinese largesse are also leaning toward statist models of development, thereby weakening democratic institutions.

From 'String of Pearls' to Maritime Silk Road: a Forward Basing Strategy?

In 2004, President Hu Jintao spoke of the 'Malacca dilemma' and the need to develop China into a maritime power. This led to speculation about Beijing's plans to develop port facilities around the Indian Ocean in a 'string of pearls' strategy to secure its own trade and energy supplies along the sea lanes dominated by the US navy. The proverbial pearls on the string included the ports in Myanmar, Bangladesh, Sri Lanka, the Maldives and Pakistan. While no official acknowledgement of such maritime ambitions was ever made, Chinese analysts and retired naval officers gradually began advocating acquisition of overseas bases to ensure stable energy supplies and to break through the perceived geopolitical encirclement of China by the US and its allies. As China's navy began taking part in anti-piracy operations off the coast of Yemen, influential Chinese voices called on Beijing to pursue formal military alliances, build overseas bases and openly compete with Washington.[33]

Coinciding with this chorus for overseas bases was a concerted effort at reclaiming and militarizing artificial islands in the SCS, which was widely viewed as a strategic stepping-stone for naval supremacy in China's own backyard and for projecting power into maritime Southeast Asia. China's 2015 Defense White Paper formalized a new maritime strategy encompassing 'open seas protection' for which its naval capacity to protect its overseas interests and assets must increase. This makes a naval presence in the Indian Ocean an integral part of China's maritime strategy.[34]

Xi's MSRI is a logical culmination of the Chinese navy's two-ocean strategy (the Pacific and Indian oceans) that will also serve to restore China's historical maritime prestige after a gap of some 600 years. Senior military officers acknowledge that the MSRI would have a 'security component'.[35] Rear Admiral (retd) Yin Zhuo has called for building 'at least five to six aircraft-carriers' in order to maintain 'two carrier strike groups in the West Pacific Ocean and two in the Indian Ocean'.[36] Within a decade, China is projected to have the largest naval and submarine fleets. Given the weak or non-existent naval capabilities of Southeast Asian countries, China's island fortifications will help the Chinese navy acquire sea denial capability that may well be more successful than the Maginot line.[37]

Still, Beijing is treading carefully to advance its goals by creating a network of 'geo-economic alliances' that will add to its strategic outreach. Despite China's propensity to conceal its naval ambitions, coupled with the rhetoric of mutually beneficial 'win–win' economic relationships, the strategic approach dominates in the SCS and the Indian Ocean. With a fusion of commercial initiatives and strategic goals, Beijing is courting many resource-rich countries and strategically located small states that may facilitate a forward presence and augment power projection capability in the future. The Belt and Road megaproject

---

[33]Yan Xuetong quoted in Nathan VanderKlippe, 'A Chinese dynasty with a 21st-century outlook', *The Globe and Mail*, (27 August 2016), available at: http://www.theglobeandmail.com/news/world/a-chinese-dynasty-with-a-21st-centuryoutlook/article31576784 (accessed 29 August 2016). Also see Xu Yao, 'Overseas military bases not alliances', *China Daily*, (14 January 2015), available at: http://usa.chinadaily.com.cn/opinion/2015-01/14/content_19312377.htm (accessed 24 August 2016); and Tu Debin, Ma Yahua *et al.*, 'Research on China's maritime transportation security' ['中国海上通道安全及保障思路研究'], *World Regional Studies* [世界地理研究] 24(2), (2015), pp. 1–10.

[34]The State Council Information Office of the PRC, *China's Military Strategy* (2015), available at: https://jamestown.org/wp-content/uploads/2016/07/China%E2%80%99s-Military-Strategy-2015.pdf (accessed 26 August 2016).

[35]Reuters, 'China stresses security needs for new Silk Road initiative', *The Express Tribune*, (5 May 2017), available at: https://tribune.com.pk/story/1401773/china-stresses-security-needs-new-silk-road-initiative (accessed 6 May 2017).

[36]Yang Sheng, 'China's navy budget based on security needs: experts', *People's Daily*, (28 February 2017), available at: http://en.people.cn/n3/2017/0228/c90000-9183488.html (accessed 28 February 2017).

[37]See Brian Wang, 'Maginot line in the South China Sea', *NextBigFuture.com*, (6 January 2015), available at: http://nextbigfuture.com/2015/01/maginot-line-in-south-china-sea.html (accessed 10 July 2015).

will create separate land and sea transportation corridors and help China thwart any encirclement by a concert of hostile powers. That is why many see it as Beijing's strategic riposte to Washington's Asia pivot. One Chinese commentary noted, 'China's "Maritime Silk Road" is not only an economic development plan, but also a strategic solution to breaking the tight US control of the Strait of Malacca'.[38] China will not spend hundreds of billions of dollars on infrastructure projects under the MSRI without the promise of future strategic benefits, and de facto control or privileged access to dual-use naval ports and airbases. 'China usually bundles military and civilian uses in a [single] project', explains naval analyst Li Jie.[39] Not just commercial ports, but nearly all infrastructure projects (e.g. telecommunications and highways) have dual use and can be upgraded to support naval operations in wartime situations.

Myanmar figures prominently in Beijing's maritime strategy as 'a strategic asset', and its long shoreline is seen as 'China's west coast' that would allow Beijing to bypass the risks associated with trade through the Malacca Straits.[40] Its significance is evident from Beijing's proposal to abandon the controversial US$3.6 billion Myitsone megadam project in return for preferential access and majority control (70–85% stake as opposed to the proposed 50/50 joint venture) in the US$7.3 billion Kyaukpyu deep-sea port on the Bay of Bengal, a move that could heighten tensions within and without.[41] Strategically, this places Myanmar as a source of energy and a trans-shipment route for China. As part of its ambition to secure more access to the Indian Ocean, China has also proposed a new trading route—a waterway from the town of Bhamo in northern Myanmar to the Irrawaddy Delta. Beijing's influence over neighboring Thailand and Cambodia also continues to grow.

Generally speaking, Beijing acts in a piecemeal, quiet and patient fashion, only bringing the pieces together 'when the conditions are ripe'. This is seen in the case of Sri Lanka where China took advantage of the Sri Lankan civil war in the mid-2000s to establish a strong foothold in that country. In return for becoming the regime's largest benefactor during its fight against Tamil separatists, China's navy obtained a strategic toehold in the critical sea lanes in the Indian Ocean through its development of the Hambantota and Colombo ports. China's strategy of fusing its maritime expansion with regional economic development and multilateral integration is yielding rich dividends. A military base in Djibouti along with major port development projects in Pakistan, the Seychelles, Sri Lanka, Myanmar, Malaysia and Cambodia define the contours of China's Maritime Silk Road—an oceanic connectivity project centered on the Indian Ocean. For Beijing, the Xinjiang–Gwadar railroad and pipeline and the Kunming–Kyaukpyu railway and pipeline constitute the two most critical veins of the 'Belt and Road' as both provide access to the Indian Ocean and help overcome the Malacca Strait strategic vulnerability.

The MSRI and new financial institutions seek to convince neighbors that they have everything to gain from cooperation with China and a lot to lose from containing China. China's global clout has ensured that adverse political change, whether in Myanmar, the Maldives or Sri Lanka, will not damage Chinese economic investments and strategic interests.

MSRI: Roadblocks, Detours, Cracks and Fault Lines

Despite its endorsement by Myanmar and 60 plus other countries, major problems confront MSRI. Whether it succeeds or falls short of its original objectives depends on how China responds to the obstacles in its path.

---

[38]'The South China Sea is China's future economic growth point', *ChinaScope.org*, (4 March 2015), available at: http://chinascope. org/main/content/view/6982/104/ (accessed 10 March 2016); 'Zhong ping: nanhai jiang shi zhongguo weilai jingji chang dian' ['The focal point of China's future economic growth is in the South China Sea'], *China Review News*, (21 February 2015), available at: http://hk.crntt.com/doc/1036/2/2/0/103622065.html (accessed 10 July 2015).
[39]Li quoted in Liu Zhen, 'Pakistan port on China's radar for naval base', *South China Morning Post*, (7 June 2017), p. 5.
[40]See Jane Perlez and Wai Moe, 'Visiting Beijing, Myanmar's Aung San Suu Kyi seeks to mend relations', *New York Times*, (17 August 2016), available at: http://www.nytimes.com/2016/08/18/world/asia/visiting-beijing-myanmars-aung-san-suu-kyi-seeks-to-mend-relations.html (accessed 17 August 2016).
[41]Yimou Lee and Saw Myint, 'China seeks up to 85 percent stake in strategic port in Myanmar', *Reuters.com*, (5 May 2017), available at: http://mobile.reuters.com/article/idUSKBN1811DF (accessed 5 May 2017).

At the geopolitical level, 'peaceful rise' and 'win–win' rhetoric notwithstanding, China arouses unease among Asian countries because of its size, history, proximity, power, and more importantly, because memories of 'the Middle Kingdom syndrome' have not dimmed. Strategic mistrust pervades bilateral relations. Given Beijing's penchant for using its economic and military muscle to intimidate others, they worry more about China than about the United States, Japan or India. Foreign Minister Yang Jiechi's statement to his Southeast Asian neighbors in 2010 that 'China is a big country and other countries are small countries and that's just a fact' still rankles with many in the region.[42] Beijing expects others to respect its core interests by placing them above their own national interests—a sort of tributary relationship that acknowledges China as the lord of Asia. Asians want to benefit from economic ties with China, but none wants to become a Chinese vassal. Against this background, linking the MSR to China's national rejuvenation as a maritime power or as part of the 'China Dream' may do more harm than good insofar as it arouses suspicions that it is 'a Trojan horse for extending geopolitical clout, and dumping excess capacity abroad as China's economy flags'.[43]

Even as governments in Myanmar and other developing countries welcome Chinese investments, opposition parties and civil society push back against Beijing's economic dominance. Chinese aid, loans and investments provide a vital lifeline to beleaguered regimes that allows their leaders to disregard human rights and good governance and become more repressive. Far from generating goodwill, the growing economic interdependence creates its own stresses and strains. Tensions center on the use of imported Chinese labor, poor environmental standards and debt accumulation by host governments. Beijing often ends up facing the consequences of cutting shady business deals with corrupt and auto-cratic leaders who get voted/booted out when citizens rise in revolt over corruption.[44]

In addition, Beijing is deeply involved in Myanmar's ethnic conflict. Several ethnic groups—the Kachin, Kokang, Shan and Palaung—fighting with the army inhabit both sides of the Sino–Myanmarese border. China officially professes its support for stability along the border, yet Beijing has played both sides for years, signing deals with the government while funding and arming rebel groups. The reason for keeping ethnic armed groups on a tight leash is to retain the option of stepping up aid to rebels to punish Myanmar if it is perceived as going too far or tilting toward 'China-wary' countries.[45] Nonetheless, border disputes, continuing ethnic strife and insurgencies threaten Beijing's MSR priorities, such as border security and connectivity projects, which require the support of the Myanmar government.

The organizing principle of Xi's BRI is a Sino-centric unipolar Asia which is diametrically opposite to the vision of a multipolar Asia held by China's rivals; its cumulative effect will be to bring Central, Southeast and South Asia closer into China's orbit, and extend its economic, diplomatic and possibly military supremacy across the entire region to disadvantage Beijing's rivals. Unfortunately for Beijing, 'China fever' of the 1990s has given way to 'China fear' in the 2000s.[46] China's irredentism encourages Asians to seek greater American, Japanese and Indian involvement in regional affairs to countervail China. In geo-strategic terms, China's success would be detrimental to the interests of Russia, the United States, Japan and India, which have long dominated these regions.[47]

Thus, China's economic and strategic forays are not without repercussions. Wherever China goes, Japan, India, Russia and the US are not far behind, offering potential partners options and opportunities to look beyond China. As China builds a north–south route to access the Indian Ocean from Yunnan, India and Japan are building the east–west route to integrate their investments in Myanmar, Thailand and Vietnam, and connect the South China Sea with the Indian Ocean. To counter China's AIIB, Japan

[42]Quoted in John Pomfret, 'US takes a tougher tone with China', *Washington Post*, (30 July 2010), p. 1.

[43]Charlie Campbell, 'China's Xi Jinping talks up "One Belt, One Road" as keynote project fizzles', *Time*, (18 August 2016), available at: http://time.com/4457044/xi-jinping-one-belt-one-road-obor-south-china-sea-economic-trade-business (accessed 25 August 2016).

[44]'An auspicious moment', *The Economist*, (15 January 2015), available at: https://www.economist.com/news/leaders/21639503-extraordinary-election-result-gives-country-chance-heal-deep-wounds-auspicious (accessed 26 August 2016).

[45]Bertil Lintner, 'China uses carrot and stick in Myanmar', *Asia Times online*, (28 February 2017), available at: http://www.atimes.com/article/china-uses-carrot-stick-myanmar (accessed 28 February 2017).

[46]For details, see Mohan Malik, 'Balancing act: the China–India–US triangle', *World Affairs* 179(1), (2016), pp. 46–57.

[47]Lucio Blanco Pitlo III, 'China's "One Belt, One Road" to where?', *The Diplomat*, (17 February 2015), available at: http://thediplomat.com/2015/02/chinas-one-belt-one-road-to-where (accessed 17 February 2015).

announced a US$110 billion 'partnership for quality infrastructure' (PQI) fund through the ADB. Japan's focus is on east–west corridors in competition with China's railroads and increasing its investments and trade with Myanmar and Indo-China.[48] The proposed Dawei SEZ project is a three-way cooperation among Myanmar, Thailand and Japan with a railroad linking up with the east–west transport corridor across Vietnam, Cambodia and Thailand to integrate southern Myanmar with Indo-China. Russia remains wary of China's ambitions to dominate the Eurasian Heartland. Though Washington is not opposed to China's infrastructure projects, provided they are transparent, environmentally sound, and promote employment and good governance, the United States continues to fortify its regional engagement. Democratizing Myanmar figures prominently in America's rebalancing strategy. Though bilateral trade remains miniscule, major US oil companies like Chevron's Unocal Myanmar Offshore Co. have re-entered the market. The US is also a more important source of FDI in ASEAN than China. In 2015, American FDI into the region accounted for US$13.6 billion, well ahead of China's US$8.3 billion. Since the new great game is about supply chain geopolitics, both China and the United States are vying for influence over the crucial industrial, financial and commercial nodes across Eurasia.[49]

Like Japan, India is deeply suspicious of a growing Chinese naval presence in the Indian Ocean and has publicly criticized MSRI.[50] Most Indian strategic analysts regard the MSR as a disguised 'String of Pearls 2.0'. As China's navy nurtures grandiose ambitions, India fears the PLA-N's artificial islands in the SCS becoming a basing point for patrolling in the Indian Ocean. The greater frequency of naval forays by Chinese warships and nuclear submarines in the Indian Ocean reinforces those suspicions and increases the risk of blowback for Beijing. Just as Myanmar is for China a critical entryway to the Indian Ocean, for India, Myanmar is the land bridge to Indo-China and Southeast Asia. It was at the India–ASEAN summit in Naypyitaw in late 2014 that Modi launched India's 'Act East' policy. As China's navy goes south to the Indian Ocean, India's navy is going east to the Pacific Ocean.[51] Beijing's MSRI has prompted the Indian navy to unveil a three-pronged strategy: fortify its defenses in the Indian Ocean by acquiring privileged access to bases in the Maldives, Mauritius, the Seychelles and Madagascar; conducting joint naval exercises in the East and South China Seas; and launching an ambitious naval expansion program. Since 2011, India's naval voyages have grown in number by 300%.[52] The US–India Logistics Exchange agreement benefits both as it provides India's navy access to American bases in Diego Garcia, Djibouti and the Pacific, while the US navy gains access to India's ports. The US–India 'Joint Strategic Vision' of 2015 mentioned 'support for regional economic integration' and 'accelerated infrastructure connectivity' suggesting that it could be further developed as a counter-point to China's MSRI.

To balance China's north–south transport corridors in Southeast Asia, rival India is pitching to gain an entry into Indo-China by building an east–west corridor cutting horizontally through Myanmar toward Thailand and on to Vietnam.[53] Also, the Kaladan multi-modal transport project would link Lawngtlai in India's state of Mizoram via a road and the River Kaladan to the deep-sea port at Sittwe in Myanmar's

[48]'Japan helps Burma tilt away from China', *The American Interest*, (12 July 2016), available at: http://www.the-american-interest.com/2016/07/12/japan-helps-burma-tilt-away-from-china (accessed 15 August 2016); Nikkei, 'Japan races China to secure Asian port rights', *Nikkei Asian Review*, (8 June 2017), available at: http://asia.nikkei.com/Politics-Economy/International-Relations/Japan-races-China-to-secure-Asian-port-rights (accessed 10 June 2017).
[49]Pepe Escobar, 'Why the New Silk Roads terrify Washington', *RT.com*, (7 October 2016), available at: https://www.rt.com/op-edge/361898-new-silk-roads-terrify (accessed 7 October 2016).
[50]Indrani Bagchi, 'India slams China's OBOR, says it violates sovereignty', *Times of India*, (14 May 2017), available at: http://timesofindia.indiatimes.com/india/china-road-initiative-is-like-a-colonial-enterprise-india/articleshow/58664098.cms (accessed 16 May 2017).
[51]Ilaria Maria Sala, 'When China bullies its neighbors, India gets more muscular', *Quartz India*, (16 December 2016), available at: http://qz.com/864961/when-china-bullies-its-neighbors-indias-narendra-modi-gets-more-muscular (accessed 16 December 2016).
[52]Manu Balachandran, 'India is flexing its maritime muscles in the Indian Ocean', *Quartz India*, (19 December 2016), available at: https://qz.com/864011/with-an-eye-on-china-india-steams-ahead-in-the-battle-for-naval-supremacy-in-the-indian-ocean (accessed 24 December 2016).
[53]See Wang Jin, 'Can China keep India silent over the South China Sea?', *The Diplomat*, (17 August 2016), available at: http://thediplomat.com/2016/08/can-china-keep-india-silent-over-the-south-china-sea/ (accessed 17 August 2016); Liu Zongyi, 'India's political goals hinder cooperation with China on "Belt, Road"', *Global Times*, (3 July 2016), available at: http://www.globaltimes.cn/content/992047.shtml (accessed 10 July 2016); 'To counter China's clout, India offers to stand by Myanmar "at every step"', *Times of India*, (30 August 2016), available at: http://timesofindia.indiatimes.com/India/To-counter-Chinas-clout-India-offers-to-stand-by-Myanmar-at-every-step/articleshow/53920012.cms (accessed 5 September 2016).

Rakhine province. India's construction of ports at Chabahar in Afghanistan and at Sittwe in Myanmar can be seen as India's counterbalance to the Chinese-built Gwadar Port (about 72 km away) where CPEC culminates and to Kyukphu port in Myanmar where the pipelines start for Kunming. With Myanmar allowing Japan and India to build ports on its Bay of Bengal coast, the prospects of China gaining unimpeded access to a western seaboard now look dim. Furthermore, India has stepped up aid and offered an alternative vision to China's MSRI with 'Project Mausam'—a counter-move by New Delhi to revive India's ancient trade routes and cultural linkages around the Indian Ocean.[54] Beijing's efforts to acquire sea-denial and sea control capabilities have thus prompted leading maritime powers (the US, Japan, Australia and India) to coalesce together to ensure that the northern Indian Ocean does not fall under Chinese hegemony.[55] While India and the US are collaborating in tracking Chinese submarines in the Indian Ocean, India and Japan plan to build a sea wall of 'hydrophones'—microphones with sensors placed on the seabed—between southern India and the northern tip of Indonesia to keep a check on Chinese submarine movement. Signs of pushback are everywhere. Neither the Belt nor the Road would succeed in completely de-coupling Asia or Europe from the United States. If anything, India, the US and Japan could block or derail China's plans.

At the economic level, China's rise has fundamentally restructured the regional political economy and made all Southeast Asian economies part of a China-led regional production network. This economic dependency creates despondency. The growing disunity within ASEAN and the loss of ASEAN centrality in regional affairs has resulted in 'China centrality in ASEAN affairs'. Many fear that large-scale investment could open the floodgates to Chinese economic dominance—as it has done in Myanmar, Cambodia and Sri Lanka—and, by extension, political influence. Numerous infrastructure projects and billion-dollar investment promises have failed to materialize. Even when they do, they tend to provoke socio-political backlash fearful of the long-term hidden costs of the panda hug. Debt for equity swaps provoke domestic backlash as they lead to foreign ownership. As noted earlier, China's growing economic and strategic foothold ignited protest among Myanmarese worried about external control over their country. One Myanmarese diplomat said: 'We don't want Myanmar interests trampled on by China on its road to greatness'.[56]

Despite Beijing's 'mutual benefit' rhetoric, and promises of unconditional aid, the recipients of Chinese largesse know that strings are always attached. Beijing warms to nations willing to co-operate with its strategic agenda, but angrily rebukes them when it is rebuffed.[57] Arguing that host countries' 'embrace of China's strategic agenda is always at the back of the mind of Chinese officials when they sit at the negotiation table', Yun Sun adds: 'China's support always comes at a price'.[58] Economic integration has strategic consequences. There is invariably a strategic element attached to enterprises that begin with commercial port construction or management and end with naval presence and long-term ownership rights. Actually,

> [t]he Gwadar template, where Beijing used its commercial knowhow and financial muscle to secure ownership over a strategic trading base, only to enlist it later into military service, has been replicated in other key locations in Sri Lanka, Greece and Djibouti.[59]

The modus operandi of Chinese SoEs in Myanmar, Laos, Cambodia, Malaysia, Sri Lanka, Kyrgyzstan and Greece holds lessons for others to avoid falling into Chinese debt traps that may end in strategic entrapment.[60] China's practice of bankrolling huge infrastructure projects through big loans with high

---

[54]Sachin Parashar, 'Narendra Modi's "Mausam" manoeuvre to check China's maritime might', *Times of India*, (16 September 2014), available at: http://timesofindia.indiatimes.com/india/Narendra-Modis-Mausam-manoeuvre-to-check-Chinas-maritime-might/articleshow/42562085.cms (accessed 20 October 2016).
[55]Wang Yiwei, 'No need for India to fall in US–Japan trap', *China Daily*, (15 March 2017), available at: http://www.chinadaily.com.cn/opinion/2017-03/15/content_28560954.htm (accessed 20 March 2017).
[56]Author's discussion with a senior Myanmarese diplomat, October 2016.
[57]Richard McGregor, 'The price tag of China's threats', *Nikkei Asian Review*, (13 October 2016), available at: http://asia.nikkei.com/Viewpoints/Viewpoints/Richard-McGregor-The-price-tag-of-China-s-threats (accessed 15 October 2016).
[58]Yun Sun, 'Suu Kyi's visit to Beijing', *Panglong.org*, (19 August 2016), available at: http://english.panglong.org/2016/08/17/aung-san-suu-kyis-visit-to-beijing-recalibrating-myanmars-china-policy (accessed 11 September 2016).
[59]James Kynge *et al.*, 'How China rules the waves', *Financial Times*, (13 January 2017), p. 1.
[60]These countries are all weighed down with heavy indebtedness due to high interest rates of 4–8% on Chinese loans.

interest rates in littoral states in return for strategic concessions causes tensions internally and anxiety externally. The greater the debt, the more leverage Beijing acquires in negotiating exclusive ownership or access to land, resources, ports and airports. Myanmar, Sri Lanka and others have expressed unease with unequal business deals that burden them with high interest loans for buying Chinese products, services and labor, yet do not alleviate unemployment, corruption or environmental degradation.

For historical reasons, Asians remain highly sensitive to foreign domination. Most nations hew closer to open market (if not, open politics) and are wary of putting all their eggs in the China basket. Faced with growing criticism of Chinese firms' work practices, trade imbalances, and demands for more transparency and high environmental standards, China's leaders have begun to acknowledge 'growing pains' in the partnerships.[61] A related problem is that MSRI projects enmesh China much more closely in other countries' domestic politics. That leads to situations where Chinese businesses bear the brunt of criticism for the governance failures of ruling elites. In Myanmar, negative portrayals of China have risen in conjunction with its increased involvement in the country. Myanmarese have become vocal in expressing what they see as 'Chinese economic colonialism plundering not just their forests, but their resources in general'.[62] The public reaction to China's environmentally and socially damaging economic activities (dams, pipelines, railroads) was a major factor behind Myanmar's political reform and overtures to the West. Concerns over China's stranglehold over the economy often generate domestic pressure for political change and restrictions on Beijing's privileged access to RMB in those countries. The cancellation of the Kunming–Kyaukpyu railway project, the lackluster performance of the China–Myanmar gas pipeline, and the offer to renegotiate dam deals show the limits of this approach. Beijing is no longer Myanmar's sole patron. Transition to a civilian government not only gives Myanmar greater strategic space to maneuver between China and other suitors but also requires China to deal with multiple power brokers such as nationalistic legislators, minorities and business lobbies contributing to Myanmar's policy decisions.[63] Thus, future bilateral relations cannot be as close as they were before 2011. Myanmar sees its national interests in counterbalancing China's influence and power through its ties with India, ASEAN, Japan and the West.

Not only that, economic slowdown coupled with dramatic falls in the Chinese currency market and in foreign exchange reserves from US$4 to US$3 trillion raise questions about the longevity of the 'China dream'.[64] Official estimates show that Xi's MSR initiative would require US$4–8 trillion of investment to bring to fruition. Some wonder if it is wise to pour such huge amounts into low-return projects and high-risk countries at risk of default when China's own debt is 250% of its GDP and climbing. Many of the infrastructure projects don't make money and remain under-utilized. Interestingly, Chinese officials privately expect to lose 80% of their investments in Pakistan, 50% in Myanmar and 30% in Central Asia.[65] In fact, Beijing may have already overreached itself by creating a far-flung empire of 'exclusive economic enclaves' as the problems of harsh terrain, political change and geopolitical rivalries add to financial woes.

Lastly, China's vision may be backed with trillions worth of investment, but money alone cannot buy love and loyalty.[66] At most, it can buy short-term influence. China's railroads, highways and pipelines may bring about physical integration with Asian countries, but the political and security integration will take place only when their interests, values and vision are in harmony with those of China's. Until then, China's neighbors will take its money but balk at allowing greater Chinese influence over policy or

[61]Ding Gang, 'Populism constitutes risks to Belt & Road', *Global Times*, (29 March 2017), available at: http://www.globaltimes.cn/content/1040213.shtml (accessed 30 March 2017).

[62]Jonathan Manthorpe, 'Burma puts the brakes on resource exports to China', *Business Vancouver*, (2 February 2015), available at: http://www.biv.com/article/2015/2/Burma-puts-the-brakes-on-resource-exports-to-China (accessed 15 September 2016).

[63]'China and Myanmar: restoring a damaged alliance', *Stratfor.com*, (17 August 2016), available at: https://worldview.stratfor.com/article/china-and-myanmar-restoring-damaged-alliance (accessed 17 August 2016).

[64]Tom Holland, 'Why China's "One Belt, One Road" plan is doomed to fail', *South China Morning Post*, (6 August 2016), available at: http://www.scmp.com/week-asia/article/1999544/why-chinas-one-belt-one-road-plan-doomed-fail (accessed 6 August 2016).

[65]Oliver Stuenkel, 'The political economy of China's New Silk Road', *Post-westernworld.com*, (6 November 2016), available at: http://www.postwesternworld.com/2016/11/06/political-economy-chinas/ (accessed 10 November 2016).

[66]Simon Denyer, 'China promotes "Asia–Pacific dream" to counter US pivot', *Washington Post*, (11 November 2014), p. 1.

granting strategic concessions to Beijing. Even some Chinese analysts question the wisdom of China's single-minded devotion to trade and commerce to the exclusion of environmental standards or local political sensibilities.[67] Zheng Wang acknowledges the limits of checkbook diplomacy: 'Influence does not derive from a country's coffers, but rather from the promotion of shared values and soft power'.[68] Suspicion and distrust mean that the MSRI would deliver less than promised. Beijing needs to outline a vision of the regional order that 'de-territorializes' bilateral relations and transcends the centrality of Chinese world order in ways that appeal to other peoples.

Conclusion

For China, Southeast Asia—via the Maritime Silk Road—is a key hub in the new connectivity game. Myanmar is a very crucial part of a trade route stretching across Asia to Africa, as well as a vital link in its oil supply chain. China's interest in staking out a presence in Myanmar, and thereby the Indian Ocean, is based on an assessment of China's strategic needs as a global trading maritime power that is increasingly dependent upon overseas resources and markets. Beijing also sees itself as being engaged in a long protracted competition with other major powers and wants Myanmar (along with Cambodia and Pakistan) to remain within its orbit. If Myanmar's attempts to steer an even-handed course undermine China's interests, Beijing could resume assistance to ethnic insurgents fighting for independence. How Myanmar deals with Beijing's blandishments and bluster would determine the future of their relations. Myanmar shows the extent and limits of China's MSRI. With the weight of money, might and technology on the Chinese side, Myanmar is unlikely to antagonize the superpower on its doorstep. In an article written in 1996, this author argued that

> the present and future Burmese leaders would find it very difficult to withdraw completely from China's sphere of influence. Nor would the Chinese government allow them to do so because Burma now occupies the same place in China's calculus of deterrence in South and Southeast Asia that Pakistan does in South and Southwest Asia.[69]

That conclusion still holds true 20 years later. Whether under Than Shwe or under Suu Kyi, Beijing's topmost priority is to have a government that maintains *paukphaw* relationship which fulfils its economic need for resources and its geo-strategic need for access toward the Bay of Bengal.

As in the past, the Silk Road is an avenue for development and expansion. Should it succeed, it would bend borders and change internal and external power dynamics. China's infrastructure diplomacy plays to its strengths and offers insights into Beijing's long-term strategy for reshaping both the landscape and the seascape of the Eurasian continent and its maritime domain. Economic dominance and geopolitical heft over China's near neighbors are the key elements. Many countries seeking to improve their living standards are tilting toward Beijing. Some are, however, uncomfortable with Beijing's checkbook/infrastructure diplomacy that invariably ends in a trail of huge debts, IOUs and strategic entrapment in the form of long-term Chinese presence. From Myanmar to Mexico, concerns over China's stranglehold over local economies often generate domestic pressure for political change and the potential loss of Beijing's privileged access to resources, markets and bases in those countries. As its experience in Myanmar and elsewhere indicates, Chinese companies will need to grapple with the additional socio-political and economic considerations and adopt international best practices, including corporate social responsibility, for sustainable development. Other major players—Japan, India and the United States—could also create major road blocks along the Silk Road if Beijing fails to get their buy-in. To be successful, OBOR may well need 'an order based on rules' (OBOR). It is worth remembering that no single country built the old Silk Road in the past; it developed organically to meet foreign demand for Chinese silk. No one country can build it alone again. Its size, contours and dimensions will be determined by the laws of supply and demand. As in the past, there will be not one but several silk, spice and cotton roads in the

[67]Yimou Lee, 'China's $10 billion strategic project in Myanmar sparks local ire', *Reuters.com*, (9 June 2017), available at: http://mobile.reuters.com/article/idUSKBN18Z327 (accessed 9 June 2107).
[68]Zheng Wang, 'China's alternative diplomacy', *The Diplomat*, (30 January 2015), available at: http://thediplomat.com/2015/01/chinas-alternative-diplomacy (accessed 15 September 2016).
[69]J. Mohan Malik, 'Burma's role in regional security: pawn or pivot?', *Contemporary Southeast Asia* 19(1), (1997), p. 52.

future. While optimists predict the Silk Road will kick-start flagging global economic growth, skeptics see it as China's play for power and influence that is doomed to fail. However, this author believes that the BRI is too big to fail completely. Beijing can take credit because China's aid stimulates development and galvanizes its rivals to step up to contribute to others' development. Since most, if not all, of the projects that sport the label would probably have been built anyway, by 2049 Beijing can proclaim success: mission accomplished!

Acknowledgements

The author thanks Jean-Marc F. Blanchard, Brent Christensen, Donald Emmerson, Thomas Fingar, Jonathan Odom, May Tan-Mullins, Meihua Roy and the editor for invaluable feedback on earlier drafts. The views expressed herein are his own.

Disclosure statement

No potential conflict of interest was reported by the author.

12 Deconstructing the China-Pakistan Economic Corridor

Pipe Dreams Versus Geopolitical Realities

Jeremy Garlick

ABSTRACT

Intense interest in the China–Pakistan Economic Corridor (CPEC) was stimulated when US$46 billion of investment agreements were signed in April 2015, a sum which two years later increased to US$62 billion. A major focus of CPEC is on developing overland transportation and pipeline links from the port of Gwadar to the Chinese province of Xinjiang as a land-based alternative to the maritime 'chokepoint' of the Straits of Malacca. This article assesses the viability of pipelines connecting China to the Indian Ocean through Pakistan via a close analysis of evidence obtained from both primary and secondary sources. It concludes that the overland connection is beset with difficulties because of geographical, economic and security problems, and that China's long-term motivations for maintaining a presence in Pakistan are likely to be chiefly geopolitical rather than geo-economic. In fact, China's primary aim with CPEC and other investments is to hedge against India by establishing a physical presence in the Indian Ocean Region (IOR), a strategy which is herein referred to as geo-positional balancing.

Introduction

The China–Pakistan Economic Corridor (CPEC) is, as part of the Belt and Road Initiative (BRI), one of Chinese President Xi Jinping's flagship projects. Announced in April 2015 as a US$46 billion agreement (an amount which had by April 2017 increased to US$62 billion),[1] CPEC is in effect a rebranding of the long-term cooperation between the two countries which has been in progress since the 1950s. This cooperation is generally characterised by the partners as an 'all-weather friendship', but has been beset by difficulties of many types since its inception. Some of the most notable nowadays are the wealth imbalance between China and Pakistan (which includes Pakistan's lack of foreign exchange reserves),[2] the frequently troublesome security situation in Pakistan, and the looming presence of India on both China and Pakistan's borders.

However, in assessing CPEC's ostensible aim of connecting Pakistan with China's northwestern Xinjiang region, it is important not to omit mention also of problems relating to the physical topography and geographical location of the China–Pakistan border region. In particular, the Karakoram Highway

---

[1]Salman Siddiqui, 'CPEC investment pushed from $55b to $62b', *The Express Tribune*, (12 April 2017), available at: https://tribune.com.pk/story/1381733/cpec-investment-pushed-55b-62b/ (accessed 22 November 2017).

[2]Pakistan's chronic shortage of foreign exchange reserves forced it to borrow US$1.2 billion from China in 2016 and early 2017. See Kiran Stacey, Farhan Bokhari and Henny Sender, 'China bails out Pakistan with $1.2 billion loans', *Financial Times*, (25 April 2017), available at: https://www.ft.com/content/3ae64c9a-ffd8-11e6-96f8-3700c5664d30 (accessed 18 September 2017).

which connects the two countries, built with great difficulty between 1959 and 1979 and now under reconstruction, passes through difficult mountain terrain and an earthquake zone. This territory is also claimed by India, meaning that any further development of the region is geopolitically sensitive. It is also potentially a transit point for Islamic insurgents such as the East Turkestan Independence Movement (ETIM) and other groups seeking the independence of the Chinese province of Xinjiang.

There are also further problems to be solved in the remainder of Pakistan. The poor state of most Pakistani infrastructure (for instance in the field of energy) and the lack of Pakistani financial resources demand massive Chinese investment with uncertain economic outcomes and doubts concerning Pakistan's ability to repay loans. In addition, amid frequent regional insurgencies and other outbreaks of violence, there is the difficulty of maintaining security around infrastructure investment projects such as the construction of factories, plants, railways and pipelines.

This article aims to continue the research initiated by Saul B. Cohen and others in reasserting the central importance of physical geography in assessing evolving global and regional geopolitics.[3] This physically-centred approach contrasts with that of critical geopoliticians who emphasise the 'discursive/representational construction of geographic space'.[4] Cohen's approach is not set up in opposition to critical geopolitics, however, but rather as an attempt to re-emphasise the importance of physical geography for the study of geopolitics.

In developing Cohen's approach, the article takes as a key discussion point David Brewster's assertion that the establishment by China of overland connections to the Indian Ocean would radically transform the geopolitics of the Indian Ocean region by opening up to Chinese influence what has been until now a closed geographical space which India has been attempting to dominate. If China becomes a major actor in the IOR, he points out, the consequences for the region are hard to predict outcomes amid radically altered geopolitical dynamics.[5] However, whether China can connect its remote interior regions (Xinjiang and Yunnan provinces) with the Indian Ocean via efficient transportation and pipeline networks remains to be seen.

This article is therefore intended to be a rich, empirically-grounded study based in the close analysis of data (to the extent that they are available) concerning the economic and logistical viability of constructing overland transportation and pipeline connections between the Indian Ocean and China's landlocked Xinjiang province via Pakistan. To examine the proposed CPEC connections, the analysis takes as a starting point Brewster's geographically-based investigation of the geopolitics of the Pakistan and Myanmar routes from China to the Indian Ocean, expanding on it by adding analysis of factors relating to logistics, economics and security.

Given the fact that oil and natural gas pipelines have already been constructed between the Chinese-developed port of Kyaukpyu in Myanmar and Yunnan province in China, the article also examines whether these pipelines can thus far be regarded as successful economically, politically and in terms of energy security. This part of the study, again based in empirical detail, strongly suggests that China's multi-billion-dollar investment in the Myanmar pipelines has thus far not produced substantial economic benefits, is problematic in terms of China's increasing entanglement in Myanmar's internal politics, and has not enhanced Chinese energy security. The analysis of the Myanmar pipeline project is intended to provide an illustrative case study concerning the potential problems of constructing a pipeline and transportation corridor from the Pakistani port of Gwadar to Kashgar in China's Xinjiang province. Myanmar and Pakistan are, of course, different in many ways, but the example of a completed pipeline project is intended to cast some light on the issues to be expected in the case of the projected CPEC link.

---

[3]See: Saul Bernard Cohen, *Geopolitics: The Geography of International Relations* (3rd edn) (Lanham, MA: Rowman & Littlefield 2015); David Brewster, 'Silk roads and strings of pearls: the strategic geography of China's new pathways in the Indian Ocean', *Geopolitics* 22(2), (2017), pp. 269–291; and Jakub J. Grygiel, *Great Powers and Geopolitical Change* (Baltimore, MD: Johns Hopkins University Press, 2006).
[4]Brewster, 'Silk roads and strings of pearls', p. 270. A notable example of critical geopolitics is Gearóid Ó Tuathail, *Critical Geopolitics: The Politics of Writing Global Space* (Minneapolis, MN: University of Minnesota Press, 1996).
[5]Brewster, 'Silk roads and strings of pearls'.

However, since the primary focus is on CPEC, the article mainly concentrates on a close study of the empirical data available concerning China's involvement in Pakistan. There is an urgent need to examine the feasibility of constructing a land corridor between Gwadar and Xinjiang using primary sources as far as possible: it is difficult to unpack the complexity of the issues involved using only the prevailingly over-optimistic local media reports and official announcements by the Chinese and Pakistani governments. Information is therefore obtained from in-depth analysis of primary sources such as the Gwadar Port Operating Authority's website and the official CPEC website, as well as secondary sources such as journal articles and policy papers.

Although there are limitations, enough information can be obtained to strongly suggest that China's primary motivation for involvement in Pakistan is geopolitical rather than geo-economic and that the reality of the proposed overland pipeline and transportation corridor is that it is more a symbol of cooperation than a fully achievable goal. The argument presented here, based on the empirical evidence, is that the central aim of China's engagement in Pakistan (as well as Myanmar) is to balance against its regional rival India by establishing and maintaining a Chinese presence in the IOR. The author proposes to call this type of balancing, based on long-term strategic assessment of physical geography, *geo-positional balancing*. This concept is based on traditional Chinese notions of geographical space,[6] and is developed, as Henry Kissinger points out, from the tactics of encirclement used in the Chinese game of *weiqi* (called *go* in Japan).[7] Geo-positional balancing is a system of putting down marker 'stones' in key geographical positions for potential future use and as a hedge against possible conflicts. The aim is for China to strengthen its long-term geopolitical position *vis-à-vis* rivals (in this case India) without great risk or, despite appearances to the contrary, excessive financial expense.

The article thus begins with an extended assessment of the background to and prospects for the CPEC land corridor, based mainly on an in-depth analysis of primary and secondary sources relating to CPEC's conception and funding, the port of Gwadar, the physical geography separating Pakistan and China, security issues, and pipeline logistics. It then continues with an analysis of the China–Myanmar pipeline project, in order to assess the extent that the project has faced problems of an economic and political nature, and whether these issues can be taken to be indicative of potential problems for the proposed CPEC pipelines and overland connection to China. Given that the sources reviewed suggest that Chinese investment in CPEC pipelines is less likely to go ahead than some commentators appear to believe, due to economic, logistical, geographical and security problems which are acknowledged by some Chinese experts, the final sections then assess China's motivations for involvement in Pakistan. The evidence assessed points, above all, to Chinese interest in offsetting India's regional dominance in the IOR through a strategy of geo-positional balancing in Pakistan, Myanmar and other nations in the Indian Ocean littoral.

The CPEC 'Land Corridor' Problem Defined

Much debate and discussion, not all of it very clear-sighted—and some of it closer in tone and content to a public relations campaign than objective analysis[8]—has swirled around the China–Pakistan Economic Corridor (CPEC) since its inception in April 2015. CPEC, ostensibly intended to connect the Persian Gulf port of Gwadar with Kashgar in northwest China's Xinjiang province, is framed as a key part of China's 'Belt and Road' Initiative (henceforth BRI), which was launched in 2013. The BRI is intended to encompass

---

[6]William Callahan notes, for instance, that the underlying basis of Zhao Tingyang's agenda-setting *tianxia* theory, which is taken from traditional Chinese philosophy, is geographical. See William A. Callahan, 'Chinese visions of world order: post-hegemonic or a new hegemony?', *International Studies Review* 10, (2008), p. 751, and also Zhao Tingyang, 'Rethinking empire from a Chinese concept "All-under-heaven" (天下)', *Social Identities* 12(1), (2006), pp. 29–41.

[7]Henry Kissinger, *On China* (London: Allen Lane, 2011), pp. 23–25. *Weiqi* is a popular Chinese strategic board game involving attempts to encircle the opponent, or to resist encirclement by the opponent by putting down black or white stones.

[8]Two examples of articles which uncritically extol CPEC's virtues are the following: in Pakistan, Jamal Hussain, 'China Pakistan economic corridor', *Defence Journal* (Karachi), (January 2016), pp. 13–21; and in China, 'Interview: China–Pakistan Economic Corridor on track: ambassador', *Xinhua News*, (25 June 2016), available at: http://news.xinhuanet.com/english/2016 06/25/c_135465494. htm (accessed 21 March 2017).

a network of projects across the Eurasian landmass and through the seas to the south, including the Indian Ocean. Apart from the land corridor aspect, CPEC also has a major focus on enhancing energy and transportation infrastructure in Pakistan. Of the 67 projects listed on the official CPEC website in December 2017, 21 are energy-related, while 20 are transportation-related.[9]

Based on an observation which was made by Chinese President Hu Jintao in 2003[10] (and which has been reiterated so often by numerous commentators that it has become something of a truism), one of the principal motivations for China's involvement in Pakistan is to establish an alternative to the usual maritime trade route via the Straits of Malacca and the South China Sea (SCS).[11] In this interpretation, the Straits of Malacca is considered a 'chokepoint' because it is a stretch of water which could hypothetically be blockaded, thus preventing vital supplies of oil and other commodities from reaching China. The point is frequently made in both the energy security literature and elsewhere that approximately 80% of China's oil supplies pass through the Straits of Malacca and the SCS on their way to Eastern China: this is termed, per Hu's coinage, the 'Malacca Dilemma'.[12] However, already prior to the advent of CPEC two authoritative studies pointed out that the danger of blockade or piracy is not as serious as it has often been said to be, since alternative sea routes can easily be found in case of disruption at Malacca and blockading all of these routes would require a massive and costly deployment of naval resources.[13]

In economic terms, one recent peer-reviewed study in a major energy journal claims that the overland route through Pakistan to Xinjiang is shorter and potentially cheaper than the sea route, and could therefore save time and money as well as provide China with enhanced energy security.[14] The fact that Gwadar is located on the Persian Gulf across the waters from Oman and the United Arab Emirates (where the Chinese oil company Sinopec owns 50% of the oil terminal at Fujairah) and next to Iran is suggestive, cartographically at least, of an intention to transport at least some crude oil into China via CPEC along with other resources and goods. The question then is whether the Chinese intention would be to construct oil and gas pipelines to Xinjiang along the lines of the recently-constructed Myanmar–China pipelines, or whether fuel could instead be viably transported by road or a new railway. However, critics doubt whether oil and gas transported via pipelines would really be cheaper than using the maritime route.[15] In addition, since large quantities of fossil fuels already pass via existing pipelines through Xinjiang on their way from Central Asia, there logically seems little need to add to these supplies at present.[16] Since Xinjiang is also 'China's largest gas producing and second largest oil producing region and has one of the largest networks of oil and gas pipelines in China',[17] the rationale for adding extra fossil fuels via a logistically difficult and probably expensive route is not clear.

The literature on CPEC which has appeared since the announcement of China's investment in April 2015 reveals that there appears to be a surprising lack of clarity and consensus to date about the practical feasibility of connecting Gwadar and Xinjiang. For instance, the study (by Shaikh et al.) referenced at the beginning of the previous paragraph set out to study the prospects for oil being transported northwards to China from Gwadar; but despite a detailed quantitative cost analysis, the authors did

---

[9]Official CPEC website, 'Progress update', available at: http://cpec.gov.pk/progress-update (accessed 4 December 2017).

[10]Marc Lanteigne, 'China's maritime security and the "Malacca Dilemma"', Asian Security 4(2), (2008), pp. 143–144.

[11]Among the many examples are the following: Jian Yang and Rashid Ahmed Siddiqi, 'About an "all-weather" relationship: security foundations of Sino–Pakistan relations since 9/11', Journal of Contemporary China 20(71), (2011), pp. 574–575; Mathias Hartpence, 'The economic dimension of Sino–Pakistani relations: an overview', Journal of Contemporary China 20(71), (2011), p. 586; Mordechai Chaziza, 'China–Pakistan relationship: a game-changer for the Middle East?', Contemporary Review of the Middle East 3(2), (2016), pp. 1–15; and Amrita Jash, 'China's 21st Century Maritime Silk road: strategy for security', in Sidda Goud and Manisha Mookherjee, eds, Sino–Indian Relations: Contemporary Perspective (New Delhi: Allied Publishers, 2016), p. 100.

[12]Lanteigne, 'China's maritime security', pp. 143–144. However, Guy C. K. Leung, 'China's energy security: perception and reality', Energy Policy 39, (2011), pp. 1330–1337, points out that 'the so-called Malacca Dilemma has been commonly exaggerated' (p. 1334).

[13]These are: Leung, 'China's energy security'; and Andrew S. Erickson and Gabriel B. Collins, 'China's oil security pipe dream: the reality, and strategic consequences, of seaborne imports', Naval War College Review 63(2), (2010), pp. 89–111.

[14]Faheemullah Shaikh, Qiang Ji and Ying Fan, 'Prospects of China–Pakistan energy and economic corridor', Renewable and Sustainable Energy Reviews 59, (2016), pp. 253–263.

[15]See Leung, 'China's energy security'; and Erickson and Collins, 'China's oil security pipe dream'.

[16]I am indebted to Kishan S. Rana of the Institute of Chinese Studies in Delhi for this observation (personal communication, March 2017).

[17]Yang and Siddiqi, 'About an "all-weather" relationship', p. 575.

not even mention the feasibility of a hypothetical pipeline in terms of non-economic issues such as the logistics of construction in the physical geography of the Himalayas, security issues relating to terrorism, the necessity of building through disputed territories in the north of Pakistan, and capacity issues relating to Gwadar port.[18] This is not the only article in a peer-reviewed journal to make the (unfounded) assumption that the geographically shorter distance to China from the Persian Gulf to Xinjiang via Pakistan must automatically mean cheaper oil.[19]

Another incorrect claim (citing a Reuters news item which does not mention the data supposedly cited) which appears in a recent peer-reviewed journal article is that '[a]s a direct consequence of the huge investment by China, Gwadar port contains 13 berths and has the capacity to hold bulk carriers of 350,000 deadweight tonnage'.[20] Examining the reality of Gwadar port's present capacity on the Gwadar Port Authority's website (as of December 2017) reveals that its capacity is currently much less than this, with three functioning multipurpose berths and the capacity to accept vessels of up to 50,000 deadweight tonnage (DWT) only.[21] These three berths were all completed in 2005 in the so-called 'Phase I' of the project to expand the port. As of March 2016, according to the Pakistani Minister for Ports and Shipping, work on the further berths which were supposed to constitute 'Phase II' had not yet begun.[22] Andrew Small, the author of the most authoritative book on China–Pakistan relations to date, confirms that from 2007 onwards, for a variety of reasons including the removal of Pervez Musharraf from office in 2008, acrimony surrounding alleged mismanagement by the Port of Singapore Authority (which had been granted the contract to run the port in 2007 but which withdrew from the project in February 2013 after extended bouts of litigation), and security issues relating to the safety of Chinese workers, 'very little of "Phase 2" was ever undertaken'.[23]

The confusion surrounding Gwadar and Sino–Pakistani relations since the launch of CPEC in 2015 means that there is a pressing need to further clarify the state of play today. As Andrew Small puts it,

> for a long time the story of the economic relationship between the two sides has been one of excitable headlines touting large numbers, ports, pipelines, and energy transit routes followed by frustration, disappointment, stalled projects, and much smaller figures buried away in statistical reports.[24]

A central aim of this article is thus to attempt to assess (or rather continue the assessment begun by others, including Small[25]) the feasibility of CPEC acting as a transportation corridor for crude oil and other commodities and goods from the IOR to western China based on a reasonably thorough examination of the primary data available (such as they are), as well as evidence provided in secondary sources, including ones which predate the advent of CPEC.

From Gwadar to Kashgar, the Hard Way

Gwadar is located in Balochistan, in the southwest of Pakistan. It is on the Arabian Sea opposite Oman and to the east of the Straits of Hormuz. About 70 kilometres to the west is the Iranian border, on the other side of which is the port of Chabahar, now being developed by India. Approximately 650 kilometres to the east of Gwadar, along the Makran Coastal Highway (construction of which was completed by China in 2004), is Pakistan's main port, Karachi, which is part-owned by China Harbor Engineering Company (CHEC).

---

[18]Shaikh *et al.*, 'Prospects of China–Pakistan energy and economic corridor'.
[19]The assumption is also made by Chaziza, 'China–Pakistan relationship', p. 4.
[20]Shawn Amirthan, 'What are India, Iran, and Afghanistan's benefits from the Chabahar Port agreement?', *Strategic Analysis* 41(1), (2016), p. 89.
[21]Gwadar Port Authority website, 'Port Profile: Current Port Infrastructure', available at: http://www.gwadarport.gov.pk/portprofile. aspx (accessed 4 December 2017).
[22]'At Gwadar port: additional multipurpose berths in offing', *The Express Tribune*, (10 March 2016), available at: https://tribune.com. pk/story/1062683/at-gwadar-port-additional-multipurpose-berths-in-offing/ (accessed 8 February 2017).
[23]Andrew Small, *The China–Pakistan Axis: Asia's New Geopolitics* (Oxford: Oxford University Press, 2015), p. 101.
[24]*Ibid.*, pp. 95–96.
[25]See: *Ibid.*; Leung, 'China's energy security'; and Erickson and Collins, 'China's oil security pipe dream'.

Gwadar was a fishing village under Omani rule until 1958, when the enclave was purchased by Pakistan for US$3 million.[26] Plans to build a deep-sea port were initiated in 1993, and construction began in 2002 using Chinese finance and labour.[27] Phase I of the project was completed in 2007, whereupon the administration of the port was handed over to the Port of Singapore Authority (PSA International) on a 40-year lease. However, PSA withdrew by mutual consent from this deal in 2012–2013, and the rights to administer the port until 2047 were sold to China Overseas Ports Holding Company Limited (COPHCL) in May 2013. PSA's withdrawal came ostensibly because Pakistan refused to transfer 584 acres of land under the control of the Pakistani Navy, although problems with security due to local Baloch militants have also been cited as an associated reason.[28]

One major impediment to Gwadar's utility as a port is geographical. Gwadar is relatively isolated from Pakistan's major population centres, and Balochistan is one of Pakistan's poorest provinces. Apart from the highway to Karachi, there is at present little else of note in the vicinity of the port in terms of infrastructure. Pakistan's main industrial centres are far away in Gujranwala, Faisalabad and Lahore.[29] For this reason, there has been an extended debate within Pakistan about whether the proposed connection from Gwadar to the Chinese border should take an eastern or western route (or both).[30] Each route would likely encounter numerous logistical problems, and each has already met with objections from factions within the country.

Either way, linking Gwadar to China over land demands crossing the entire length of Pakistan, including the Karakoram Mountains in the north. The Karakoram Highway, completed in 1979, crosses into China through the Khunjerab Pass, at an altitude of 4,693 metres. Topographical maps, photographs and tourist films reveal that the pass, located on the border, is wide, but the road which winds up to it through Pakistani territory is precariously cut into the mountainside above the Khunjerab river, which is the headwaters of the Hunza river.[31] As the highway passes from the Khunjerab Pass down into Pakistan, its 'main geomorphic features include hanging valleys, waterfalls, glaciers, snow-fields, lateral and terminal moraines and cirques':[32] in other words, extremely difficult terrain for the building and maintenance of pipelines. Sections of the highway are subject to frequent landslides and rockslides since it crosses a geological fault line where the Eurasian and Indian plates collide. More than 1,000 Pakistani and Chinese workers died during the construction of the highway due to landslides.[33] A major landslide in 2010 caused the closure of a section of road due to the formation of a new lake, until the completion in 2015 of 24 kilometres of bridges and tunnels which restored the road link. The geological instability of Pakistan's northern region, allied with difficult terrain, high altitudes, the possibility of insurgency and the fact that the border region is disputed with India, mean that adding any further infrastructure alongside the highway (such as a railway or pipeline) is fraught with risk and extreme difficulty in terms of maintenance and construction, including extensive high-altitude tunnelling.

The prohibitive cost of constructing high-altitude pipelines is another factor against the proposed project. In November 2016, Mei Xinyu, a Chinese Academy of International Trade and Economic Cooperation research fellow and representative of the Chinese Ministry of Commerce, commented in the state-endorsed newspaper *Global Times* that since high-altitude pipelines 'need extra heating and insulating equipment as well as high-power pumping stations' to pump fuel uphill, the costs of

[26]Small, *The China–Pakistan Axis*, p. 100.
[27]Tim Willasey-Wilsey, 'Gwadar and the "string of pearls"', *Gateway House: Indian Council on Global Relations*, (28 January 2016), available at: http://www.gatewayhouse.in/gwadar-and-the-string-of-pearls-2/ (accessed 6 February 2017).
[28]Syed Fazl-e-Haider, 'China set to run Gwadar port as Singapore quits', *Asia Times*, (5 September 2012), available at: http://www.atimes.com/atimes/China_Business/NI05Cb01.html (accessed 6 February 2017).
[29]Filippo Boni, 'Civil–military relations in Pakistan: a case study of Sino–Pakistani relations and the port of Gwadar', *Commonwealth & Comparative Politics* 54(4), (2016), p. 512.
[30]See for instance: Syed Irfan Raza, 'Eastern route not part of economic corridor, claims NHA chief', *Dawn*, (5 July 2016), available at: https://www.dawn.com/news/1269102; and Maryam Usman and Sardar Sikander, 'CPEC's western route to be ready by 2018', *The Express Tribune*, (16 June 2016), available at: https://tribune.com.pk/story/1123811/western-route-ready-2018-ahsan/ (accessed 22 March 2017).
[31]A good range of maps, photographs and videos can be found online by Googling such terms as 'Khunjerab Pass' and 'Karakoram Highway topographical map'.
[32]Sharad Singh Negi, *Himalayan Rivers, Lakes and Glaciers* (New Delhi: Indus Publishing Company, 1991), pp. 86–87.
[33]Small, *The China–Pakistan Axis*, p. 99.

transporting oil over the Himalayas to Xinjiang would be approximately 16.6 times higher than the conventional route from Saudi Arabia to Eastern China by tanker. Mei concluded that '[f]or the same amount of investment, it's more economically viable to build very large crude carriers than oil pipelines'. Comparative analysis conducted by Erickson and Collins in 2011 reveals that oil transported by pipeline from Angarsk in Russia to Daqing in northern China via relatively flat terrain is around double (US$2.41 per barrel) that of oil transported from Saudi Arabia to Ningbo (US$1.25 per barrel), even though the distance covered is less than half (3,200 km versus 7,000 km).[34] This indicates beyond reasonable doubt that the cost of fuel transported through the proposed CPEC pipelines would be substantially higher than that transported by existing routes.

Another question surrounds the draft—defined as the dredged depth—of Gwadar port. As previously stated, the port can currently receive vessels up to 50,000 DWT, with a draft of 12.5 metres. Gwadar has three 200-metre berths plus a 100-metre service berth.[35] This capacity is insufficient to receive even mid-sized cargo carriers and oil tankers, severely limiting the utility and commercial success of the port at present.[36] Further dredging of the approach channels and port is scheduled, but so far the depth to be dredged has not been specified.[37] Since all models of large cargo carriers and oil tankers are over 200 metres in length and have drafts of between 16 metres and 35 metres, to receive even those of medium size the entry to Gwadar port needs not only to be dredged further, but its berths also need to be extended or new ones built.[38] According to the official CPEC website, as of early February 2017 COPHCL's draft business plan for port improvements was still under review by the Pakistani Ministry of Ports and Shipping.[39] Wu Minghua, a shipping analyst, also noted that Gwadar Port had a handling capacity of 1 million tons per year in 2016, while China's total oil imports were 335.5 million tons in 2015, further casting doubt on the practical value and cost-effectiveness of offloading and transporting oil supplies by this route.[40]

A further problem for both Gwadar and CPEC is security. The security situation in Pakistan has been highly unstable for years, with terrorism and regional insurgencies producing violent attacks across the nation, not least in Balochistan, 'an area over which Islamabad's political hold has weakened substantially since 2007'.[41] Three Chinese engineers were killed in a 2004 bomb attack at Gwadar by Baloch separatists, and nine more were injured.[42] In 2017 a Chinese couple was kidnapped near Gwadar in Quetta by separatists and eventually killed.[43] A recent *Foreign Policy* article suggests that the Balochi separatist issue is not likely to go away soon, and that the security situation may even worsen.[44]

The remainder of Pakistan is also not noted for its safety. Indeed, more Chinese were targeted in terrorist attacks in Pakistan between 2004 and 2010 than anywhere else in the world.[45] There were further attacks on Chinese nationals, including a group of engineers, in 2013, resulting in several fatalities.[46] The

[34]Erickson and Collins, 'China's oil security pipe dream', p. 92.
[35]Gwadar Port Authority website, 'Port Profile: Current Port Infrastructure'.
[36]According to information on ship sizes obtained from Maritime Connector website, available at: http://maritime-connector.com/wiki/ship-sizes/ (accessed 7 February 2017).
[37]Official CPEC website, 'Dredging of berthing areas & channels', available at: http://cpec.gov.pk/project-details/35 (accessed 4 December 2017).
[38]Hofstra University website, 'The geography of transport systems', available at: https://people.hofstra.edu/geotrans/eng/ch5en/appl5en/tankers.html (accessed 7 February 2017).
[39]CPEC website, 'Progress update'.
[40]Li Xuanmin, 'Gwadar Port benefits to China limited', *Global Times*, (23 November 2016), available at: http://www.globaltimes.cn/content/1019840.shtml (accessed 7 February 2017).
[41]Hartpence, 'The economic dimension of Sino–Pakistani relations', p. 598.
[42]Small, *The China–Pakistan Axis*, p. 102.
[43]Salman Masood, 'Chinese couple abducted in Pakistan have been killed, officials say', *New York Times*, (12 June 2017).
[44]Emily Whalen, 'Balochistan looks ready to blow, and when it does, it likely will spill over', *Foreign Policy*, (9 February 2017), available at: http://foreignpolicy.com/2017/02/09/bolochistan-looks-ready-to-blow-and-when-it-does-it-likely-will-spill-over/ (accessed 22 March 2017).
[45]Mathieu Duchâtel, 'The terrorist risk and China's policy towards Pakistan: strategic reassurance and the "United Front"', *Journal of Contemporary China* 20(71), (2011), p. 543.
[46]Small, *The China–Pakistan Axis*, pp. 171–173.

security situation has become so unstable that the Pakistani cricket team has played almost all its 'home' matches in the United Arab Emirates since a terrorist attack on the visiting Sri Lankan team in 2009.[47]

The difficulty of ensuring security means that constructing any hypothetical transportation and pipeline corridor to China which crosses the length of Pakistan is a risky enterprise demanding a high level of security manpower and placing a heavy load on the Pakistani armed forces. Exacerbating these concerns as far as China is concerned is the possibility of Islamic insurgents crossing into restive Xinjiang from Pakistan. Indeed, China tightened security at the Khunjerab Pass in January 2017 in an attempt to prevent militants from entering Chinese territory.[48] There was also an upsurge in violence inside Pakistan in the first two months of 2017, with Pakistani security forces seen as struggling to cope.[49] In short, it is far from clear that CPEC could provide a more secure route for fossil fuels from the IOR to China than the existing maritime one via Malacca. Indeed, it would be more likely to add to China's energy security headache rather than to alleviate it.

An alternative solution for connecting Gwadar to Xinjiang is to cross the nearby border into Iran and/or Afghanistan and then go through the Central Asian states of Turkmenistan and Kazakhstan.[50] Three gas pipelines originating in Turkmenistan already supply natural gas to China, so there might be a possibility of linking Gwadar with Turkmenistan via a more secure route at lower altitude, although it is not clear that this would make any economic or logistical sense. An alternative proposal for a Turkmenistan–Afghanistan–Pakistan–India pipeline (TAPI) is already on the table, but is reportedly beset with difficulties and delays.[51] In 2015, with the lifting of sanctions on Iran, an Iran–Pakistan gas pipeline to be built by China was proposed. This is intended to pass through Gwadar on its way to Nawabshah in southeastern Pakistan.[52] As of November 2016, the Iranian section of the pipeline was reportedly already constructed, but construction of the Pakistani section was delayed due to the lack of funds on the Pakistani side.[53]

All in all, there are a number of serious logistical problems facing the hypothetical project of enhancing Gwadar to Xinjiang connections by adding to the existing road link. While the upgrading of the Karakoram Highway continues, proposals for pipelines and a railway have not yet got off the drawing board, and the absence of references to them in Chinese media in 2017 suggests that they are likely to have been quietly shelved. Pakistan appears to be constantly short of hard currency and dependent on Chinese loans or investment, implying that China will have a near-monopoly on decision-making in CPEC. This means that if the Chinese government and Chinese companies decide that certain aspects of CPEC are not economically viable, they will not be funded. Given the fact that a Chinese state newspaper has reported serious Chinese doubts about the profitability of supplying oil through pipelines to Xinjiang,[54] and since even Pakistani experts have expressed doubts about Gwadar's economic viability,[55] it seems unlikely that such a difficult project will find a place high on China's list of potential investments in the foreseeable future. The comments of two Chinese experts in *Global Times* undermine the assertion of Shaikh *et al.* that an oil pipeline is cost-effective and feasible, and confirm that Gwadar

[47]Mike Selvey, 'Pakistan cricket can never have home advantage in soulless Emirates', *The Guardian*, (11 January 2012), available at: https://www.theguardian.com/sport/blog/2012/jan/11/pakistan-cricket-emirates (accessed 21 March 2017).
[48]Saibal Dasgupta, 'China to seal border with Pakistan to curb terror', *The Times of India*, (11 January 2017), available at: http://timesofindia.indiatimes.com/world/china/china-to-seal-border-with-pakistan-to-curb-terror/articleshow/56468455.cms (accessed 2 April 2017).
[49]Daud Khattak, 'New wave of terrorist attacks casts doubt on Pakistan's security forces', *The Diplomat*, (15 February 2017), available at: http://thediplomat.com/2017/02/new-wave-of-terrorist-attacks-casts-doubt-on-pakistans-security-forces/?utm_content=bufferf0e19&utm_medium=social&utm_source=facebook.com&utm_campaign=buffer (accessed 22 March 2017).
[50]Chaziza, 'China–Pakistan relationship', pp. 8–9.
[51]Casey Michel, 'TAPI and CASA-1000 remain in project purgatory', *The Diplomat*, (10 July 2017), available at: http://thediplomat.com/2017/07/tapi-and-casa-1000-remain-in-project-purgatory/ (accessed 25 September 2017).
[52]Saeed Shah, 'China to build pipeline from Iran to Pakistan', *The Wall Street Journal*, (9 April 2015), available at: https://www.wsj.com/articles/china-to-build-pipeline-from-iran-to-pakistan-1428515277 (accessed 7 February 2017).
[53]Daniel J. Graeber, 'Iran emerges with claim of Pakistani pipeline interest', *United Press International*, (4 November 2016), available at: http://www.upi.com/Iran-emerges-with-claim-of-Pakistani-pipeline-interest/2581478260003/ (accessed 7 February 2017).
[54]Li Xuanmin, 'Gwadar Port benefits to China limited'.
[55]Boni, 'Civil–military relations in Pakistan', p. 512.

Port does not at present have the capacity to transfer oil from tankers to shore in anything other than relatively small quantities.[56]

A Salutary Tale: Lessons from the China–Myanmar Pipeline

China's first attempt to bypass the Malacca 'chokepoint' in the wake of Hu Jintao's 2003 comments took shape in 2004 when talks were opened with Myanmar on constructing an oil pipeline to Kunming. Then in December 2005 a contract between the then Burmese government and PetroChina to deliver 6.5 trillion cubic feet of natural gas to Yunnan over 30 years was signed.[57] Interest in exploiting the Shwe gas field drove the project to its next stage, and agreements to build both natural gas and oil pipelines were drawn up in 2008 and 2009. Construction of the crude oil pipeline commenced on 31 October 2009.[58]

The project consists of two pipelines. One is for natural gas and one for crude oil. They were constructed between 2009 and 2014, and pass in parallel through Myanmar on their way to Kunming in China's southwestern Yunnan province. The gas pipeline, which originates at Kyaukpyu port, is intended to exploit the Shwe gas field in the Andaman Sea, while the oil pipeline begins at a new deep water port on nearby Maday (or Made) Island, at which tankers from the Middle East can dock and offload crude oil.[59] While the gas pipeline has reportedly been in operation since October 2013,[60] the oil pipeline took longer to build, was 'essentially completed' in early 2015, but was beset by delays, questions concerning economic viability and disputes over terms.[61] The fact that, according to Chinese state media, the first delivery of oil from a tanker occurred only in April 2017 underlines the fact that the oil pipeline lay unused for more than two years after its construction was completed.[62] A proposal to construct a railway along the pipeline route between Kunming and Kyaukpyu was also put forward, but this was cancelled by the Myanmar government in July 2014 due to the pressure of negative public opinion concerning perceived Chinese exploitation of Myanmar's resources.[63]

The two pipelines reportedly cost a total of US$2.45 billion to build. However, while the gas pipeline began pumping fuel after its completion, the 771-kilometre oil pipeline lay unused during 2015, due, according to a Myanmar Oil and Gas Enterprise official, to a number of reasons including the following: disagreements over fees and taxes, probably due to the fact that the Myanmar government had changed between drawing up the contracts and the completion of the pipeline; the fact that construction of the refinery at the Yunnan end of the pipeline which was due to process the crude oil had not been completed; and low oil prices making operations unprofitable.[64] Even after completion of the Yunnan refinery in July 2016, oil did not start pumping until 2017 due to continuing disputes over the level of taxes to be paid by China, revealing this to be a central reason for the ongoing delay:

---

[56]Li Xuanmin, 'Gwadar Port benefits to China limited'; Shaikh *et al.*, 'Prospects of China–Pakistan energy and economic corridor'.

[57]Ian Storey, 'China's "Malacca Dilemma"', *China Brief* 6(8) (The Jamestown Foundation), (12 April 2006), available at: https://jamestown. org/program/chinas-malacca-dilemma/ (accessed 8 February 2017).

[58]'Constructions begin on wharf for China–Myanmar crude oil pipeline', *Xinhua Economic News*, (3 November 2009), available on *Downstream Today* website at: http://downstreamtoday.com/news/article.aspx?a_id=19041 (accessed 8 February 2017).

[59]Eric Meyer, 'With oil and gas pipelines, China takes a shortcut through Myanmar', *Forbes*, (9 February 2015), available at: http://www. forbes.com/sites/ericrmeyer/2015/02/09/oil-and-gas-china-takes-a-shortcut/#5fb8ca892d40 (accessed 2 April 2017).

[60]Aung Shin, 'Controversial pipeline now fully operational', *Myanmar Times*, (27 October 2013), available at: http://www.mmtimes. com/index.php/business/8583-controversial-pipeline-now-fully-operational.html (accessed 3 April 2017).

[61]See: Chen Aizhu and Aung Hla Tun, 'New China refinery faces delay as Myanmar seeks extra oil tax: sources', *Reuters*, (10 October 2016), available at: http://www.reuters.com/article/us-china-myanmar-oil-idUSKCN12A0JF (accessed 8 February 2017); and Shwee Yee Saw Myint and Henning Gloystein, 'First oil for long-awaited Myanmar pipeline to China delayed again', *Reuters*, (24 March 2017), available at: http://www.reuters.com/article/myanmar-china-oil-idUSL3N1H13NV?rpc=401& (accessed 3 April 2017).

[62]This information is obtained from official reports in the Chinese state-endorsed newspaper *Global Times* and confirmed by reports in Western news outlets such as *Bloomberg News*. See: Cao Siqi and You Ma, 'China, Myanmar ink oil pipeline deal', *Global Times*, (10 April 2017), available at: http://www.globaltimes.cn/content/1041785.shtml (accessed 18 September 2017); Cao Siqi and Shan Jie, 'Sino–Myanmar oil pipeline launch a good signal: experts', *Global Times*, (28 March 2017), available at: http://www.globaltimes. cn/content/1039861.shtml (accessed 18 September 2017); and 'China opens delayed Myanmar oil pipeline to get Mideast crude faster', *Bloomberg News*, (11 April 2017), available at: https://www.bloomberg.com/news/articles/2017-04-11/china-opens-de-layed-myanmar-oil-link-to-get-mideast-crude-faster (accessed 18 September 2017).

[63]Adam Pasick, 'China's cancelled Burma railway is its latest derailment in southeast Asia', *Quartz*, (25 July 2014), available at: https:// qz.com/240436/chinas-cancelled-burma-railway-is-its-latest-derailment-in-southeast-asia/ (accessed 0 February 2017).

[64]*Ibid*.

the Myanmar government wanted an extra 5% tax on top of the earlier agreed transit fee and pipeline tariff.[65] A tanker which was due to deliver oil to Kyaukpyu for the first time in March 2017 was unable to deliver its load due to yet another breakdown in negotiations between PetroChina and the Myanmar government.[66] After the first delivery in April 2017, oil started flowing through the pipeline in early May,[67] and 2 million tonnes were transferred in the four months to September.[68] However, the cost of the oil is high, with Myanmar set to collect US$13 million per year from China as a Right-Of-Way (ROW) easement payment, plus two custom duties whose exact amount has not yet been decided.[69] It is also important to note that the tankers delivering crude to Kyaukpyu port for the transfer would otherwise take the oil to ports in mainland China where there would be no payments or duties. Thus, the costs associated with the running of the pipeline cast doubt on its economic efficacy.

The reaction to the Chinese pipelines in local Myanmar communities has also impacted their operation to a degree. The widespread civic protests which led to the cancellation of the railway project from Yunnan to Kyaukpyu in 2014 may have been a factor in the delay to the commencement of the operation of the oil pipeline: local inhabitants were outraged that they had not been consulted and had not benefitted from the pipelines, and also that energy resources were being diverted to China when most of Myanmar lacks electricity.[70] Then, in early 2017, violence between Buddhists and the minority Muslim Rohingya group in the state of Rakhine, which includes Kyaukpyu port and the pipelines, put the operation of the Chinese enterprises in further doubt.[71] An article by a freelance Burmese photojournalist in November 2015 reveals a picture of growing disillusionment among local people on Maday Island concerning the economic benefits of the Chinese-funded oil pipeline and terminal.[72]

It is not possible at this stage to assess the impact on the pipelines of local protests and complex outbreaks of sectarian violence in firmly quantitative terms. However, it can be stated that the Chinese involvement with successive Myanmar regimes means that the pipelines have a political and social impact which demands further research since it affects the local environment within which the pipelines are operated. These issues have also added an extra layer of insecurity to the Chinese energy security equation rather than significantly alleviating the situation.

In short, the problems inherent in the China–Myanmar pipeline project are surely instructive as regards the potential construction of a pipeline between Gwadar and Kashgar. Indeed, the remarkable Chinese capacity for learning valuable lessons from failed projects in a timely fashion (precisely according to Deng Xiaoping's dictum of 'crossing the river by feeling for the stones') appears to have led in late 2016 to China quietly shelving CPEC's pipeline project in the customary low-key manner adopted by the Chinese authorities when dealing with failure, disappointment or tragedy: without fanfare or publicity.

So What is CPEC for?

If the notion of constructing pipelines (and perhaps also a railway) from Gwadar to Kashgar appears impractical, as the above analysis suggests, then four questions need answering. First, why is China involved in Gwadar? Second, what does China hope to gain from CPEC? Third, what are China's overall intentions with regard to its 'all-weather friend' Pakistan? And fourth, what does Pakistan expect from China?

[65]Chen and Tun, 'New China refinery faces delay as Myanmar seeks extra oil tax'.
[66]Myint and Gloystein, 'First oil for long-awaited Myanmar pipeline to China delayed again'.
[67]'CNPC loads first crude oil into Myanmar–China pipeline', Reuters, (3 May 2017), available at: http://www.reuters.com/article/china-myanmar-oil/cnpc-loads-first-crude-oil-into-myanmar-china-pipeline-idUSL1N1I504H (accessed 21 September 2017).
[68]Chan Mya Htwe, 'Myanmar exports 2 m tonnes of oil via pipeline over 4 months', Myanmar Times, (21 September 2017), available at: https://www.mmtimes.com/news/myanmar-exports-2 m-tonnes-oil-pipeline-over-4-months.html (accessed 22 November 2017).
[69]Ibid.
[70]Pasick, 'China's cancelled Burma railway is its latest derailment in southeast Asia'.
[71]Ding Gang, 'China, India could help stabilize Myanmar's conflict-ridden Rakhine state', Global Times, (8 February 2017), available at: http://www.globaltimes.cn/content/1032014.shtml (accessed 9 February 2017).
[72]Yu Yu Myint Than, 'Myanmar pipeline brings gas to China, hardship to villagers', National Resource Governance Institute (NRGI) website, (5 November 2015), available at: http://www.resourcegovernance.org/blog/myanmar-pipeline-brings-gas-china-hardship-villagers (accessed 8 March 2017).

It is likely that the answers to all these questions are interlinked. It is also likely, given the complexity of the issues involved, that, as the authors of a 2016 study put it, 'China's motives in pursuing CPEC are variegated'.[73] Filippo Boni, who conducted field research in Pakistan, concurs in stating that security, economics and foreign policy are 'inextricably intertwined when it comes to the development of the port of Gwadar and, by and large, Pakistan–China relations'.[74] However, the argument developed in this section is that China's involvement in Pakistan is primarily motivated by considerations of geopolitics based on physical geography (geo-positional balancing), particularly with respect to the most significant nation located in the IOR, India, and it is this which brings China and Pakistan's interests into alignment.

Geo-positional balancing differs from other forms of balancing (such as classical hard balancing, soft balancing and offshore balancing) in that the strategic actor, in this case China, prioritises geographical factors. Classical hard (or external) balancing involves states forming military alliances to ensure that stronger states do not achieve a dominant position, while in soft balancing weaker states employ economic and diplomatic means to equalise their position *vis-à-vis* a potentially hegemonic state. Offshore balancing, as outlined by Stephen Walt and John Mearsheimer, is a strategy recommended for the United States specifically: it entails encouraging allies to build up their own defences instead of the US maintaining an onshore military presence.[75] In contrast with these other forms of balancing, geo-positional balancing aims to establish physical footholds in selected countries (in this case Pakistan and Myanmar) with a view to establishing a stronger long-term geo-strategic position with regard to a regionally more powerful rival (in this case India). The aim of geo-positional balancing, in this conception, is neither to build up onshore military bases nor to remain entirely offshore, but instead to establish a non-military presence at selected sites (such as commercial ports). These can be maintained long-term for the purpose of keeping a powerful rival geopolitically honest by making it aware of the incoming actor's presence. At the same time, onshore economic investment and infrastructure building give the balancer influence in the host country by building up a degree of soft power through enhanced economic connections.

In this reading of the situation, Gwadar is a geo-strategic 'place marker' or, as Henry Kissinger would have it, a metaphorical *weiqi* stone: the utility of the 'stone' may not yet be clear, but Beijing appears to believe that it is better to seize the opportunity.[76] If China intends to be an actor of significance in the IOR and South Asia, as well as to shore up its existing position, it needs to hedge against Indian activity (for instance investment in Chabahar port along the coast in Iran) as well as the US naval presence in the region (based in Diego Garcia). Given that India and China have not exactly had close relations since the 1962 border war between them, and amid ongoing territorial tensions along their extended frontier, including Indian claims on the Karakoram territory which connects Pakistan with China geographically, China seeks to ensure that it has as many strategic footholds in the region as possible.[77] US intentions in the region have been unclear in recent years, but there is always the chance that the Americans will re-engage: China therefore needs to hedge against that possibility as well.

Viewing China's port-building programme in the IOR as geo-positional balancing permits a more nuanced understanding of Chinese activity than simple aggression or hard balancing. In essence, China intends to establish a physical presence to enhance its overall long-term defensive security rather than aiming to directly challenge or threaten India, a goal which is currently unrealistic in terms of maritime power projection, particularly given the continuing American military presence in the IOR. The nuclear rivalry between Pakistan and India and the ongoing Sino–Indian border tensions contribute to the

---

[73]Hamzah Rifaat and Tridivesh Singh Maini, *The China–Pakistan Economic Corridor: Strategic Rationales, External Perspectives, and Challenges to Effective Implementation*, Visiting Fellow Working Paper (Washington, DC: The Stimson Center, 2016).
[74]Boni, 'Civil–military relations in Pakistan', p. 500.
[75]John J. Mearsheimer and Stephen M. Walt, 'The case for offshore balancing: a superior U.S. grand strategy', *Foreign Affairs*, (July/August 2016), pp. 70–83.
[76]Kissinger, *On China*, pp. 23–25.
[77]Huang Junbao *et al.*, 'Con zhanlue gaodu renshi he shenghua yu Bajisitan de quanmian hezuo' ['To look at and deepen China's comprehensive cooperation with Pakistan from a strategic perspective'], *Yatai Jingji* [*Asia Pacific Economy*] 2, (2008), p. 64, cited by Yang and Siddiqi, 'About an "all-weather" relationship', p. 575.

assessment that geo-positional balancing in Gwadar is a strategy which is intended to serve China's long-term security interests in the sense of what China terms 'active defence'.[78]

In this light, it is of course to be expected that China refutes claims that it is out to 'encircle' India. Yet suspicions remain. On the other hand, extended supply lines which stretch for thousands of kilometres from China's southernmost naval base on Hainan Island mean that China's People's Liberation Army Navy (PLAN) is not yet able to rival India's navy in the IOR.[79] China's geo-positional strategy takes account of this fact by attempting to gradually build up a network of commercial ports around the IOR while occasional activity from the PLAN, such as a visit by Chinese warships to Karachi in June 2017, remains relatively low-key.[80]

This is not to say that what can be termed China's port-of-entry strategy has been entirely smooth sailing. Not all efforts by China to incorporate ports in other IOR countries into its so-called 'string of pearls' have come to fruition, and even those that have are often controversial. For instance, a Chinese bid to develop a port in Bangladesh was quietly rejected in 2016 by the Bangladeshi authorities (probably due to behind-the-scenes pressure from India, the US and Japan, which had already been developing a port),[81] while two Chinese port construction projects in Sri Lanka, at Colombo Port City and Hambantota, have developed in fits and starts as Sri Lankan governments have come and gone (or changed policy). Concern about Chinese loans being converted into Chinese equity, and ports potentially being used for military purposes have not been eased by Chinese insistence that the investments are purely commercial in nature, as a senior Indian scholar has noted.[82] Stopovers in Sri Lanka by Chinese submarines have understandably led to Indian howls of protest, with a 2017 proposed docking rejected by Sri Lanka under pressure from India.[83] The Sino–Indian geopolitical rivalry in the IOR means that all Chinese port projects stir suspicion on the part of India, as well as other regional actors, most notably the US and Japan. Such considerations explain why India also continues to reject Chinese invitations to join the BRI.

Several observers (Andrew Small, Ye Hailin, Mathieu Duchâtel) who have interviewed or maintain contacts with Chinese foreign policy makers have noted that according to their sources China's long-term priority in Pakistan has been to prioritise security concerns over economic ones.[84] Duchâtel's anonymous source, interviewed in 2009, reveals China's long-term geopolitical strategy with regard to Pakistan and so is worth quoting in full:

> If projects progress too slowly or if they are threatened by insecurity, it's easy: we stall them. The energy-and-trade corridor has only little importance and security costs are high. Pakistan has no resources, no gas, no oil, *only a geographical position* [italics added]. Pakistan insists that China should invest in this project, but China is now a market economy and seeks returns on [its] investments. China was considering the construction of this corridor under Musharraf because there was a sufficient degree of security and economic growth, but today it is meaningless.[85]

Another area in which China seeks to enhance its security in Pakistan is the aforementioned issue of containing threats to the stability of Xinjiang province caused by possible transnational flows of (or support for) Muslim insurgents. In fact, Pakistan has been playing a key role in actively quelling Uighur

---

[78]See China's Defence White Paper: *China's Military Strategy*, The State Council Information Office of the People's Republic of China, Beijing, (May 2015), Section III. Full English text, available at: http://www.chinadaily.com.cn/china/2015-05/26/content_20820628.htm (accessed 22 March 2017).

[79]Lanteigne, 'China's maritime security', p. 148.

[80]Shailaja Neelakantani, 'Four Chinese warships arrive on shores of "all-weather friend" Pakistan for "training" mission', *Times of India*, (11 June 2017), available at: http://timesofindia.indiatimes.com/world/pakistan/four-chinese-warships-arrive-on-shores-of-all-weather-friend-pakistan-for-training-mission/articleshow/59093648.cms (accessed 29 September 2017).

[81]Indrana Bagchi, 'Dhaka cancels port to be built by China, India eyes another', *Times of India*, (8 February 2016), available at: http://timesofindia.indiatimes.com/india/Dhaka-cancels-port-to-be-built-by-China-India-eyes-another/articleshow/50894554.cms (accessed 28 September 2017).

[82]Swaran Singh, 'Why is India worried about China consolidating in Sri Lanka?', *The Sunday Leader*, (13 August 2017), available at: http://www.thesundayleader.lk/2017/08/13/why-is-india-worried-about-china-consolidating-in-sri-lanka/ (accessed 28 September 2017).

[83]Shihar Aneez and Ranga Sirilal, 'Sri Lanka rejects Chinese request for submarine visit: sources', *Reuters*, (11 May 2017), available at: https://www.reuters.com/article/us-sri-lanka-china-submarine/sri-lanka-rejects-chinese-request-for-submarine-visit-sources-idUSKBN1871P9 (accessed 29 September 2017).

[84]See: Ye Hailin, 'China–Pakistan relationship'; Andrew Small, 'China's caution on Afghanistan–Pakistan', *The Washington Quarterly* 33(3), (2010), pp. 01–97, Duchâtel, 'The terrorist risk and China's policy towards Pakistan'.

[85]Duchâtel, 'The terrorist risk and China's policy towards Pakistan', p. 557.

separatist elements [such as the East Turkestan Islamic Movement (ETIM)] on China's behalf for some years already.[86] Thus, a secondary motivation for involvement in Pakistan is to attempt to contain the Muslim separatist threat to China's northwest security outside Chinese borders as far as possible.

The nature of Chinese investments constitutes another aspect of CPEC which is problematic since they are made up of loans which have to be repaid sooner or later. Used worldwide, China's 'debt-based model for infrastructure development'[87] gives the impression that investment is being used as a tool to promote geopolitical interests as much as economic ones. For instance, by looking to swap debt for real estate down the line, as happened with a Sri Lankan port in 2017,[88] China gains long-term control over physical assets in strategic locations. In this sense, the use of loans as investment instruments is suggestive of geopolitical goals being at least as important as economic ones in China's long-term strategic approach.

There are also doubts concerning the extent to which Chinese investment projects can progress smoothly and at the expected rate. Scrutiny of the official CPEC website run by the Pakistani government reveals that, as of December 2017, work had not yet begun on more than half of the 67 projects listed.[89] In these cases, individual projects are still at the planning or feasibility study stage and the timeline for substantive progress is unclear. On the other hand, China's increased pledges of cash for Pakistani energy and transport infrastructure projects in 2017 indicate firm, ongoing commitment to these aspects of CPEC. Nonetheless, it is significant that the possibility of constructing pipelines and railways between China and Pakistan was no longer being discussed in the Chinese media or other official sources in 2017. The notion of Pakistan further adding to its debt by taking on Chinese loans to pay for CPEC infrastructure is a further problem which can only exacerbate the imbalance in economic relations, and is likely to be the source of yet more financial problems for Pakistan in future.[90]

It might be hypothesised that China is genuinely seeking to increase economic ties with Pakistan and to boost Pakistan's economy. While this may be true, and it would seem to be in China's interest to ensure that Pakistan's economy does not completely collapse, it seems unlikely that Sino–Pakistan trade is ever going to constitute a significant proportion of China's foreign business. Pakistan's share of Chinese trade compares unfavourably with India, Vietnam and even the Philippines.[91] Pakistan also has a massive trade deficit with China, importing more than six times what it exported in 2015,[92] principally because China is the main supplier of military hardware and nuclear technology to Pakistan.[93] The fact that China's GDP per capita was lower than Pakistan's in 1968, but in 2012 was five times higher, further illustrates the growing gulf in economic potency between the partners.[94] The evidence therefore suggests that there is limited potential for Pakistan to become a major trade partner for China and that attempting the Sisyphean task of transforming it into one is not likely to be China's main goal in promoting CPEC cooperation. Pakistan's weakness and dependency also play into Chinese hands in geopolitical terms, once the strategy of geo-positional balancing is taken into account. A dependent, needy Pakistan is, in fact, an ideal ally for a China intending to expand its geopolitical interests and hedge via geo-positional balancing against future conflicts with its most significant regional rival, India.

Finally, China's position regarding the potential for growth in Sino–Pakistani trade and economic interactions is summed up by an anonymous Chinese senior specialist on South Asia interviewed by Mathieu Duchâtel:

Pakistan is a minor market for China. Economic and trade issues have only a marginal influence on the relationship.[95]

[86]Yang and Siddiqi, 'About an "all-weather" relationship', pp. 576–577.
[87]Jakub Jakóbowski and Marcin Kaczmarski, *Beijing's Mistaken Offer: The '16+1' and China's Policy towards the European Union*, OSW (Centre for Eastern Studies) Commentary No. 250 (15 September 2017), p. 3.
[88]Singh, 'Why is India worried about China consolidating in Sri Lanka?'.
[89]See Note 39.
[90]K. S. Venkatachalam, 'Can Pakistan afford CPEC?', *The Diplomat*, (16 June 2017), available at: https://thediplomat.com/2017/06/can-pakistan-afford-cpec/ (accessed 22 November 2017).
[91]Small, *The China–Pakistan Axis*, p. 96.
[92]National Bureau of Statistics of China, *China Statistical Yearbook 2016*, Section 11–6.
[93]Ye Hailin, 'China–Pakistan relationship', p. 110.
[94]Small, *The China–Pakistan Axis*, p. 95.
[95]See Note 85.

In other words, geopolitical considerations are paramount for China *vis-à-vis* Pakistan, and economic diplomacy is mainly used as a tool to achieve the goal of bolstering China's position with regard to India in the IOR.

Pakistan's motivations for encouraging Chinese involvement in Gwadar, and for promoting CPEC generally, can be listed as follows. Above all, there is the desire to continue what it regards as a key partnership which enables it to resist pressure from its historical enemy, India.[96] Pakistani military strategists keenly recall the December 1971 war with India, when the Indian Navy inflicted massive damage on the Pakistani Navy in Karachi port in two attacks.[97] Second, the present government believes it can score points with the electorate by cultivating a Chinese business presence. Third, Pakistan is desperately short of hard currency, so seeks to obtain funds and assistance from China. And fourth, Pakistan's energy infrastructure needs an overhaul, so Chinese expertise and investment in this area are welcome. All these factors mean that Pakistan's government is generally enthusiastic about its Chinese connection, even if not all the promised investment materialises.

Overall, then, China's engagement in Pakistan at present suits both parties and in particular serves China's geopolitical interests. China gets away with maintaining the partnership through loans which have to be repaid either in cash or equity in the projects constructed by Chinese firms (which thereby benefit), and Chinese strategists see the investment as worthwhile in order to establish a position of 'active defence' in the IOR and South Asia. Essentially, China views Pakistan principally as a counter in a larger geopolitical game aimed at geo-positionally balancing other actors in the region such as India and the US. A secondary aim is to contain Islamic fundamentalism, which could threaten China's internal security, outside its borders. Economic factors, the 'face value' aspect of CPEC, are therefore far less significant in reality than geopolitical and security issues.

Conclusion

The evidence presented in this article suggests that China's intentions with CPEC are primarily geopolitical rather than geo-economic. Geographical difficulties, cost calculations and security problems make further development of the overland connection between China and Pakistan unrealistic and unattractive, particularly with regard to the construction of oil and natural gas pipelines. Rather than taking the stated geo-economic objectives and the Malacca dilemma at face value, viewing CPEC through a geographically-focused lens which evaluates Chinese motivations in terms of geo-positional balancing presents a clearer picture of what CPEC is primarily intended to accomplish. Balancing against the regional rival India via attempts to establish footholds on the IOR littoral can thus be seen as China's paramount goal, with the rather fanciful notion of economically cost-effective and security-enhancing (rather than insecure) overland corridors fading into the background as geographical and geo-economic realities dawn on Chinese policymakers.

The comparison between the proposed CPEC pipelines and completed Myanmar ones is also instructive. Despite claims to the contrary, Chinese investment in the Myanmar pipeline project has not proved to be particularly profitable nor to have significantly enhanced China's energy security. Since the empirical evidence reviewed indicates that building pipelines across Pakistan would meet with far more problems, ranging from security issues to geographical difficulties to irrational amounts of money spent on construction and maintenance, it is highly likely that this part of the CPEC project has already been quietly shelved. Indeed, in 2017 official Chinese sources continued to emphasise investment in Pakistani energy projects while mention of pipelines and the overland connection to Xinjiang was conspicuously absent from published material.

Yet the Chinese interest in the port of Gwadar remains, even though the port has not been developed much since Phase I was completed in 2007. This article's argument is that the Chinese interest

[96]See Note 74.
[97]Tariq Ali, *Can Pakistan Survive? The Death of a State* (New York: Penguin, 1983), p. 95; 'Indo–Pakistani War of 1971', *GlobalSecurity. org*, available at: http://www.globalsecurity.org/military/world/war/indo-pak_1971.htm (accessed 2 April 2017).

in Gwadar, and other IOR ports such as Kyaukpyu and Hambantota, is primarily due to the strategy of geo-positional balancing with regard to India and, to an extent, the US. Converting debt to equity, as China has recently done in Sri Lanka by acquiring a 70% stake in Hambantota Port,[98] gives China a maritime presence which it had previously lacked. In this interpretation, CPEC is more about bolstering China's position in Pakistan than about economic cooperation, although in fact security goals can be achieved alongside economic ones because commercial 'facilities could be quickly flipped for military application'.[99]

In the end, the reality of China's involvement in Pakistan consists mainly of efforts to sustain the footholds in the IOR gained so far as an insurance policy against as-yet-unknown future eventualities, rather than being the tale of large-scale geo-economic expansion that is told by some over-optimistic commentators. In essence, as geopolitical realities confront impractical pipeline fantasies, CPEC is, for the most part, the acceptable face of China's attempt at establishing a geo-positional balancing act in the Indian Ocean.

Disclosure statement

No potential conflict of interest was reported by the author.

Funding

This work was supported by the Internal Grant Agency of the Faculty of International Relations, University of Economics, Prague, as part of the research project 'The New Silk Road Initiative as a New Stage of Chinese Global Activity', project no. F2/32/2017.

---

[98]See Note 88.
[99]Jessica Drun, 'China's maritime ambitions: a sinister string of pearls or a benevolent Silk Road (or both)?', *Party Watch Initiative*, (5 December 2017), available at: https://www.ccpwatch.org/single post/2017/12/05/China%E2%80%99s-Maritime-Ambitions-a-Sinister-String-of-Pearls-or-a-Benevolent-Silk-Road-or-Both (accessed 7 December 2017).

Index

Note: Page numbers in *italic* refer to Figures; page numbers in **bold** refer to Tables

Abe, Shinzo 32
Action Plan *see* Vision and Actions on Jointly
   Building Silk Road Economic Belt and
   21st-Century Maritime Silk Road
ADB (Asian Development Bank) 9, 10, 11, 12, 22, 26,
   34, 78, 84
AIIB (Asian Infrastructure Investment Bank) 1,
   4, 8–12, 15, 16–17, 19, 21–28, 29, 30–34, 39,
   48–49, 50, 58, 71–72, 77–85, 177
Alfred Thayer Mahan, Alfred Thayer 182
Allison, Graham 5
Anglo-Saxon Doctrine 123
APD (Asian Port Doctrine) 123
APEC (Asia-Pacific Economic Cooperation) 6
ASEAN (Association of Southeast Asian Nations)
   8, 13–14, 15, 34, 44–45, 146, 148, **149**, 151,
   182–183, 187
ASEAN Plus China (10+1) Expo 6
Asia 6, 7, 8, 17, 34, 52–55, *56*, 57, 69, 151, 185
Asian countries 4, 8, 13, 14, 29, *59*; FDI
   63–64, **65**, 66; infrastructure development
   7, 9–10; international trade 60–61, *62*; OBOR
   initiatives 14; ODA 66–69
Asian Development Bank *see* ADB (Asian
   Development Bank)
Asian development model 58
Asian Infrastructure Investment Bank *see* AIIB (Asian
   Infrastructure Investment Bank)
Asia-Pacific region 29, 30–31
Association of Southeast Asian Nations *see* ASEAN
   (Association of Southeast Asian Nations)
Australia 11, 48, 82, 117

Baldwin, Richard 42–43
Bandar Malaysia 159, 164, 166–167, 170, 171, 172
bandwagoning 143, 177
Bangladesh–China–India–Myanmar Economic
   Corridor 16, 21, 40, 41, 47
bargaining theory 72
Beeson, Mark 160
Belt and Road Forum for International Cooperation
   (2017) 39, 46, 50, 87, 107

Bernard, Mitchell 116
bilateral relations 13, 15, 31, 87, 88, 90, 91
Boni, Filippo 201
Bremmer, Ian 113
Bretton Woods institutions 38, 48, 71, 72, 78, 80
Brewster, David 192
BRI (Belt and Road Initiative) 1–2, 4, 43–47, 48,
   49, 50, 58–60, 104–108, 115–116, 117–119,
   140, 158–159, 160–162, 193–194; control
   mechanisms 113–114, 117, 118; external dissent
   114–115; foreign policy 36–37, 39–41, 182,
   183–184; international trade 43, *44*, 51–53, 55,
   60–61, 69, 81; LSGs 109; Malaysia 159–160, 162,
   164, 170, 172; mobilisation 109–113, 117, 118;
   port development 126, 137; soft balancing 42;
   Southeast Asia 173, 176
BRICS countries (Brazil, Russia, India, China and
   South Africa) 10
Brunei–Guangxi Economic Corridor 143
Brzezinski, Zbigniew 40
Burma *see* Myanmar
Bush administration 151

Calderón, César 7
Callahan, William A. 160
Cambodia 9, 54, 143, 144, 146, 152, 154, 155,
   157, 178
Canada 48, 123
Central Asia 30, 34; SREB 87–88, 90, 91,
   100–102, 103
Cheng-Chwee, Kuik 142
China 1–2, 4, 5–6, 7, 10, 12, 36, 55, 57; FDI 7, 8,
   80, 117–118, 144, 148, 162–163, 177, 179–180,
   188–189; ODA 67–68, 69; OFDI 16
China-ASEAN (Association of Southeast Asian
   Nations) 6
China-Central and West Asia Economic Corridor
   21, 40, 41
China Development Bank 21, 22, 80
China Development Forum (2015) 49
China Export and Credit Insurance Corporation 22
China–India–Nepal Economic Corridor 40

China–Indo–China Peninsula Economic
    Corridor 21, 40
China Merchants Port Holdings Company
    Limited 126
China–Mongolia–Russia Economic Corridor
    21, 40, 47
China–Myanmar partnership 47
China–Myanmar Pipeline 193, 199–200
coastal ports 7, 120–122, 124–125, 126, 128, **132**
Cohen, Saul B. 192
colonization 182
commitment problems 72, 73, 74, 75, 77, 85
Community of Common Destiny 47
constructivism 38–39
container ports 7, 10, **11**, 120–121, 123, 124–125
control mechanisms 113–114, 117, 118
COSCO Shipping Group 112
COSCO Shipping Ports Limited 126
CPEC (China–Pakistan Economic Corridor)
    21, 22, 28, 33, 40, 41, 50, 105, 117, 191,
    192–195, 196–197, 198, 200–203, 204–205
credible threats *see* threat credibility

Dalian Port 135, 136
democracy index 152
Deng Xiaoping 6, 7, 27, 33, 41–42, 51
domestic economy 6, 8, 10, 29
domestic politics 1, 105–106, 115–116, 118
dominant states 74, 90
Duterte, Rodrigo 34, 45, 154, 155

EAEU (Eurasian Economic Union) 34
East Coast Rail Link *see* ECRL (East Coast Rail Link)
economic cooperation 34, 51–52
economic corridors 21, 40, 41, 104, 120
economic development 1–2, 25–26, 27, 33, 52, 116
economic growth 6, 7, 8, 25–26, 33, 39–40, 45, 52,
    57–58, 69, 104
ECRL (East Coast Rail Link), Malaysia 159, 164–166,
    170, 171, 172
emerging powers 48, 78
established powers 48, 72, 73, 74, 75
EU (European Union) 44
Eurasian Economic Union *see* EAEU (Eurasian
    Economic Union)
European Doctrine (Continental) 122–123
Export-Import Bank of China 22, 80, 112
external dissent 114–115

Fallon, Theresa 105
FDI (Foreign Direct Investment) 43, 144, **145–146**,
    148, **150**, 157
Five Principles of Peaceful Coexistence 46, 47
Flynn, Matthew 123
foreign policy 5–7, 12, 17, 19, 27, 34, 36–37, 39–42,
    46, 106–107, 108, 182, 183–184, 202
Forest City, Malaysia 159, 164, 167–169, 170,
    171, 172
founding members *see* PFMs (Prospective
    Founding Members)
Four Asian Tigers 55, 57

France 11, 48, 82
Fravel, Taylor 6
Fujian Province 110
Fuzhou Port 135–136
fuzzy clustering analysis model 131, 137,
    138–139

gas pipelines *see* Myanmar–China pipelines
geoeconomics 1, 4, 34
geopolitics 1, 4, 5, 34
geo-positional balancing 193, 201–202, 205
Germany 11, 48, 82
Gilpin, Robert 47
global governance 1, 10, 22, 26, 27, 42,
    47–48, 49, 50
GMS (Greater Mekong Sub-region Economic
    Cooperation) 6
'going global strategy' 121–122, 124, 125, 126, 128,
    129, 133–135, 137
Graham, Euan 150–151
Guangdong Province 110–111
Guangxi Province 13, 14, 110, 111
Guangzhou Port 134
Gwadar Deep-water Port, Pakistan 17, 28, 41, 126,
    187, 192, 193, 194, 195–196, 197, 198–199,
    204–205

Haikou Port 136
Hambantota Port, Sri Lanka 41
hard balancing 201
Harmonious World 47
hedging 143
Hirschman, Albert 73
Hu Jintao 47, 183, 194

Ikenberry, G. John 76, 85
IMF (International Monetary Fund) 10, 11, 22, 26,
    48, 77, 78, 79
India 16, 34, 50, 54, 177–178, 181, 182, 185,
    186–187, 192, 193, 201–202; AIIB 32; OBOR
    initiatives 13, 16, 32–33
Indian Ocean 16, 41, 182, 184, 192, 202
Indonesia 9, 143, 144, 146, 153–154, 157
'Indo-Pacific' concept 28, 31
infrastructure 7
infrastructure development 1, 7, 9, 33, 105, 123,
    125, 126, 180–181
infrastructure investment 2, 8, 120–122
infrastructure projects 2, 10–11, 22, 28–29, 176,
    177–178, 184, 187–188
institutional reforms 74–77, 85
international economic system 26
international institutions 38, 72, 73, 76, 84–85
international ports 126
international relations 105–106
international trade 10, 27, 43, *44*, 51–53, 55, 60–61,
    62, 69, 81
inter-regional infrastructure 7, 8, 13, 17
Iran–Pakistan gas pipeline 198
Israel 11, 48, 82
Italy 11, 82

Jackson, Jay 45
Jackson, Van 143
Japan 10, 15–16, 27, 31–32, 34, 54, 55, 57, 78, 181,
    185–186, 187; AIIB 15, 30, 31, 32, 81; BRI 117;
    OBOR initiatives 13, 15, 30, 31, 32; ODA 69;
    OFDI 16
Johnson, Christopher K. 106

Karakoram Highway, Pakistan 191–192, 196, 198
Kazakhstan 91–93, 103, 117
Keohane, Robert O. 38
Kyaukpyu Port, Myanmar 41
Kyrgyzstan 93–95, 103, 114

Lam, Jasmine Siu Lee 123
Land Silk Road 41, 51
Laos 143, 144, 152, 154, 157, 178
Lee, Paul Tae-Woo 123
Lim, Guanie 161
LSGs (Leading Small Groups) 108–109

Mackinder, Halford 40, 182
Malaysia 9, 143, 144, 146, 150, 152, 153, 155,
    156, 157, 159–160, 162–164, 172–173; Bandar
    Malaysia 159, 164, 166–167, 170, 171, 172; ECRL
    159, 164–166, 170, 171, 172; Forest City 159, 164,
    167–169, 170, 171, 172
maritime trade shipping 7
Marshall Plan 8, 118
MDBs (multilateral development banks) 72, 80
Mearsheimer, John 201
Mei Xinyu 196–197
Melaka Gateway Port, Malaysia 22, 28
Middle East 54
ministerial mobilisation 109–110
mobilisation 109–113, 117, 118
Mohan, Raja 16
MSR (Maritime Silk Road) 3, 41, 50, 51, 120, 121,
    123, 125
MSRI (Maritime Silk Road Initiative) 140–144, **147**,
    148, 150, 152–157, 158, 176, 177, 183–189
multilateral development banks *see* MDBs
    (multilateral development banks)
multilateral institutions 48, 49, 72–73, 75–77
multilateralism 73
Myanmar 146, 161, 174–176, 178, 179–181, 182,
    185, 186–187, 188, 189; BRI 143; MSRI 144, 154,
    156, 157, 184
Myanmar–China pipelines 192, 194–195, 204
Myitsone hydropower project, Myanmar 17, 114,
    161, 175, 184

Nanjing Port 135, 136
NDRC (National Development and Reform
    Commission) 5, 13
neoliberalism 38
neorealism 38
Nepal 66, 161
New Development Bank 34, 78
New Eurasian Land Bridge corridor 21, 40, 41
New Silk Road Economic Belt 140

Ningbo-Zhoushan Port 135, 136
normative power 45, 46, 50
Notteboom, Theo 125

Obama, Barack 12, 49, 82, 151
Obama administration 27, 30–31, 151
OBOR (One Belt One Road) initiatives 3–6,
    7–8, 10, 13, 14, 15, 17–18, 19–21, 22, 25–30,
    33–34, 40, 106, 189; projects 22, **23–24**,
    25, 28–29, 33; *see also* BRI (Belt and Road
    Initiative)
OBOR Forum (2017) 21, 29, 31, 32
ODA (Official Developmental Assistance) 66–69
OFDI (outward foreign direct investment) 8, 10, 43,
    44, 52–53, 62–64, **65**, 177; BRI investment 58, 60,
    62–64, **65**, 66
offshore balancing 201
oil pipelines *see* Myanmar–China pipelines

Pakistan 17, 28, 34, 115, 117, 191–192, 195–198,
    202–203, 204, 205
Pakistan pipeline project 192
Pan Qi 176
Papua New Guinea 114
Peaceful Development 47
Peaceful Rise 47
PFMs (Prospective Founding Members) 12, 16,
    21, 81, 82
Philippines 9, 13, 14, 34, 45, 143, 144, 148, 154,
    155, 157
'Pivot to Asia' strategy 14, 15, 27, 28, 41, 42
port development 122–123, 126, 128–131,
    133–135, 137, 201
port enterprises 126, **127–128**
port governance 122–125, 128, 137
Port of Yantai Group 126
provincial mobilisation 110–111
Pu, Xiaoyu 47–48
Putin, Vladimir 47
Putnam, Robert D. 105–106

Qingdao Port 135, 136

Ravenhill, John 116
regional cooperation 6, 7, 34
regional multilateral institutions 38
regional multilateralism 36, 37, 38–39, 40, 42, 43,
    45, 47, 49–50
relationalism 87, 88, **89**, 90–91, 101–102, 103
rising powers 38, 72, 73, 74, 75, 76–77, 85, 142;
    China 12, 17, 36, 42, 45
Rizhao Port 135, 136
RMB (Renminbi) 21, 27, 48
Russia 34, 185, 186

SAARC (South Asian Association for Regional
    Cooperation) 34
Saudi Arabia 54
Schweller, Randall 47–48
SCO (Shanghai Cooperation Organization) 6,
    34, 101

SCS (South China Sea) 13–14, 27, 28, 34, 43–45, 50, 148, 150, 157, 183
Servén, Luis 7
Shanghai 7, 121
Shanghai Cooperation Organization see SCO (Shanghai Cooperation Organization)
Shanghai International Port Group 126
Shanghai Port 134, 135
Shantou Port 136
Shenzhen Port 135
Silk Road countries 5, 8, 10
Silk Road Economic Belt see SREB (Silk Road Economic Belt)
Silk Road Fund 21, 22, 39, 177
Silk Road initiatives 5, 7, 8, 17–18, 189–190
Silk Road routes 3–4, 5
Singapore 28, 143, 144, 146, 154, 156, 157
Small, Andrew 195
small states 142, 143, 173
SOEs (state-owned enterprises) 53, 105, 111–113, 117, 177
soft balancing 42, 43, 143, 201
soft power 45–46, 47
South Asian Association for Regional Cooperation see SAARC (South Asian Association for Regional Cooperation)
South China Sea see SCS (South China Sea)
Southeast Asia 4, 55, 158, 161–162, 173, 176, 177–178, 189
Southeast Asian (SEA) countries 8, 140–142, 143–144, **145–146**, **147**, 148, 150, 151–156, 157
South Korea 11, 48, 82
Soviet Union 54
SREB (Silk Road Economic Belt) 3, 87–88, 90, 91, 100–102, 103, 158, 176; Kazakhstan 91–93, 103, 117; Kyrgyzstan 93–95, 103; Tajikistan 95–97, 103; Turkmenistan 97–98, 103; Uzbekistan 99–100, 103
Sri Lanka 114, 184, 202, 205
state-owned enterprises see SOEs (state-owned enterprises)
Straits of Malacca 28–29, 194
Sub-Saharan Africa 7
Summers, Lawrence 12
Suu Kyi, Aung San 174, 175

Tajikistan 95–97, 103
TAPI (Turkmenistan–Afghanistan–Pakistan–India pipeline) 198
territorial disputes 13, 14, 16, 27, 28, 31, 34, 50, 148, 150, 153, 155, 157
Thailand 9, 143, 144, 146, 153, 155, 157, 178
threat credibility 72, 73–74, 75, 77, 79, 80, 85
Tianjin Port 135
TPP (Trans-Pacific Partnership) 32, 41, 42, 49
Trump, Donald J. 28, 31, 32

Trump administration 28, 31, 32, 50, 151, 156
TTIP (Transatlantic Trade and Investment Partnership) 42
Turkmenistan 97–98, 103
Turkmenistan–Afghanistan–Pakistan–India pipeline see TAPI (Turkmenistan–Afghanistan–Pakistan–India pipeline)

UK (United Kingdom): AIIB 11, 48, 82, 83; port development 122
UN Development Program 29
US (United States) 10, 12, 14–15, 26, 29, 34, 44, 78–79, 116–117, 150, 185, 186, 187, 201; AIIB 11, 30, 31, 48, 81, 82; FDI 186; 'Indo-Pacific' concept 28, 31; Marshall Plan 8, 118; OBOR initiatives 13, 30–31; OFDI 16; 'Pivot to Asia' strategy 14, 15, 27, 28, 41, 42; Southeast Asia 151, 157
Uzbekistan 99–100, 103

Vietnam 13, 14, 143, 144, 146, 148, 150, 152, 154, 155–156, 157
Vision and Actions on Jointly Building Silk Road Economic Belt and 21st-Century Maritime Silk Road (2015) 53, 120

Walt, Stephen 201
Wang, Gungwu 4
Wang, Jisi 13
Wang, Zheng 189
Western Development Strategy (1999) 39, 110
Westphalian sovereignty 46
World Bank 9, 10, 11, 12, 22, 26, 34, 48–49, 77, 78, 84

Xi administration 87, 88, 91, 176; Kazakhstan 91, 92–93; Kyrgyzstan 93–94, 95; SREB 100–102, 103; Tajikistan 96, 97; Turkmenistan 97; Uzbekistan 99, 100
Xiamen Port 135–136
Xi Jingping 3, 7, 14, 16, 27, 33, 37, 47, 48, 106, 158; AIIB 9, 17, 21; BRI 1, 39, 46, 107, 108, 140; foreign policy 6, 19, 29, 42, 107; Kazakhstan 91; Kyrgyzstan 94; OBOR initiatives 8, 20; port development 120, 126; Silk Road Fund 21; SREB 158, 176; Tajikistan 95, 96; Turkmenistan 97; Uzbekistan 99–100
Xinjiang Province 8, 110, 191–192, 193, 194

Yang, Zhongzhen 125
Yantai Port 135, 136
Yunnan Province 8, 13, 111, 176

Zhao, Kejin 113
Zhao, Suisheng 6
Zheng He 4

For Product Safety Concerns and Information please contact our EU
representative GPSR@taylorandfrancis.com
Taylor & Francis Verlag GmbH, Kaufingerstraße 24, 80331 München, Germany

www.ingramcontent.com/pod-product-compliance
Ingram Content Group UK Ltd.
Pitfield, Milton Keynes, MK11 3LW, UK
UKHW031833180425
457613UK00023B/1267